Accidentally on Purpose

AN AUTOBIOGRAPHY

MICHAEL YORK

Simon & Schuster

NEW YORK LONDON TORONTO SYDNEY TOKYO SINGAPORE

SIMON & SCHUSTER
Simon & Schuster Building
Rockefeller Center
1230 Avenue of the Americas
New York, New York 10020

Originally published in Great Britain by Headline Book Publishing PLC
under the title *Travelling Player*.
SIMON & SCHUSTER and colophon are registered trademarks of
Simon & Schuster Inc.

Designed by Caroline Cunningham

Manufactured in the United States of America

1   3   5   7   9   10   8   6   4   2

Library of Congress Cataloging in Publication Data
York, Michael.
Accidentally on purpose: an autobiography/Michael York.
p.   cm.
Simultaneously published: Travelling player. London:
Headline Book Pub., 1991.
Includes index.
1. York, Michael.
2. Motion picture actors and actresses—Great Britain—Biography.
I. Title.
PN2598.Y68A3   1991
791.43′028′092—dc20
[B]   91-40708
CIP
ISBN: 0-671-68940-1

This book is dedicated to all its Dramatis Personae—heroes, villains and walk-ons—but especially to those leading luminaries, my wife, my parents, and my family.

Acknowledgments

S pecial thanks to Phillip Berman, the editor of *The Courage of Conviction*, who first suggested I write a larger contribution; to Jim Bates, who put it all on his word processor; to Adrian Brine, who, in his self-appointed role as that pseudo-Shakespearean character "Don Adriano, A Pedant," scrutinized the finished results; and of course, as always, to Pat, for . . . well, everything.

Permission to quote from the letters of Tennessee Williams on pages 252, 259 and 274 is granted by Maria St. Just and John Eastman, Trustees of the Tennessee Williams Estate.

Every reasonable effort has been made to trace the copyright holders on material contained within this book. However, if there has been any accidental omission, the author and publishers would be glad to rectify it in future editions of the book.

Contents

C O N T E N T S

Prologue

The phone in my Tel Aviv hotel rang just before midnight. "My government has just ordered me home." Liv Ullmann's lilting tones were traced with sadness. The next morning we were both due to resume work on a film we had started in Hungary, and five weeks of filming lay ahead in Israel. But nearby, a five minutes' missile flight away, was Iraq, whose dictator, defying reason and world opinion, threatened the world with a bloody Armageddon. "I'll see you on the set tomorrow," Liv murmured, curtailing further speculation.

Pat, my wife, had flown in earlier that evening on an empty plane that, after hastily refueling, had sped back to a less vulnerable world. There was talk of all further flights being suspended. What do we do? My job was unpredictable and insecure at the best of times. But at the worst? Sleep came fitfully. Words from the long, crucial speech I had to perform in a few hours' time mingled with musings on our plight and, ringing tauntingly amongst them, was that old adage about the show having to go on. But, as Noël Coward had observed, why must it?

We headed for Jerusalem in the chilly morning dark, passing on the way the wreckage of previous wars that had secured the nation's survival, and arrived in the ancient stone city just after dawn. This was the sacred time, when the Greeks used to attend their theater. I wondered what kind of drama lay ahead.

Our first film location was the Yad Vashem Museum, itself a memorial to past aggression. In costume and makeup, I became another victim, a Hungarian Jew who had survived the death camps and sought refuge in Israel. Now the impending danger gave my words and emotions a new resonance. Filming went well.

Afterward we decided to go along with the scheduled plan and drive down to our next location, Eilat, on the Red Sea. Anyway, we had no passports. They had been collected so that our gas masks could be issued. Skirting a now ominous-sounding Dead Sea, we passed beneath the fortress rock of Masada, where patriots had perished before a previous foreign assault. Crossing a wilderness where John the Baptist, another character in my repertoire, had surely roamed, brought to mind the nearby desert and the mad scorpion that menaced within.

That evening we assembled to discuss the situation. Like so many film units we were an international group, but one that the crisis had made unusually close and everyone loathed the prospect of creative momentum being stopped. However, to continue, it was agreed, would perhaps be irresponsible. It was especially difficult to justify staying on to loved ones overseas. My own increasingly anxious family repeatedly faxed their fears. As Vilmos Zsigmond, our warm and talented director, remarked gnomically in his inimitable Hungarian-American accent: "This is bigger than lunch!"

For our Israeli producer there was a certain business-as-usual calmness. He had seen it all before, having fought the British as well as the Arabs. There was a good deal of gallows humor and much play on the word *shooting*. Our problems were appreciated and, should regular flights be suspended, a charter plane was arranged to fly us out the day before the UN deadline. We agreed to stay on and work till then when, as the world hoped, there would be a peaceful diplomatic solution.

Our new film set was a spectacular desert park, its backdrop of mountains changing colors with a surreal cartoonlike intensity and rapidity as the day progressed. This peaceful, arid Eden became our new reality. Away from the strident, alarmist babble of the cable news service, the immediate demands of the film provided our only truth.

Here, too, the distant dictator took on a histrionic dimension—not the heroic bravura of a Shakespeare villain but rather the caricatured evil of the bad guy from some shoot-'em-up movie.

Arrangements were made for instruction about gas masks and chemical warfare later that evening. Born in the countryside during the Second World War, I had always felt slightly cheated that I had been denied the gas mask issued to the city children I later saw in newsreels. Now that I had one I could feel little pleasure—just a certain morbid curiosity. Carefully putting down his gun, the Israeli army major introduced his lieutenant, a beautiful girl named Talia, in a tight-fitting uniform. She demonstrated the mysteries, and one by one we obediently followed her example.

We were also shown how to inject ourselves against poison gas, holding the automatic dispenser like a child's toy, with its yellow top to the sun and its green bottom to the hopefully still vegetable ground. Instructed to seal doors and windows, I anticipated a run on that other indispensable film-set item, gaffer's tape.

All our spirits were lifted when Liv reported that a dove had flown into her room and had refused to leave. The next day we were plunged into symbolic gloom when it sickened, and relieved anew when it recovered and flew away. In the midst of all this, a fax marked "urgent" arrived containing an elaborate entreaty to subscribe to a tribute to a Hollywood star who was being honored at a banquet for his humanitarian contribution to mankind. I tore it up. It intruded the phony values of my present home town, where wars were fought for box-office profits. But it provided a useful cue. Waiting in ambush for us on the set the next morning was a newsreel crew, the now universal busybodies, purveyors of half-truths and instant opinions. With a plea for peace, I said I hoped all wars would in future be in costume and makeup.

Word came for our Hungarian companions to return home. Next advised to leave were the Americans, followed, with a reluctance that would have pleased Lawrence of Arabia, by the British, whose consul, rising enthusiastically to the crisis in the manner of his countrymen, had already contacted us about a Dunkirk-style evacuation down the Red Sea by gunboat. Assembled at a last supper, our producer regretfully requested us to leave—the first time my contract's vague force majeure clause had become a reality.

The next morning at five our Longest Day began with a dark winding drive up the windswept hills to Arad, where we were to complete the present filming. The BBC news on the car radio confirmed the worsening situation. Though constantly interrupted by jets streaking overhead and their distant sonic booms, two days' work was crammed into one. After the final "Cut!" there were emotional speeches and defiant promises of "Next week in Jerusalem." Throwing our things in a car we set off into the night back to Tel Aviv. At the airport, a British charter plane was still on the ground. Even more fortunate, there was space aboard.

Since the worsening of the Gulf crisis I had witnessed a display of emotions that for the past twenty years I had spent my professional life trying to emulate—anxiety, hope, bravado, courage and the disguise of fair nature with hard-favored rage. Joining the patient line clutching precious boarding passes, I knew I had played this scene many times before. Would life never stop imitating art? I would like to have improvised a different reality. In almost thirty years as a professional actor I had grown used to the constant assembly and disbanding of comradeship that is a stock-in-trade. But this was different. Perfectly expressing my own inexpressible feelings, Pat burst into tears bidding farewell to our colleagues who had coaxed this miracle of a film into existence on the slimmest of budgets and the largest of expectations.

The plane was a flying nursery full of innocents fleeing the wrath of a new Herod. Later, installed in a London hotel, we put a grateful end to a day that had lasted twenty minutes short of twenty-four hours. Soon afterward a message came from Liv, now in New York: "We have really shared an extraordinary thing together, and I have a gut feeling that it is not over. We must continue to believe in it and wait for it, and live our lives as if this is just an intermission in a play that has many more acts." Then came news of the first missile attacks on the friends we had so recently left behind. Anxious to do something positive, and possibly creative, in the face of burgeoning negativity and destructiveness, I pulled out of my suitcase the papers that, crushed and tattered, have been my traveling companions for the past two years. Arranging them into the acts leading up to this enforced intermission, I wrote this overture. So, houselights down and curtain up . . . !

Act 1 – Beginner

C H A P T E R   O N E

I started performing on the world stage with a borrowed silver spoon in my mouth, for I made my first entrance into Fulmer Chase, a grand English manor house. Situated in the village of Fulmer in the southeastern county of Buckinghamshire, it had been converted to wartime use as a maternity home for the wives of young army officers. The time was five past five in the morning of March 27, 1942 —midway through the saga of alarms and excursions then exciting offstage attention.

Not insignificantly as it turned out, my birthplace was situated a mere stone's throw from the gates of Pinewood Film Studios, the scene of many subsequent entrances and exits. In those bleak days of rationing and deprivation the house was an oasis of peace and plenty, with its own farm supplying butter, cream and eggs. I mention a silver spoon not only because my parents' circumstances were far less luxurious than those in which I initially found myself, but also because it symbolizes a good fortune that I have enjoyed from that day on. In the first place, I was enormously lucky to have been born at all. Britain was embattled and my father was a serving officer. I was apparently conceived on a brief leave much to the disapproval of my mother's parents, who considered such behavior irresponsible.

My appearance failed to elicit an overly favorable notice from the midwife. I was skinny but solid, attributes that I can at least boast of today. Picking me up to weigh me she made some insensitive remark about my physical endowments that upset my proud mother who was further dismayed by the arrival of a telegram: "The cock croweth and the hen delivereth the goods." These were my father's exultant congratulations unwisely composed and sent in the course of a boozy celebration in the mess during army maneuvers. It was not well received, nor at first was he, when he followed this up with a personal visit on a forty-eight-hour compassionate leave.

My birth was registered on April Fool's Day, in Burnham, a subdistrict of Eton. The certificate read: "Michael Hugh Johnson, boy, son of Joseph Gwynne Johnson and Florence Edith May Johnson formerly Chown. Father 2nd Lieutenant R.A. and manager of multiple domestic store of 20 The Garth, Yarnton, Nr Oxford." The registrar, I hope prophetically for me, was called A. N. Goodchild. My name was intended originally to be Michael Peter Johnson but, at the time of my arrival, my mother was engrossed in a book whose dashing hero was called Hugh and she persuaded my father to change my middle name. So I have an archangel's and a hero's name. As for "York"... I'll come to that later. Suffice to say that it was my own contribution to the nomenclature!

My father, as his own middle name suggests, came from Welsh stock. In fact, he used nothing but Welsh until he was four years old. Later, when requested to speak it, his native tongue had become horribly, if impressively, entangled with German, a language learned from his wartime work with British Intelligence. His father, Joseph, whom I never met, was a house painter and lived with his wife Rachel and the family in Llandovery in the rural heartland of Wales. On his mother's side was a long line of Nonconformist ministers.

Another ancestor was Ephraim Palfrey. Of Jewish descent, he apparently had a successful carpet manufacturing business in the Midlands. Cheated by his partners, however, including his sister, who used the family fortune to found a lace factory in Philadelphia, Ephraim had abandoned commerce for art by running off to Wales to join a circus. Like me, he also changed his name. Not only does his precedent help to justify my own choice of career, but the influx of such exotic blood enlivened our somewhat plebeian stock and helps to explain my somewhat un-English looks. I was delighted to learn of Ephraim, a skeleton who had been unjustly locked in the family closet.

My father, who went to a local college on a scholarship, excelled both in the classroom and on the sports field. His short, strong build made him an excellent fly half and he played rugby both for his college and for Wales. Later he went on to Oriel College, Oxford, where he continued his studies of classical Greek and Latin and rugby lore. His intention, or rather that of his parents, was to become a minister and it was toward the goal of eventual ordination that the path of his studies lay. Knowing my father as I now do, I would say that he was temperamentally unsuited for this spiritual vocation. But this judgment is made with hindsight of him as a successful soldier and businessman, his personality forged in the crucible of war both on the battlefield and in the boardroom.

My parents met when my father went to lodge as a student in the Oxford house where my mother lived with her own parents and younger sister, Irene. May, as my mother preferred to be called—appropriately, since she was delicate, gentle and pretty—was the eldest child of Amos Chown and his wife, Mabel. Amos had been an orphan but came from a line of Oxfordshire farmers and laborers. He was a keen cyclist and a good one, as testified by the photograph of him crouched over his machine in racing style surrounded by a shiny array of trophies.

Professionally, Amos worked his way up from assistant to head of the pathology department at Oxford's Radcliffe Infirmary. There he had helped the famous Dr. Florey, handling the first batch of penicillin to be used for healing. He told me later how venereal victims had besieged him for samples of the new miracle cure. Amos was later offered an honorary degree but, with characteristic bluffness, turned it down as it represented no financial reward.

His wife, Mabel Emily Higginbottom, was six years older. This discrepancy in age, nowadays more fashionable, was due to a promise she had made to look after the orphaned Amos. She kept her word to the end of her life, perhaps because she herself came from a broken home. Her father was a drunk who abandoned his family, forcing them to fend for themselves in a small cottage.

Mabel's birthplace, however, had been Bermondsey in London, enabling her to claim herself a true cockney as she had been born, as the definition demanded, within the sound of Bow bells. Both she and her sisters had found employment "in service," an experience that, it seems, left its scars. My grandmother never ever spoke about this time. Certainly she kept an immaculate house—and a sober one, too. The demon drink made only rare appearances at Christmas time or for strictly medicinal purposes.

My parents had married on Monday, September 4, 1939, the day after war broke out, their vows being made against a background of broken international promises. Their honeymoon in their new house in Swindon was interrupted by the sound of marching feet assembling at the railway station. My father's joined them soon afterward. By this time he was earning his living, as my birth certificate states, as an assistant manager of the Swindon branch of Marks and Spencer, the "multiple domestic store" that was then well into its astonishing growth from a Manchester market stall ("Don't ask the price, it's a penny!"), to today's international conglomerate.

He had joined the company as a managerial trainee, starting work as a lowly porter. My mother was left, if not as poor as the proverbial church mouse that his intended profession might have guaranteed, then certainly with little more than the £3 a week of his income plus an extra ten shillings from his army allowance. Soon there was another mouth to feed. A baby girl, Penelope Anne, was born in August 1940. My father was away by then, training this time to be a gunner at Woolwich barracks and finding the lack of privacy, his hard boots and the hot weather all equally uncomfortable. May, for her part, loathed her lonely penury in Swindon.

She was rescued from it by her father, who arranged her removal to a house in his own village. Yarnton, north of Oxford on the road to Woodstock was a rather nondescript place, boasting a manor house where good Queen Bess was reputed to have slept, an ancient parish church and other buildings made of the honey-colored stone and thatch that characterize the area. My grandfather's house, however, was a modern semidetached one facing a busy bypass. Its grounds bloomed with flowers, especially the roses that were his abiding passion, for he was an instinctive, brilliant gardener. At the back was a lawn graced by a comfortable canopied swing. Behind some bowery trellises lay a large kitchen garden where, among myriad other vegetables, grew the horseradishes to which my mother was addicted while expecting me. Beyond this were fields bordered by a new street of squat brick houses called The Garth. Number 20 was my first real home.

Dislodged from my aristocratic birthplace, I was brought rudely back to reality in this unlovely but practical house. Like its uniform neighbors it had a modest garden and, though my father was soon to begin a long apprenticeship in green-thumbed lore under the tutelage of his father-in-law, it was still too early for greenery to have grown up to obfuscate its raw, unstuccoed redness. The sitting room led through French windows to a pocket-handkerchief-sized terrace and a small lawn that on Mondays bloomed with washing. In those dig-for-victory days, there was also the inevitable vegetable patch and compost heap. The last was my unofficial playground. Penny—as Penelope was always called—spent much of the time with her grand-mother, who would hang a white handkerchief out of a window of her house to show when she was at home. With my mother restored to the immediate bosom of her caring family we lacked for nothing, or so it seemed.

A few years ago I was working in Santa Fe, New Mexico, an area famed for the natural physicians attracted by the cosmic energy abun-dant in this extraordinary part of the world. A psychic healer told me that I had suffered a traumatic experience at the age of three. The mathematics was easy and the reason inescapable: 1945, the end of the war, and thus the return of my father to his family. I can only assume that I resented his intrusion into the matriarchal calm of our fatherless society. Certainly Penny is reported to have asked her be-loved grandmother, "Nana, when is that man going back?"

The stranger brought me presents. As befitted his recent warrior status, these were suitably martial and masculine—some clockwork battle tanks with twin turrets and treads. Within a short time, they, too, were victims of war, smashed and eviscerated with all the gleeful violence that a little boy can wreak. How I wish he had kept them for later. A painted wooden train set made by O. Blow, a gentle village character whose most caustic cuss earned him his nickname, proved more durable. My father's medals were locked away in a drawer; pulling out his handkerchief, he fashioned it, to my delight, into a jumping mouse. The Major became Daddy.

One other memorable present he brought home for all of us was an infectious rash. Treatment involved standing naked in the bath while being liberally soaked in a lotion that stung with a fiery antiseptic fury. I remember howling alongside my screaming sister. Later I learned that the lady next door was given an even more devastating gift by her homecoming spouse. Syphilis made her hair fall out.

Although rationing was still in full effect, we were extremely well provided for from the fruits of my grandfather's labors. I remember teas with tomatoes warm from the greenhouse and huge stalks of celery served with salt in cut-glass bowls. My grandmother also baked wonderful cakes, and pies with china blackbirds pecking through the crust. One Christmas, Penny and I were given the ultimate treat—a banana, the likes of which had not been seen since Hitler's U-boats had first terrorized the Atlantic trade. We were both bitterly disappointed with this marvel, spitting it out and complaining of its lack of juice. But I cannot remember a Christmas without a tangerine at the bottom of my stocking. To this day, that tangy, pungent smell evokes powerful memories of sleepless vigils and dawn delights.

My father's return to the domestic hearth had a much-needed disciplinary effect on his only son. I was, it seems, somewhat badly behaved. Although mindful of the Apostle John's observation: "The son can do nothing of himself, but what he seeth the father do: for what things soever he doeth, then also doeth the son likewise," I think I was merely high-spirited and not intrinsically belligerent. In my repertoire of less desirable habits was one where, perched on my grandparents' knees, I would snatch off their spectacles and gleefully hurl them away. But at least I was not underhandedly bad-mannered as the evacuees billeted on them, who would hide uneaten food inside cushions. I was certainly a little pyromaniac and delighted in the recent Hitlerian habit of book burning. At the age of three I entertained my sister with a conflagration of our father's library. Half a dozen volumes had been added to the pyre, spilling from the open hearth to smolder on the carpet before my crime was discovered. O. Blow was instructed to make an immovable fire screen, which was installed too late to prevent the similar immolation of May's knitting.

Where the rod had been spared it was now applied in the shape of my father's army baton. This rather alarmed the gentle, protective May, who had seen her scholar husband go off to the wars and return a hardened man. Joe told me later that he had enjoyed the military, which had forced him to grow up quickly. His unit had been stationed in Berlin. He recounted being responsible for the appalling task of clearing the city's Underground after its flooding by the Nazis in a last-ditch resistance with huge numbers of the population still huddling below for shelter. I remember asking him if he had ever killed and his reproach, justifiable I think, for the unfairness of my question.

If his treatment of me was strict, it was merited, and, in retrospect, fair. While he was away fighting the German menace, I had developed into a little local tyrant. True to my Aries birth sign, I was leader of the gang and full of mischief. My domain was the cornfield separating the two family houses. I ordered my minions to trample down the precious crop into corridors leading to even vaster rooms that served as my headquarters. My second-in-command and best friend was Kenneth. Our total disdain for food shortages was further manifest in our chosen weaponry: gobbling biscuits and bombarding each other with jets of crumbs. My crimes were soon discovered and, arrested by the local policeman, I was hauled before my grandfather, then *in loco parentis,* for sentencing.

Then a severe, punctilious man, who extended the disciplines of hospital life to his own household, Amos could invariably be found at home at lunchtime. Meals were served as the clock struck or the radio announcer began intoning the news, never a minute before or after. I can't remember him ever laying an angry hand on me, but my memory has been seduced by images of the sweet and gentle old man that he grew to be. In general he indulged me—for I was the son he never had. Besides some Cotswold nursery rhymes he taught me, his linguistic influence betrayed itself when, denied some sweets for continued bad behavior, I upbraided my assembled aunts with a withering cry of "You greedy buggers!"

When I was still only three I attempted to fly from the coal-house roof and landed—badly—on the concrete path. My overweening ambition—or was it overwhelming imagination—was rewarded with a broken nose. Once put out of joint, it remained vulnerable and troublesome, although others have later claimed that this lopsided, improbable proboscis made my fortune!

I am unsure if I manifested any infant signs of my dramatic destiny, although I am told that an early and much-iterated word in my vocabulary was "Watch!" I loved to dress up in my mother's beads and run wild in full redskin gear with bonnet and tomahawk that was almost de rigueur for little boys of that era before Batman and Superman had inflicted a cult sartorial change. Later, Penny and I used to put two mattresses together to form a stage for Christmas nativity plays for parents and neighbors. She was always the director and it was Penny who first officially performed. I remember watching her in her school garden as, dressed in diaphanous robes, she went through some Isadora Duncan routine. I was filled with a mixture of curiosity and, yes, envy.

Photographs record the progress of a happy and uneventful childhood. An early one shows me grinning in my baby carriage, little knowing then that I was practicing a routine for the camera that would become a fixture of my life. Another, of my family, reminds me that I have inherited both my father's strong mouth and my mother's deep-set eyes.

There are also pictures of picnics in the country with rugs, primus stoves, teakettles, baskets and dogs. Nan, ever camera-shy, can be seen peeking around the corner of a car. There are photos of family seaside holidays with the shore still bristling with wartime barbed barriers. There's Penny in ribbons and bows and myself in long drooping shorts, entranced in front of a Punch and Judy show and another of us with my cousins down on the farm in Herefordshire. It was here that one of my uncle's horses kicked me, instilling an equine antipathy that persists despite subsequent professional encounters where I have valiantly simulated ease and enthusiasm.

Yarnton was an agreeable place to grow up in. Not far from Shakespeare country where "oxlips and the nodding violet grows," it was surrounded by the kind of green fields, soggy with rivers, about which Falstaff had babbled. There were bluebells in the woods, slow-moving streams full of tadpoles and cress and trees filled with juicy elderberries. We discovered how to make daisy chains, calm nettle stings with dock leaves and nibble on hawthorn berries and cow parsley roots when hungry. Despite the coming and going of teeth, I learned to whistle loudly, although another ambition—to coo dovelike through thumbs and palms—still eludes me. I also mastered that magic trick of reading, and delighted in the adventures of Thomas the Tank Engine. The great steam train era was ending and I used to love to wait on bridges for the thundering monsters to pass under me, spewing up their smoky volcanoes.

Bicycle trips into Oxford were great adventures. Penny and I would sit behind in little basketwork seats. A car ride was an even greater thrill. We eventually had our own—EMD 313, a secondhand, bottle-green Ford convertible. Once, however, alone with my father, I fell out into the road as the car rounded a bend but survived to face my mother's protective fury. But there were times when even she would countenance Joe's treatment of me when I was insufferably naughty in the car. He would stop, put me out and drive on. I would chase whimperingly after the departing vehicle to be recovered suitably chastened a few yards—but to my mind a million miles—farther along.

Childhood traumas were rare and they seemed to leave no permanent scars of negativity. I learned to respect, if a little to fear, my father. Starting school, though, was a major upset. My formal education began when I was four years old at the local village school, a solid Victorian building near the church and the outlying fields. I have an impression of a row of jam jars full of dead flowers ranged on a windowsill that indelibly symbolizes the utter misery of that first day. But I can remember nothing of my academic initiation apart from fighting in the hard paved playground and eating processed peas for midday "dinner." I would walk there and back unescorted, something considered unthinkable in these more sinister times.

In 1947, when I was five, my younger sister Caroline was born. From the start she was a sickly child. Her twin sister Bridget had died after being negligently left out in a draughty hospital corridor. I remember watching May breast-feeding her precious surviving baby and going to visit Caroline when she was back in hospital. Suffering from something called Pink's Disease, she was devotedly nursed by nuns whose somber habits alarmed me. A convent schoolgirl herself, Penny filled me with recondite religious lore, such as that all nuns wore flannel underwear as bright red as Jesus's heart. However clad, Caroline's nuns were skillful. She survived and thrived, but not without an abiding sense of loss for her twin sister.

When Caroline was six weeks old we moved to the London suburb of Merton Park near Wimbledon. Again there was a film studio in the vicinity, Merton Park's being famous for cranking out a plethora of "B" movies. Our new house was in Aylward Road, a leafy street of identical semidetached homes. My father was now working at the head office of Marks and Spencer and his rise in fortune and need to travel to London was reflected in this new home, which was bigger than its predecessor and close to the local station. In fact, the electric railway line flashed by at the bottom of our back garden.

My new best friend was Peter Kingham. His father was a sailor with huge hairy arms like Popeye's and a leopardskin watchstrap. The Kinghams kept chickens at the bottom of their garden and the smell of the evening feed was horribly offensive. Peter himself, I noticed enviously, was daily dosed with Virol, a kind of thick sweet syrup. Our household favored cod-liver oil sucked reluctantly from the spoon.

Food was still rationed, with books of coupons required for basic shopping needs, and my father cultivated an allotment of land that provided him with weekend exercise and fresh vegetables. My mother had inherited her mother's culinary skills and, like most of the country, we mostly ate at home. Special treats were fish and chips and a block of ice cream, both brought home wrapped in newspaper. On Sundays there would be a lunchtime joint of meat. It was an era blissfully free of cholesterol consciousness, one that would countenance fried and fatty foods such as pork with its irresistible crackling. There was always a pudding with custard or—a sign of returning prosperity— cream, delivered in a horsedrawn cart. On really special days I was allowed to ride along and help the milkman with deliveries.

There were parties with quivering jellies and opalescent blanc-manges, chocolate cookies and iced cakes. "Mrs. Bowdrie's slices" were the less than generous portions served by this local lady, and festivities at her house were accepted with some reluctance. We played Sardines, Musical Chairs, and other old favorites still unthreatened by the upcoming electronic revolution that would soon plant a cathode-ray-tube entertainer in every front room.

The local children's meeting place was the recreation ground, a little gray-green outpost in the encroaching suburban sprawl. Here we paraded our seasonal chestnuts, prizing the champions hardened in combat and the family oven. Marbles flew, balls bounced and we hopscotched over the chalky numbers, trying to avoid the cracks in the paving stones.

One day I swapped a water pistol for a cart made of baby carriage wheels and wooden crates. In that pre-skateboard era it was a major thrill to hurtle down the station hill in this boxcar bobsled loaded with screaming children. My daredevilry took a bolder form—climbing out of my top bedroom window onto the roof of the house. One unfortunate day I was spotted scaling the tiles by the guard of a passing train. He informed on me to my father who brought me firmly down to earth with a beating. On another occasion I came home dreadfully late from school after wandering the streets, a tourist in embryo, but my frantic mother was too relieved to punish me. Further chastisement, however, came when, imprudently secreting the embers of yet another illicit fire, I burned down a neighbor's fence. I longed for the legitimate fireworks and bonfires of Guy Fawkes Day.

My inexorable growth could be witnessed from my green skeletal feet viewed in the shoeshop X-ray machines before nuclear nervousness consigned these marvels to the rubbish heap. I was also making strides at the local primary school, triumphing even on the sports field amidst the jolly sack and egg-and-spoon races. I won the boys' kangaroo race and still have the yellowing parchment to prove it.

It was at Merton Park that Thespis first seduced me into a lifetime's fascination with performing. In the Music Club competition for 1949 I recited a ditty called "Cherry Stones." The adjudicator's critique provided a perfect blueprint for future professional performance: "Speech: Make sure of the words. You have a good voice. Interpretation: Good, but not knowing the words showed this up. Facial Expression: Don't look so worried. Stance: Don't fidget."

Our class also performed a version of *Little Red Riding Hood,* and I was given a little triangle to tinkle in the infant orchestra. I remember the seething envy that overwhelmed me watching the lucky boy playing the Wolf as he huffed and puffed his stuff on the stage. I longed to be in his hairy skin and knew absolutely that I could do better. I prayed for sickness to incapacitate him and, in the time-honored cliché, for me to put down my piffling instrument and tread the boards in triumph. I played this scenario in my head with such conviction that I'm confused as to whether it actually took place.

What I am certain of is that I was hooked. Peter Kingham and I organized several shows for which we demanded an entrance fee, an early initiation into the inextricable consanguinity of art and money. I singed my eyebrows with an inevitable fire-eating act and made my first toy puppet theater from an empty soapflakes packet. At the pantomime in Wimbledon, where we had all sung—feelingly in my case —"All I Want for Christmas Is My Two Front Teeth," the arrival of Cinderella's fairy godmother in the fireplace in a smoky flash made an incandescent impression.

Television was then in its infancy and few households possessed a set. For the most part, entertainment was provided by the cozy Uncles and Aunts of the BBC's Children's Hour on the wireless. The music played was often genteel and improving although the Laughing Policeman could be heard cackling ad nauseam. Sentimental favorites were a staple at Sunday lunchtimes, when the nation was kept in touch with its military forces that were still attempting, valiantly but vainly, to hold the far-flung Empire together.

One day I was invited by our neighbors across the road, the Suttons, to see a film, a Mickey Mouse cartoon projected clankingly on the sitting-room wall. This thrilling cinematic initiation was followed by regular outings to the Saturday-morning pictures at the local Odeon. For sixpence we visited strange planets, rode the range and assisted Dick Barton and Sherlock Holmes vocally in their ceaseless combat with crime. Penny and I were reduced to tears by Bambi's brutal death scene. *Little Women,* though, met with unequivocal approval, unlike the incomprehensible homespun un-fairy *Tales of Hoffman.* We read *Film Fun* comics and film annuals and I prized the gift of an old album of thirties film stars who smiled out in sepia, airbrushed perfection.

For the most part life was unremittingly pleasant. All things were bright and beautiful, as we chorused every morning. God was the benign Great Uncle who arranged, as noted in another hymn, for the rich man to live in his castle and the poor man to stand at his gate. Death was a distant abstract, manifest in black mourning armbands and the removal of hats at passing funerals.

I now had a growing awareness of an outside world. Mrs. Simeon, who lived opposite, gave me stamps amassed by her husband whose work involved him in much international correspondence. There was our King, God-saved but aging, the disembodied voice of the solemn Christmas Day broadcasts, emblazoned regally on the stamps of his still numerous colonies. Their names, now vanished or replaced, became familiar—Nyasaland, Gold Coast, Rhodesia and many with that proud, possessive prefix "British." I became a passionate collector and appropriated my father's album. To this day, I cannot throw away a stamp and fortunately have found philanthropic use for this magpie habit.

At school we explored the imagination and the world further. Besides conventional lessons, we were given special projects to study. One about Australia planted the seeds of an insatiable desire, happily now realized, to visit the distant continent whose shape we carefully cut out and embellished with drawings of koalas, dingoes and the inevitable kangaroo.

A Transport project, researched some time in 1949, contains an essay entitled "A Car Ride" and is revealing of more than just vehicular matters.

> When I went in a car I saw all the towns and roads. I went to oxford and hurn bay. When I went to oxford I saw all the aerplanes. Our car is green. Our car is a ford. Once when we were on a journey we came back in the dark and the babey was tired. Once when we went to the sea-side we bumped into a car and an old man came out and he was deaf. Daddy went past the trafick lights. One day daddy went down a no entrey road.

Daddy's crimes obviously loomed larger than my own but went spectacularly unpunished. The fascination for "aeroplanes" has not left me, and even today when jet travel is no longer for the jet set, that childhood excitement flares fitfully every time I step aboard.

Thanks to the green Ford, seaside holidays and trips became a feature of our lives. I have memories of a bungalow with huge, odorous mushrooms in its poppy-filled fields. Another year it was a seaman's cottage in Lyme Regis, also on the south coast. Small and filthy with a Stygian kitchen, it was wonderfully situated on the lovely harbor. As Caroline was still a fragile baby, Penny and I often had to amuse ourselves. I went fishing with a bent pin for a hook, but without success until one memorable day when into the harbor swarmed a school of frantic shiny mackerel that could be fished out with a shoelace.

It was at "hurn bay," the unremarkable Kentish resort of Herne Bay situated on the flat muddy estuary of the Thames, that our annual seaside holiday became a regular fixture. We shared a bungalow with the Sutton family, who were now friends as well as neighbors. Greta was the matriarch of this lovely brood. She was now husbandless, so all masculine duties had devolved to her good-looking eldest son, Hilary, who was much older, already into long trousers and with a driving ambition to own a car. Then there were the twins, Ann and Jill, who didn't resemble each other at all and finally Imelda, who was Penny's age and her inseparable companion. Unlike the real twins, they managed to look alike, even dressing identically.

To get to Herne Bay, Joe would attach a trailer to the car and fill it with carriages, bags, and buckets. We children rode in the back with Judy, our equally excited Sealyham, entertaining ourselves by pulling faces at other motorists and vying for the honor of being the first to see the sea. We all thrived in the jumbled informality of our holiday home, which was ideally situated on the low-slung seafront. We were given specific jobs: girls washed up and made beds, boys peeled potatoes. Trawling the endlessly shallow waters for shrimps, squealing as they tickled our feet, we would return our bounty to the communal kitchen and watch the sand-colored creatures turn deathly pink in the steaming pot.

When the tide allowed we swam in the muddy brine or floated out on inflated inner tubes toward the distant wartime gun emplacements. Jellyfish stings were avenged with a ritual melting of the offender. For there was sun, albeit a hazy infrequent English one, but one that could redden and peel white schoolboy skin as surely as a shrimp's plopped into boiling water. I appropriated my father's leather-flapped, Wehrmacht-issue sunglasses and goggled at the damp sands like Rommel musing over Alamein.

A long Victorian pier paraded far out to sea on spindly legs with a palace of entertainment at its end. Leading up to it were amusement arcades and carnivals where live goldfish and coconuts could be won. There was also a ghost train and little theatrical showcases containing famous horrors—beheadings, hangings and the unspeakable but irresistible activities of Jack the Ripper. Fortune tellers could be found appropriately amidst the endless games of chance where the penny-in-the-slot machines were genuine antiques. I was a great collector of equally ancient "bun" pennies depicting Queen Victoria in her youthful hairstyle. Worn into smooth thin disks, they are still in the box I used to collect money for the Mission to Seamen. For a penny a demure vintage beauty could be coaxed, in a whirl of flying frayed cards, to perform a chaste striptease.

For there was an innocence about it all. We all stalked Hilary when he found a girlfriend and dropped wet seaweed on other courting couples. Even the secret games we played at night in bed were free from guilt. Certainly Ann Sutton displayed no inkling of her future vocation as a nun in the worldly things she showed me under the sheets. I once surprised Greta in the bathroom in all her generous Rubenesque splendor. Yet like Ann's budding anatomy she was more an object of curiosity than sensuality, especially as she had recently caused a stir by catching a fish in her cleavage. Female nakedness in these pretopless days was still the smirking province of saucy seaside postcards.

The continuity of the annual Herne Bay holiday was not threatened by another move the family made in 1951 when I was nine, for we remained in the prosperous southeast corner of England. My father's new promotion to Assistant Manager took him to Brighton, that twin-piered Regency town on the Sussex coast. Packing up our house the moving men made me a present of an antique sun helmet found in their van. It turned out to be a rather prophetic symbol both of a future life of travel and exploration and of the kind of house into which we next moved.

Brighton

*B*urgess Hill, a place as bourgeois as its name, was formerly a sleepy rural hamlet that the arrival of the steam train had transformed into a dormitory for both London and Brighton. The progressive ugly urbanization did much to justify its local sobriquet of "Bugger's Hole."

Our new home, though, number 28 Park Road, was solid, generous and full of character. Wisteria cascaded in front, fuchsia and fruit trees blossomed in the back alongside a rockery and a fishless pond full of mosquito larvae. There was an adjacent field, soon to flower with its own crop of bright brick dwellings. Built in the heyday of Empire, our house was large and rambling, with such luxuries as a breakfast room as well as a dining room. It was also full of the jetsam of bygone taste —stag antlers and stuffed birds that the previous owners had left behind. I appropriated these for my bedroom, which lay under the eaves with a dormer window commanding panoramic views of the soft, sculptured South Downs that rose up like a long green wave to separate us from the sea. Surveying my new horizons with my brass sailor's telescope, I was on top of my own little world. The adjacent room was left empty. Musty and dark, it contained shelves of pungent, wrinkly dried apples and an alarming old water tank that growled, hissed and gurgled. We called it the "Witches' Bedroom" and avoided it, especially at night.

Park Road was a definite cut above Aylward Road. An aura of gentility still hovered about the neat rows of villas, the Gothic Revival church and the village green where ladies played a maidenly game of stool ball. The forested V planted in the flank of the downs to commemorate Victoria's Jubilee symbolized the prevailing respectability. Two Scottish ladies, Miggie and Jane, lived next door. I would have described them as "elderly" but for the sobering realization they must have then been about the age I am now.

A few houses farther up lived my first girlfriend, Anne. Our initial tryst ended in tears. True to my terrorist nature, I inadvertently kicked her while playing Tarzan to her well-bred Jane and swinging on the rafters of her parents' garage. But her nosebleed was forgiven. I was allowed back into the garden—even to climb some giant fir trees that enclosed the property, daring me to the challenge. Lithe and fearless, I claimed these swaying eyries for my new kingdom. We soon became involved in our new environment and made new friends, setting a pattern that has endured all my working life. Then, as now, the bed-rock of family provided security in the face of successive disruptions.

In summer there was swimming at the open-air pool on the green —or rather, there was a great deal of rowdy jumping, knees tucked under chin, from its high board. The thrill of dive-bombing the denizens of the deep end, however, barely survived the stinging rush of chlorinated water up the nostrils. I once saw a girl swallow-diving from the same heights and, true to my Icarus nature, tried to emulate this winged beauty—with a red-battered belly as a result. Even as late as 1980, when in Paris training for a film version of *Robinson Crusoe,* I could never quite master this longed-for flight from the high board. More recently, I was told by a psychic that I had been one of Leonardo Da Vinci's assistants in a previous life, helping him with his flying machines. I had apparently suffered an accident, so perhaps my failure is attributable not to arrant cowardice but to some persistent, deep-rooted psychic scarring!

Certainly that early obsession with "aerplanes" persisted. I became an avid model-plane enthusiast, especially for those proven successes of my Renaissance mentor, gliders. The heavy, metal Meccano models bristling with screws and washers were set aside and my room became a glue-scented shrine to this new passion. Squadrons of aircraft pictures lined the walls and spotter's guides filled my bookshelves. In addition to my own creations, I prized the models of a Spitfire and a German "doodlebug" given to me by my father along with his Russian sector armband emblazoned with hammer and sickle.

I even worshipped at that Holy of aviation Holies, the Farnborough Air Show, where, on another occasion, the test pilot John Derry was killed. I kept a scrapbook of the event, cutting pictures of the wreckage from the *Illustrated London News* and adding a suitably solemn tribute. The realization that these glorious objects were fallible made a profound impression. So did the film *The Sound Barrier,* where I rode in the cockpit alongside another doomed hero as, joystick juddering uselessly, he smashed brutally to earth.

In 1951 we were taken to London to the Festival of Britain, an optimistic monument to the spirit of regeneration after the bleak destructive years of war. On the desolate south bank of the Thames amidst its dying dockside where Shakespeare had first performed his plays, this was an attempt to bring culture to an area that had once witnessed its flowering. A modern concert hall was erected as well as the towering Skylon that pointed to a future of space and technology. There was also a film theater that would later figure prominently in my own future. London was then, however, a foreign country, unrecognizably grand and different from the unprepossessing suburbs in which I had so far been raised.

At least our house was in the center of town. School was a short walk away and the local Anglican church of St. John was just around the corner. True to his unspoken vow not to unleash on his children the spiritual fascism he had suffered, my father made church-going a matter of personal choice rather than obligation. He had seen his own father die, possibly as a result of Welsh Grandma's inflexible Christian Scientism. This had turned her wits so that she herself had to seek medical treatment. On the rare occasions she visited us she seemed stricken by an aura of sadness and never appeared to be quite there.

It was a time of growing religious fascination for me. On the way to school one day, someone showed me a postcard of the Crucifixion scene from a Passion Play—probably Oberammergau's. The sight of the suffering Christ, graphically portrayed as a man, churned up the fermenting brew of emotional and spiritual fervor. This was further intensified when I joined the church choir. I had originally done so for entirely materialistic reasons—the half-crown pay that boosted my modest weekly allowance. But later, other forces took over that shaped an enduring aesthetic.

In happier days, I found out, Welsh Grandma had once sung in chapel choirs, too, and at local Eisteddfods where my father had also been a competitor. He won several prizes of money wrapped in velvet embroidered bags—which were all thrown away when he traded the church for commerce. He could still croon a pleasing version of "You Are My Sunshine." My mother was a competent pianist and violinist who as a teenager had played regularly in the Oxford Chamber Orchestra, performing at the Albert Hall and in Gilbert and Sullivan operas. Now her prize piece was "Für Elise," for which we demanded frequent encores. Despite these roots we were not an overly musical family. Penny and I started piano lessons but, on my part, a typical impatience with technique prevented any real progress.

Our new school was Junction Road County Primary School. Its different grades and classes were demarcated by a chivalric system that belied the school's plebeian name. Starting as a Page, you progressed to Squire and achieved maturity as a Knight. This was all the more ironic as many of the children so ennobled came from the poorest families. They were pale, thin and hollow-chested and there were running noses, floods of tears and other more drastic "accidents." I became aware for the first time that the Johnsons were somehow better off.

The theme of accessible nobility was also evident in the school play I remember seeing, which was about Bonnie Prince Charlie. Again, swathed in tartan and sprigs of heather, it was Penny who got to perform. Again I was in the audience—but biding my time. I had to wait forty years before I could don the most dazzling of Highland costumes in a film of *The Master of Ballantrae* and finally achieve this most wished-for fantasy. Meanwhile I requested an Archie Andrews ventriloquist doll as a present and invested pocket money in a clumsy gadget for throwing the voice. Opportunities for further showing off were provided by local festivals, where fancy-dress competitions were still in vogue. I was a pipe-smoking pirate alongside a gypsified cross-my-palm-with-silver Penny. I can still taste the thrill of applying that big black burned-cork mustache. There was frequent reiteration of that early command, "Watch!"

I did eventually get to perform on stage. I had become a Cub Scout. The costume, with its exotic toggles, garters and badges, was part of the attraction, although the new law of Arkela with its Grand Howl and dib, dib, dibbing was enjoyable stuff, too. It was the concert party, however, that made the whole Baden-Powellite rigmarole worthwhile. I was chosen to play in a sketch entitled "Bathing the Baby" where, for the first time, I had the thrill of hearing laughter engendered by the apt delivery of a line of dialogue.

Life was pleasant. It was a time of increasing plenty for both the nation and our family. Rationing was almost a thing of the past and books of coupons, like prefabricated houses and demob suits, were disappearing. Only a trip to the local gasworks during a particularly cold winter to line up for a sack of coke to heat the house stays in the mind as a relic of bleaker times. We still joined my parents in their warm bed for a Sunday-morning lie-in. My father encouraged discussion around the weekend lunch table but forbade any intrusion on his sacred afternoon nap.

May and Joe rarely quarreled, though there was one memorable mealtime when my angered mother was moved to hurl a strawberry at my father, leaving a pink spot on the wall as a souvenir of this rare disharmony. Frequently unwell, and not very robust, May was treated with a certain circumspection. We were told never to upset her, with the result that, despite my father's bullish assertiveness, she became the real power center. When she was ill Joe would cook meals, forcing me at one point to eat his burned fare by holding my ungrateful nose! He even made me a birthday cake, decorating it for some reason with green icing and thistles.

EMD 313 still toiled regularly to the seaside and there was one unforgettable occasion when its ancient brakes failed when negotiating the road past the Jack-and-Jill windmills on the suddenly aptly named Downs. The trips to Oxford decreased when my grandparents came to live nearby. Amos was supposedly in failing health and had decided to take early retirement. They bought a house at Telscombe, a sprawling windswept development on the chalky cliffs to the east of Brighton. Amos also acquired an adjoining lot in which to use his last asthmatic breaths to re-create his garden. But he had not reckoned on the invigorating power of that Sussex air, for twenty years later he would still be harvesting his broad beans and sweet peas and pruning his beloved roses.

Our happiness was complete when sugar was de-rationed. I could now walk into a confectioner's shop and, incredibly and unprecedentedly, buy whatever I wanted! I even won a competition—the first fruits of literary ambition—where the prize was a visit to the Cadbury factory at Bournville and a year's supply of its delectable output. The correlation to all this sweet indulgence was that my teeth began instantly to rot. Luckily my dentist had rigged his office with a projector and as his drill whirled, so did a cartoon film through this magical machine that had the power to exchange pain for laughter. I wanted one, too! One birthday, my ever-generous parents presented me with a "Mini-Cine." It had a real electric beam, the single strip of film being animated by turning a handle. The images that danced their Technicolor way across the screen were mostly American cartoon favorites such as Br'er Rabbit and Jose Carioca. No matter! I was at the center of my own entertainment world. I called the tune, albeit an endlessly repeated one.

Perhaps wishing me to share some of the academic privileges he had known as a boy, my father determined that part of my education at least should be outside the state system. So, at the age of nine, I was enrolled in the preparatory school of Hurstpierpoint College, a handsome flint-faced establishment that lay a few miles to the south in deep countryside. I was fitted out with a complete new uniform, ritually identified with name tags. It included a cap and that indispensable cult object sacred to British academic life, a school tie. There was also a gym kit, football boots, cricketing whites and a large shiny satchel for all the new books that included, for the first time, a slim Latin primer. *Gaudeamus igitur!*

As a day boy I acquired a solid, reliable bicycle with which to make the daily commute. There were a few other "Day Bugs" as we were dubbed by the boarders, and we rode together in a slow convoy led by Woodcock, a solid, reliable senior boy. For the first time I encountered the team ethic that is such a feature of public-school life. The junior school was divided into two houses, York and Lancaster. I was put into York. In my case, allegiance to this ancient name went beyond mere superficial house spirit. It filtered its way into my subconscious to emerge usefully and dramatically decades later.

England in the early 1950s was, for all its postwar egalitarian posturing, a hopelessly class-ridden society and the school was a microcosm of these larger issues. The British, as it has been observed, are the only people to have been branded on the tongue. Most of the boys were from well-to-do families and spoke with the ringing confident tones of their class. The antique academic ethos found in countless fictitious school sagas was still largely intact, as was its accompanying patois. Presence at the morning roll call was confirmed with an *"adsum."* *"Cave"* we cried in warning and *"Ego"* to the demand *"Quis?"* Brothers were distinguished by the suffixes "Major" and "Minor." Even my father was affected: I have a letter from that era signed "Pater."

I was initiated into a serious new sporting life that included, to Pater's delight, rugby football. Freezing winter mud-caked scrimmages alternated with the pavilioned splendors of summer cricket. The roar of the touchline crowd was exchanged for the crack of leather on willow, polite applause and the odd "Well played there!" Footballers were called Colts and we were rounded up in buses to play other frisky, lean-limbed small boys at similar schools in Ardingly and Lancing. Although competent and furiously keen, I was not an outstanding sportsman. "Johnson in the York goal gave a very brave display," the college magazine commented generously on a game our house lost by seven goals to nil. The choice of the word *display* is perhaps significant in the light of subsequent developments! There was a house cricket match in which I tasted the heady sweet smell of success by hitting a six before being quickly bowled out. I had to wait years before returning to the wicket and repeating my triumph, but this time for an incalculable audience of spectators. In Joseph Losey's *Accident* I filmed a cricketing sequence at Oxford in which my prowess was a triumph of edited ease. "Oh, well played!" indeed.

At the beginning of my first term at Hurst, I was cycling home one evening when a herd of cows blocking my path forced me to stop. A fellow schoolboy was similarly halted and cracked a joke about our situation. We started to talk and when the road was clear again, rode on together. He, too, was a Day Bug, it turned out, and also lived in Burgess Hill. His name was Frederick Linnell. I had never met anyone remotely like him before. His round face was emphasized by round glasses and offset by a mop of spiky blond hair; he was intelligent without being pretentious, and eccentric without being insufferable. He called me Johnny; he was always Freddy.

I discovered that his hobby was collecting arms and armor. A first manifestation of our burgeoning friendship was the gift of an antique sword. Freddy and his brother Marcus—who would go on, quite appropriately, to become a director of Sotheby's—had a collection that included whole suits of armor. As a great favor, I was allowed to help polish it. Their bedroom was lined with a complete set of G. A. Henty's historical novels, adding to the atmosphere of cultured adventure. I looked forward to our daily bike rides together, even caped against the rain and in the winter dark when our whirring dynamos would light a path through the hedgerows. Freddy illuminated further the enduring mysteries of mathematics and helped me with my Latin homework. He taught me to play chess and let me beat him. I was enthralled by my new friend.

I welcomed all the new intellectual stimuli. I found I could write a good English essay, once composing a mystery story that, through lack of time I hope rather than of imagination, I failed to complete. It was read aloud and I had the satisfaction of being begged by my clamoring classmates to reveal the ending and what lay behind the two giant doors covered with butterfly emblems. I would still be curious to know! I even mastered the violin and played in the school orchestra, preferring uncharacteristically to allow my single sawing dissonance to be subsumed by the anonymous whole. In the music room I piped other more delicate odes. "My Love's an Arbutus," I declared, wondering what on earth that could be.

Our schoolmasters were mostly sympathetic, their billowing black gowns sitting easily on their youthful frames. However, there was one significant exception. The horror of his memory has wiped away any record of what he actually taught, if anything, apart from fear and loathing. We called him Monty Bear because of his shuffling hunch-backed gait and growling nasal voice. His particular circus trick was to insert a pencil in his chosen victim's hair and twist, almost deracin-ating the overwound strand. I was the frequent object of these sadistic ploys. Under his painful interrogation, I remember babbling about how exactly I had spent my weekend without managing to complete a homework task. The forced revelation to the class that I had spent some time washing up dishes was the final humiliation. But at Hurst such educational barbarities were mercifully rare. True, the Headmas-ter was given to administering canings on the behind, but this was still standard practice. Through tear-bleared eyes, I would watch up-side down between my legs in pained fascination as the dust rose in staccato clouds.

My voice responded to the more "cultured" tones of my environ-ment, dispelling once and for all any Oxfordshire burr and lazy sub-urban drawl. I found that I was good at reciting and was often called upon to read the lesson in Chapel at the Christmas carol services. Again, the church was my stage: "In the beginning was the word," I intoned prophetically. It was interesting to hear this same strong, muscular language used in an actual theater, for it was at Hurst that I saw my first Shakespeare play, a college production of *Cymbeline*. Despite not quite following the plot—I still don't—I was mesmerized by this story of headless bodies and magic potions and boys dressed as girls disguised as boys. I longed to emulate those lucky seniors now wildly garbed as Romans and ancient Britons.

Apart from the daily reminder of the Wars of the Roses, history was strongly featured at school. Roman legionnaires bestriding their northern walls looked down on us from their picture frames as we paraded for watery morning milk. A lecturer came to talk about the local Iron Age remains and suddenly history was wrenched from the musty realm of the textbook and made immediate. I felt the same thrill that holding Freddy's sword had given me, the double-moon insignia on its dark, sharp blade hinting at unlimited mystery and excitement.

Then one day history itself was made. The old King, prematurely worn out by the war and Britain's Pyrrhic victory, fell ill and died. His beautiful daughter rushed home from Africa and became our new Queen. Coronation Day was a national holiday and the event was celebrated in every aspect of British life. We were given china mugs and I hoarded stamps and even chocolate labels that were similarly exceptional commemorative issues, storing them with the aviation and Festival of Britain memorabilia. There they are today, together with a photo of the Queen given to us at school, imprinted with the request "to pray for me that God may give me wisdom and strength . . . that I may faithfully serve Him and you all the days of my life."

The great day itself, June 2, 1953, was spent around one of the rare television sets to be found in the neighborhood, watching the glorious ritual inauguration of the new Elizabethan age. Simultaneously, Mount Everest was climbed and we were later trooped off to see the film of this other momentous event. There were shots of Nepal in all its exotic splendor and I vowed one day to go there, too. A few years ago I had the good fortune to trek into the same Himalayan foothills while filming and, pitching camp on this roof of the world, I marveled again at its extravagant beauty.

Under the polished veneer of my schooling I was beginning to lose some of my wild ways. The only crime I can remember committing, apart from the petty infringements of academic law, was the stealing of a single walnut from a local greengrocer's shop. I was unaware, however, of my biggest crime—that I was in danger of turning into an insufferable little snob.

Cycling back from school one day, I stopped at the brook that ran by the road. On summer evenings we would often lark about on its grassy banks, but on this particular occasion I slipped and fell in. I made my dripping way home and, to explain my soaked and shivering state, concocted a story that I had been set upon and thrown in by "villageites," as we condescendingly called the local lads. I even elaborated the fantasy by describing the vivid red hair of one of them. To my consternation, my father reacted by calling the local police to instigate a manhunt for this carroty thug and his gang. Drowned in sympathy, I was sent to bed.

In the morning my father greeted me with a changed, pained face. This was a thousand times worse than the wrathful one I had at first fearfully expected. He had discovered the truth and made his disappointment plain. He had been paying for an expensive education and failed to see any positive results. I made my tearful apologies and vowed from that moment never to tell another lie. To a large extent, this Washingtonian imperative has been obeyed. It was a wretched but instructive time for us both for, after this episode, my father rarely punished me, nor did I give him much cause to.

I was maturing physically too, although my newly accented voice had not broken and I was still in short trousers hitched up with a snake's-head belt. I was hardened by sport and cycling and radiant from the buzzing school sun-ray lamp before which we were periodically paraded like observers at the current atom bomb tests. Photos show baby-fine hair blown into a permanent state of dishevelment— an enduring condition.

On the sexual front things were quiet. Then one day Barnet, another Day Bug, also in mid-transition from villageite to gentleman, asked me back to his home after school. There, he engaged in a form of quasi-copulation with his compliant younger sister. I was invited to watch and then to participate. Although I had perused the medical books in my father's library, gloating guiltily over their graphic pictures, I was unable to relate their specifics to reality. And Barnet's jolly sister proved no help.

Penny, and especially the Sutton girls, had given useful hints about the mechanics of the business, but the flesh was as yet too inadequate to perform the puzzling mysteries. In due course came the proof that one could actually procreate life, this revelation trailing clouds of solemnity and awe, but singularly failing to stop further "self-abuse," as it was censoriously termed.

A more pertinent rite of passage was the transition to secondary education and the choice of progressing in the rarefied fee-paying atmosphere of the public school or returning to the state system. My father decided upon the latter. His choice was partly motivated by financial considerations but mostly by the promotional exigencies of Marks and Spencer. Ascending their ladder meant a willingness to move around the nationwide network of stores. Joe wanted any residential relocation to be made as a complete family with the assurance that the state would provide a good grammar school education wherever we went—as proved the case.

So I exchanged the gray uniform of Hurstpierpoint for the navy blue one of Hove County Grammar School. A railway season ticket replaced the bike, for my new school required a trip down the Brighton line with a walk to and from the stations at both ends. A prewar brick building, it was perched on the Downs above Hove near an old windmill that featured on the school's crest. Indeed, life here was industrious and breezy with an expanded curriculum all supervised by a headmaster of such an energetic disposition that he was nicknamed "The Bouncer." But it was still very much a segregated boys' school with girls sequestered nearby in sister establishments. Anyway, our crushes were on the patrician senior boys. We longed to do them favors and, in return, bask in the warmth of their favorable regard.

In class I shared a desk with Gilbert McGinn, a darkly handsome Scot. "Tusks" McNaughton sat behind flashing two enormous front teeth, one of which I later knocked out in a playground tussle. The horror is with me still and through a thousand subsequent stage fights I have always dreaded the thought of doing someone similar accidental harm. I did once break an actor's nose but he was effusively thankful afterward, claiming that for the first time he was able to breathe freely!

In Hove County's larger classes I found that I was frequently among the first with a "Please, sir!" and a ceiling-stabbing hand to answer a question or tell a story. I was elected form captain and, as a term report grandly noted, "fulfilled admirably the office." I was enjoying myself. There were new things to learn: woodwork, pungent with glue and sawdust; physics and chemistry, with blue-flamed bunsen burners, explosions and boiling retorts. I started French, the first halting steps of an adventure that would bring me eventually before the cameras of a French film unit and to a home near the south of France.

Another new subject, art, became a favorite and facilities matched tuition in excellence. I discovered I had a talent, and learned to develop it with such new techniques as lino cuts and scraper boards. I also took a course in calligraphy and for a time wrote with a slow but elegant italic hand. As anyone who has had to unscramble and decode my present scrawl will attest, this did not last. My excuse for abandoning this new penmanship was that my mother had objected. When pressed by an incredulous art teacher, I couldn't say why. I still can't, except that I must confess to an ongoing impatience that undermined such mandarin dedication.

There were other failures. Latin America, for example, came up in an essay question and not one of us knew where or what it was. Our world was still agreeably small.

If Brighton with its *jolie-laide* seafront, its Regency and Victorian mishmash of architecture, its antique and shellfish stalls, its flamboyant Pavilion and narrow lanes was our new stomping ground, then the train was our new playground. We would dare each other to risky exploits until one day Boxall cracked his head on the entrance to Clayton Tunnel and a stunned sobriety ensued.

I once left my satchel on the train and was thrilled to see from the labels fixed to it on its return that it had traveled to Paris on the Golden Arrow. "Abroad" was still a myth, the romantic province of the privileged few, more the subject of a geography lesson than a family holiday. This was the era before the burgeoning middle class had begun a mass transformation of the travel market, making Barcelona as accessible as Bournemouth.

As for our own annual jaunt, in 1953 we exchanged the familiar mudflats of Herne Bay for the distant rocky shores of Cornwall, taking a house in St. Ives and including Amos and Mabel in our family party. My new box Brownie dutifully recorded suntans and seascapes.

On another occasion, staying with friends at Bacton on the Norfolk coast, I improved my smoking skills. As neither of my parents indulged, these were patiently and painfully self-acquired. I had started with rolled-up newspapers in the appropriate fume-filled fug of the Witches' Bedroom. Now I graduated to the real thing, inhaling secretively with equal appropriateness beneath the stack of pipes that were soon to suck natural gas from the North Sea. We used the cheapest of "fags"—usually Wills Woodbines in packets of five—and, I now squirm at the thought, butts harvested from the street. At this time, Freddy's father, a heavy smoker, died of lung cancer and we attended his memorial service in Southwark Cathedral. But the connection between his death and his tobacco had not yet been drawn or certainly not popularized. Cigarette cards and advertisements abounded. The London air had not been cleansed by law of its foul smoky fogs and its buildings were still clad in an ancient patina of soot.

Life was very much circumscribed by the parochial routine of Burgess Hill. I still scouted and choired. St. John's was high Anglican, possessing a wealth of Victorian carved wood, candles, stained glass and a plethora of quasi-Catholic rituals. Incense wafted from a swaying censer, Latin was invoked and the priest celebrated communion clad in gorgeous garments. Our own choirboys' robes were no less impressive—cassock, surplice and ruff off-set with a blue-ribboned medallion. I enjoyed this ceremonious showing-off. I welcomed filing in with voice and silver crucifix uplifted to the sacred skirl of the organ pipes. I liked performing for this captive audience and would not hesitate to put in extra time at weddings and funerals and weekly practice. Payment no longer mattered: I looked forward to the sheer pleasure of singing.

At this time I shocked my family by refusing to be confirmed into the Anglican Church. I wanted this to be a considered act of faith, not an automatic conveyor-belt process. I failed, moreover, to experience Cardinal Newman's criterion for conversion—"cumulative probability leading to subjective certainty." But I did accept the offer of another initiation rite.

Donning my first pair of long trousers I was sent off to Haywards Heath to learn to ballroom dance. In that nebulous era, dance was in a Terpsichorean time warp waiting for the imminent arrival of rock and roll to shake it free of its genteel restraints. True, my mother had taught me a nifty charleston, and I could conga like a dervish, but it was the waltz and the ladies' excuse-me that set the general tone. Ironically, the only places where I could practice my newfound expertise were local church socials. I very nearly gave up attending such functions when, in mid-dance, an unlucky forfeit forced me to sing "If You Were the Only Girl in the World" to an equally embarrassed partner.

All three of us children were growing up fast. Penny, buxom and boyfriended, was poised on the threshold of womanhood and great beauty. She shocked me with her pubescent revelations, filling my ears with innuendoes and unimaginable information. She was still strong-willed and yet showed the firm compassion that would later steer her toward a remarkable career in nursing. It was she who put our pet mice out of their suffering when they contracted some horrible disfiguring disease. As Caroline and I stood squeamishly by, Penny, caring and practical, quickly dispatched them. It was me, ever the romantic dreamer, who followed through with the elaborate funeral and grave ceremonies.

We were not, however, especially close as children. Penny attributes this partly to being forced to read and comment on my school report cards, a practice that inevitably turned her into a rival. She also tells me it was impossible for me to keep a secret. We would spend hours making or choosing presents and I would then infuriate her by giving out elaborate clues as to the nature of our bounty. I also teased her unmercifully, once hiding her library book until she threatened to throw herself from a window unless it was returned. It was only when her legs were alarmingly hanging over the ledge that I lost my nerve and produced it.

Caroline was now a beguiling combination of delicacy and robustness, enjoying that extra attention reserved for the baby of the family and especially for one who had beaten the odds. We would cycle together into the country, sometimes as far as Ditchling at the foot of the Downs to get frogspawn from its pond. But when a jet plane crashed locally I insisted on going off on my own to track it down. In scenes spared us in *The Sound Barrier* film, there were reports of shredded flesh hanging from the trees and someone claimed to have found a whole finger with a gold ring still on it. I failed to discover the gruesome site of all this carnage and I think I was glad.

My friendship with Freddy flourished. He, too, had left Hurst and was now at a grammar school in Brighton, and so our joint morning journeys continued. He continued to impress me, this time by reading the *Daily Telegraph* on the train. I was a devotee of the new *Eagle* comic and especially its adventures of Dan Dare in that postatomic frontier, outer space. But Freddy's precocity was no longer surprising. The fact that he had just received an axe—and not an antique one—for a birthday present seemed entirely normal.

It was he who introduced me to the greater glories of that quintessential English establishment, the garden. Raised in tightly fenced plots, I had come to regard my grandfather's green acres as the last word in horticultural expansiveness. I now marveled at the landscaped beauties of such local Sussex gardens as Nymans, with its shrubberies, rose gardens and majestic avenues of lime and beech. Freddy's own house was surrounded by trees and lawns and I loved to go there for tea where it was served on antique china.

In a nearby field we practiced archery using cowpats as targets. Laurence Olivier's film of *Henry V* had just been playing at the local Odeon and we had been to see it. It was a revelation. I had almost fallen out of my seat with excitement. There was Freddy's beloved armor in action. There was that thrilling thrum of a thousand Agincourt arrows hurled aloft on the strings of Walton's mighty score. And there was that opening sequence in that wooden O of a theater with painted actors imploring me to employ my "imaginary forces." I hardly needed such bidding. Shakespeare, gagged and misunderstood in the classroom, was speaking to me directly, making the short hairs stand up on end and the pulse race. Under his guidance I was traveling effortlessly abroad for the first time: "And thence to France shall we convey you safe, And bring you back, charming the narrow seas to give you gentle pass."

Later we were taken to the Tower of London. There in the armory were the steel suits we had just witnessed being winched on to horses, the lethal blades and proud banners. Suddenly it was all making sense. The drama, hitherto kept somewhat at arm's length by academic propriety, could be as accessible and as enjoyable as, say, *The Sign of the Pagan,* a film that the whole class had rushed to see during the holidays.

Culturally, things were improving all round. A television set now reduced us to silence, its novelty threatening the radio's long-standing sovereignty. Its programs reflected the mostly suburban mores, with the Grove Family Granny, incorruptible policemen as well as a legion of other entertainers and educators who stepped into our living room. Here's adventure! Here's romance!

The wireless's *The Archers,* though, remained a weekly fixture, and I remember still the imaginary forces shocking us with the immediacy of Grace Archer's fiery death. Later my father gave me his old battery radio that, in those pretransistor days, glowed heatedly from a multiplicity of valves. I was overwhelmingly moved by a play about the Crimean War, emphasizing radio's unique ability to embellish both educative thought and emotional feeling. Yet I saw my first opera on television: Menotti's *Amahl and the Night Visitors.* It was a civilized time for the medium. There was even an interval during which horses plowed fields and potters molded clay. Known as the "Toddlers Truce," it allowed parents to wean their offspring from their monochrome mesmerization and get them to bed.

This flood in the tide of my affairs ebbed briefly when an inflamed appendix sent me into hospital in Haywards Heath. The surgeon was quick—he apparently held a record of four minutes for this operation —and I was soon home again. Then it was May's turn to be hospitalized. My sisters remained at home with my father, Penny virtually taking over, at the age of fourteen, the running of the household. To relieve the domestic pressure I was sent to stay with my grandparents by the sea.

I had a new kingdom to rule, and an unpeopled one, for Telscombe was where, to the shrieking delight of innumerable swooping gulls, the Brighton sewer poured oilily into the sea. Apart from myself and the odd fisherman, the beach was rarely visited. No wonder. It was littered with the flushed-away detritus of distant civilization. I puzzled innocently over some of the objects found amidst the tar and seaweed —the dozens of slim, knotted balloons, for example. Other treasures were more identifiable: round green glass floats miraculously washed up on the pounded pebbles like so many mermaids' crystal balls and also some rocket distress flares, saved to brighten a later Fifth of November.

I became an avid beachcomber. In this isolated amphitheater under the towering cliffs I invented fantastic stories and recited them animatedly aloud. I imagined finding the dead bodies of spies and pirates, of pilots wrapped in unopened parachutes. I was the hero of countless daring exploits. The driftwood at my feet was Thor Heyerdahl's balsa raft and I was with him on the endless Pacific. The incoming tide beat at my feet forcing me to scale the cliff, its chalk transformed into a sheer ice face, and myself into Scott, snow-blind in Antarctica. At its beetling top I would dare myself to look down over Everest, feeling the wind pummeling my back, trying to push me into that fearful longed-for flight.

At night, we gathered around the fireplace, Amos wheezing asthmatically over his Pools coupons, Nan clicking away with her knitting and myself consuming cocoa and a book. I was reading my way through my grandfather's library, especially his Book Club selections, from *The Forsyte Saga* to *Whisky Galore*. I discovered Somerset Maugham, Erskine Caldwell, Mazo de la Roche and even Elizabeth Taylor.

For a treat Nan filled a plate with her pickled onions, which I would chomp and crunch with vinegary zest. After the ritual evening news there was bed with an old-fashioned stone hot-water bottle if it was cold. I slept surprisingly soundly, despite the wind whipping at the window and inside my gurgling stomach. Before putting out the light

I continued reading, often from the encyclopedic volumes of *Peoples of All Nations*. This was a world glimpsed through a patronizing imperial prism showing the natives with their quaint costumes and customs. But the most exciting discovery was that the dusky belles and bare-breasted maidens were starting to provoke a physical response that was unwonted if not unwanted.

I now made the journey to school on the green Southdown bus. The scenic ride along the swayback cliffs was spectacular and I always tried to sit in the top front-row seat. The ugly brick and stucco sprawl of Telscombe gave way to Saltdean and its 1930s pavilion, followed by a glimpse of Roedean School in maiden isolation behind its prim wall; on past St. Dunstan's with its railed cliff walks for the blind, skirting Rottingdean and so to Black Rock and along the shingly beachfront into Brighton. At the bus terminus, a window displaying cheek-melting mounds of iced coconut proved almost as impossible to pass as the joke shop with its itching powders, fake nails through fingers and plastic dog droppings.

I did my homework on the dining-room table beneath the goldfish tank with its two china children looking down. Nan brought me tea and cakes and I gave her company. She seemed a lonely woman and, I suspect, not a happy one, although she had obeyed her vows scrupulously, keeping a spotless house and a well-filled table. With tremulous fingers fidgeting at her mouth and gray hair, she confided how difficult life could be. I am sure that she and Amos were fond of each other, but they tended to keep to separate rooms and she apparently had no other friends. Penny had long ago sided with her grandmother against the strict and unbending Amos, but I kept an uncomfortable neutrality.

Amos could be found in the living room sitting in his high-backed favorite chair by the wireless. The walls were hung with oil paintings of roses done by an Oxford neighbor and some splendid Victorian watercolors that I have now inherited. He was most at home, however, in his garden, with its greenhouse and marrow frames, bonfires and compost heaps and a shed where he kept his tools and paints, his packets of seeds and jam jars full of screws. Here Nan also housed her massive clothes mangle with its iron handle and wooden rollers. She refused to trade in this ancient relic for a modern counterpart, thereby betraying that streak of masochism that would eventually compromise her life.

Though I enjoyed their company, I discovered that, on the whole, I was quite happy to be by myself. This new feeling of self-sufficiency was compounded shortly afterward when, at the end of term, I was sent away with a mob of classmates to the school's junior summer camp. "Good old Sussex by the sea" we roared out from the back of a truck as we skirted its shoreline to the New Forest where the camp was pitched amidst trees, sandy bracken, and wandering wild ponies. My first taste of life under canvas with its smoky fires and primitive ablutions was agreeably different. It held some of the romance of Arthur Ransome's enchanting *Swallows and Amazons,* with trees to climb, forest walks to explore and nature to study at close hand.

There were team games, with a gargantuan tug of war, and even an art competition of sorts where we were asked to model something in mud. Inspired by recent reading about the elephants used to maneuver logs in Asian jungles, I fashioned a mixed-media group of mud tuskers lifting whole trees with their trunks and dragging them with ropes of string. Thrilled with the result, all my enthusiasm was rudely dashed when the prize was given to a boy who had made a small, plain ashtray. It was incomprehension rather than disappointment that engulfed me. An ashtray!

Then one night as I lay in my tent I had an insistent feeling that I was somehow "different" from the other boys there. I could play their games and laugh at their jokes, but I somehow wasn't entirely comfortable in their company. The feeling became so overwhelming that I had to get up and leave the tent and be by myself in the sheltering darkness.

Bromley

CHAPTER THREE

S uch self-indulgent reverie was banished by the demands of yet
another move. Although I had no hint at this stage that it
would be ideal training for a would-be actor, we were uprooted again,
my father having been promoted to the management of his own store
at Bromley in Kent.

Mention of this county, also tucked away tidily in the southeastern
corner of England, usually conjures up images of gardens and fields,
of sunlit crops and horticultural abundance. But Bromley was then on
its way to joining its cockney namesake as a suburb of London, and
our new house in Blackbrook Lane was in that blurred no-man's-land
between town and country. Though detached, its cheek-by-jowl placement in the tree-lined road gave our new home continuity with its
predecessors. Slightly disappointing us children with its unopenable
roof, a shiny new Vauxhall sedan stood in the garage to complete the
picture of maturing prosperity.

Bromley was the town H. G. Wells used as a model for his *Kipps*
and, despite a market square now fighting its slow and inevitable
metamorphosis into a traffic island, it still retained some Edwardian

charm. Shops of the "Old Curiosity" variety survived—especially the booksellers with floor-to-ceiling stacks of dusty treasures that could be had for sixpence.

My new school was Bromley Grammar School, a handsome, neo-Georgian edifice set amidst playing fields on the town's edge, in busy Hayes Lane, its name redolent of vanished rustic simplicities. Also trickling past it into an open landscape of scruffy woods and fields was the river Ravensbourne, immortalized as "the stream" in the *Just William* stories of Richmal Crompton, who had lived close by. The school had been founded in 1911 and a patina of quasi–public school tradition overlay everything. There were houses, each with an emblazoned escutcheon, gowned prefects and sportsmen swaggering in their coveted, candy-striped house colors. Incised wooden notice boards commemorated the dead of two wars and the successful scholars of the ongoing academic battle. Even the school desks celebrated this theme of hallowed antiquity, being stained and carved with the self-aggrandizing memorializations of succeeding generations. There was morning assembly in a magnificent stucco-ceilinged hall with imprecation both secular and religious and wistful hymns harking back to dominion over palm and pine. All this was conducted from a large, curtained stage at one end with a balcony at the other, the significance of which eluded me for the first few unfamiliar terms.

Slowly I picked up and rewove the threads of my interrupted education, noticing in the continuing weft of subjects the same persistent highlights. I seemed to excel in written subjects, especially English and history, was competent in the sciences, but still woefully inadequate at mathematics. Although proficient at sports, even swimming for the school, I preferred the pursuits that could be crammed into that grab-bag labeled "Arts." I made new schedules—and friends.

The boys whose company I enjoyed most invariably shared a common bond—a passion for the wireless's futuristic *Journey into Space* and *The Goon Show,* especially the latter, which had just erupted on the scene. The ludicrous anarchic wit of Peter Sellers, Harry Secombe and Spike Milligan was slowly and rudely pulling the rug from underneath the old Establishment humor, fashioning a whole new revolutionary brand. Here was Aunty BBC, of all people, dropping her sacred knickers and mooning at her delighted public. And yet there was a double standard. We discussed the second television channel that had just started broadcasting, challenging Aunty's monopoly and style with its blatant commercials, and regretted this pollution of the pure Reithian cultural stream.

The timidity and hero-worshiping of earlier years vanished as we probed and tested the authority of masters and older boys, feeling the confidence of comradeship. "Master baiting," the elderly Latin master remarked, to a chorus of sniggers, "is not to be tolerated." Hayward would entertain us all by igniting his farts and more conventional smokers lit up in the Bogs, as the lavatories were poetically and justifiably described. One day their doors were found sawn in two with the lower half removed, presumably to stop this, and other, more sinister, practices.

In these pre–"Thatcher-Milk-Snatcher" days, the state provided milk as a mid-morning refreshment and perhaps to guarantee the final banishment of such Dickensian diseases as rickets. Smelly and repulsive in summer, it was only enjoyable in the winter when the caretaker carried in the icy bottles, semifrozen. He also sold soft drinks that, primed with sugar, were deployed as a weapon of sticky terrorism against the scourge of high-flying water bombs. Punishment was physical, administered either by the Headmaster's cane or by the inevitable school bullies. I was once made to lie flat on the playing fields while some sideburned, drainpipe-trousered delinquent practiced hurling a flick knife past my perilously protruding ears. More innocent diversions were yo-yos and 3-D comics, but, like the craze for hula hoops, they came and went.

We lunched in the smaller hall that made the fourth side of the Quad around which we would ramble in postprandial disputation. The food was hot and filling, especially the mounds of custard-drowned English puddings. Certain of our number volunteered as servers, but their benevolence was cloaked in greed and even sadism. Old scores could be settled by withholding bounty or by pouring hot gravy over fingers and thumbs.

In the afternoon the hands of the overwatched clock crept round to release inmates just before they pointed at four. I reverted to commuting to school by bicycle, this time a new racing one with drop handlebars and purring multiple gears, developing an iron-wristed grip on my briefcase as it began to bulge with knowledge. Once at home, I would be greeted with a cup of tea and a slice of cake—a custom I have delighted in ever since—served by the cheery Mrs. Carr, an M & S cleaner seconded to Blackbrook Lane to help my mother with the housework. As I sipped my Ty-Phoo brew, I glanced through the *Daily Mirror* and discussed the latest scandals with her before retiring upstairs with Freddy's old vade mecum, the *Daily Telegraph*. Large and airy with an old desk and bookcase, my new room overlooked the usual suburban rectangle of a back garden, now the disputed domain of our new puppy, a delightful Shih Tzu called Ming whose hair was only marginally more unkempt than mine.

Homework kept me desk-bound until the family gathered for dinner or until my concentration was dissipated by an irresistible appeal from the mumbling television set below. On Sundays, we watched the Variety Show from the London Palladium, eating delicious fried-egg-and-bacon sandwiches that calorie-carefulness now forbids. There were many transatlantic television imports and Eisenhower's America was portrayed as a curious blend of Norman Rockwell innocent plenty and unbridled criminality. A great fan of *Dragnet* and its Los Angeles setting, I had a glimpse of the city that twenty years later was to become my home. Later at night, when reception was clearest, I lay in bed and tried to tune in to this distant world on an erratic crystal set.

My father had become a Rotarian and roundly successful. My mother joined him in a new wheel of friends and associates. She was now well again, restored by a family holiday at a convalescent home in Chichester. We had also gone to Ireland, staying on a farm near Dún Laoghaire where the children still believed in fairies. It was all cozy warmth and comfort with piglets in the kitchen and hot bread to eat. At the Guinness brewery we inhaled the fumes of stout, guaranteeing us a year free of colds; our good fortune was further enhanced by shaking the bony hand of a mummified crusader knight who lay shriveled and outraged in his crypt.

Joining the local library, I extended my parents' and my grandfather's bookshelves a thousandfold. I was obsessed by a current national trend—the reexamination of the Second World War and its reenactment in every aspect of the media. My bedside table was stacked with titles such as *Cheshire V.C.* and *The Scourge of the Swastika*. With the same patriotic passion that Olivier's *Henry V* had ignited, I watched a generation of stiff-upper-lipped officers and their hearts-of-oak subordinates act out the conflict in films such as *The Dam Busters* and *The Cruel Sea*.

I was fascinated by the cache of photographs my father had brought back along with the Meissen figurines that were more elegant, and certainly less disturbing, spoils of war. Another album emblazoned with a silver swastika and marked "Berlin Diary" portrayed his service days. The confident comradely poses of his fellow officers contrasted strongly with the blank hopeless stares of their vanquished foe. Scenes of celebration followed scenes of devastation. I was later to reenact such episodes myself and these sad testimonials branded a searing truth on my awakening consciousness.

My father promised he would take us to Germany, where all this had happened, when I was thirteen years old. He kept his word, realizing for both of us long-standing ambitions: he to return to his old battleground and me to take wings and fly. My old mentor Leonardo would surely have been amused to see me elatedly strap myself into the Silver City Airways freighter transporting me and our car into the reality of a hitherto dream world. Airborne, this roaring ugly duckling became a graceful swan and even when we came down to earth in Le Touquet, along the shore where Hitler's armies had been halted by other feats of aerial daring, I was still in the metaphorical clouds.

The splendors of Paris, not to mention the heights of the Eiffel Tower, sustained the mood. The hours spent wrestling with irregular French verbs were vindicated in minutes of halting conversation as we found our way around streets and menus. French plumbing, though, provided a new challenge, especially those sinister malodorous lavatories with two slippery porcelain footrests and a gaping hole. When it was learned that that other receptacle was for washing not feet or socks but inflamed sexual organs, the legend of Latin lovers' prowess seemed positively understated.

Already familiar from photographs and from an oil painting my father had also brought back of a landscape of ordered fields and farmhouses, Germany was no disappointment. *"Zimmer Frei"* notices led us to simple lodgings in a variety of similar farmhouses. We also stayed with the family of my sister's pen pal in Bönnigheim amidst the vineyards of the Neckar Valley. Delighting in this picturesque, industrious land of reviving plenty, we drove up through the cool alpine meadows and mountains and home again. By a strange irony, imports from our former enemy were beginning to infiltrate British markets. A shiny new German refrigerator, curiously called a "Bosch," inhabited our kitchen. The famous Messerschmitt name, however, formerly emblazoned on fearsome fighter planes, was now reduced to labeling a squat, pipsqueak motor car.

The following year, 1956, we went in search of the sun. Like thousands of our invading fellow countrymen, we abandoned the uncertain skies of England for the cheap and dependable sun of Spain. The Mediterranean was the new playground and scampi the vogue food although the ever insular British insisted on eating it with chips. Driving through France, we found modest accommodations and I often slept in a room with my father, while mother and daughters shared another. In Carcassonne, in a stifling cork-lined bedroom, I paid him back for keeping me awake with his snores by getting hopelessly drunk for the first time and laughing equally loudly and uncontrollably.

The sight of the Hotel Marinada in Tarragona just below Barcelona, however, sobered us all up. With its dingy rooms, fly-blown kitchen and oily food, it spoke, not of mantillaed, castanet-clicking romance but of deprivation and depression. This was still very much Franco's Spain, before prosperity and democracy wrested the stubborn country from its long, stunned, feudal sleep after the catastrophe of Civil War. My father protested, but he had prepaid his bill in England, so we decided to stick it out.

The beach was nearby and the old city with its wine bars was a cool refuge at night. We explored the castle, the cathedral and the local Roman ruins, even penetrating the broiling heat of Barcelona to watch from cheap "sol" seats that almost mandatory tourist spectacle, the bullfight. Then a shadow fell on things. Caroline became ill with a burning temperature. There were anxious consultations with a doctor in her sweltering little room. My father's anger simmered: he was running out of patience and money.

As soon as Caroline was well enough we set off home, crossing back into France, and picnicking and sleeping in the car to save money. Then, just outside Orléans, Joan of Arc took ghostly revenge on us British. My father was overtaking a truck loaded with milk when, without warning, it suddenly veered to the left across his path, heading down a side road. A collision was inevitable. There was a stunning noise followed by an electric silence as we bumped and ground to a long, shocked halt. Fortunately, our car was strong enough to save us, but not itself. The sight of its broken glass and mangled metal was horrific enough to provoke three passing cars to crash into each other and a motorist to ask me darkly if there were any dead bodies. Not even one milk bottle, though, was broken on the truck.

It was the aftermath of the accident that showed the human spirit in all its contradictory lights. Another passing motorist gave my father money to complete our journey to a channel port, and on the train a young man, hearing our story, insisted that we stay with his family in

Calais. At Dover, however, as we huddled before him with our tattered baggage, hungry and exhausted, the British Railways clerk refused to bend his rules and allow my father to pay by check for tickets. The pent-up anger roared, to no avail. When we finally reached Victoria my father had an inspiration that threw us, yet again, on the kindness of strangers. He led his refugee band round the back of the station to a cafe run by a Pole who had been under his wartime command. We were immediately taken in and treated to a cornucopian breakfast. Flush with food and finance we at last reached home again.

The crash left no bruised memories. Rather, it nurtured in me an undying affection for France and the company of her vivacious citizens. My thirst for foreign travel remained unquenched and I shall always be grateful to my parents for awakening and encouraging this when so many of my friends had yet to venture out of England. But there was a fine residue of fear. At night I would lie anxiously awake for the sound of the new car in the garage to signal my parents' safe return. In time, I, too, learned to drive, reveling in the four-wheeled freedom. I even had the good fortune to survive several subsequent collisions. Each close encounter with extinction revived a certain wariness, but the joy of driving was so intoxicating that I soon forgot— as one does the everyday presence of ultimate death—such morbid, realistic thoughts.

Geography classes at school kept a window open to the outside world and it was no coincidence that a favorite book in English class was Conrad's *The Rover*. Life was now routine, with masters becoming friends rather than inquisitors. It was at this time that I encountered two teachers whose influence was strong and lasting. One was Grahame Drew, the assistant art master. Unusually, he was a product of an English public school and, with his instinctive confidence, "Danny" Drew exemplified the easygoing charm of his class. The cloth cap he affected—the stock-in-trade of the lesser orders—became on him an article of distinction, tweedily redolent of grouse moors and other icons of prosperous country life. The overcultured tones of his accent immediately set him apart, like a polite officer in a rowdy sergeants' mess.

He taught us the principles of academic drawing and perspective. A practicing artist himself, he took us to the studios of friends such as the painter Keith Vaughan. His major contribution, though, as far as I was concerned, was to organize school parties to numerous exhibitions and galleries. The marvels of the National Gallery, the National

Portrait Gallery, the Tate, the Courtauld Institute and the Royal Academy became ours, as a succession of other masters, old and young, paraded their achievements before our astonished eyes. The discovery of Impressionism was exciting enough, but to see London and its dreary southern suburbs through Monet's magic, transforming eye was thrilling. Above all, Mr. Drew shaped in me a discerning sensibility and sparked an aesthetic fire that has illuminated my life ever since.

At home I decorated my room with two eighteenth-century prints discovered in Brighton. Both my grandfather and I were great browsers in the Lanes, the picturesque quarter of antique and junk shops. He once picked up a filthy brass pot that, cleaned up, was revealed to be of exquisite cloisonné. Not to be outdone, I found an old grimy canvas in the street that had been discarded or lost. I cleaned it superficially and, with mounting excitement, uncovered the signature "Corot" in the artist's characteristic style. Putting the treasure carefully under my bed for safekeeping, I made plans to have my newly discovered masterpiece professionally restored. Going to retrieve the picture, I discovered it was missing and when I asked my mother for its whereabouts, found she had "thrown the filthy thing away!" I shall never know if, with it, went a small fortune, and I never fail to look at a Corot now without a feeling of dispossession!

The other great influence on me was Grace Collett-Franklin, the only lady teacher on the staff. She was a handsome woman, of certain years, with hair rather too severely drawn back in a school-marm bun and a rich humorous voice. As well as instructing the junior school, she also produced and directed the school plays. In addition, she was involved in the running of the semiprofessional Bromley Little Theatre and so, as well as enthusiasm, she brought a great deal of expertise to her school dramatics. Fortunately, she was encouraged by the Headmaster, who, unusually for those times, allowed two full-scale productions a year.

In the autumn of 1956 I appeared—at last—in my first theatrical production. *The Yellow Jacket* was a play that drew on the traditions of the Chinese classical theater, with its stylized mime and decor, rather in the vein of *Lady Precious Stream*. As Moy Fah Loy, the merchant's daughter, I was cast headlong into a whirlwind of joyous activity. There were rehearsals and fittings and an introduction to an unfamiliar world backstage. Crudely lit mirrors reflected mounting excitement. There were paints and powder, wigs and costumes. On stage, the heady smell of paint on scenery and the murmur of an assembling

audience. Curtains parted. Lights dazzled. A pulse-racing rush of terror and exhilaration. I was immediately addicted. The drug was in my
blood. And I was home. I belonged. The unlimited boundaries of the
stage were instinctively *terra cognita*. At last I had found my wings.

The school magazine gave me my first good review. The whole
family, who had nursed me through psychosomatic sore throats, unlearned lines and nerves, came to see the finished result, the first in a
long, long line of unstinted support. I would like to feel that my
parents' interest in playgoing intensified at this time, so that I gave
back a little of their bounty.

But there was still time for other things. A continued fascination
with flight lured me to the RAF station at Biggin Hill to watch the
screaming jets swoop in to land. There were fish ponds nearby at
Keston and on summer evenings I cycled up there with school friends
to try my luck. This incarnation as a fisherman was brief but passionate. I loved the ritual and the paraphernalia of the sport—tying hooks
and weighting lines under my school desk, buying sixpennyworth of
squirming maggots and watching the bright floats bob and quiver with
every nibble, enjoying the shriek of whirling reels when a large pike
would sportingly take the bait and rush madly round before slipping
free to provide another fishy story.

Another great friend, Dick Vane-Wright, tried to interest me in
bugs and butterflies, which he hunted in the surrounding woods and
commons. The great Darwin himself, who had first theorized about
their origins, had lived locally at Down House. I wasn't interested but
Dick went on to become one of Britain's leading lepidopterists and—
after eating some of his beloved bugs on a TV show—one of its more
colorful characters! He had always been that. Tall, gangling and unconventional, he had stood for Sinn Féin in the school mock parliamentary elections when my own political sensibilities were less
confirmed. Despite the Welsh background there was no history of
embattled labor struggles in our family, although my parents, in common with most of the country, had voted in the socialist utopia at the
end of the war. Increasing plenty and the natural political pendulum
swing inclined them to a conservatism that would become ever more
deeply blue and ingrained.

My great hunting ground was London, its center a fast fifteen minutes away by train. From an early age I enjoyed going up alone for
the day to "mooch," as my mother called it, through the junk shops
and markets and the latest exhibitions. I would finish up at the stall

under Charing Cross Bridge for a mug of cheap chicoried coffee and something disguised as a sausage roll. Again, I was happy to be by myself, to invent and improve on the scenarios that had flared my imagination under Telscombe's cliffs.

Then, one day, the boy who had acted a Chinese conjurer in the school play performed an act of pure magic, introducing me to the National Film Theatre on the South Bank. In its hallowed hollow shell of a theater I discovered some of the glories of world cinema from Eisenstein to Welles, embarking on an unofficial university course that remains unfinished.

Penny was not without her admirers as her beauty and character matured. She was invited back to Germany to stay with her pen pal's family. But, as the correspondence had now been taken over by the brother Jörg, a handsome man in his late teens, I accompanied her as a sort of chaperon. Before leaving we both took German lessons from Mrs. Poske, a native exiled across the road.

Clad in the latest fashion of bright "dayglo" yellow socks I performed my task as knight-errant with some diligence. Our sea crossing was so rough that the boat was forced to cling to the battered shore before making a mad headlong dash for the Continent across the broiling Channel. Staggering on to the bucking deck into the extremely fresh air to minimize queasy feelings, I remember gallantly enfolding us both in my raincoat as a protection from the drenching spray and flying vomit. Later that night on the train we were interrogated at the German border by the police. Had we anything to declare? As it happened we were smuggling in some packets of tea for our hosts. The German economic miracle was not then fully complete and such items were still luxuries. Using my new-fangled Thespian skills, I successfully feigned sleepy incomprehension.

In Bönnigheim we stayed at the village parsonage, for Jörg's father was its pastor. Our gift was gratefully received and, indeed, we thanked God at length for every mouthful. Stars twinkled in the clean air and a large romantic harvest moon hung over the landscape. The grapes were ripening; so was my sister's friendship now that ink and paper could be set aside. I kept a tolerant eye on things. I liked Jörg, too. He showed me both the old and the new Germany. We gazed over the blend of neat fields and bustling towns from the top of Stuttgart's new concrete television tower. We drove down to Lake Constance through towns such as Tübingen whose picturesque medievalism was still intact. I safely returned my charge after a painless, nay enjoyable, period of playing gooseberry in the vineyards.

The following year, 1957, Grahame Drew offered to enlarge our classical studies even further by taking a party of boys to Greece for the Easter holiday. Asked to go, I was wildly enthusiastic and pressed my parents to agree. For some reason, though, our Greek destination fell through, as did our school party. It ended up with just myself and Mr. Drew heading off for Italy.

At the Gare du Nord we took the overnight express and I remember the thrill of waking up to a pristine alpine landscape. We dined at a table set with silver, crystal and flowers as "Lombardy, that fruitful garden of great Italy," as I was later to enthuse, flashed by the curtained window and Rome, our first destination, was reached by sunset. Everything enchanted. Everywhere there were sermons in stone. Tedious Latin textbooks came alive as the monuments spoke of a history that still compelled. The Vatican overwhelmed with its treasures. Even the weather was perfect.

Later a coach took us along the ancient Roman road, still bordered with original paving stones, to Florence where Leonardo, my airy mentor, gave cause for further homage. I began to become aware of the astonishing fact that this country was an elongated treasure chest containing over half the world's works of art created prior to our own century. We admired the Giottos in Siena and the frescoes and spectacular setting of Assisi. This glorious Renaissance landscape would become familiar years later when Franco Zeffirelli re-created it for the screen, inviting me to figure in it. We next withdrew into the Canaletto cityscape of Venice, staying in a little pensione in an alley that reeked of canals and sweet cakes. I little realized then that I was in the footsteps of a legion of other privileged young English gentlemen making a similar Grand Tour.

Unlike most of these predecessors I brought back nothing of great material value, but the spiritual baggage was of inestimable worth. Grahame Drew was an ideal guide and tutor—knowledgeable and witty, allowing me to think for myself, form my own viewpoint rather than unthinkingly mimic his opinions. He provoked new perceptions and a new maturity. On the way home I read the new James Bond thriller, *From Russia With Love*. By an extraordinary coincidence I found that the train's progress matched that of Bond's. We were both traveling north on the Orient Express. At one point I glanced up to gulp a breath in all the fast-paced action to find that we were in Bardonecchio. At that same instant, Ian Fleming's fictional train raced through the same border station. I have often subsequently been aware of this force of synchronicity. What I was unaware of at the time was that James Bond would sweep the world—I would even be approached about playing him.

As with Bond, sex was now a factor of major significance. With the new hormonal symphony playing rousing overtures in my blood, it was becoming an everyday obsession. Outwardly, it could be heard in the vocal seesawing between uncertain manhood and boyish treble and was rawly visible in a pimply visage. At this time, I became aware of the full significance of the homosexual alternative. Although my father had expressed his intolerance of this sexual persuasion now newly legalized, I certainly experimented with it, briefly and unsuccessfully, pressured as much by curiosity as by others to explore this classical ideal. It was not for me. Subsequently, though, many of my dearest friends were homosexual and I was given many professional opportunities to understand and portray their kind.

I decided to stop kissing my father, although in retrospect I deplore the curtailment of this intimacy. Then, however, a masculine-man-to-man handshake seemed to be more consonant with the new maturity. We became friendly rivals waging bets on the most abstruse subjects, such as whether a plane existed capable of carrying a bus. I won. On aerial matters I was usually invincible.

Women now became the exclusive object of desire. I began to have lusty, unrequited longings, especially in summer when clothes were minimal and, as Shakespeare so accurately observed, "then is the mad blood stirring." Underclad models in my mother's magazines provided early titillation and, in the house opposite, a young woman who preened in her bedroom window as I sat trying to concentrate at my desk provoked spasms of guiltily enjoyable voyeurism. I was enchanted, too, by Brigitte Bardot, then similarly pouting her way to international fame as a "sex kitten," and, in response to my drooling request, received her signed photograph.

Not long afterward I had a chance to be a lover—and to revisit the Rialto. *The Merchant of Venice* provide my first "starring" role—Bassanio, Portia's successful suitor. It was also my first Shakespeare production and my entré to the world of doublet and hose and pentameter rhyme first glimpsed at Hurstpierpoint. Grace Collett-Franklin taught us a rudimentary stagecraft which I'm still polishing and improving. We learned the physical reality behind the admirable facade of a Shakespeare speech and how to steer the meaning through the intricate labyrinth of words. Grace demonstrated how to suit the action to the word and where the strongest stage position could be found. Also, how to pick up cues and make a pause speak louder than words. We were taught not to tread upon laughter but, I must confess, laughs were few and forced. The subtleties of this awkward play then escaped me and I am unsure if it was recent revelations about the Holocaust that made its anti-Semitic bent so uncomfortable. Certainly its language seeped in, bloating my limited vocabulary. "So may the outward shows be least themselves," I find myself still musing, although, as with most roles, the lines have evaporated from memory, to be reheard, like old jokes long forgotten, with the keenest of rediscovered pleasure.

Grahame Drew took me to my first live opera performance, a jewel-bright production of Mozart's *Die Entführung aus dem Serail*, at Glyndebourne, whose bucolic setting vied with Oliver Messel's decor for romantic escapism. As in the plot, I felt myself being abducted from a closed world of parochial values into a wider one of creative largesse. Seeing Wagner's gargantuan *Götterdämmerung* at Covent Garden, more scales fell from my astonished eyes. Soon after, I remember an encounter with a beautiful French woman while on another holiday in a hotel in the west of Ireland. We argued passionately about the respective merits of Mozart and Beethoven, a fervor inflamed on my part at least by the syncopated rhythms filtering through her adjoining bedroom door at night.

Even in popular music, good golly Miss Molly, my tastes were changing. I no longer held the snobbish view that the invasion of rock and roll music was socially destabilizing. I no longer derided the cult of Elvis Presley or fellow students who paid him homage with their blue suede shoes and duck's-arse haircuts. I enthused over Johnnie Ray's sobbing version of "Cry" and even went with Penny to see Chubby Checker twisting live at Croydon. Later I was secretly pleased to be nicknamed Adam at school because of a passing resemblance to Adam Faith, the new teenage pop idol.

Dick Vane-Wright, temporarily forsaking his butterfly net, had once shoved a trumpet mouthpiece down a section of scrap-metal lead pipe and entertained us all to an impromptu concert on his self-styled "sponosphone." Others had joined in on makeshift instruments, which had led to a serious interest in making music and a progression to real instruments. I had tried to make a guitar but failed to coax such a delicate instrument to life. After toying with a borrowed one, I abandoned ambitions as a musical performer, even though skiffle was then the rage, with every other youth making music from tea-chest basses and maternal washboards. Although fascinated by the louche world of London's coffee bars, such as the Two I's that had made famous such homegrown talent as Tommy Steele, my own growing preference was for classical music. The experience of my first Bach Passion was an overwhelming revelation.

Jazz provided other pleasurable new insights into the American cultural mainstream, and I especially liked Duke Ellington's interpretation of Shakespearean themes, "Such Sweet Thunder." I encouraged the formation of a film society at school. We screened *The Cabinet of Dr. Caligari* and *The Battleship Potemkin* and started the first hard stumbling steps down the twisted road of cinema criticism. I wrote argumentative letters to the local paper, one of which was published.

As a "healthy-minded" teenager I was exasperated by the sheer fatuity of the letter written by your understandably anonymous correspondent concerning Alfred Hitchcock's recent film *Psycho*. Not only did I and most of my friends, who prefer to treat the cinema as a creative art rather than a weekly entertainment, find this film emotionally stimulating—its fundamental purpose—but also our enjoyment was enhanced by its technical brilliance. I suggest that these squawking teenagers were attracted into the cinema, not by Mr. Hitchcock's considerable reputation, but by the scantily dressed girl on the poster.

Such extracurricular joys, however, were circumscribed by the impending threat of academic examination. The O level was the second great national hurdle. I attempted nine fences and fell at only one, the notorious slough of mathematics, cleared miraculously the following year. How important it all seemed at the time and how sweet the relief when it was all over!

I celebrated the temporary freedom from scholastic duress in a now characteristic way—performing in the summer school play. "Every time you write to me you seem to be in a play!" a letter from my Burgess Hill girlfriend Anne Dunnett commented. "Are you a gifted actor or what? Congratulations on getting 'a good part.' I hope the local grammar school girls live up to the honour that has been thrust upon them!" *My Three Angels* by Sam and Bella Spewack was a comedy and this time the laughs were long and genuine. I was the unsympathetic Paul and relished the new sensation of playing a "villain." Well, was I a serious actor? I certainly enjoyed discovering the mysteries of this new craft under Grace's tutelage. It was preferable to kicking or thwacking a ball around after school and I did seem to have a facility for it. I had won the school speech prize and, moreover, the local newspaper had said that our performance was "up to professional standards." But as a future career? I hardly dared dream so far. Actors were mythical creatures like Olivier and Marilyn Monroe, currently generating attention by filming together in England.

Asked about future employment I had nonplussed the careers master by telling him I wanted to be a couturier, but at the time it was a genuine, if curious, ambition. Design fascinated me and I was a frequent visitor at London's Design Centre, where it was celebrated in every aspect of life. I had thoughts of becoming an architect but, like the character in the Peter Cook sketch who laments "I could have been a judge but I didn't have the Latin," I knew that mathematics would be my pitfall.

To earn extra money I worked, like my father before me, as a porter at Marks and Spencer, but with no ambitions of this leading to a similar career. I was soon bored with my backstage role crushing boxes and sweeping floors, and one day promoted myself to the shopfloor. Furiously selling fruit, I found that eye contact could stop customers in their tracks—a discovery later put to good professional use —and that if you actually presented a bunch of apples, overemphasizing their weight with an actorly skill and flourish, a sale was almost guaranteed.

I took every advantage of more school parties to see plays. We were spellbound by John Gielgud's magisterial silver-voiced Prospero. In contrast, Robert Atkins's production of *Hamlet* was notable for his loud whispering of stage directions to his cast. It was to be expected, even welcomed, for, like Gielgud, he was already in the pantheon of the legendary, his eccentricity the source of many stories. Whatever the play at hand, "Couch we awhile and mark" was the invariable signal that he had "dried" on his lines, whereupon he would shuffle down to the prompt corner for enlightenment and carry on until the next uncertainty brought him back there again. We enjoyed the Royal Academy of Dramatic Arts's public offerings and my longing to emulate grew apace, although university and not drama school still remained my goal.

In the summer school play of 1959, I played the Russian Ambassador in Peter Ustinov's *Romanoff and Juliet;* although made up with deep purple age lines, I looked more like a kabuki actor. The first in a seemingly endless line of parts requiring an Eastern European accent, it was also an introduction to the work of a man whose humor and humanity I admire inordinately, and whom, on several occasions, I have been privileged to call a colleague. My U.S. counterpart, the prototype of the patronizing, overaffluent American then current, was played in broad transatlantic tones by Tony Dear. Tall and elegant, he was offstage invariably draped in an immaculate silver-buttoned double-breasted jacket fastidiously devoid of scholastic adornment. Almost in contradiction, he was obsessed with Kerouac, the American Beat movement and the Existentialists. I became infected with his antiestablishment enthusiasms. "Bourgeois" became the ultimate insult, although in my new tweed jacket, gray flannel trousers and daring suede shoes I was, like Tony, its living embodiment.

Youth Theatre

CHAPTER FOUR

*I*n the summer of 1959 I made my West End theatrical debut. As the ambassador Voltemand in *Hamlet* I had one line: "In that and all things will I show my duty." It was a fitting credo for a neophyte and I wrung every possible subtlety and variety from it. Performing in London, the Parnassus of British theatrical culture, was a swift fulfillment of a schoolboy's dream.

It had all happened when I chanced to read a notice on the school board from someone called Michael Croft inviting people to take part in a production by an organization called the Youth Theatre. Noting the details, I got in touch and duly found myself one February afternoon in London undergoing that quintessential and theatrical experience—the audition.

Michael Croft turned out to be a short, untidy, sandy-haired man with quizzical, ironic eyes set in a square head and a cigarette permanently clenched between stubby fingers. Between vigorous inhalations, he spoke with a slow Northern accent. He was unintimidating and friendly and there seemed to be a constant, unstated, wry amusement behind every word. We had been asked to prepare two contrasting speeches from *Hamlet* and to bear in mind that the main qualities looked for were clarity, dramatic sense and liveliness. "Pleasant elocution is not enough." The cautionary warning continued: "Only those with a real sense of team spirit are required—who enjoy taking part in a dramatic production in however humble a capacity and who will carry out cheerfully any job however mundane which is given them."

Waiting with the other young hopefuls I must have chewed on my nether lip in nervous anticipation because, glancing down to recheck my lines for the thousandth time, I noticed that the trembling text was, as Shakespeare would have put it, incarnadined. This rite of blood-bonding to the Bard seemed, however, fortuitous. I was accepted into the company to play Voltemand and his one unmemorable line and to understudy Horatio. I was humble and very cheerful.

The Youth Theatre had been recently formed from a nucleus of boys Michael Croft had taught at Alleyn's, a south London school named appropriately after Edward Alleyn, the great Elizabethan actor. Croft demonstrated that a large-cast Shakespeare production could make up in energy and enthusiasm—and sheer numbers—for what it lacked in professional polish and skill. At the same time, it fulfilled the old Aristotelian precept of learning by doing. After a successful start, he was now expanding his net, drawing young actors from London and the Home Counties, thereby setting his fledgling company on the long vicissitudinous path to royal patronage and recognition as the National Youth Theatre of Great Britain.

Hamlet was staged at the Queen's Theatre, newly remodeled with a glass front and foyer. We followed Sir John Gielgud's one-man Shakespeare recitation *The Ages of Man,* and so a formidably high standard had been invisibly set. Gielgud's great friend and colleague Sir Ralph Richardson was our patron and would occasionally attend rehearsals and meetings. Like a benevolent great uncle, he inspired and enchanted. "That boy has a face for Horatio," he remarked of me in eccentric, oft-imitated tones. I am still uncertain whether to accept it as a compliment!

The production was run on military lines, discipline and initiative being expected of recruits both on and off the stage. Grants from educational authorities were few and we were expected to earn our keep. Fortunately, Grahame Drew, away on holiday, lent me his Kensington flat and the means to eschew the standard scenario for the budding artist of starving picturesquely in a garret. A star system was rigorously discouraged, the fiction being maintained that the person bearing fardels was as important as the person playing Hamlet. Nonetheless, stellar talents appeared inevitably and involuntarily.

At that time the company was still all male, with boys playing female roles as in the Elizabethan theater. The mother of Richard Hampton who played Hamlet, however, was the wardrobe mistress, assisted by the enchantingly nubile Jane Merrow, who would later blossom into an admired actress. Then, too, she was the object of a mass male admiration that bordered on unmitigated lust. Her chosen escort was Simon Ward who, with his wide almond eyes and sensual lips, had just graduated from playing beautiful maidens to the role of Rosencrantz—or was it Guildenstern? Hywel Bennett was a ravishing blonde-wigged Ophelia and Kenneth Farrington a bearded, foxy Claudius.

Croft rehearsed as if with a soccer team, stating expressly that he wanted acting to be "as natural as playing football and just as exciting." We were his lads whose natural habitat when not kicking around on stage was in the Duke of Wellington pub next door. This brisk no-nonsense approach would reach its apotheosis in 1967 with *Zigger Zagger,* a play about football teams and fans that the National Youth Theatre made internationally famous. But Croft's approach—a fast, unfussy reading of the text—obeyed Hamlet's own strictures to his players, which, in my estimation, is still one of the best acting lessons ever devised. The result was a critical and financial success.

I hadn't realized then that the whole future of the Youth Theatre was hanging in the balance and this approbation ensured the continuance of a splendid idea. I witnessed for myself its social value. Energy that might otherwise have been self-destructively employed was redirected to positive ends. At first reluctantly holding spears, potential thugs found unsuspected seeds of creativity within which bloomed as their lives were turned around. Audiences responded to the verve and clarity of these contemporary "little eyases." As for me, acting in the West End brought added confidence. It was a thrill just to pass through the stage door. Even sleeping on the foyer floor after an all-night technical rehearsal seemed impossibly glamorous. It was also the beginning of an enduring love affair with this haunting, unforgettable play.

At the end of the week we transferred to Cambridge for another week's run at the Arts Theatre, affording tantalizing glimpses of undergraduate life. My father, while approving my dramatic holiday, continued to emphasize how much he would like me to follow in his academic footsteps and not be sidetracked down some glittering show-biz path. Seduced over the years by his crested college photographs, and now by academic reality, I hardly needed encouragement. But all that lay ahead. Now I was a touring actor with theatrical digs, pub lunches and moonlight dips in the river to enjoy.

The curtain having rung down on these pleasures, there remained the rest of the long summer to spend "resting." With a schoolfriend, Peter Fenwick, I followed in Laertes's footsteps to a France still characterized by berets, baguettes and coffee drunk by the bowlful. Exploring the byways of Normandy and Brittany by bicycle, our progress was unreliable as we invariably drank too much cheap wine for lunch. We slept it off under haystacks in the shade of farmhouse walls covered with huge alcoholic inducements such as the *"Du, Dubon, Dubonnet"* that looked like a drunkard's stumbling attempts to read the famous sign. We stayed in youth hostels where the heavy-handed "humor" during the evening's entertainment could sometimes be "de trop."

We stayed in a minute tent until a latent and unsuspected sybaritism made us settle in a small hotel in St. Brieuc. Apart from swallowing all our savings, there were other consuming problems. We were both served with our first artichoke and sat there bewildered by this culinary stranger. Covert observation of our fellow diners showed us the way and from then on I have been a passionate stripper of this delectable vegetable. Here we also learned to lotus-eat for, having stopped our *tour sportif*, we lolled lazily in the sun reading avidly. Ever since, books and beach have constituted my recipe for a good holiday. So thorough was our physical decline that we even stashed our bicycles on the plane and flew home.

This trip demonstrated a tendency that was to persist. In the headlong rush south I was to know Europe before my own country. Whole tracts of the English Midlands and the North, not to mention Scotland, remained unexplored. Only now am I beginning to reverse the trend and to realize what I was missing. But then it was a glorious time to be abroad in Europe, before travel was packaged into a stressful industry. Even Penny, on leaving school, had moved to the Continent, taking a temporary job as a secretary in Zurich and sending back details of her enviable adventures there.

Exploring equally unfamiliar territory back at school, I graduated to the sixth form and, as a prefect, joined in the school government.

Befitting the quasi–public school ethos, we wore gowns and were allowed to administer punishment—usually in the form of endlessly repeated lines. I was also a librarian and welcomed the inclusion on the shelves of the new unexpurgated version of James Joyce's *Ulysses.* It was joined by D. H. Lawrence's *Lady Chatterley's Lover,* which the British courts had just absolved of charges of obscenity, a brouhaha that had diverted the entire nation and guaranteed best-sellerdom for the book.

I found the sharper focus on my chosen subjects—English literature, history, French and art—to be enormously satisfying although, in retrospect, regret the severing of all science subjects. I wish I had learned economics, as history studies seem to emphasize that the world was shaped as much by these forces as military ones. But this modern world, unfortunately, seemed to insist on specialization. I kept a diary that recorded in minute, spidery writing my curriculum and weekly, nay daily, essay tasks. I doubt now whether I could tell you if the Revocation of the Edict of Nantes was a turning point in the reign of Louis XIV but I could then. I marvel now at the multiplicity of my intellectual tasks and the mental stamina they developed.

It was a time when the First World War was receiving renewed scrutiny as the beginning of our New Age. I had been enormously affected by Joan Littlewood's monumental musical show *Oh! What a Lovely War,* which counterpointed the death and destruction of the 1914–1918 war with the jaunty music-hall songs of the era. I made a special study of the poets who, energized by the prevailing horror and hypocrisy, had mostly died like cattle before the youthful promise I now sensed had been fulfilled. I felt a morbid kinship with Owen and Sassoon.

My generation was almost the first to miss out on military National Service although, ironically, most of us went around looking like conscripts in cast-off naval duffel coats and Eighth Army desert boots. Whether we benefited from this failure to serve Queen and country makes fruitless speculation. I would get to fight my war, glorifying and vilifying it, in stage and film roles. Meanwhile there was a growing pacifist, and especially antinuclear, movement. While the military still talked of "winning" limited nuclear engagements, the reality of possible mass obliteration was engendering a nervous nihilism, especially in the children.

Protests became widespread and vociferous with a national campaign for nuclear disarmament and annual marches from the atomic weapons establishment at Aldermaston. I was sent this note at school:

> Would you confirm that you are joining the Easter March please? We are to leave on Good Friday and the demonstration will finish on the Monday afternoon in Trafalgar Square. Accommodation is in large schools, food is provided at a reasonable cost, and everybody's baggage is transported during the day to the evening's halt. This may sound stupid but you'll need twice as many pairs of socks as normal. Should your parents be concerned about the length of your jail sentence, you can assure them the problem will not arise. The campaign is on very good terms with the police.

The perfect suburban rebellion, well mannered and well fed with baggage service and plenty of clean socks!

I didn't get to march and was subsequently never much of a political activist. On the party-political front my zealotry was defused by a persistent ability to see both sides of an argument. Then, however, I was ill placed to disagree with the Prime Minister, Harold Macmillan, when he assured us that "we had never had it so good."

But I also listened to the strident, urgent voices of the new playwrights who preached another gospel, one that tried to shake Britain from its smug postcolonial slumber. The Suez fiasco had bred uncertainty about our future role in the world, especially now that we possessed the power to destroy the latter entirely. At home, John Osborne, Colin Wilson and other Angry Young Men were fanning the fires of literary, if not social, rebellion. Abroad, the New Wave was reinventing cinema. Life was getting exciting!

For the moment, the academic and theatrical stage preempted any major performances in the larger arena of life, though I did get my first opportunity to play a soldier: "The British soldier can stand up to anything except the British War Office," was my laconic comment as the suave, worldlywise General Burgoyne witnessing the start of the American Revolution in Shaw's *The Devil's Disciple*. We later made a trip to Stratford-upon-Avon to observe the vengeful fate of another soldier, Coriolanus. There was a huge groan of disappointment when it was learned that an understudy would be substituting for Laurence Olivier, who had injured his leg doing a characteristically spectacular backward death fall. This, however, turned out to be a fiery young actor named Albert Finney, and his dynamic interpretation left none of us disappointed. He was in the slips of stardom, and I admired the way this future colleague seized and glorified his chance.

Mine came soon afterward when I followed my father's suggestion to sit the scholarship examination at Cambridge University. It was a trifle premature, he reasoned, but it would give invaluable practice and experience. With the Headmaster's approval a small group of us duly went up to try our luck. I remember with sinking heart the small room at Pembroke College smelling of socks and gas, and the insomnia borne of strangeness and anxiety.

What made this whole trip unforgettable, however, was meeting with E. M. Forster in his rooms at King's College. This had been arranged by a friend of Grahame Drew, ever my benefactor though now gone from Bromley to spread enlightenment among his social peers at Winchester College. Mindful of Polonius's observation that "The apparel oft proclaims the man," I rose sartorially to the occasion by purchasing my first shirt with detachable collar, studs and links, forgetting that Forster had mocked such craven conformism: "All men are born equal—all men that is to say, who possess umbrellas." Spry and polite, he was surrounded by a bevy of handsome young men. We took tea and listened to bel canto arias on his gramophone. The next day I rushed out to buy his *A Passage to India* and inscribed my copy in honor of this meeting. I remained a devotee of his work, at one point, when filming in India, even trying to purchase the screen rights to *Passage,* so strongly had its theme ignited my imagination.

This term-time glimpse of the gowned and scarved student world only intensified my longing to join it. Shortly afterward I learned that one of our group, Christopher Hill, had won an open scholarship in history to Corpus Christi College. My father's suggestion had paid off handsomely, but his son was filled with an envy that astonished with the degree of its ferocity. Then news came that I had been offered a place to read history at Pembroke, which calmed the green-eyed monster. Although he never raised this matter, I felt an obligation to free my father of any future fee-paying, setting my sights on a state scholarship and switching allegiance to an Oxford award.

The year ended on an unexpectedly frivolous note after all this fierce ambition with another, this time minor, competition. My recent encounter with the wit and wisdom of Bernard Shaw had prompted me to enter a quotation of his in a newspaper contest for the best New Year's resolution. "Without good manners, human society becomes intolerable and impossible," I smugly offered, still desperately trying to put this into practice vis-à-vis Chris Hill's academic triumph. A letter of congratulations informing me that I was "one of the lucky one hundred out of many thousands of entrants" preceded another requesting measurements for a dinner suit. Revealingly, it also contained a check for £10 "to enable your companion to buy her ball dress"—a sum that today would barely purchase the zipper on it! In the upshot I invited and gowned Penny's best friend Di, a fellow student at King's College Hospital, where they had both just started nursing careers. We enjoyed a most soigné evening at the Waldorf hotel, where we also stayed—in chaste separate rooms. I little realized then that such unaccustomed splendor would one day become a welcome part of my working life.

Girlfriends were now a necessity rather than a luxury, but there was no one special in my life. We had all been seduced and devastated by Simone Signoret's sensual performance in *Room at the Top*. Here was the woman of our dreams: older, competent, and exotic. Then, in Soho on one of my continuing London "mooches," I felt the thrill of maturity when I was accosted by a whore for the first time. This was somewhat deflated when she added that she "did student rates."

For the time being the women in my life reverted to being boys in "drag." The Youth Theatre had been invited to Holland to tour its production of *Hamlet*. The previous summer's success had not gone unnoted. We were now under the patronage of the British ambassador to Holland and supported by the British Council. In the letter inviting renewed participation in the production, a challenge was thrown out: "There will be a number of special performances for schools and colleges. Most Dutch schoolboys speak English fluently and some will know the play a good deal better than many English schoolboys." It all suggested a kind of cultural athletics match, the Lads versus the Jonkheers.

Our first performance in The Hague on April 19, 1960, was warmly received, especially by Dutch schoolgirls. Far from assaulting us with textual criticism, they showed the kind of teenage enthusiasm that would later be showered on pop groups. Accommodation en route was haphazard. In that first venue I found myself sharing not only a room, but also the bed of my gangly schoolboy host. "I could be bounded in a nutshell, and count myself a King of infinite space, were it not that I have bad dreams," I ruefully mused, trying to sleep. At least his mother brought us a breakfast in bed of sugared white bread. Although I continue to find this practice vastly overrated, it was preferable to the lot of another boy billeted with a family who insisted on hymns and prayers between courses! At Eindhoven I luxuriated in the elegant mansion of an executive of the local Philips conglomerate, while in Amsterdam I stayed with a charming old lady in a houseboat moored on a canal.

By this time our tour had attracted more camp followers, mostly girls, who would assemble at the stage door for autographs. Barbara was one of them. Bright and flaxen-haired, she almost approximated the kind of young critic we had been warned of in the fluency of her bubbling English and her enthusiasm for the play. When I took her back to my floating digs, textual examination was the last thing on my mind. Fortunately, the old lady slept soundly while Barbara and I spent the whole night furthering Anglo-Dutch relations. She had to disappear reluctantly at dawn to appear at her family breakfast table leaving me to devour my unsuspecting hostess's cheese and ham and black bread with an unusually wolfish appetite.

The tour, with sixteen performances in nine towns, gave some indication of the rigors of professional theatrical life. There were the exhausting get-ins and get-outs, the dawn assemblies and late nights, the endless technical rehearsals and the packing and repacking. I loved it. Not long afterward we were invited to Paris to present *Hamlet* at the Théâtre des Nations Festival, and were the first amateur company to be afforded official status. We flew there in a chartered plane of such decrepitude that, with the weight of all our costumes and company, "the undiscovered country from whose bourn no traveller returns" very nearly became our destination. We played at the old dusty Théâtre Sarah Bernhardt, and it was as thrilling to glimpse a floodlit Paris through an open dressing-room window as it was to be representing one's country again on the international stage.

Back at school, the A level examinations loomed with the same portentousness as the ghost of Hamlet's father. So intensely prepared for, undergoing them came almost as a relief, like the actuality of performing after a bout of anticipatory stage fright. In the English paper I answered just one question with an essay on my beloved *A Passage to India*. It seemed to pay off, for I passed with a distinction. In the history paper, however, possibly because I had alluded to contemporary phenomena such as beatniks, the same honor eluded me and, as a result, so did the coveted state scholarship. A momentary disenchantment with Oxbridge elitism drove me to apply to Keele University in Staffordshire for their liberal arts course. I had become a *New Statesman*–reading "left-winger" in temporary rebellion against the affluence in which I had been brought up. Reading philosophy at a Midlands redbrick had an evangelical feel.

My preferred gospel, though, was preached elsewhere. I was soon back in a familiar haunt—London's West End, where the Youth Theatre presented a modern-dress version of *Julius Caesar*. It was ideally suited to the company's large-cast policy, as the mob had a starring role. Moreover, the updated approach demanded a degree of realism and so girls were admitted for the first time. The casting net was spread wider, too, and youth from Croft's beloved North Country was recruited. I was detailed to meet Ian McShane at Euston and enjoyed his wide-eyed pleasure at being in the Big Smoke for the first time.

It was a thrill to be performing again in the West End alongside such professionals as Rex Harrison, currently the source of much theater gossip for his temperamental antics in *My Fair Lady*. Again we were expected to earn our keep during rehearsals and performances and I was lucky to be able to commute from home. That introductory caveat about being cheerful and humble rang tauntingly in my ears for I was playing Messala, another small part. In combat gear and slouch hat, I was nightly reminded that "lowliness is young ambition's ladder." As of old, however, I longed to play the wolf.

Biding my time, I was rewarded with an important precept. Shakespeare's wisdom and insights seeped into the subconscious in a subtle osmosis, and I took to heart Brutus's observation: "There is a tide in the affairs of men / Which, taken at the flood, leads on to fortune / Omitted, all the voyage of their life / Is bound in shallows and in miseries." I forced myself to wait for the tide that had momentarily becalmed my academic, dramatic and even libidinous craft.

I sensed it starting to flow not long afterward. My final stage appearance at school was as Michael O'Riordan in Joseph O'Conor's *The Iron Harp*, a drama about the Troubles that dealt with conflicting loyalties, both personal and political. Does the true patriot put his country before everything, or should a man value friendship at a higher rate? This was a question that E. M. Forster had already answered with his extraordinary wartime affirmation that he would sooner betray his country than his friend.

The play was well received and not least by a correspondent of *The Times* who, for some reason, reviewed a performance.

It is a brave English school which would think of tackling an Irish play at all, with all the difficulties of accent and background involved. But to choose, moreover, a straight drama, without the ready-made appeal of dialect comedy would seem to be carrying bravery to the verge of foolhardy.... The producer was blessed with at least two excellent actors as the leading rebels, O'Riordan and Kelley (the former especially has a fully professional style and presence, and managed a remarkable Irish accent). The whole evening was as enjoyable as it was unusual.

With such encouragement, I allowed myself to entertain, for the first time, the possibility of becoming a professional actor.

I declared as much in a lunchtime speech to the local Bromley Chamber of Commerce. A group of sixth formers had been asked to talk of our career plans and, to my relief, my ambition was politely received. Even the school magazine echoed the inevitability of my choice, publishing my future curriculum vitae:

Sir Michael Johnson rose rapidly to national fame through his brilliant performance in TV commercials, and was duly knighted in '68. 1972 became a Director of X.T.V. 1977 bought the Old Vic for use as a T.V. studio. 1979 Chairman of X.T.V. also part owner of a number of charm schools throughout the length and breadth of South London.

At about this time the flood tide of fortune brought Lesley into my life. Introduced at a party, we continued to meet casually at other social events. Striking and vivacious, she was also wonderfully outgoing and uninhibited. She taught me to hand-jive, the latest American craze, and I took her for coffee at the new transatlantically styled Waggon Wheel Restaurant in the High Street. Together we listened to records, especially to the soundtrack of the film *High Society* that seemed an infinitely desirable amalgam of all that mythical Hollywood and Cafe Society had to offer. She, too, was in the throes of examinations and university entrance but we made time for other things. Meetings became more frequent and passionate.

With customary capriciousness I decided to switch my entrance exam subject from history to English. "I'm glad you have changed over though I fear you may be disillusioned," wrote Chris Hill from his academic ivory tower.

The Tripos isn't all Huxley and Waugh. It contains just as much grind as history. However, I'm sure that you will succeed despite

Lesley. A most charming girl. If you do come up to see me next term, pray bring her along. Never fear, she would never desert her shag-haired golden boy from Bromley! You don't change much— always this frantic rush, this zeal to cram twenty years' experience into as many months—it makes me feel quite sentimental.

Eventually I found myself at the "other place," eager for academic bounty and looking like a banker in my new custom-made three-piece suit. I had chosen Oxford's University College deliberately, motivated by more than scholastic considerations. It was then known as an actors' college and, in fact, included Richard Hampton, our Youth Theatre Hamlet, among its undergraduates. He left greetings and encouragement: the readiness was all. After the written exam, I was selected for an interview and held my breath. I recalled how a former Bromley pupil had spent his entire interview talking about daffodils and wondered if I could parlay myself into favor with similar abstruse musings. I was offered a place to study English. Though not a scholarship, it was still a consummation devoutly to be wished and, like Hamlet, I was blasted with ecstasy.

When Grace asked me to join the cast of *My Three Angels* that she was directing at the Bromley Little Theatre, I responded immediately and positively and not only because she was offering one of the leading convict roles. This studio theater and its semiprofessional company had a considerable reputation. It was run by an extraordinary old lady, Betty Pinchard, who was as dynamic as she was opinionated. She had once sent a note round to Laurence Olivier in the middle of a performance claiming she couldn't hear him and had received an apology. "We shall probably have to keep some of this activity dark so far as the senior English and history men are concerned," Grace concluded conspiratorially.

It was an interesting change to work alongside mature and experienced actors. I picked up many of their habits and especially their time-honored superstitions. Whistling in the dressing room and, most heinous of all, quoting even the name of Shakespeare's "Scottish play" was strictly forbidden. Infringement of these fusty rules was punished with arcane rituals involving turning in circles outside the door and knocking to beg readmittance.

My former part was played by a young man with the face of a bemused, naughty cherub called Adrian Brine. Wearing an "arty" bow tie, he was just down from Oxford where he'd set the town alight with several acclaimed productions and was poised on the threshold of a theatrical career both as actor and director. Adrian and I hit it off immediately. We still do. It was the start of a long and cherished friendship. We talked endlessly of the theater and cinema and of our ambitions, and found we had much in common. We almost shared a birthday and definitely shared a choice of favorite film—Renoir's *La Règle du Jeu*. Adrian's enthusiasm was infectious, his opinions intelligent and irreverent. The same things we found amusing, and we laughed a great deal.

The following year the school celebrated its Jubilee and I penned a pious tribute including the following wish-fulfillment: "Rather than mass-producing spurious symbols of academic success the school concerns itself with the moulding of real and interesting people." I fervently hoped the combined influence of Grahame Drew and Grace had steered me from the standard norm, allowing that odd early sense of feeling different from others to be transmuted into a genuine individuality. Notwithstanding that, for the time being my surging tide continued to flow along mainstream channels. I was made School Captain. O heavy honor! I chose to operate as an éminence grise— more Horatio than Hamlet.

The updrafts of freedom, though, were swelling my wings. I longed for release from schoolboy constraints, even though I knew that I owed the school a great deal. And Grace even more. She wanted me for her Jubilee school production, but the thought of marking time till the summer was anathema. It was a pattern that was to become familiar over the years. No sooner has a project terminated—and in my trade they have been necessarily numerous—than I have to cut loose, dismiss it with unsentimental gratitude and move on to the next. Around my birthday, always a time of transition and new beginnings, I finally left school without a backward glance.

I had until the start of the Oxford Michaelmas term of 1961 to get a taste of the world before being retied with restrictive academic bonds —and to earn some money. Up in London, I had some interesting chance encounters. A rather pompous gentleman stopped me in the street, complimented me on my dress and appearance and invited me back to the Public Schools Club in Piccadilly for tea and an introduction to its hushed, closed world of privilege. It was the Establishment at its most fossilized. We discussed my employment prospects but his old school tie looked more like a noose. I wanted something that was artistic and well paid—an automatic contradiction in terms!

A more promising meeting was with Anton Dolin, who invited me to the Athenaeum for a drink. Offering me a job with his ballet company, he jetéed across the room with a phone so that I could there and then tell my parents of my new employment. But I needed to widen my world. I went in search of Forster's India with the British India Steam Navigation Company but there were no vacancies for a job. I applied for one on the railway with the Pullman Car Company hoping, at a blow, to make up for my lack of funds and of familiarity with my native land.

At the same time a letter arrived from Michael Croft saying that the Youth Theatre had been invited to the United States and to Italy and requesting us not to make any holiday arrangements. There was also talk of a return to Paris and Holland. Here was my ticket to ride! We had been brought up on a transatlantic culture. *West Side Story* was the new "cool" West End sensation. To visit America would be exciting enough, but to perform there quite extraordinary. In the upshot, the U.S. tour fell by the wayside and an Italian one took its place.

We set off in early April to Florence where we performed *Julius Caesar* in the Teatro Pergola. Despite the barrage of noise from the simultaneous translation, or perhaps because of our "fascist" interpretation of the play, its reception was enthusiastic. Old memories must have been stirred by the sight of jack boots, banners and the passionate roar of manipulative speech. We swept down to Rome where between performances I managed to see the Pope and review the marvels of the Vatican. Then, during one interval of the play at the Teatro Sistina, there was a strike, occasioned by the Italian impresario's failure to pay her staff. It went on so long that the audience threatened to "cry havoc," their abusive protests outdoing those of our own vociferous Roman mob. Michael Croft had warned that our budget was "suicidal" but even so our fee was reduced and, at one point in mid-tour, we were even canceled. Lean and hungry looks were assuaged and we went on to Perugia and Genoa where, due to the continuing chaos, we were put up in a brothel—the most comfortable bed I have ever slept in.

We traveled the long distances by coach, engulfed at times in another more subtle kind of mob violence. Youth can be savagely cruel. One young man in the company had an emotional problem that he confided to me. Inexperienced in these matters myself, I turned to that fount of wisdom, Shakespeare, and found help: "This above all: to thine own self be true / And it must follow, as the night the day /

Thou canst not then be false to any man." Our companionship was misinterpreted and our coach turned into a wheeled *huis clos*. That old sense of incompatibility flared briefly and to this day I have never been much of a company man, preferring the more individual pursuits of my freewheeling trade. We finished up in Turin and headed home. Years afterward, veterans of this tour still referred to it as "The Italian Campaign."

The urgency to earn money was alleviated somewhat when my father offered to pay me to paint the house. I just managed to finish before boredom finished me. Turning to scene painting at the Little Theatre, I became involved in other productions including Pinero's *The Schoolmistress,* which Adrian directed. I saw at once why his theatrical reputation had preceded him. He was witty and committed and, above all, talented.

Adrian was now a co-director of a new touring company called Prospect Productions, based at the Oxford Playhouse, and suggested that, to gain experience as well as funds, I sign on as an assistant stage manager for his forthcoming production there of *Whiteman* and its curtain-raiser *Sammy*. We took digs in St. John Street, around the corner from the theater, giving me another brief, scintillating foretaste of undergraduate life.

Whiteman was an incendiary play about a smoldering social issue, South African apartheid, while *Sammy* consisted of a cockney crook's increasingly desperate monologue as he tried to talk his way out of an ever-tightening corner. By a remarkable coincidence my stepson, Rick, found the latter obscure piece decades later to use as a screenplay for his first effort at film school.

As a student ASM I was, I confess, undistinguished. I became so fascinated with the acting that I would forget to give cues. At one point in *Whiteman,* Brian Blessed sang to the accompaniment of an accordion but was left squeezing his silent prop instrument while I frantically fumbled for its taped music. But even in so menial a capacity I was thrilled to belong, at last, to this real theatrical community with its extrovert bonhomie, gossip and good fellowship. After the last curtain call, Adrian and I both decided to abandon our tight little spotlit world and hitchhike abroad, where horizons were unpainted and unlimited. Europe, having teased with seductive glimpses, lay waiting to be ravished. So did Lesley. She was spending the summer with her family in Italy and wrote enticingly from the warm Mediterranean.

It was a chilling northern downpour that drenched our departure, pursuing us all the way to Brussels. The next day was the Fourteenth of July and the beer flowed freely—in marked contrast to our halting progress, which was more hitch than hike. A woman who picked us up as we neared the Black Forest even demanded payment for her trouble. The Germans could sometimes be so inexplicably strange. Penny's affair with Jörg had ended in England after some minor argument. To our utter astonishment he had suddenly erupted in a burst of histrionic emotion declaring that "all his hopes and dreams had died forever in 1945."

Germany, however, has always been beneficent for me and this time was no exception. Finishing up on the piney shores of the emerald Schluchsee, we put up at a farmhouse and began to enjoy ourselves. There were forest walks and other healthy exercises of intellect and imagination. I had packed a copy of Milton's *Paradise Lost,* still a prerequisite for the Oxford preliminary examination, and busied myself with "things unattempted yet in prose or rhyme." Cream cakes and more material pleasures were to be had in the local gingerbread town.

This sunny, smiling summer interlude reflected our shared enthusiasm for the films of Ingmar Bergman, then undergoing savage critical reassessment in such heavyweight journals as *Encounter.* The whole film-as-style school of *Cahiers du Cinéma* was against Bergman's romantic photoplay form. But to hell with camera angles! Seeing his films, we agreed, made you feel you had lived a little longer and more intensely. That wonderful, easy unspoken accord that is the hallmark of friendship engulfed us and a gentle *gemütlichkeit* reigned over those hiatus days.

Adrian had to return to England and I pressed on south. Hostels were full, so I was reluctantly obliged to use my little tent for shelter, even sharing it on the long, halting trek through Switzerland. The tourist season was in full spate and my kindness to strangers was only fitfully reciprocated by motorists until I encountered an enchanting girl of radiant, traffic-stopping beauty. We joined forces and progress speeded up miraculously. Then, on the steps of Milan's Duomo, she vanished as abruptly as she had appeared, like a good angel.

At Alessandria characteristic impatience prevailed and I caught the milk train to the coast. There, on the still seafront at Alassio, the sand was being raked and towels and umbrellas positioned. Finding the hotel where Lesley was staying, I lurked outside until she eventually appeared. Accosted in pseudo stage Italian, it was delicious to watch her set English *noli me tangere* face dissolve into incredulity, then delight, as I kissed my *bella signorina* in the pellucid morning light. Pitching my tent in the local camping ground, I found myself back in a small corner of a foreign field that was forever England, surrounded by cheerful cockney families offering endless tea and sympathy. In a repetition of previous sybaritic indulgence, I rented a small room in town and there discovered the true meaning and practice of *la dolce far niente.*

On my return to England, there was a notice from the Youth Theatre saying that *Julius Caesar* had been invited to the Berlin Festival and was I prepared to repeat my role? Was I ever! My wanderlust was growing fast by what it fed on. But enthusiasm was swiftly dampened. Penny was celebrating her twenty-first birthday at the end of August with a party in a chic London restaurant—in direct conflict with the Berlin dates. For my parents, the occasion had ballooned into a Major Event and they felt that I should be part of it. I did, too, except that the privilege of representing one's country at an international cultural festival was not to be so easily denied.

I decided to ask Penny herself if my absence would spoil her evening. She expressed a disappointment but did not insist. It was an irresistible response. Anger would have been my easy passport. Bidding farewell to Berlin and hello to family fellowship, I slunk obediently back to the fold. As comfortable and valued as it was, I was becoming ever more impatient to leave it. However, owing my parents so much, I was unwilling to put stain or strain on our relationship.

The party at the Ecu de France turned out to be fun. Moreover, the news that one of my *Caesar* co-conspirators had succumbed to a mild case of clap somewhat eased the nagging regret. I was not to know then that I would get to perform in Berlin in a starring role, sharing my father's affection for this schizoid city so battered into modernity. Having turned Bromley into one of M & S's most successful stores, he was now working at its head office with nationwide responsibilities. I joined him on a business trip to Edinburgh where, at the Festival, I saw the Old Vic company perform Schiller's *Maria Stuart* in the Usher Hall. There, like Hamlet sitting at another play, with a growing conviction and excitement, I knew my course.

O x f o r d

C H A P T E R F I V E

"*I* am wondering whether you would like to face your first Oxford
audition soon. OUDS are putting on *The Devil's Disciple* in the
third week of next term. Normally, of course, freshmen could not get
into this, but as your worth is known, the producer would be willing
and pleased to see you." The invitation had come even before my
arrival for the new term at Oxford, sent by Peter Lee, another Youth
Theatre colleague and an undergraduate at Keble College. My worthi-
ness ensured that I was cast in the small part of the priest and that a
pattern of Oxford life for the next three years was set almost from the
first day.

Apart from academic study, the university seemed to provide something for everyone, from beagling to boogie. *Cherwell* and *Isis* bred
future journalists and the Union provided that first push up the greasy
pole of politics. There was also the Playhouse. This was the theater
on Beaumont Street shared by professional town and amateur gown.
Without any hesitation or sideways glances, it was my mecca.

Student theater was dominated by the Oxford University Dramatic
Society and the Experimental Theatre Club. I joined both. As their

names suggest, the former was more "establishment," the ETC having been founded by Nevill Coghill in the thirties to get away from the OUDS's dual reputation as a dining club, and to involve all aspects of the theater arts. This demarcation, though, was now blurred. Both enjoyed a national reputation, nurturing some of the country's major talent. Distinguished professionals such as John Gielgud, Peggy Ashcroft and Maggie Smith had worked with the student ensembles, and guest speakers and directors were a constant feature. Performing plays seemed a natural adjunct to their academic study.

University College is situated "branchy between towers and towery between branches" in one of Oxford's most busy and beautiful thoroughfares, the High Street. One of the University's oldest institutions, claiming Alfred the Great as a founder and his martlets on its arms, it was built around two ancient quadrangles that extend through a honeycomb of rooms above the High Street's banks and shops to more modern buildings in the back.

I was lucky enough to be given rooms on the top floor of the handsome main quad. The leaded back window faced on to the Fellows' Garden, which was shaded by a giant tulip tree that flamed in spring like a monstrous candelabra. It was rumored these rooms had been Shelley's during his brief, inglorious university career. If so, all traces of his metaphysical experiments or presence had vanished. He lay drowned next door in marble effigy in a little mausoleum, the target for generations of irreverent daubers.

The name freshly painted alongside mine outside the door belonged to another grammar-school pupil, a tall, slim, suede-shod historian. He rejoiced in the name Wildgoose that seemed even more exotic when elongated by his native Sheffield accent. We each had a bedroom —mine overlooked the grassed square of the front quad whose stones were then black and rotting with age—and shared a sitting room furnished with equally timeworn sofa, desks and armchairs.

An ancient scout called Percy looked after us. I was uncomfortable with the whole question of servants, having been raised without them. The cheerful Mrs. Carr could hardly have been called a family retainer and, although from the same "working class," as it was still bizarrely called, had little else in common with this man as old as my grandfather. Short of breath and stature, Percy was obviously ill and would wheeze and cough his painful way about his daily tasks. I have always been reluctant to have people do things for me, although then, as now, I enjoyed the luxury of retiring to a well-made bed.

Having a servant was something else, like being addressed as "sir," that I would have to get used to—things that boys from public schools seemed to take in their well-tailored stride. And that was another change to be absorbed: we were no longer "boys" but "gentlemen." Douglas, the bluff, outspoken head porter, however, made no bones about the fact that indeed "fucking schoolboys" were now passing through his lodge gate whereas, a few years before, men hardened by National Service and war had preceded them.

My fellow undergraduates were the privileged products of both the state and the private school systems with the odd American Rhodes scholar thrown in to modulate the blend of accents. Smooth, "upper-class" tones-prevailed, although rough Northern timbres, redolent of smokestacks and moors, could be heard, too, amidst the nasal brays and clenched vowels, especially in the college beer cellar where prized Newcastle brown ale was dispensed. Three-piece Savile Row suits were as common as corduroy jackets and new-fangled jeans, although photos of this era reveal an almost universal espousal of the tie. Silkily encrusted with crests and insignia, they were as abundant as striped college scarves, for Oxford was then very much a traditional place. London lay cut off at a distance along clogged, inadequate highways. College co-education was unknown. The winds of academic change were blowing, but as a mild invigorating breeze.

Modern buildings were few in this miraculously unbombed city whose laboratories had helped unlock the power that had terrified the world into a truculent peace. Oxford, with its otherworldly seat of learning yoked to a modern industrial complex, seemed less rarefied than Cambridge, although a hothouse intellectual atmosphere bred a certain quaintness and eccentricity. There was a learned professor who placed saucers beneath the electric points in his house to catch the electricity that escaped during the night and solemnly emptied their invisible contents the following morning. I saw a similar old gentleman peering into a shop window, Sherlock Holmes style, through a large magnifying glass.

I was happy to have some old friends "up" at Oxford. Freddy was at Wadham and Peter Fenwick at Worcester. Peter seemed especially glad to see me and talked volubly. Inevitably one made new friends in this radically new milieu. Michael Emrys-Jones and Braham Murray were both University College freshmen reading English and, like me, ambitious for a theatrical career. They were a study in contrasts. Emrys-Jones was a tall, good-looking Marlburian given to Prince-of-

Wales check suits and a devastating charm; Murray, also a public-
school product, was a short, volatile, opinionated Jew and very dapper
in the narrow-tailored style of the day. We became inseparable.

Matriculated together in a little Latin ceremony, we formally entered this closed world ruled by an intellectual mafia of dons and
policed by their bowler-hatted Bulldogs. With our spiritual well-being
supposedly in the care of a moral tutor, our academic tutors were
Peter Bayley, an amiable, owlish man besotted with Spenser, for literature, and, for linguistics, Christopher Tolkien, the son of the world-
beloved author J. R. R. Tolkien. Their two tutorials provided the only
academic obligation of the week. Just two hours! This was another
difference from school. Success, fulfillment and happiness were entirely in our own hands and obtaining a degree—the ostensible object
of the three-year course—entirely dependent on self-administered industry. There was no punishment: again that was self-inflicted.

Basically there were essays to research and write and lectures to
attend. Robert Graves had just been appointed Professor of Poetry
and, with his silvered locks and craggy mien, was something of a star
attraction. His lectures, however, were more remarkable for their style
than for their content. Besides, books could be read independently of
fixed schedules and locations.

It was everywhere evident that students were meant to do more
than study. Extracurricular activity was an essential, perhaps the most
important, part of an Oxford education. It provided a rich patina and
polish on the character impossible to obtain by mechanical means.
The University, despite its ivory-tower elitism, was a microcosm of
the establishment world beyond its towers and spires. You had to play
the game—literally or metaphorically.

Despite my father's reputation on the rugby field I had no intention
of following anywhere close to his studded footsteps or of striking a
ball of any kind. Rowing was a glamorous, clamorous alternative,
possibly because the Boat Race featured so strongly in the televised
sporting life of the nation, but nothing would induce me to endure the
hours of frigid, backbreaking slog and the inevitable hearty team spirit,
even though during Eights Week crews were given extra-nourishing
food. It was not that I had the aesthete's disdain for exercise ingrained
in Max Beerbohm's remark, "Whenever I have an urge to exercise I
lie down until it passes." My principal interest, the theater, was far too
physically intense.

Had I realized that Stephen Hawking, then the cox of the college crew, would go on to become the greatest contemporary theoretical physicist, I might have revised my dismissive attitude. Moreover, my contemporary, Jeffrey Archer, managed to become not only a decorated sportsman but also a canny politician while at the same time laying the foundation, no doubt, for another career as a storyteller. Certainly a story that Jeffrey now tells about me is pure fiction. He claims that, hesitating between political and theatrical stardom, he finally opted for the former, thus making way for his "understudy"—me—to shine. His brilliant telling of this fable, however, suggests that the theater did indeed miss out on a most worthy recruit.

After the initial shock of so many new things at once, life settled into an approximation of a routine. Although never one for staying up late—I'm still not—I usually rose too late for breakfast, a practice I now deplore. Mornings were spent studying in the Radcliffe Camera, Christopher Wren's extraordinary birdcage rotunda on the other side of the High. Not only was it a distinct pleasure to be in the aesthetic heart of the city, but there it was possible to work alongside female students. The masculinity of the all-male colleges could sometimes overwhelm, and I have never been entirely comfortable in the exclusive company of men. Even today my spirits droop at dinner parties when the ladies are dismissed, leaving the men to their strong liquor and stronger conversation. Besides, the Camera was a natural pickup place. The birdcage contained "birds," as women were now slangily called. There would be invitations for coffee and leisurely repair to one of the city's many teashops. At the Kemp, Alan Bennett could be glimpsed, duffel-coated and famous from his continuing West End triumph in *Beyond the Fringe,* snatches of which were everywhere imitated.

Lunch was usually in liquid form in the Gloucester Arms, or "Glock," the actors' pub, strategically placed a few steps from the Playhouse's stage door. I am now astonished that brain cells could function on their rough diet of beer and stodgy pies. The afternoons were for rehearsals or for responding to the crisp, crested social invitations parading on the mantelpiece. Tea was a quasi-sacred ritual. As the day slipped languidly into the evening, there were sherry parties at which whole cellars of the stuff were sipped and swallowed.

In the college hall, where an ancient ineradicable smell of food warred for supremacy with one of polish, dinner was taken under the oiled, unsmiling gaze of benefactors and other worthies. White-jacketed scouts served gowned undergraduates and a high table of dons and Master. There were certain unspoken rules of conduct. Conversation was supposed to exclude three cardinal topics: Politics, Religion and Women. As these constituted the cornerstones of any interesting and worthwhile exchange, social intercourse was superficial to say the least. Those who transgressed these time-honored rules could be punished with a "sconce"—a curious ritual involving the imbibing of unnatural quantities of beer. Postprandial coffee was obtained in the Junior Common Room along with the national newspapers and magazines. I can't remember seeing a television set or even thinking this absence odd. The theater—of stage or screen—was our entertainment.

I would pick my bicycle from the hundreds that festooned the outer lodge walls like a spiky metal fungus, and pedal off to pleasure. Filmgoing was still a passionate activity in this age of New Wave and Free Cinema. At the racily named La Scala and Moulin Rouge cinemas foreign films were greedily devoured. A particular favorite of mine was the Andrzej Wajda film *Ashes and Diamonds,* and posters of its charismatic star, Zbigniew Cybulski—his fatally myopic good looks enhanced by dark glasses—were on every other wall. Another new pinup was Monica Vitti. Antonioni's *L'Avventura* and *La Notte,* together with Godard's *À Bout de Souffle,* had rewritten the rules, redefining romanticism and showing life at an intense twenty-four frames per second. Our prim Oxford routines seemed, in contrast, desperately prosaic.

The theater, however, fed this imaginative lust. Michael, Braham and I were cast in our college production of John Arden's *Serjeant Musgrave's Dance.* But this dour antiwar play was memorable in only one respect: it taught me the value of an external "prop" in creating a role. I was having trouble in playing the Mayor. "It's bad, it's bloody bad," I intoned in Wildgoosean accents, but this was more a reflection on my performance than an authentic characterization. It was only when, in desperation, I gummed a large walrus mustache on my face that the whole part slipped magically into place and focus. It was a valuable lesson and, ever since, I have looked for "the Mayor's mustache" in every role. I was also involved in the ETC's lavish twenty-fifth anniversary production of *Peer Gynt* and trolled alongside Rachel Packenham and other well-bred dancing girls who daringly exposed their navels to the autumn chill.

Lesley wrote from Queen Mary College at London University to describe her own theatrical initiations. She had the leading role in *The*

Good Woman of Setzuan and wrote vividly about the rehearsal process, and particularly how her director had bullied her into a tearful break-down in an attempt to rid her of her "westernization" and "sophistication." Sadly, these depredations left little time for her to come up to Oxford as planned.

Toward the end of this first term, I was walking up the High Street when I caught a glimpse of a girl who literally stopped me in my tracks. She was wearing an elegant checked coat and her hair piled up in the fashionable beehive style. I was so arrested by her looks that I followed her up the busy street. I crossed the road when she crossed. Desperately trying to think of a remark that would allow me to speak to her, I lost my nerve and opportunity and she merged with the crowd, leaving me curiously bereft. So this is how Dante felt after glimpsing Beatrice!

Then a few weeks later, after a performance of *Peer Gynt,* there backstage in the center of a group of people was my Beatrice, my lady of the checked coat. Again I was halted. Again I fought fiercely for an appropriate opening gambit. I smiled. Our eyes met. She gave me an opaque stare. I was in despair. It was only later that I learned that, without glasses, she saw nothing clearly. Suddenly, someone was introducing us and—miraculously—we were talking.

Her name was Julia Parker. She was also reading English, at St. Hilda's. We arranged to meet in the Bodleian and go for coffee. She was a new breed for me—a blue stocking raised in the rarefied atmosphere of an exclusive girls' public school. I was invited to her neat rooms for the inevitable sherry and to listen to music. There, she also played the piano for me with accomplishment. She had a shyness that emphasized her beauty and masked her formidable intelligence. I delighted in her company.

The next term the OUDS invited Peter Dews to "produce," as it was still called, their major production of both parts of Shakespeare's *Henry IV.* This followed a long-standing and valued tradition of guest directors: Michael Croft had produced a characteristically vigorous *Richard II* the previous year. Peter Dews was freshly laurel-wreathed from his *The Age of Kings,* a dynamic compilation of Shakespeare's history plays for the BBC in which Sean Connery had played a memorable Hotspur.

Like many of his fellow Yorkshiremen, Dews loathed pretentiousness. His style was straightforward and honest and we were dragooned with a combination of hot temper and wit. He had a weakness for jokes and was adept at finding the odd extra characters buried in the text—the film director who appears shouting for "more rushes, more rushes" and the two disreputable bookmakers, "Unworthy Urn" and "Monty Cheval." He cast me as the icy, dangerous Prince John. A pudding-basin Plantagenet haircut left ears and self exposed to some offstage ribaldry, but in the floodlit clearing of Gaultree Forest it was good to feel cold steel in the voice as well as the hand. I was happy, too, to be able to show off to Grace the fruits of her teaching as she sat in the audience with Digby, her husband and my fellow Little Theatre co-star.

I saw Julia as frequently as Bard and Bodley allowed. I discovered she had a remarkable singing voice and had even considered having it trained. Knowing my own delight in performing, I encouraged her to do likewise. She took me to concerts and I escorted her to the cinema. We occasionally went out for dinner but this stretched my stressed finances to near breaking point. Tea was the perfect solution.

We were both preoccupied with Prelims—the imminent Preliminary Exam that provided the term's most dramatic undertaking, and the first of the many crises that characterized the year. The Oxford English syllabus at the time was still redolent of its medieval heritage. At least two of the papers were not in English, but in Latin and Anglo-Saxon. The latter had actually been a pleasurable revelation. Far from being the product of a barbarous dark age, the literature seemed sophisticated, often witty, and shot through with a hard-edged beauty. *Beowulf* was a twilight cinerama epic, a Bergmanesque saga to be shouted aloud in all its alliterative allure. The Latin, on the other hand, was a bore—a compulsory flat-footed tour of Virgil's *Aeneid,* which, after the rich, spittled, throat-clearing rasp of Anglo-Saxon, seemed the last gasping yawn of a dead aestheticism. *"Arma virumque cano Troia"*—but I sang in vain, failing to elicit favorable notices from the examiners. As did Braham and Michael and even our English scholar. "Lif," as the Anglo-Saxon writer had mourned, "is laene."

A stern letter arrived from the senior tutor informing me that the college would allow a second attempt at the end of next term.

You must, however, make sure of passing then, as it is a college requirement that anyone who is not completely through his prelims by the end of the first year must go down. I hope you will make no mistake about this.

This failure cast a gloom over a return trip to Holland with the Youth Theatre in a production of *Richard II.* I was playing Aumerle—another

"Horatio" part—thereby seeming to confirm the chilling accuracy of Sir Ralph's prognostication. The role was a walking shadow, one of those Shakespeare characters who do much without making any impression.

The tour was superficially enjoyable. In Amsterdam I even met up with Barbara again and took her dancing at the Lucky Star. Certain members of the cast appeared on stage wearing clogs and despite—or maybe because of—this, we were well received as a tortuous translation of the review in the *Gelderlander* testified:

> *Richard II* bij English gentlemanplayers under the exemplary stage management of Michael Croft, gave a beautiful performance before the eyes of a very passable occupied house, in which beside the polished saying of the poetry, the qualities of his art for managing very striked. One could see in the play of the juvenal players those nearly disciplinary perceptible presence of Croft who it is true advocated in the play of the principle part of the hegemony, but had a sufficient attention for the interpretation of the minor parts. He had given his juvenile interpreters much concious accuracy of fire, which one cannot miss when one don't like to be wooden on the stage. The audience was sympathising with the play, and was reacting and thanking enthousiastic.

However, I too had been "very striked" by Michael Croft, who had unwittingly hurt my feelings by suggesting that I was being unreasonably optimistic in entertaining thoughts of a professional career as an actor. My wounded spirits flared like the phlegmatic, colorless Aumerle's. "What answer shall I make to this base man? / Shall I so much dishonour my fair stars, / On equal terms to give him chastisement? / Either I must, or have mine honour soil'd / With the attainder of his sland'rous lips!" I determined to prove him wrong, however long that took.

My own melancholy and the subdued mood of the play with its talk of graves, worms and epitaphs was further emphasized by a backstage accident in one of the theaters. A loaded steel lighting bar, falling from the flies, poleaxed a technician who mischanced to be beneath it, collapsing him in a pool of blood. Ever since I have been wary on stage of the potential catastrophe that hangs, like the Damoclean sword, overhead. Julia wrote from the Lake District and the vastness of some "huge wuthering house for undergraduates who want solitude to stride through the rain in quest of Wordsworthian realities." She added, "Anyway, if I find the answer to life, I'll lend you my notes!"

And I had need of them. The year of crisis, with its cold, contrary, undermining currents, continued its destructive theme. There was an estrangement with my father, probably occasioned by my exam failure, but aggravated by the fact that I still relied on him for financial assistance. Our coolness infected his own relationship with May, threatening the precious family unity that had survived war and sickness. In another exchange of letters I repeated that the state's unfair insistence that he pay for the means of my Oxford education gave him no control over the ways. Joe magnanimously conceded that I had a right to look after my own affairs. We both implicitly agreed that our family's shared trust and happiness should not be lightly undervalued or undermined. Penny wrote from King's College Hospital saying how relieved she was that I had made my peace and commented on the restored domestic harmony. She had other good news, asking me to look for an announcement in *The Times:* "You will find an unpronounceable name coupled with mine in the forthcoming marriage column." Thus the future Mrs. Marek Cwynarski announced herself.

Joe showed his renewed support by driving the family to Oxford to see me in Braham's ETC production of Brendan Behan's *The Hostage.* This was extraordinary as my involvement in the play had been another factor in our quarrel. Even Adrian had counseled caution.

If you fail prelims again, you'll be out of Oxford with no more experience behind you than the boy in *The Hostage* which no one will have seen as it's not a new play—it's in all the reps. You must ensure you pass at all costs, then you have 2½ years to make your dramatic mark.

But Braham's offer had proved irresistible. The young "gorblimey" cockney soldier was a strong contrast to all the "fucking around in tights" parts that I had hitherto played. He had some good songs and was the quiet, emotional and dramatic focus amidst all the raucous goings-on in the Dublin whorehouse. Performing, I reasoned, provided an incentive to work even harder academically, the discipline of the stage hopefully animating that of the study. Even the wretched Virgil himself had urged "Fortune sides with him who dares."

And discipline was all. We took ourselves very seriously indeed. Classes were organized in improvisation and movement, inspired by the example of Theatre Workshop that had spawned the original production. Perfectly suited to the festive atmosphere of Eights Week, the play drew good reviews and business. I felt I had made my "dramatic mark," and, a hostage to fortune, awaited the second exam results with the same mixture of bravado and trepidation with which Behan's young soldier had awaited his fate.

Punishment for my hubris came from a different quarter. There was another storm in a domestic teacup, but this one blew into a hurricane of hurt feelings. It all started when I returned briefly to Bromley to see Lesley. It so happened her parents were away and I spent an unpremeditated night at their house. We were spied on by a neighbor and reported. Perhaps because he had recently been ill, Lesley's father overreacted, determining that I had seduced and ravished his daughter. My parents were summoned and ordered to punish their Lothario of a son.

By this time I, too, was away from home, working during the vacation as an assistant stage manager, again for Prospect Productions. I wrote to Lesley's parents, but my long letter of explanation and apology was returned unopened. Protesting that the most heinous criminal was given a hearing, I asked why they would scruple to read this letter as they had read all my others that they found in a pile at Lesley's bedside.

Furthermore, in a scenario beloved of many contemporary stage and film dramas, Lesley thought that she might be pregnant. I determined to "do the right thing" and marry her. To support our child I was unsure whether to leave university and get a job or stay on and add to the small number of married undergraduates, some with young children. Lesley joined me at Cambridge, where I was back at the Arts Theatre, and the beauty of the city and the summer served as a balm for inflamed feelings. We boated on the river in strange time-warped anticipation of a scene that I was soon to film in Joseph Losey's *Accident*. The mood was curiously idyllic.

The pregnancy scare, already drawn out by the prevailing tension, proved eventually to be a false alarm. Further relieving good news came from Oxford. The exam scare, too, was over: I had passed. Through all these uncertainties, May and Joe had been unconditionally supportive. Still estranged from her parents, Lesley was now at the Edinburgh Festival appearing in a play with her university company and was anxious for me to join her as soon as I finished the tour. Her digs turned out to be a crowded flat in drafty Windmill Street in the ancient part of the city. It was as cramped as a slum, but to my mind as romantic as the garret in *La Bohème*. I readily exchanged the over-solicitous mothering of theatrical landladies for more basic communal fare and especially the opportunity to share love, bread and bed. We held each other tight and tried to plan a responsible future—and to enjoy ourselves.

Together we sampled life on the Fringe where, among a myriad of eclectic offerings, chums from Oxford were daring lightning to strike twice in another late-night cabaret. Edinburgh teemed with rain and activity, its dour old granite countenance blasted with wind and the outpouring of energy from the many artistic worshipers at this improbable cultural shrine. In her new play, Lesley was powerful and moving. I gave her a locket inscribed *"numquam illegitimis carborundum,"* which my newly approved Latin skills translated as "Don't let the bastards grind you down!" But I had a troubled feeling that our two households, so unalike in dignity, had effectively doomed our love to be star-crossed.

Elsewhere, it flourished. In September, Penny married her unpronounceable doctor at the Catholic church in Soho Square. Marek was of Polish extraction, dark and good-looking, and Penny had converted to his faith. As it merged with another, our family was reunited *en fête*.

Before thankfully returning to Oxford as a student, I went back there to play at being one. A film called *The Mindbenders* was using the university as a location and had invited real undergraduates to re-create their roles. I duly appeared with my now standard uniform of cardigan, jeans, gown and bicycle and made my cinematic debut.

The film's star was Dirk Bogarde, then very much in favor for such recent films as *Victim* in which, in a fan-busting reversal of his anodyne image, he trespassed on forbidden cinema territory by playing a homosexual lawyer. I enjoyed the "hurry up and wait" atmosphere of the film set and seeing friends enacting little vignettes of university life. Again, I was strangely anticipating the future. Just four years later I would be back in Oxford filming with Dirk Bogarde, but this time having donned the same student clothes in a star dressing room and earning significantly more than the modest fee I then gratefully received.

Second Year

CHAPTER SIX

*M*ichaelmas Term 1962 started on a note of crisis—indeed, one of world significance. The Russians were found to be harboring ballistic missiles in Cuba that were rudely pointed at the nearby American heartland, and were ordered by President Kennedy to remove them—or else. As the deadline was reached we solemnly bought our final rounds of drinks in the Glock as free men before the impending holocaust called a universal last orders. But good sense and fortune prevailed and we returned with relief to Jane Austen's little closed world where war had no place, and to the Wanderer's lyric lamentations on the fate we had all just escaped.

Such tranquil studies, however, were to be short-lived. Another crisis loomed like a well-aimed missile. The University Players, our college dramatic society, had reserved the Playhouse for a production in the second week of the new term. Unfortunately, its intended director decided not to return to Oxford as anticipated. Even more unfortunately, he somehow forgot to cancel this booking. Contacted during the vacation by the Playhouse for details of our imminent production, I explained the changed circumstances. Although sympathetic, the management was insistent that University Players should honor their commitment. As President, I was suddenly responsible, financially and entrepreneurially, for finding a play. And quickly, too.

I set to work in a frenzy, writing to the diaspora of college theatrical talent. Braham, the obvious choice, was busy planning his own production of Lope de Vega's *Fuenteovejuna.* Response elsewhere was lukewarm, especially from technicians who felt that backstage work was as unglamorous as it was time-consuming. I was smitten with another horribly subtle version of the actor's nightmare—of being on stage and not knowing the play. I soon realized that I must be director, producer and general factotum. But what play?

I toyed with the idea of *Waiting for Godot.* Then Adrian suggested another play with a tramp called *A Man Has Two Fathers,* written by John McGrath. First presented by OUDS with a cast that included Dudley Moore and Adrian himself, the play had attracted warm notices from the national critics, including the current darling, Ken Tynan, who called it "An undergraduate play of extraordinary quality imposing in its own right." I read it with mounting excitement. It seemed to reflect my own, and yet a universal, situation—the ongoing war between parental authority and one's own maturing liberal instincts and attitudes. Outrageously funny and alive, mixing serious talk with sensationalism, it was essentially an allegory containing sparkling diatribes against the Church in particular and cant in general. In fact, it was a typical undergraduate play, choked with ideas that flew off in many directions at once. But it was ideal. It had a small cast and modern dress. I set to work at once.

I applied to the Lord Chamberlain—as was still the antiquated custom—for a license to perform. It was granted with the proviso that in Act III page 2, I "omit the words 'Jesus Christ.'" For an antireligious diatribe, this was being let off easily. As building a set was out of the question, a system of back projections—now in vogue in every nightclub and disco—that could flood huge areas with rapidly changing light and patterns was devised. It left the stage unconstricted and the surrealism worked for the story. I found that every waking moment was consumed in the production—the play was entirely the thing. Adrian, ever supportive and concerned, came up and gave unlimited practical advice, his experience of weekly rep helping the impossibly limited schedule to stretch to its full value. The pressure focused the work most powerfully. Then, suddenly, we were on.

"Considering that it was mounted in a fortnight, the production is a miracle," commented the *Isis* critic. Jubilation mixed with relief! John McGrath himself came to a performance and said how horrified he was to meet himself of four years ago and how glad he was that I had mocked his student sententiousness. The symbolism had been heavy, but effective, and I was particularly pleased with the notion of man as a creature of contrary impulses, represented by the two fathers see-sawing on a plank hitherto used to keep them poles apart. Balance, equipoise. The golden mean. It was a theme that was to become a guiding factor in my life.

Real life returned. For the first time, I took stock of my new sur-roundings. I had now moved to the adjacent Radcliffe Quad with rooms on the top floor overlooking the leafy Master's garden and the chapel with its wonderful stained-glass windows. C. S. Lewis had once lived on the same staircase. I loved my new quarters. The sitting room had a fire for toasting cold air and crumpets, with a coiled rope by the window for escaping greater conflagrations. The bedroom was a cu-rious wedge shape, and, luxury of luxuries, there was a bathroom with a massive claw-footed tub within shivering distance in the vaulted basement. Most importantly, I was now on my own, no longer depen-dent on an awkward social arrangement for sharing. I could "sport my oak" at will—shut my door on the whole world.

College life took on a new freedom born of familiarity. Friends had fallen into cliques and education into routine. Even though we were still locked in at night there was an accepted climbing-in spot that authority condoned, perhaps because it represented such a ferocious test of character, involving scaling a wall and circumnavigating some fearsome spikes. I was delighted to see Julia back at the Bodleian's massive tables. In the vacation she had written to me saying she was pleased that I would be returning.

Free again, I embraced the actor's life wholeheartedly "as he that leaves / a shallow plash to plunge him in the deep, / and with satiety seeks to quench his thirst." Another theater workshop was established to rehearse Braham's production of *Fuenteovejuna*. Again, we took our-selves very seriously indeed, trying to find an epic style for this play, so rarely performed in English. A product of De Vega's "Golden Age," it was a kaleidoscopic exploration of contemporary notions of honor and justice and of the rights of the common people, such as the peasant Frondoso whom I played with hair dyed a ferocious raven hue. So much high-flying ambition set us up for a precipitous fall.

It all started when a piece of scenery stuck, eliciting inevitable giggles. These turned to outright laughter as the declamatory style of acting kept the alienated audience at arm's length and free to indulge to a point where every line was provoking howls of unrestrained mirth. Indeed, Sheridan Morley in *Cherwell,* the university newspaper, confessed he was unsure whether to review the play or the audience. I realized with a shock of horror that we were getting "the bird." Anger as black as my dyed and painted looks swept through me. I had a crossbow in my hand and, turning it on the raucous mob, threatened them into silence. Michael Palin, a fellow peasant in this farrago, no doubt took a lesson from it, as I did, about the dangers of undergraduate pretentiousness, later bursting such swollen balloons of conceit to great comic effect. But, at that time, I think it was essential that ambition should vault. The university experience was one of coming to grips with ideas and either challenging or embracing them. Besides, since then I have always learned more from disaster than success.

Certainly, Brecht's undoubted influence was not wholly to blame. First encountered in a radio broadcast of *The Exception and the Rule* while I was still at school, his influence was now the rule. Perhaps this was because his style seemed itself to have been influenced by the great mass artistic medium of our time, the cinema, with its borrowing of subtitles and use of a revolve as a change of focus. He was very much a cult figure. Stratford astonished with *The Wars of the Roses,* Peter Hall's stark minimalist account of Shakespeare's history plays that I saw played all together on one thrilling, unforgettable day. Peter Brook responded with a similar *King Lear* set on an empty stage that reduced the characters to "poor, bare fork'd animals." The sight of the blinded Gloucester crawling helplessly around the stage during the intermission as the audience departed uncomfortably for their drinks and ice cream is still seared on my mind.

Many times during this strange year I had felt a kinship with "unaccommodated man" and never more so than at its end, when I submitted myself to the surgeon's knife. I had been plagued with persistent sore throats and colds. Many were psychosomatic, the inevitable first night doppelgänger, but it was considered that my broken, blocked nose was much to blame. Surrounded by Penny's nursing friends giving comfort, cheer and anesthetic, I was operated on at King's College Hospital. Darkness, discomfort and hope.

I returned to Oxford, gratefully and uninhibitedly breathing in its damp foggy air. Now that I was assured of tenure, the final examinations seemed far away. There was time to enjoy traditional leisurely undergraduate pursuits. At black-tie dinners in paneled rooms, where candlelight glinted off antique silver, I was initiated into such mysteries as which direction the port should take in its perambulation around the table. There were "smokers," as the ribald concert parties were still called in those days, before tobacco became taboo and women invaded this bastion of male chauvinism.

After the academic depredations of the previous term I found the perfect way to assuage my tutor's concern—by acting alongside him. In a college production of Robert Bolt's *A Man for All Seasons,* Braham cleverly cast Peter Bayley in the role of Wolsey. I was his nemesis, Henry VIII, and Emrys-Jones as Norfolk completed the conspiracy. Tutorials were converted into rehearsals as we put Peter through his paces and, turning the tables, demanded textual perfection.

In genuflection to the great god Brecht, Bolt had created a Common Man role as an ironic intermediary between the audience and the historic events it was watching. To my delight this was played by Adrian, who was back in Oxford to direct a major OUDS production of *Othello.* He had originally wanted to do *Antony and Cleopatra* but, in a story that reverberated around the national press, claimed he could find no one to incarnate the Egyptian Queen. "She was a woman who had a tremendous experience of sex. And she was also a woman who changed her mind again and again. Oxford girls aren't like that. They seem to know just what they want!"

I suspect, with hindsight, that it was more the recent scandalous, expensive film with Elizabeth Taylor that had cast a pall over the play rather than the unsexual, resolute nature of our student Cleopatras. But at least Adrian seemed to know what he wanted. The play was to be performed at great speed, putting into useful practice his observation in a recent rep Shakespeare production that, whenever the cast had a train to catch or a matinee to squeeze in, the performance improved immeasurably.

In an interview during rehearsals he revealed other discoveries:

> Professional actors are like a machine: you start them acting and then you have to slow the machine down, put the brake on. Here in Oxford you have to wind the machine up to get it going. Very few have the freedom to just go through a scene and let it happen to them. They're all the time stopping in the middle and accusing themselves of doing something wrong. On the other hand, the enormous amount of work and thought they put into a production makes them very valuable to work with.

Again, the main problem was finding a style—this time one that could reconcile handkerchiefs with anthropophagi, the sharp modern conversational exchanges with the great sweeping poetic passages. This was compounded by the fact that a literary approach was an almost inevitable result of so much digging in the local academic soil where, as one wag put it, "There are footnotes at the bottom of my Arden."

I was reminded of Max Beerbohm's fervent plea for a Shakespeare moratorium—that he not be performed again for at least fifty years. Only after a period of unfamiliarity, he argued, could the plays be accepted as plays and not as a kind of show-jumping event where horse and rider—the role and its actor—negotiated the well-known course and tried for a clear round. Moreover, the advent of cinema had indelibly stamped roles other than Cleopatra: it was hard to conceive of Henry V or Richard III, for example, in any way but Olivier's.

We acquitted ourselves creditably. Indeed, Oliver Ford-Davies and Giles Block, our Othello and Iago, would go on to grace the concrete portals of the National Theatre, and our Desdemona, Annabel Leventon, would sing wilder ditties than her chaste Willow Song. I played Roderigo, Desdemona's thwarted suitor and another pawn in Iago's malevolent grip. One directorial felicity was my arrival in Cyprus rolled up in a carpet. I also had an alarmingly vivid duel, the first in a long line of staged swordsmanship.

In the vacation the production was taken on tour to France, and it was here that I celebrated my twenty-first birthday. I was staying in Lyon at the time with the British Consul and he kindly arranged a jolly dinner party, blessed with a bishop and other dignitaries, to fete my majority. It seemed symbolic and significant that I should come of age while on tour with a theater company; moreover, in a year fraught with historic moment for, in 1963, the European Common Market was founded. Britain tended to ignore the significance of this event as it has tried—less and less successfully—to do ever since.

The celebrations continued. The new term began auspiciously with choirboys traditionally heralding the summer from the lofty tower of Magdalen College. Julia and I were there with the other May-morning revelers, drifting on the river in the misty dawn with the slowly warming sun a symbol of our growing friendship. Although, like me, she was involved romantically with someone else, I was also encouraging her relationship with her Muse, for a distinct talent as a performer was emerging from her shyness and inexperience.

My own talents were challenged with the offer of my first starring role in an OUDS production. With wonderful appropriateness for a reformed pyromaniac, this was the title role in *Prometheus Bound*. Here the classical connotation ceased. The Aeschylus play was directed by John Duncan, a long-limbed, long-haired graduate of my college who had astounded with his productions of *Tamburlaine* and of the medieval mystery plays of his native Yorkshire. Now a producer of one of the new television satire shows, the same irreverence infected his demeanor and work. At college he was also famous for an incident where, a notorious imbiber, he had unearthed an ancient college statute guaranteeing him a supply of ale while undergoing academic examinations. The authorities had acknowledged his right on the condition he complied with the letter of their law by taking his alcoholic due in full academic dress. Duncan agreed, only to be informed that the vintage statute required full doublet and hose, spurs and dress sword!

He staged the production, glass of ale still in hand, in New College garden. Providing the weather conformed, college gardens were ideal for theatrical performances. The previous summer Nevill Coghill had produced a memorable *Tempest* where Ariel ran magically over the moonlit Worcester College lake by means of an ingenious network of boards beneath its surface. There was nothing so ethereal or elegant for our production: New College garden resembled more a scrapdealer's yard with an assortment of crashed cars, old bedsteads, a concrete mixer and tin baths strewn about.

Prometheus's rock was a scaffolding structure to which I was chained almost naked some twenty feet up in the air while "vultures gnawed at my liver" as I paid for my crime of stealing fire and hope, the twin requisites for progress. For the finale, when a gold-lamé-suited messenger from the tyrannical Zeus, having failed to intercede, was sent packing, I was sent literally spinning down to my doom. The chorus was deformalized and disunited, crawling its fragmented way through a nightmare Hieronymous Bosch world of wrecked civilization. I trained body, voice and liver for the ordeal. It was fitting that this prototypical drama should provide a role where, for the first time, I could examine and attempt to synthesize the two opposing forces at work at the heart of the actor's art—or was it craft?—the Dionysiac impulse that is kept in check with Apollonian control.

The play was generally regarded as unperformable. But, characteristically stating a preference for inspired amateurism over professional expertise, Duncan animated the whole evening with gratifying results.

The analogy to the crucified Christ was not lost on the audience. "You could almost call it Rebel Without a Cross," Duncan mischievously confirmed. The best and most cherished review came from my mother: "You have no idea how impressive the whole scene looked, with the spotlight on you and you spoke so beautifully too. Grandad, the following day, rather staggered us by saying that when you started to speak he had a lump in his throat—he tried to laugh it off by saying how bloody silly he was, but I know how he felt."

One piece of unexpected excitement was the visit of Elizabeth Taylor and Richard Burton to Oxford to see the performance. The Egyptian Queen had come to reign undisputed over this city of non-Cleopatras, just as she now was the undisputed monarch of the media. But the local gods protested this effrontery and the evening was a dank washout. "You should have invited Esther Williams," Burton cheerfully remarked. An impromptu performance of Skelton's *Magnyfycence,* the other "unperformable" half of the evening's double bill, was improvised for our special guests. Like everyone else I stared in fascination at them as they huddled under raincoats and umbrellas that failed to dampen their glamour. I had no idea that I was encountering my future employers.

The gods did smile, however, on my blossoming romance with Julia. Her previous relationship had ended—as had mine. Lesley had written informing me that she was now happily involved in another of her own. "I'm ready for an idyll," I said to Julia. "So am I," she replied. And so it was.

An exotic gardenia in her hair, we danced all night at the college Commemoration Ball to jazz and steel bands and to the rhythms of a mutual compatibility. I was held by her aura, and the spell remained unbroken as we walked back in the soft dawn over Magdalen Bridge, willing the night to slow down. We boated on the languid river and strolled arm in arm across Port Meadow as my parents must have done as lovers.

Almost too tritely appropriate for the mood, I was asked to play Romeo in a university production of *Romeo and Juliet.* Calling ourselves the Oxford University Players, we performed first at the Minack Theatre in the farthest rocky tip of Cornwall which, like a trick of King Arthur's Merlin, had been carved out of a solid cliff face. The work had been done stone by stone over the years by another magician, a remarkable old lady called Rowena Cade. Assisted by her gardener, Billy—her cook was apparently fired when he refused to help—she had created a wildly romantic theater where the backdrop to the circular stage was the moody Atlantic and its reflected skyscape. Deceptively frail-looking, Miss Cade did more than just beat the Greek and Roman theater builders at their own game. She was manager, publicist, program seller, general factotum and *genius loci,* too!

It *was* idyllic. Julia came with me, staying with the women of the company in a little wind-washed seaside bungalow. The men camped —often in both senses of the word—in the local village hall where we lived off Spam, baked beans and white bread. The play, acted with a simplicity and directness that the open setting demanded, was well received by a crowd braving both dog-day heat and English summer chills.

I found Romeo to be a disappointing part—far too "wimpish," as we would say today. Showing a directness of passion and purpose, Juliet made his maudlin adolescent outbursts, his "heart-sick groans," seem intolerable. But, Romeo being a substantial role, it was interesting to note that its cumulative effect was better when these emotions were played passage by passage rather than line by line. Coloring each speech were certain key words that, when stressed, illuminated the sense.

We took some textual liberties for which I must now apologize. Emrys-Jones was our Mercutio and, after his death, he changed costume and reappeared as the Old Apothecary. "Costume" is perhaps a misnomer. He would shuffle in wrapped in an old cloak that, with his back to the audience, he would open to remove the poisons to give to Romeo. I would await with some trepidation the revelation that ensued. Some times he was stark naked, at others clad only with a girlie centerfold poster. There were flashing lights and other unmentionable distractions. All this was a good test for grace under pressure and I could usually survive the visual assault.

The only difficulty was his line, "My poverty but not my will consents," which invariably emerged, even as he handed over the fatal drug, as "My woverty but not my pill consents." All very well. Almost plausible in fact and far more comprehensible than the play's "skains-mates" and "flirt-gills." The problem was my rejoinder, which now had to emerge as "I pay thy woverty and not thy pill." The audience seemed unfazed by the textual nonsense, which reminds me of a story that John Gielgud told me of a hot matinee at Stratford where he was moved to intone in that parabolic swoop of a voice, "Angels and Ministers of Grace defend us. Get me a cup of tea!" Again, no untoward reaction. I have heard Laurence Olivier, too, lose his way in a Shakespeare play and, without so much as dropping a meter, take strange but definite detours through other texts until he found his triumphant way back.

If we sounded strange, we certainly looked magnificent, having rented the costumes used in the recent, now legendary, Old Vic production of the play by the young Florentine, Franco Zeffirelli. He had thrilled his English audiences by bringing out the Italian qualities of the drama so that you saw the hot, heavy summer light and felt the mad blood stirring. I little realized that wearing these garments was my first association with a great artist who would profoundly affect my life.

It was strange how the play seemed to set a mood over the whole year. The previous one had had the psychological mindset of the prison with its hostage, mind-benders and schizoid two-fathered man. Now romance was all. I remember gazing up at the star-filled Cornish sky, arm around Julia while Mozart's Clarinet Concerto played somewhere in the velvet darkness, and being overwhelmed by an intense feeling of happiness. "How silver-sweet sound lovers' tongues by night, / Like softest music to attending ears." Indeed, the "yoke of inauspicious stars" seemed to have been lifted. A new band called the Beatles had a hit single called "She Loves You" that was on everyone's, and especially my, delighted lips. Yeah! Yeah!

One small sadness was that Julia could not come with us to Israel, where we had been invited to take the play. Woverty was all, but just enough money had been raised to present one performance in Jerusalem and the rest on a tour of kibbutzim. We left behind the gray coolness of a typical English summer where, in fact, my only photograph of the production shows me sheltering my Juliet under an umbrella.

Traveling overland, the real broiling Italian heat that we had been so carefully simulating came as a shock. Nearing the real Verona, we desperately rushed out at every train station for water until we gasped into Venice. There, in the warm evening air smelling of stale canals and the cheesy pizza then almost unknown at home, we boarded a Greek cruise ship and sailed off farther south. Accommodation was a sleeping bag on the open deck. We ate leftovers and whatever the kindhearted crew could spare. Though my air mattress was punctured, I was always able to get to sleep before it deflated me on to the throbbing deck. We organized a cabaret for the first-class passengers and, by demanding endless rehearsals in their quarters, managed to spend the entire voyage in comparative comfort. Sheridan Morley, our Capulet, was indeed "the very pink of courtesy" after contriving to bathe in the Captain's cabin, a rite of our ragtag passage he took as his patrician due.

We cruised smoothly into the sharp Aegean light and I understood at once the clear hard-edged quality of Hellenic art that produced a nation of sculptors rather than painters. After the tedious literary wanderings of Aeneas, here at last was the real thing. Following his passage over the wine-dark sea, we traced the shadow of Othello's passion in the dust of Cyprus and felt that old English surge of enthusiasm for the Isles of Greece that were too soon left behind. So, too, was the suspended reality of the mood.

At Haifa we discovered our costumes had been left behind in Venice. There was nothing for it but to improvise with what we had, transforming our performance into a kind of homage to *West Side Story* with Capulets and Montagues as Jets and Sharks. In one respect it was a relief to be free of rented costumes, that, no matter how scrupulously cleaned, always tend to reveal, in the heat of the aromatic moment, the presence of their previous wearers. Our modern dress production charmed audiences who seemed grateful for this cross-cultural manna in their desert, discussing the play afterward with an infectious enthusiasm and passionate intelligence. Traveling by truck from kibbutz to kibbutz, we helped out on farms to earn our keep, cutting bananas by day and courtly capers by night. I felt extraordinarily well and alert, an effect that Israel has continued to exert. In Jerusalem we performed in a theater where Adolf Eichmann had recently been tried. Its dressing rooms were barred cells, ominous and depressing. In Galilee, Syrian jets roared over the Golan Heights reminding us of the universality of the two foes that "from ancient grudge break to new mutiny."

On our return we were invited to another old battleground, Dublin, to present *A Man for All Seasons* at the Theatre Festival. Again the budget was derisory. Taking the night ferry from Liverpool, we put up around the corner from the Abbey Theatre at Noonan's Bed and Breakfast. Here, the management assured us, unlike neighboring establishments, there were no "hoppers." The reason was not hard to find—a flea would have had claustrophobia in the tiny garret room into which we crammed. Trains thundered by a few feet from the grimy back window. I even shared a cramped bed with Peter Sissons who, as a celebrated television journalist, would go on to report far more weighty horrors. Julia's letters were a balm: "O Michael, if the women in Dublin are so gorgeous don't get too deep in your part. Off with their heads if you do!"

Though we acted on a tiny stage in Trinity College, the great joy of performing there was the huge feedback from the audience, similar to the reaction of the kibbutzniks—an unforced enthusiasm and curiosity. Dublin working men would linger afterward to discuss the play, and particularly the moral and ecclesiastical issues it raised. It made the work seem both pleasurable and worthwhile.

At home, there were some new developments. May and Joe had moved up even further in the world to a substantial house in elevated, salubrious Tunbridge Wells. Though still at school Caroline was starting to trade horses for boyfriends. I made my debut as Uncle Michael to Penny and Marek's first baby, Paul, and finished the summer with gainful employment—first in a bookshop and then working in the props department at the new BBC Television Centre. These were heady days for British television. "Aunty" was being ruthlessly eased upstairs. The satirical bent of the times, reflected in such irreverent shows as *That Was the Week That Was,* paralleled the work being gleefully presented in London's newly established Establishment Club and, of course, in countless student cabarets.

My job, however, was in contrast very mundane. As well as backstage toil, I went all over London collecting and returning furniture and firearms, books and bibelots.

We worked a shift system, and sometimes it was possible to finish the graveyard one curled up on a sofa asleep. During the day, under the guise of doing something useful—carrying a cable or a book—I could walk from studio to studio watching rehearsals. I saw the dour, beloved Tony Hancock performing live and Petula Clark sang to me of her favorite things. The only karmic consequence for me was that I was fated to return and put in my full time at these studios, this time legitimately, and on the other side of the cameras.

Finals

I returned to familiar Oxford territory, renting a top-floor room at 18 St. John Street, where I had lived as a stage manager, thereby preserving a continuity in eyries. It overlooked the narrow street and its slate rooftops. I painted one wall a bright orange as if to compensate for the new seriousness of life.

It was now the autumn of 1963 and next year's final examinations loomed menacingly, though sufficiently far away for me to consider further dramatic indulgence. But even my grandmother wrote to remind me of the new realities. "You must get down to work now that the play is over, for you must get through and get a degree. Once you have that, well, you can more or less please yourself." She astonished me, though, by adding, "I really hope you will take up acting. I'm sure you are cut out for it and I haven't the slightest thought that you won't get on." I cherished these words of encouragement. Others came from our new Master, John Maude, perhaps because his own daughter was an actress with the Royal Shakespeare Company. My father, however, thought that I should at least consider a career at Marks and Spencer as its chairman, Lord Marks, was favorably disposed to the sons of senior executives.

College was no longer a safe, closed community. Eating out was not without its problems, and not just the expense. The cheap hot dogs sold by itinerant vendors were as repulsive as their smell wafting unfittingly down the noble High Street, so I took to eating in equally inexpensive Chinese and Pakistani restaurants. Once I witnessed an amazing scene over my chicken vindaloo. Its irate cook emerged from the kitchen brandishing a fearsome carving knife at an employee and, with a blood-curdling oath, pinned him to the floor. Not one diner so much as paused with fork in air as this murderous scene was enacted. You had to have a strong stomach for the fiery food but this English sangfroid was even more breathtaking!

University Players presented a college production of Ionesco's *Rhinoceros* in which, by some curious irony, I used my now functioning proboscis to turn into a rhinoceros onstage, dispensing with the masks usually employed to facilitate this transformation. My character Jean's trumpeting of his bourgeois respectability that turns into the wild cries of an outraged animal—"the swamps, the swamps!"—was done in front of the audience in a stylized, brilliant production by Braham.

Our Oxford success encouraged us to take the production to the National Student Drama Festival at Aberystwyth in Wales. The *Guardian* thought that we were "the best thing in the Festival" and I was pleased to be considered its best actor in an unofficial student poll. But it was the veteran *Sunday Times* critic Harold Hobson who was the official adjudicator. He cast his laurels elsewhere claiming, with his usual Francophile bias, to miss in our production the horror induced in him in the original by the sight of a horn emerging from Jean's bathroom.

The year ended on a note of true horror. I had gone out one night to buy a six-penny carton of milk from a machine, picking up on the way back a late edition of the evening newspaper. By chance, I noticed in the Stop Press column the unbelievable words, "Kennedy Assassinated." The grim morning confirmed my worst fears. The tragedy was so universally and intensely felt that afterward everyone would similarly remember their personal circumstances on hearing the news. Adrian wrote to me about the production of *The Hostage* he was directing at a London drama school at the time:

> We were rehearsing the scene where news comes over the radio that the boy in Belfast jail has been refused a reprieve and they all make "remarks characteristic of themselves" when someone burst in with news about Kennedy which they'd just heard on the wire-

less. The rehearsal was thrown into confusion. But the actors suddenly saw how they should have played the scene.

Jack Ruby's execution of the prime suspect in the assassination was tacitly approved until theories about a possible conspiracy began to emerge. Coincidentally, a show about capital punishment called *Hang Down Your Head and Die* was created at Oxford amidst similar controversy. I appeared in it briefly during a week's engagement at the Memorial Theatre at Stratford-upon-Avon where it was exciting just to sit in a star dressing room imagining the scenes that had previously poured tinnily from its loudspeaker. Emrys-Jones and myself played ringmasters who, outside the theater, cheerily dragooned the unsuspecting audience inside. Here the facts of judicial murder were presented in a vivid, chilling entertainment, similar to the way that Joan Littlewood had conveyed the true horror of the First World War in its music-hall songs and dances.

There was a swing number called "An Innocent Man Is Never Hanged," which reflected the recent exculpation of Timothy Evans, hanged for the murders at 10 Rillington Place. One of the most telling moments was an unnerving, almost unendurable fifty-seven-second pause in the action that duplicated the exact time it had taken to execute the Rosenbergs in the electric chair. The show later went on to further acclaim on Broadway, the very thin end of a wedge of British musicals that would, several decades later, rule the Great White Way.

Living out of college meant greater freedom. Besides being together every day, Julia could now stay overnight with me, although this was still strictly illegal. Discovery could result in instant banishment. I certainly felt responsible for my own amatory actions. I had received no guidance on these matters, though, from my morals tutor, his purpose and presence remaining a mystery. Ironically he might have been useful in discouraging amorous advances from his own number, particularly dons involved in the already homosexually intensive arena of theater!

I had an understanding German landlady who would invariably complain, "Ach! Dis raum ist all at sexes und sevenz!": a dress rehearsal for the Berlin landlady who later did so much to enhance my cinematic good fortune. As with Herr Issyvoo and Sally Bowles, a discreet blind eye was turned on all this divine decadence. The threat of premature academic withdrawal should have made for a neurotic sex life, but it didn't seem to thwart our growing affair. Warmed by the orange walls and the electric fire and serenaded by Julia's beloved music, we glowed in our mutual company. I was Papageno to her Papagena, a role she had recently sung in public. Our heads were full of airy, bookish notions of courtly love and gallant troubadour songs but our arms were full of the reality of this extraordinary emotion that had the power to supercharge every instant.

Again, as if to encapsulate the mood, to prolong this indulgence in the food of love, I was cast as Orsino in my last undergraduate play. This *Twelfth Night* not only celebrated Shakespeare's four hundredth birthday but was also the first university production in the reconstructed Playhouse. Michael Rudman, a Texan with an amiable grin and an enviable Volvo, was now the president of OUDS, and directed a company that included David Aukin, Annabel Leventon, Doug Fisher and Michael Emrys-Jones. All of us were now committed to a life in the professional theater. I was too poor and impatient to be a student any longer, so going on to drama school was definitely discounted. Besides, I had become increasingly convinced that acting, as in the Youth Theatre, could best be learned from experience.

I had considered working elsewhere in the media—in print and television journalism. But fundamentally I was unwilling to live my life with any gnawing thoughts that I could have been a performer and hadn't dared. As I have now confirmed over the years, I would rather rue the sins of commission than those of omission. Moreover, I had been taught by so many academics who at one point, I felt, had faced a similar choice between the wild, untamed wasteland of the professional theater and the familiar walled groves of Academe. They had settled for the safer option and were left to indulge their theatrical passions vicariously through their pupils.

As *Twelfth Night* was the final shop window displaying our theatrical wares, I set about inviting agents and casting directors to the performance. Vernon Dobtcheff, an ex-President of OUDS and now a professional actor, generously showed me the best way to get photos printed and letters sent. Then as now, he was supportive and omnipresent, forever sending good wishes and delivering them in person. Indeed, legend has it that a small corps of identical Dobtcheffs exists that, beetle-browed and blackly clad, are sent out daily from some central headquarters to Thespis's farthest reaches to spread counsel and cheer.

The response to my letters and to my swan song was gratifying.

Deciding to engage a director of London Artists, Philip Pearman, as my agent, I put my career into distinguished hands. His first advice was that I should audition for the Birmingham Rep and the Royal Shakespeare Company. As a result, the latter offered me a spear-carrying role from June to December. "On the face of it it looks rather tempting," Philip wrote, "but I think you might get terribly depressed coming down from Oxford where you have been, let's face it, something of a local star and finding yourself plunged into a crowd. Unless you are very anxious to do this, I would have thought it better to wait and go to Stratford later on a higher level."

I agreed and Adrian suggested that I audition for Scotland's Dundee Repertory Company, where he had recently worked, finding its new policy of doing plays in repertoire to be most stimulating. I prepared two contrasting pieces—Romeo's bravura final speech and Bolt's cheeky Common Man—and performed them at a London audition. I was accepted, and my delight was doubled when I learned that Adrian himself would be joining the company for part of the season as co-director. The timing was perfect. The start of rehearsals coincided almost exactly with my last day at Oxford. Moreover, they were offering a starting salary of £15 a week!

Such pleasant considerations paled beside the now terrifying immediacy of finals. A note Michael Rudman had sent thanking me for my Orsino finished with the injunction "and keep swingin wit dat poesie, man!" I now did so with a vengeance. During this final vacation I stayed with Julia at her beautiful home in a West Country village. We read and revised, encouraged and bullied, inseparable in our mutual anxiety and ardor. Back in Oxford I became a bookwormed swot. Life was viewed through a haze of half-remembered quotations and a chorus of thick-tongued guttural words.

The exams, preoccupying the next two weeks, were a form of sadistic torment. In the middle of summer we victims were required to dress up in a "subfusc" outfit of dark suit, white tie, gown and mortar board. The first morning my concentration was not helped by the fact that the Chinese gentleman in the room next door had been inconsiderately and loudly celebrating the conclusion of his torture all night long. So intense was the tension that several undergraduates completed their papers behind the bars of the local lunatic asylum. One hot day in the middle of a room full of scribbling, cogitating black and white bodies, a lonely gowned figure stood up, exited and strode along to Magdalen Bridge, where, like a bat descending into hell, he hurled himself into the cold oblivion of the river.

Then, for all of us, it was over. I can't remember how we celebrated our release. There was no raucous high jinks nor wistful winding-down. It was a mood that I have since often encountered at the end of a play or film engagement—a combination of relief and regret and a keen anticipation of what lies ahead. It was time to pack. I was a hired hand.

As a graduation present—and to get me to Scotland—my grand-father gave me his old Riley car. She was a beauty to look at, a bitch to drive. Scented leather and veneered woods luxuriated inside, but the most notable feature of the engine was the cloud of foul smoke that trailed behind. Jerkily, gingerly, I drove from Brighton to say goodbye to Julia at Oxford where she was rehearsing for a tour of Turkey with *A Winter's Tale*. The car was as reluctant as I was to leave her, breaking down repeatedly. My arrival in Dundee would have to be in more reliable, if less flamboyant style.

The train rattled over the Tay Bridge after its long night journey and I took my first look at the severe, granite city that would be my first professional home. Amongst my baggage I had brought with me a new name. Michael Johnson was already listed on Equity's books. Reluctantly I had had to call myself something else. In the same situation, Michael Emrys-Jones had chosen the stage name Michael Elwyn. It was only when faced with giving up my name that I realized the importance of something I had taken for granted. Johnson might have been common and undistinguished, but it was mine. My recent studies reminded me of the power that the Anglo-Saxons considered intrinsic in a name and that a rose would certainly not smell as sweet if called something less euphonious.

I toyed with the idea of promoting my middle name, but Hugh Johnson sounded like a well-born confidence trickster. Ancestral names were equally unsatisfactory. Palfrey and Chown were too strange and Higginbottom too earthy. Then, about this time, two new brands of cigarette appeared—Richmond and York. Their names had obviously been researched for their market appeal. Besides, if Olivier could have his own personal brand, then so could I. An actor friend who faced the same problem chose one and announced himself as Michael Richmond. I became Michael York.

Dundee

CHAPTER EIGHT

S o Dundee's Holy Trinity of Js—Jam, Jute and Journalism—
remained without another J. This old industrial powerhouse
had slowed down somewhat and now its tired, dirty heart was being
revitalized with clean new hotels and shopping centers. Grim tenements were being torn down, although the survival of such places as
Reform and Temperance Street, as well as the publess Sunday, gave
clues to its recent sclerotic Presbyterian past.

Its setting, however, remained spectacular. The silvery Tay flowed
broadly between outlying farmland and low wooded hills and under
McGonagall's famous bridge, which seemed to anchor Dundee to the
populated south and prevent it from drifting off northwards into the
limitless Highlands. At night it shimmered with lights like a lakeside
resort. I found digs in a house in Osborne Place with Adrian and other
members of the company. The rent was £4 a week for a shared top-
floor front room and a gruesome communal kitchen.

The theater turned out to be a converted church in the Lochee Road
as its predecessor, a famous nursery of talent, had burned down. It
had a cramped backstage area and dressing rooms: the wardrobe mistress even had to minister from the belfry. She was also a part-time

fire-eater, which threatened to condemn this theater to the other's fiery fate. The stage was generously aproned and situated appropriately where the altar used to be. In this temple I began to practice the mysteries of my craft.

I bought myself a professional makeup kit, a tin box containing the tubes of greasepaint—the 5 and 9, carmine and lake—as well as cream to remove them. Arranging the tools of my new trade on a folded towel, I looked searchingly in the lighted mirror for Michael York. The life of rehearsals, pub lunches and performances was certainly not a new one. But it was now my living. My future. And the face that stared back at me positively beamed with contentment.

Shaw's *Arms and the Man* was the first play we rehearsed and in it I played Olivier's old part of Sergius Saranoff. The Chocolate Cream Soldier himself was Sam Walters, a fellow Oxford graduate and ETC's recent Peer Gynt. The company was young and enthusiastic.

Julia wrote from Turkey about her grueling tour with *A Winter's Tale* and particularly of her new experiences as a performer:

Darling, the play was marvellous last night in Ankara. By the trial scene all the emotion of a full heart was in my mouth. I walked on with no deliberation, conscious technique or mental intention. It was not a part in a play—it was an event of my life. The stage was small; I could see Leontes' face, his eyes and the drops of sweat on his forehead. My gown was dark red and black; my hair was loose. The people were staring. I spoke of my childbirth, my baby's murder, my own public shame. When Leontes denied the truth of the oracle I fainted—truly—of exhaustion and heat. I went off in tears. Someone took me to the dressing room where I gradually realised who I was. It's never happened before. I was afraid because I couldn't judge what effect I had made. I thought my performance had seemed out of control. But people came to me and said that I had moved them, that they had wept when I fainted. What does that mean? I couldn't do it again unless I did it again by *chance*. I have no technique, no knowledge, no deliberation. But it worked last night, just as if I had possession of those arts. Tell me how *you* act. It's a strange mystery to me. Have you been a success? Are you moved? You must have felt another person in *Rhinoceros*. Most of the time it is technique—but just occasionally a miracle, a spark of God-given genius? Who would *presume* to have had that?

Before I could put my own presumption to the test in the artistic arena I was recalled to exercise it in the academic one. There was a summons from Oxford for a viva voce examination implying that, as a result of the written papers, I was a borderline case. I was faced with the task of talking my way up or down a class or, indeed, into any sort of degree at all.

It was odd to be so soon back in college and receiving instruction from my tutor about this other kind of audition. I entered the examination room with heavy heart. How could I possibly remember my lines after this interval? One of the examiners, Dr. Helen Gardner, looked up and observed brightly, "Oh, it's Orsino." I felt my drooping spirits perk and fervently hoped that her recognition of my Thespian skills would not alert her to the fact that I was now using every one of them in earnest. Nerves were channeled into positive ends, widening the smile and, hopefully, sharpening the wit. The telling pause followed instant improvisation, the whole performance larded with charm and faked sincerity. I focused on my champion, Dr. Gardner, imagining our eyeballs strung sympathetically together like the conceit of one of her beloved metaphysical poets.

A few weeks later, I read in *The Times* one of the most generous notices I had yet received: I had been awarded a second-class honors degree. The actor's award was usually a third. Julia had been similarly adjudged and I silently praised her for her eleventh-hour coaching and Orsino for his last-minute seduction. I splurged on a bottle of Veuve Cliquot to celebrate this unexpected good fortune, though my cup of contentment was now brimful.

One night after rehearsals I was invited to a seance, one of my first encounters with the supernatural. Years earlier, there had been a ghostly visitation at the Bromley Little Theatre where Adrian and I had been working late. The silence was eerily interrupted by shuffling, muffled footsteps and we both felt a sudden distinct chill in the air. Perhaps it was just tiredness, but it certainly "froze our young blood and made each particular hair to stand on end," in vivid confirmation of Hamlet Senior's experience.

This seance had the same results. I was spellbound by the wildly gyrating glass and the coherent messages it was spelling out from the circles of letters, especially when George Bernard Shaw announced himself. Taking advantage of his spectral presence we questioned him about our interpretation of his play. He had started to respond when, suddenly behind me, there was a loud crash as books cascaded from their shelves, leaving just one with a photograph of Shaw on it staring at us. I fled.

So, for two nights, did my ability to sleep. One of the girls later made me promise never to repeat this experience. There were good and bad spirits abroad, she gravely explained, and it was difficult to determine which kind would appear. I obeyed her injunction, although a persistent curiosity has led me to echo Hamlet Junior's discovery that there are more things in heaven and earth than are dreamed of in the average man's philosophy.

Julia returned from Turkey after a nightmare journey in a crowded train where, falling ill, she was allowed the special favor of sleeping in the luggage rack. Her enthusiasm was infectious.

> Michael, you are so lucky to have chosen such a rewarding career ... Just looking back on our small venture, and seeing how consistent the play was with reality; how at times the answer to life's confusions and mysteries lay in the text so that the play held more reality than life itself—all this strengthens my belief in art, as a necessity. God bless your aspirations, my precious actor! I'm glad I attempted Hermione, to know a small something of your activity. Keep me at singing, Michael—*Please* keep me at it.

Soon the first plays in the repertoire were ready for performance and I set about honing my skills in the traditional way—Shakespeare one night, a modern comedy the next. I played the callow Claudio in *Much Ado,* our little contribution to the Bard's Big Birthday. It felt good to have become a professional actor in this celebratory year. The first reviews made that cup run over. "To stand out in this new-look rep is difficult. The team has suddenly become more outstandingly proficient than it has been for months." Michael York was complimented for his "considerable comic gifts" though deemed to be playing Saranoff as "a kind of Ruritanian mixed-up kid." I had, in fact, borrowed Olivier's business of falling over his entangled spurs, and dedicated the guaranteed laughter to his inspiring genius. Michael Johnson stood on the receding shore of amateurdom and waved a fond farewell as my renamed barque sailed sprightly into the crosscurrents of "the business."

I repeated my lucky cockney soldier in *The Hostage,* maintaining— now with more certainty—that "There was no place on earth like the world." Our production became an unscheduled tribute to Brendan Behan, who had just died at the tragically early age of forty-one. His humor, foaming naturally in his language like stout in a glass, was his guarantee of immortality. Death's sting-a-ling was elsewhere evident in the equally untimely passing of my agent, Philip Pearman. My career was handed over to his youthful colleague, Michael Anderson.

Julia was now back in Oxford, teaching to provide the financial wherewithal for her singing vocation. "I hate the word *career,*" she wrote. "Singing I have loved in my heart; no public job could ever draw me like this. Music is an instinct to me. So is acting for you— you don't analyse, you *do.*"

In fact, I had just had a chance to analyze my motivations. We put on Julian Slade's fifties musical *Salad Days* in which I was reasonably typecast as Timothy, the young man just down from university. The story had an agreeable old-fashioned quality; in it the word *gay* could be used without fear of ambiguity. It did seem, however, to anticipate a growing cult of youth that would soon make universally poignant the lament, "We don't understand our children." At its heart was a magic piano that set everyone dancing and this grail equivalent corresponded to my own search for significance in what I was doing. I sang feelingly of three perfect years—"The dons we placated, the lectures we missed"—and vowed never to look back. But, asked to write an article for the theater program, I seized the opportunity to retrospectively take stock, anatomize my feelings and look to the future. The resultant self-centered cerebrations appeared under the title "On being an actor" and included the following:

> Acting can never be just a job: it's a way of life. For me at least it is a toy in the blood, something I have not been able to purge, and therefore have come to acknowledge and respect. Frequently I have had to justify my action in not putting my university degree to a more apparently practical use, in joining the ranks of this much-maligned, traditionally despised, overcrowded and underpaid profession. Although my ideas are still in their own salad days, I hope they are not glamorised by false romanticism. . . .
>
> I feel strongly that theatre is important because it helps us to understand not only what stuff dreams are made on but also what stuff man is made on. Sir Laurence Olivier has said that the actor should command the same respect from society as the doctor or the solicitor, for like them, he helps man to understand his problems and to know himself. Man, exposed and isolated on the stage and illuminated by the spotlight, can be seen in all his paradoxical attitudes: an object of terror and ridicule, of laughter and compassion. . . .
>
> But all is nothing unless, like a good doctor, we sense the pulse

of our audience and command their respect and confidence: otherwise the theatre becomes a cultural ghetto peopled by a community totally out of touch with the outside world. Yeats once wrote that in the poet's church there was an altar but no pulpit; in the actor's church, a far more public place, both are indispensable. More—they are virtually indistinguishable.

My parents came for a visit. Seeing my happiness and dedication, Joe, ever magnanimous, conceded that I had made the right choice.

I telephoned Julia regularly from a lonely box that stood in the center of the empty riverside green. The plonk of falling coins counted out the hours and miles of our separation. "O this waiting, waiting, like vegetating! When will it end?" Julia wrote. "I have ringing through my ears a beautiful Old English ballad which goes—'O that my love were in my arms'—It's about winter and absence and loneliness."

At weekends, when not involved in special Sunday night experimental productions, Adrian and I devoured the newspapers with their new American-style supplements and listened to music before the gas fire's asthmatic hiss. Scarved against tear-jerking wind we walked beside the leaden river and its millipedal bridge, and scootered up corn-smudged hills to where the Highlands blazed with autumnal colors. There was something clean and antiseptic about Scotland. Its people were straightforward and kind. But outside of the theater I was rather antisocial, especially when Adrian was away directing other projects. As of old, when not with someone special, I enjoyed being on my own.

I have continued to be an untypical company man. Not for me the endless retelling of theatrical stories in smoky, cacophonous bars. The preceding generation of actors was famously wild and self-destructive but I felt only the occasional urge to test liver and wit in bibulous company. I still dread running the gauntlet of location hotel bars and being caught in a net of camaraderie, to hear the chimes at midnight spell out another pleasant but vacuous evening.

This puritanical attitude to what was generally accepted as pleasure perhaps contributed to the fact that, by the end of the year, I was exhausted. Certainly so much continuous and varied work on top of the summer's examination effort began to tell and the management decided to give me a break. I was excused from the forthcoming Christmas pantomime, although I still regret never having had a chance subsequently to participate in this quintessential English entertainment. Oh no you don't—oh yes I *do!* Like Dick Whittington I headed for London. En route I stopped in Oxford where, finally, Julia and I were in each other's arms.

In London, Michael Anderson suggested I should take advantage of being there and audition for the two major companies, the Royal Shakespeare and the National Theatre. I polished up Prince John's Gaultree Forest speech and, in contrast, Bolt's Common Man was also allowed a rude reappearance. At the Old Vic rehearsal room I came face to face with my idol, Olivier. He sat surrounded by his co-directors and staff, like a king on his throne. I wanted to kneel at his feet. His charisma was magnetic and yet he possessed that sure touch of greatness—the ability to put others at ease, me included. At least my common man could look him in the eye.

I heard first from the Royal Shakespeare Company. Philip Pearman's strategy seemed to have paid off, for they asked me to join them to play a range of small but significant parts. This excitement was matched when Michael Anderson called to say the National Theatre had also requested my services—in fact, I could join next Monday walking on in a production of *Much Ado About Nothing* to be directed by Franco Zeffirelli.

I was faced with a fundamental feature of my new profession—choice. There was no blueprint for a career, or logical progression from role to role, nor guaranteed reaction to a given action. Or obvious options. You were left with the task of developing sensitive antennae joined to a network of instincts that, when primed and energized, would generate the most propitious decision. Sometimes the most important things were subtended from the thin thread of accident. Like Hamlet, though, I believe in that divinity that shapes our ends and, on occasions, confusingly rough-hews them, too.

All I knew then was that every immature instinct urged the apparent illogic of accepting the National's offer. Moreover, this was made possible when the Dundee management kindly agreed to release me from my contract. I rushed back north on the last day of the year in a train full of cheery revelers, packed my things, and thanked providence for such a splendid professional initiation and for the prospect of a very Happy New Year.

National Service

*T*he National Theatre was then but a few years old, having grown out of the company that Olivier had gathered as director of the new Chichester Festival Theatre. A permanent building was still a decade away so it was temporarily housed in the historic Old Vic, the scene of so many of his former triumphs—and current successes. Instantly applauded, the new company had settled down to a repertoire of classic revivals, such as Oliver's *Othello,* and new plays like Peter Schaffer's *The Royal Hunt of the Sun,* that would earn this period the warm retrospective title of the Golden Years.

I joined the company on January 4, 1965. So did Ian McKellen and Albert Finney. My Coriolanus had lived up to that early promise and become an international screen idol with such films as *Saturday Night and Sunday Morning* and *Tom Jones,* an image enhanced by long cigars and a plush motor car. Ian, a fellow Oxbridge graduate, was vaulting up the professional ladder. Dashing between capitals and from triumph to triumph in the new jet-set style, Zeffirelli was the current darling of the theater and opera world. A trim neat man in his boyish forties, he addressed the assembled company in accented but collo-

quial English, wearing a navy blue cashmere sweater and wreaths of
smoke from a constant cigarette. He stressed that he wanted *Much Ado*
to be fun and to emphasize its Italian elements. At one point our eyes
met and I had an instant intuitive flash that this encounter would not
be without significance.

I again found lodgings with Adrian, this time in a basement flat in
Earls Court, an area in West London dubbed "Kangaroo Alley" for
its predominance of antipodean settlers. My new home was remarkable for several eccentric features that would have defied the hyper-
boles of the most persuasive real estate agent. For one, it had an
outside lavatory installed as a civilized afterthought in what once had
been the coal hole. Often during naked nocturnal dashes to this dank
freezing chamber, I speculated on the bizarre consequences of the front
door blowing closed. Gray daylight filtered down the basement well
to the barred front window facing the rickety steps and a wall. The
bedroom was windowless and airless, as was the bathroom, whose
antique gas water heater provided atmospheric lighting and noises.
The living room had one electrical outlet so plugged and socketed
with adaptors and extensions that it buzzed and glowed like an atomic
pile. A tiny, immemorially greasy kitchen with an ancient, museum-
quality gas stove, made up the accommodation. It was cheap and ideal.

I was frequently on my own as Adrian was elsewhere consolidating
his reputation as an international director. He was now working more
and more in Belgium and Holland, winning admiration and awards.
My subterranean life extended to the daily journey to work by Underground to Waterloo where I would immure myself in the venerable
fastness of the Vic. True to form, I had been assigned a dressing room
on the top floor under the roof, which I shared with other young
members of the company, including Michael Gambon and Christopher
Timothy.

It was a full and pleasurable life. Apart from the daily rehearsals
there were classes in voice, movement and fencing, the latter conducted by Bill Hobbs, who years later would provide the swash and
buckle for my D'Artagnan. Classes were democratic: you could find
yourself doing knee-bends alongside Olivier, who inspired the company with his zeal and fitness. I learned to breathe from the diaphragm
and, in many other ways, tried to make up for technical weaknesses
in my actor's armory.

There was much ado about *Much Ado*. Zeffirelli had given it a
nineteenth-century Sicilian setting, inspired by contemporary gaudy
sugar dolls and puppet shows so that it looked, and often sounded,

like an extravagant "opera buffa." Nino Rota had provided music to be oompah-pahed by a brass band with "Sigh No More, Ladies" turned into a larynx-wobbling love song. Robert Graves had even been called in to make some textual amendments in the interests of englightenment. However, at some point a decision had been made for the Spaniards, Don Pedro and Don John, to speak with Spanish accents. This had unleashed a verbal avalanche, for Dogberry and the other rustics were allowed to trade their customary stage "Mummerset" for a thick potpourri of stage Italian in which snatches of *La Traviata* could even be heard.

There was a crisis of confidence. I was a mere walk-on—albeit in a jet black wig and mafioso mustache—privy only to the endless rumors and not the facts of the case. Ken Tynan, now the National's brilliant dramaturge, was, it was said, threatening to resign and Robert Graves to sue. Many were made nervous by Zeffirelli's pragmatic style of direction—to be later so brilliantly suited to the less formal medium of film—and cautioned that the young tyro was not infallible with Shakespeare, pointing out his recent setback with a Stratford *Othello*. Eventually it was resolved that England's premier company could present its premier playwright in an "accented" version.

It was a measure of Shakespeare's genius that it worked triumphantly. The play could rarely have exerted more joie de vivre, especially from Maggie Smith in a real star-dancing turn as Beatrice. Nor could there have been such shocking menace as when, eyes flashing in flaring anger, she hurled out her uncomfortable order "Kill Claudio," which, as a vendetta, suddenly made sense. I loved the sunny exuberance, the constant inventiveness and good humor that made even the curtain call entertaining!

During the rehearsals I had had two significant encounters. One was with John Dexter, who, after many successes with the work of contemporary playwrights, had been recruited as a co-director of the company. He had a fearsome reputation as a demanding martinet and, with his dark, scowling looks, seemed like a naughty boy permanently on the point of saying something very rude. He took me for champagne cocktails and dinner and flattered me by inquiring how NT and MY could best ally their initials. The second was with Zeffirelli himself. We met by chance at the same table in the Old Vic's minuscule canteen. He asked me if I had ever made any films. I told him no, but that this was a dream ambition. "Maybe someday you should," he rejoined enigmatically.

I was cast in other plays in the repertoire and understudied other roles, covering "Simon" in Noël Coward's masterful production of his *Hay Fever*. Nightly I marveled at the sheer ensemble brilliance of the company, led by the incomparable Edith Evans as Judith Bliss, and shared the audience's ecstatic laughter. It was sobering to realize that Coward had so recently been out of favor and that I had entered a career in which fickle fashion played a far too prominent role.

I became an Inca in *The Royal Hunt of the Sun*. My main memory of this visually arresting play was the nightly royal hunt for a spare shower and bottle of Fairy Liquid, the only reliable means of scouring off the coating of native "bole" while leaving the skin intact. Another was the occasion when an explosive fart made all the other upturned bottoms prostrated in silent reverence before Atahualpa quiver in mirthful sympathy. "Corpsing" on stage was as enjoyable as it was painful and I was relieved to witness the greatest in our company having to turn upstage like crass amateurs to allow the paroxysms of suppressed laughter to subside and fatal eye contact to disconnect.

My especial friend in the company was Derek Jacobi, one of its founding members, having played Laertes in the inaugural production of *Hamlet*. A former Youth Theatre player, he and I had first met briefly backstage at the Arts Theatre in Cambridge, the scene of his student triumphs. Blond and friendly, he was then a star at the Birmingham Rep. It was now odd to see his striking looks and powerful voice masked by the facial tics and thick accent of his latest role—the villainous Don John in *Much Ado*.

The immediate future seemed assured. "It is a mistake to look too far ahead. Only one link in the chain of destiny can be handled at a time," Winston Churchill had once observed. A dramatic highlight of this time was the death of this great man. He was mourned and buried with great pomp and moving ceremony—in its way the last act of the old order. A new tune was being played and the sixties, led by those mop-headed pied pipers from Liverpool, were starting to swing to its rhythm, leaving profound changes in customs, costumes and mores in their wake. Macmillan's winds of change were blowing here as well as in Africa.

My Aunt Irene came for a visit from Southern Rhodesia, a country where she had long lived and one undergoing massive, irreversible changes. We argued passionately about apartheid, she chiding me for my unrealistic idealism while I countered that distance made objectivity easier and the moral imperative stronger. Our differences were ingrained: we dined off corn on the cob, a relative luxury for me, cattle-feed for her! The boast of her country's founder, Cecil Rhodes, that to be born an Englishman was to win first prize in the lottery of life now echoed hollowly. England was beginning to shake off such arrogant assumptions.

London was suddenly the place to be and I reveled in my new colleagues and routine. The Royal Academy's Bonnard exhibition warmed a cold gray January. Adrian returned and we translated a Feydeau farce for simultaneous broadcast at the World Theatre season at the Aldwych. I continued my education at the National Film Theatre. Once, at a rare screening of Johnstone Forbes-Robertson's rather geriatric *Hamlet,* I was amused, then moved, to hear behind me an old buffer cry out to his companion during the graveyard scene, "Good Heavens! There's C. Rivers Gadsby!" Was this the writing on my wall? Was this the symbolic graveyard where all small-part players, clinging but to the muddied hem of their muse, go to mourn? But even in so humble a role, the cinema had provided a sort of immortality. I longed to make the medium mine.

Worn down by her enforced ascetic life-style, Julia fell ill. I went to see her in hospital in Bristol and tried to share the good cheer that was being heaped on me. I had just been assigned some significant roles in the National's forthcoming summer season at the Chichester Festival Theatre and looked forward to her joining me in this enchanting corner of the Sussex coast.

Founded by the Romans, Chichester lay at the farthest reach of the sheltered sea. Derek and I decided to share digs, managing to rent Garnet Cottage situated amidst tranquil fields on the road south to Selsey. Its ancient framework contrasted strongly with the concrete and glass modernity of the theater, which sat like a vast spaceship in the middle of a city park. One of the new generation of playhouses, its audience was seated in tiers around an open stage. Backstage facilities were starkly efficient, contrasting favorably with the antediluvian Vic with its warren of cramped rooms and echoing, institutional corridors.

The plays to be presented that season were Pinero's *Trelawney of the "Wells,"* *Armstrong's Last Goodnight* by John Arden (like Bolt, another Brecht disciple) and a double bill of *Miss Julie* and *Black Comedy,* a new play by Peter Shaffer here receiving its world premiere. Just as *Trelawney* highlighted the differences between the old-fashioned and the newer realistic drama, so *Armstrong* presented another total contrast. *Trelawney* was an unabashed vintage valentine to the theater and in it

I was promoted to playing Arthur Gower, the "juve lead" and Rose Trelawney's young lover. Its story of a well-brought-up young man who gives up respectability for the life of a stage "gypsy" had echoes of my own experience. Perhaps fed up with kitchen sinks, our audiences took it to their hearts.

Armstrong's Last Goodnight, written in an impenetrable sixteenth-century Scots dialect, concerned a freebooter called Johnny Armstrong, played by Albert Finney. In wild wig and wilder accent, I fulfilled a long-cherished ambition to work with this charismatic actor by playing his leather-clad brother. Albert had a tangible aura of star power—even when ambling on stage chewing on a great meaty bone and announcing his satisfaction of appetite with the words: "Ma waim nickers nae langer." The play's barbaric events and uncouth shaggy-haired actors speaking raw, abrasive language was like an Anglo-Saxon epic performed on some mad Burns' Night.

Black Comedy, in contrast, was an undisputed triumph. Understudying Derek, who was playing the leading role, I watched it evolve from a basic sketch to a complete play thanks to John Dexter's inspired direction and Peter Shaffer's inventive ear. In fact, the whole company contributed suggestions and business, the perfect example of collaborative theater. The initial conceit, borrowed from the Chinese theater, of the stage being in darkness when it was light and vice versa, was stretched to its full comic potential. You could see—and enjoy—Derek's Brindsley Miller staggering in the "dark" from crisis to crisis during the course of an endlessly vicissitudinous evening.

Louise Purnell, my Trelawney, played a leggy, debby type with a chandelier-shattering Kensington accent. Albert Finney exchanged dreadlocks for camp looks as a limp-wristed antique dealer while Maggie Smith was in her farcical element as Brindsley's spurned mistress masquerading as the cleaning woman. I never hope to see the play better performed.

It was a happy summer. Derek was a delightful companion—witty, warm and wise, as might have been expected from someone raised in a close, loving family in the unpretentious East End of London. Although obviously marked for greatness, he shared the usual actor's insecurities. As well as chain-smoking, a certain self-deprecation made him go out of his way to avoid being photographed. Even later when film acting inevitably embraced him, he would refuse to watch his performance at the rushes.

Friends came to performances and to stay. There was croquet and tea on the sunny lawns of the cathedral deanery. My parents began an association with the Chichester Theatre that persists—they have since then never missed a season. Julia came as often as she could and in July we decided to put an end to the uncertainty and separation by becoming engaged to be married. I wrote formally for her hand to her parents. Soon after this I encountered unawares my future spouse. It was at a local restaurant after a performance where I happened to notice the American author Irwin Shaw dining with others at an adjacent table. Pat, my eventual wife, later confirmed that she had been among them.

This coincidence and its attendant laws proved inexorable. Fate slowly dress-rehearsed the future. At the end of the summer Julia requested a delay in our proposed nuptials. She was now a student again, of singing, at the Royal College of Music. At least we could look forward to the shared harmony of being together in London. Meanwhile, the season finished, the company was given a brief holiday and Derek and I decided to drive to the real Mediterranean. Top down, we whirled through France in his sporty Triumph Herald, past my future home in Monaco, and along the Italian Riviera, the scene of bygone romance, finishing up in a pensione in Amalfi. Here an andante atmosphere compared favorably to the brio we had been creating all year.

That autumn the Chichester plays were integrated into the Old Vic repertoire. Albert himself restaged *Armstrong* to fit the gilded proscenium that now suited *Trelawney* to perfection. Playing to a London audience, I felt my assurance grow and I was especially pleased to receive a very complimentary letter from Michael Croft.

My only slight regret was that the company, for administrative purposes, was divided into two. One half stayed at home while the other toured. As a result I never realized another cherished ambition of actually sharing the stage with Olivier. He apparently approved of my apprenticeship, however, asking me to stay on in the company. At Christmas there was another note attached to a bottle in his characteristic baroque style: "A nip of astonishing modesty to bring thoughts of most grateful size to you on Xmas Eve. L.O."

We went on tour to the Midlands and to genteel out-of-season Bournemouth where even Pinero seemed avant-garde. I remember how privileged I felt riding in the same train compartment as Maggie Smith, who was idolized as much by the company as by her public, and to share taxis and billing with other great artists such as Celia

Johnson. I reentered the tight little world of the theatrical landlady first experienced on tour with Prospect. One prototypical lace-curtained establishment was even called Vaude-Villa and was full of doilies and pictures of Ivor Novello on the piano. Adrian had a theory that Harold Pinter had written *The Birthday Party* while in digs, as their mood of claustrophobic respectability had been so perfectly captured.

It was in Glasgow that I received an urgent request to send a photograph immediately to a casting director in Rome regarding an imminent but secret film project. Consternation! I had no photograph with me. Moreover, the message specified it had to be of the entire body unclad as much as modesty would allow. Between rehearsals and performances I rushed from one photographic studio to another, but none could provide a quick service. In desperation I persuaded an instant passport photographer to change focus to accommodate a full-length pose and, braving old-fashioned looks and goosepimples, I stripped down to my underwear and sheepishly adopted a suitable Mr. Universe stance. After I expressed the results to Rome, the reply came that Dino de Laurentiis had found me "interessantissimo" and John Huston, "a very fascinating character." This gave a clue to the project. It was well known—Mr. de Laurentiis being a master of the arts of publicity—that both filmmakers were planning a cinematic version of the Bible and I instantly cast myself in the Sodom and Gomorrah sequence. But their interest and fascination was short-lived.

The excitement this episode engendered, however, was intoxicating. As I had told Zeffirelli, to act in films was a powerful ambition for most young actors of my generation. A saturnine Welshman called Anthony Hopkins, a new recruit to the company, gave stupendous impressions of his fellow countryman, Richard Burton, in the stage-door pub where postperformance adrenaline as much as alcohol kept the proceedings lively. We were inspired by the example of our immediate predecessors, Finney, Stamp, Harris, O'Toole, Bates and Courtenay, who were winning their spurs on international cinema fields.

As if counterbalancing any ambitious notions I might currently be entertaining about myself, there occurred a dismal time at work. Specifically, I could do nothing right for John Dexter. He had a reputation as a task master, his brilliant ends invariably justifying his sometimes unorthodox means. For some reason I was singled out for special punishment. "An actor exists to be criticized": I acknowledge the truth of Stanislavsky's harsh dictum. Dexter's censure, however, was excessive. Besides, theater has existed for some two thousand years and only in the last fifty have there been nonacting directors. Monty Bear was back, metaphorically twisting hairs. Perhaps he was merely testing my mettle. If so, it upset the company and complaints went to the top. "Oh, it's a hateful profession." Avonia Bunn's exasperated cry in *Trelawney of the "Wells"* rang loudly in my ears.

After one particularly humiliating session I stormed off the stage, banged into my dressing room, threw my things into a bag and made a dramatic, if uncharacteristic, final exit through the stage door. In the cold light of the Waterloo Road reality and reason returned. The old instincts urged caution, reminding me of the opportunity I was so impetuously throwing away. Swallowing hurt pride, I went silently back to my place in the rehearsal. A few weeks later my humility was rewarded. Franco Zeffirelli asked me to audition for his forthcoming film of *The Taming of the Shrew* starring Elizabeth Taylor and her husband, Hopkins's roaring hero, Richard Burton. He wanted more than a photo. It was to be the real thing, a filmed test in Rome.

On the early morning plane winging south over the Alps were three other young hopefuls—Ian Ogilvy, Natasha Pyne and Fionnuala Flanagan. We eyed each other furtively and appraisingly over our bacon and eggs and began to chat tentatively. I think we all realized that the impending trial could alter at least one of our lives. Finding ourselves booked into the same hotel, we continued to communicate, a luxury usually denied in the normal conveyor-belt process of the audition with its packed anteroom of mumbling preoccupied penitents. After dining—and especially wining—we agreed with sporting, if hypocritical, largesse that as we all liked each other so much it didn't matter who won the roles.

The tests were filmed at the new Dino de Laurentiis studio in the countryside outside Rome. Rumor had it that it had been constructed one centimeter across the line that arbitrarily divided the impoverished South from the affluent North, thus qualifying for government aid. Its facilities were lavish and nothing was spared: I was in costume and makeup and in a properly lit set. I tried to keep my face as relaxed as possible, realizing that it was now my principal actor's tool, the eyes being the chief source of emotional communication. Playing to the glittering impersonal eye of the camera lens was enjoyable and Zeffirelli seemed satisfied with my efforts. With breath bated and fingers crossed I returned to London.

The good news came soon afterward. It was even announced in the newspapers—an instant foretaste of the kind of celebrity afforded by the cinema. Natasha and I had been chosen to play the young lovers, Bianca and Lucentio. Moreover, the National was prepared to release me for the film. Columbia Pictures insisted on my signing a long-term contract with them and I felt honored to join a distinguished roster of actors that included Cary Grant, William Holden, Rosalind Russell and Jack Lemmon—all of whom later became acquaintances.

One morning, a few weeks before my departure for Rome, on March 10 to be exact, a day that will also live in infamy, I turned up for work as usual. Coming through the stage door, I was buttonholed by an anxious stage manager who informed me that Derek was sick and that I was on for the matinee performance of *Black Comedy*. Also, the Queen was coming to the evening performance so I had better be good. Imperturbably, I informed him that he was speaking to the wrong person. Another actor had taken over as understudy when the play was first presented earlier that year at the Vic.

"Yes. But he doesn't know it."

"Well, neither do I," I protested. "It's been ages since I last covered the part at Chichester."

"But John Dexter insists that you go on!"

The penny dropped with a sickening, stomach-wrenching thud. So my mettle was to be tested to the bitter end in a real-life black comedy. Personal humiliation and professional embarrassment would engulf me in a tidal wave that would sweep away all vestiges of my presence as a National Theatre player. Weak-kneed, I staggered up to my dressing room. There, anxious colleagues rehearsed my moves and drummed in the half-remembered text along with endless cups of tea. There was barely time to make up and change. I was led down to the stage like a convict to an execution.

When I set foot on the set it was for the very first time. I was in the dark in every possible way. Louise Purnell was there. We had the opening dialogue. I heard the curtain rise. The anticipatory mumblings of the audience subsided. Nothing happened. Somehow Louise didn't give me the first cue. Waiting alongside this stranger she must have been as nervous as I was. Perhaps the blood pounding in my ears had made me miss it. Or was it my line first? Panic engulfed me. All I could see were the illuminated exit signs at the back of the auditorium. I made a quick desperate plan to creep into the stalls and head for them. And then keep on going. The management would just have to

explain. The extra burst of adrenaline induced by this frantic ratiocin-
ation gave the stunned brain cells an extra fillip and out popped the
first line, "Well, what do you think of the room?" provoking the first
big laugh.

The rest of the cast was similarly keyed up, whispering cues, steering me around the stage and masking my inadequacies. Fortunately,
the groping, uncertain action of the character perfectly matched my
real predicament. I began to settle down, even to enjoy myself and the
applause at the end gave emphatic proof that we had all pulled it off.
I was congratulated. The measure of my success was that I was forbidden to go on for the evening performance and a feverish Derek
was dragged from his bed to amuse his monarch.

The nervous consequences were considerable and enduring. Even
after all these years I still dream of being on that empty stage, not
knowing what to say or do. I wake in the same cold sweat and to the
same delicious overwhelming relief.

Film Star!

CHAPTER TEN

*I*n Rome I was plunged into a plethora of preparations. There were wardrobe fittings and makeup tests. At a ladies' hair salon, alongside some amused matrons, my hair was bleached and permed, and at a stable, alongside some indifferent horses, I was taught the rudiments of riding. I waited anxiously for Zeffirelli's call, expecting that he would want to rehearse. Finally, on the Sunday before the first day of shooting, I was invited to lunch at his comfy, old-fashioned apartment in the via Due Macelli.

Ever convivial, Franco presided over a large round table of family and friends that included Edward Albee as well as that pole star of the ballet world, Eric Bruhn, and its sensational new comet Rudolf Nureyev. Our host could have been relaxing on holiday rather than about to embark on his first multimillion-dollar film. I continued to wait with mounting anxiety. Then, as daylight faded, he took me aside and briefly outlined his intentions for the role. His approach was essentially pragmatic yet obviously grounded on thorough preparation—one that I share and try to emulate. Above all I valued his implicit trust.

After a fitful sleep, I was driven out to the de Laurentiis Studios in the predawn quiet. To see the great cities of the world before they have come fully awake is one of the unexpected treats that cinema affords. The view of the Colosseum rising dreamlike against a purple pink sky was no exception.

The brightness of the busy makeup room came as a shock. I was sat down in a chair and with a Borgia malevolence my sleepy face was shocked awake with a coating of strong-smelling spirit gum. To this, a beard was laboriously fixed, glued on hair by hair, protracting the torment. Hot, smoking tongs then curled the appended fuzz as well as my unnaturally blonded head. To this day the merest whiff of spirit gum awakens memories of those hours spent squirming and gagging in that torturer's chair, and the revulsion revives.

On that first morning I was in the very first shot of the film. There was an electric air of expectancy. Time was now a measure not of minutes but of dollars. Bundled into doublet and tights, the last of my innumerable bows and laces were being tied as I was escorted to a set that swarmed with activity. Speedily hatted and cloaked, I was thrust onto my horse. *"Silenzio!"* The hubbub abated. *"Motore!"* The camera started to whir and my horse quivered with a contained excitement. Conspicuously more experienced than I was, at *"Azzione!"* it moved off and, utterly contemptuous of all my energetic spurring, went at its own pace precisely to its marks.

I was grateful for such assured professionalism for the shot required me to ride down a steeply raked street into Padua while quoting a sizable passage of Shakespearean verse. Fortunately, reality assisted illusion. I was meant to be overwhelmed with excitement and antici-pation and that is exactly how I felt. So much so, in fact, that Zeffirelli had to keep directing me to look less pop-eyed! By nine o'clock he had ordered "Print" and my screen baptism was over. There had simply been no time to be nervous.

That whole day I felt supremely alive. My love at first sight for Bianca was matched by my own for this new medium. I knew instinc-tively that I belonged to its world of lenses and lights just as surely as my name belonged on the canvas chair to which it was now proudly affixed. Everything delighted and the work flowed with an intuitive ease. Dining that evening with Alfred Lynch, who played my servant Tranio, I poured out my enthusiasm with the celebratory Chianti, totally intoxicated by the day's adventures.

I seemed to adjust quickly to the demands of the camera, never finding its presence intrusive or disturbing. I didn't mind the frequent repetition, although it surprised me at first to see how much coverage was required for even a relatively simple sequence. Franco was constantly inventive, cleverly suiting the action to the actor's intrinsic nature so that his direction seemed unforced. For fun he would ask for one take to be filmed in a restrained "English" style, and the next in a flamboyant "Italian" manner with gestured, extrovert behavior. His best effects were achieved through a synthesis of the two. I could understand why he liked working with English actors; their cool sangfroid neutralized his slightly operatic excesses.

He was a visual perfectionist. Renzo Mongiardino had re-created medieval Padua within the giant enclosed space. Its patinaed walls, courtyards and cobbled streets were lit day-bright by batteries of overhead lights, creating an out-of-season summer and much thirsting and fanning. Extras were handpicked, Franco even using some light-skinned blond people from a nearby village, formerly imported by Mussolini from the north to work the rice fields, for his Lombards. The youthful hordes of long-haired "Capelloni" haunting the Spanish Steps were also rounded up and, along with others, including his own dear aunt and the young Burton children, were costumed and co-opted to his lively creation.

A few weeks later the Burtons started work and I was moved to learn that some of their initial footage was later reshot. Realizing that even these consummately experienced actors could experience unease, I felt pangs of nerves. For our stars, the fantasies and pageantry of the set were matched by their life off it. Chauffeured to work by Rolls-Royce, they were there ministered to by maids, secretaries and butlers as well as hairdressers and makeup artists. Their suite of dressing rooms was palatial, replete with kitchen and office and carpeted throughout with virgin whiteness. I was happy to have my own modest dressing room where, between takes, I taught myself to speak Italian, learning as with all languages the rude words first.

The Burtons also held court to legions of visitors and journalists including the legendary Sheilah Graham who, flatteringly, found time to chat to me too. They were like gods to be showered with offerings. I remember finding a rare book of bawdy lyrics in a street market and showing it to Richard. "Thank you!" he said, accepting the volume, which was never returned. My wife later told me that the same thing happened to David Bailey when he imprudently demonstrated a new camera. They gave a lavish party at their rented villa on the Appia

Antica and it was good to experience at firsthand the exotic dolce vita hitherto but glimpsed at in the films of Fellini and Antonioni. Both Elizabeth and Richard were enormously kind and I am forever indebted to them for agreeing, as producers, to have me in their film.

I moved from my hotel in the modern suburbs to the timeworn center of town, putting up at a famous actors' haunt, the Pensione Riviera, run by the ebullient Contessa Bimbi. Vernon Dobtcheff, or at least one of them, was also in residence and playing my spurious film father.

"I can't honestly imagine what your life is like," wrote Julia. "But from your letter I can guess a little. It must be exciting to have such diverse and colorful impressions dancing round you and to be in such a glorious place with such bright and beautiful people, and to be occupied with such a great play." I looked forward to her joining me to share this bounty. Meanwhile, memory of her fueled my performance. I imagined it was Julia I was looking at when I had to gaze in rapture at Bianca.

Derek, then inexperienced in these matters, was fascinated with the technique of filming:

> What you've told me is very interesting. I think it's quite significant that Franco is not rehearsing you, but directing you on the spot, so preventing you from letting your theatre technique blur your photographic image. In other words *his* is the technique, *yours* the expression. . . . Michael Caine said on the steam radio today that an actor's achievements and success in theatre and television have nothing to do with what he can do in films. As the medium is so individual, what the actor requires *above all* is the intangible "it"— which I, and I'm sure many others, tell you that you've got.

I was anxious to ascertain if I did indeed have "it." There were occasional hints of approval. "How very nice to hear from you," Laurence Olivier wrote. "I am so glad you are enjoying the picture. I hear from Zeff that in his opinion you have a big future in the medium and am equally overjoyed to pass this news on to you."

Easter with paschal lamb and *vin' santo* was celebrated around Zeff's equally generous table. He also gave me a twenty-fourth birthday party, but afterward, as the film concentrated on the delineation of its title, we inevitably saw less of each other. The filming process was a daily revelation of new pleasures and disciplines but the initial excitement had abated somewhat. I was now just one of the cast—the "English lot," as the Burtons called us. I enjoyed the civilized company of Michael Hordern, the saucy charm of Victor Spinetti and the cynical Irish wit of Cyril Cusack, who brought his brood of daughters to the set, including in schoolgirl embryo a future co-star, the lovely Sinead.

My especial friend was a young American called Ed Limato. An assistant director on the film, he had come over from the States by ship with his big red convertible Pontiac in the hold. In it, all Rome was ours. Hood down, sunglasses on, we would motor through the narrow streets and, wind whipping hair, streak out to the beach at Ostia for lunch and a swim. The nearby hills with their rustic villages and local wines were another cool retreat. We explored Spoleto and its lively arts festival. We ordered handmade shirts and soft leather shoes, for this was the tail end of a tailored era soon to be transformed by a universal uniform of T-shirt and jeans.

We found a tiny workmen's trattoria in an obscure street by the Trevi Fountain, "the little old lady's place." Despite pasta's present global popularity, I have yet to eat any that matched her homemade marvels. At night we sat in one of the cafes on the via Veneto, sipping flaming sambuca and tasting the heady joy that Italians were finding in their postwar affluence. There were occasional sorties to the "in" Piper Club to dance over the lighted glass floor. Here, and in magazine photographs, I was once amused to find myself gyrating alongside Nureyev, especially as, a year later, I was asked to impersonate him in a film about a defecting Russian ballet dancer. Now you would have to pay a small fortune to seduce me into the hellish smoke and noise of a nightclub, though I still love dancing.

We were an odd couple. Ed would regale me with tales of Broadway which I would swap with London theater talk. Fascinated with showbiz, he perused its bible, *Variety,* with fervor, informing me of the "boffo confabs," the "hit pix" and other arcane mysteries. At the end of the summer I insisted he put all this enthusiasm to good use by returning to New York and becoming an agent. He did. Starting in the lowly mail room, he worked his way up to become one of the most powerful Hollywood agents. He's still mine, I'm delighted to say.

Through the Rome *Daily American,* I found a bijou apartment just off the via Veneto. Its actual rooms were insignificant, but its terrace was wide and generous and overlooked a roofscape of similar softly stuccoed buildings. Pots of gardenias bloomed in sultry profusion and in the jasmine-scented dusk flocks of darting swifts shrieked delightedly around a burnt orange sky. In this romantic setting, Julia at last came to see for herself and to discover, among other things, her familiar Michael now disguised with a curly thatch of straw-colored hair and a straggling mustache grown to minimize the horrors of the daily bearding. Adrian, too, came to stay and, as with Julia, I felt proud to be able to introduce him to my new worlds of studio fantasy and Roman reality.

May and Joe were also welcome visitors. Ed obliged as chauffeur, terrifying my mother at one point by leaping out of the car and remonstrating Italian style, voice and fists raised, with a traffic policeman. They received the grand tour—from prosciutto and figs by the gurgling little fountain at Othello's to the full watery panache of the Villa d'Este. When Joe left for a prearranged holiday in Yugoslavia, May moved in with me and I was delighted, at last, to be able to return a degree of her lifetime's hospitality.

Toward the end of the *Shrew* schedule, Joseph Losey asked me to meet him in Cannes where his latest film, *Modesty Blaise,* was in competition at the film festival. I had apparently been recommended to him by a casting director who had seen my work at the National. Losey was planning a new film entitled *Accident,* with the same creative team responsible for his previous success, *The Servant*—Harold Pinter as screenwriter and Dirk Bogarde as star. The screenplay turned out to be brilliant, its leanness of dialogue matching an intensity of meaning—all in strong contrast to my present florid undertaking. The role of William, the doomed aristocratic student, was a key one and I yearned to do it. Ed in his fledgling capacity of agent also advised me to take the meeting.

I caught an early morning flight to Nice and taxied up through rose-scented roads to the Colombe d'Or in the ancient huddled hill town of St. Paul de Vence where Losey and Bogarde were staying. My first time in the South of France, I was overwhelmed by its fresh morning beauty. At the old hostelry, upstairs shutters opened to reveal Losey, a large shy man with a remarkable sculptured face. Bogarde was equally affable and welcoming, joining us for breakfast under the vines of the dove-haunted terrace. I felt guilty for intruding upon all this hushed tranquility with rude news of the outside world, for I had brought with me the English Sunday papers. These were seized upon with masochistic avidity, and I witnessed the unnerving spectacle of the success of so many months of their painstaking work hanging in the balance of a few brief reviews.

Another unavoidable stock-in-trade was the press conference. I was invited to the one for *Modesty Blaise* in Cannes where a variety of questions, both hostile and flattering, was fielded with native bluntness by Losey and characteristic debonair charm by Bogarde. Escaping from this madhouse of flashing cameras and intrusive microphones, Losey and I walked along the sunny Croisette and talked about *Accident*. If this was an audition, I seemed to pass, for word came through soon afterward that the part was mine. Dirk told me later that he had argued all night to persuade Losey that English aristocrats *can* have broken noses.

Unfortunately, our *Shrew* proved to be an unconscionable time a-taming and my participation in *Accident* became questionable. Zeffirelli, ever an arbiter of my destiny, kindly finished me off in time. My end was my beginning, riding through the gates of Padua and onward to London where I started work for Losey that same afternoon. With me was Franco's farewell gift of an old glass painting of San Michele, who protects me to this day, and a silver framed photograph inscribed: "Dear Michael, you will tread greater boards than these. If not, we shall want to know the reason why. Love, Richard and Elizabeth."

Accident started filming in Oxford and it was good to be in residence again. My first shots, like those in *Shrew,* even had a university setting, emphasizing the sense of continuity. The scene was a tutorial with Bogarde as tutor. I even got to wear my old college tie and gown. My *Shrew* experience, I soon realized, was not exceptional. On the first day, nay first hour, I plunged straight in, instinctively establishing the character.

What was a new departure for me was, at the end of work, going to see the day's rushes projected on the large screen at the local Odeon after the last performance. I was horrified. My giant head seemed to react grotesquely and my amplified voice appalled. Back at the Randolph Hotel, a sleepless night ensued as I thought of ways to remedy this disastrous beginning. The next morning I put these into practice. Scathingly, Losey asked me what the hell I thought I was doing, retorting to my explanation in his most bluff and unadorned way that *he* was the director. It was a useful lesson in required objectivity and I have since learned to treat rushes as a creative process rather than as entertainment or, at worst, a confidence-sapping ordeal.

Experience has also familiarized me with the acting demands that Derek tried to analyze. Just as someone once defined poetry as the best words in the best order, so film is the finest frames in the finest order. It is constructed of whole sequences of little moments and looks in which a raised eyebrow can speak more than a ranting speech. This was especially true of Pinter's minimalist style, where what was said between the words—frequently in those famous pauses—was often of more import than the dialogue itself. Arranging this selection of filmed felicities, an editor abandoned the failures to his fabled cutting-room floor and assembled the rest. This process was powerfully illustrated in the cricketing scenes. It had been years since I last wielded a bat and yet these sequences portray a veritable champion. I noticed that Pinter, incidentally, like other English playwrights such as Tom Stoppard and Simon Gray, was obsessed with cricket and no doubt some day there will be a learned article on the influence of the sport on modern English drama.

Dirk became my tutor in more than just screen terms. He taught me about film acting both by instruction and example. His own method was a fine blend of intense concentration and instinct. Cinema, it has always seemed to me, is essentially filmed thought, and you could almost hear Dirk thinking. Concentration was essential and the slightest peripheral disturbance—a technician yawning or some unnecessary movement—could demolish it, making it vital to clear, or at least stabilize, the actor's eyeline. Indeed, the eyes were the essential doors to the soul of the film. Playing a scene together, Dirk instructed me how to look at the eye of his nearest camera so that both of mine could be captured on film.

He also taught me other technical matters, especially about camera lenses and the importance of knowing which one was being used so that the performance could be adjusted accordingly. He elaborated on the ever-puzzling mysteries of "crossing the line" that determined at which side of the camera one entered, exited and looked. It was a return to the old Apollo-Dionysus synthesis. One half of the brain monitored physical movement to critically exact marks, timing and looks while the other attempted to allow the god to speak. I became aware of the subtle symbiosis of actor and writer where the choice of inflection or suggestion of an alternative word could immeasurably illuminate the work. Dirk also insisted on the supremacy of the script and how important it was to keep referring to it, not only at night when one rehearsed the next day's dialogue but constantly on the set. I am now never without the text, or at least bits of it, smudged from ceaseless reference and annotation, folded up in my pockets.

He further impressed me by wearing a fine old tweed jacket that had already done duty in many films and I longed for a veteran wardrobe that would see such continued and varied active service. In keeping with current film realism he wore little or no makeup. This was a world away from the time when his matinee-idol looks had been photographed from only one profile—an era of charm schools and fan clubs and the whole studio-based paraphernalia that went toward the manufacture of "stars."

The language of film, so imperfectly if delightedly learned in Rome, was now given an English accent—and often a cockney one, for rhyming slang had become a staple of the British film set. Summoned by the "dog and bone," one was driven to work in a "jam jar" where "Rosie Lee" was provided by the potful. Hairdressers fixed "barnets" (Barnet Fair—hair) while makeup artists embellished "boat races." I became aware of the hierarchy of assistant directors, and that the real place to go for inside information was the makeup room. I also tasted for the first time that gastronomic miracle the bacon sandwich, and the mere memory of the smell still has the power to set the gastric juices flooding. In the afternoon there would be an elaborate tea with sandwiches, cream cakes and other childhood delights. Somehow the length and intensity of the work neutralized this caloric holocaust.

I was also a frequent guest in Dirk's trailer, where I sampled his habit of a medicinal mid-morning Guinness poured by his friend and manager, Tony Forward. I also had a stand-in who would look after me, fetching tea and even lunch if requested. But as with Percy of old, I was reluctant to be fussed over. I found refuge and real pleasure being alone in that contractual obligation, a dressing room of my own. Then, as now, I considered this a vital necessity, not a luxury. Film sequences are rarely rehearsed, so this is best done in privacy or in isolation on the set. That is why visitors who outstay their welcome are such an infernal nuisance. Like the person from Porlock, their intrusiveness can unwittingly interrupt or destroy an essential play of ideas. In those endless, unavoidable pauses between set-ups when technical changes are made, it may seem that nothing much is going on. However, these can be the most creative moments of the whole process.

The summer of 1966 taxed creative ingenuity to the limit. It was gray and gloomy with only fitful fine patches. As one of the major sequences of the film, where the main characters' destinies were sealed, took place on a long, hot Sunday, this presented problems. The sun would appear weakly, often first thing in the morning, and there would be a manic dash to maximize its uncertain presence before the drizzle returned. No sooner had the decision been taken to move inside to shoot interiors than, maddeningly, it would reappear to mock our studio-bound labors. One could understand why the industry had started in the pellucid, reliable light of California and why so much film product was factory-bound. And why the English were so perpetually obsessed with their weather.

The film became a patchwork of those little sunny moments. The pressure to produce footage was so great that during one long night-shooting sequence, Losey even filmed some close-ups of Jacqueline Sassard as she lay on the damp lawn basking in the light from a battery of arc lamps operated by electricians clad in parkas and thermal underwear. Rain, unless back-lit, does not show up on film and one wet afternoon, the carpenters erected a false kitchen window for me to look through. I was wearing a thick roll-neck sweater against the chill, a garment that appears absolutely nowhere else in the film—a detail that still bothers me but, apparently, no one else.

All this I learned was par for the course in filmmaking, where logic and rationality have little place and trompe l'oeil is all. It seems that if a film's center is solid and persuasive, then audiences will overlook any number of weaknesses at its edge—as witness the airplane that flies unremarked through a particularly dramatic moment in *Ben Hur*. Our film was shot out of sequence, which I liked. It seemed to more accurately reflect life where, from one day to the next, there is no logical progression of behavior or feeling.

Through all this I developed a profound respect for Losey. He was a man of cast-iron integrity and refused to compromise his vision. Given neither to hyperbole nor euphemism, he was frank about my performance and accordingly very helpful. He had a taciturn shyness, however, that exacerbated my own. Dirk told me that you might hear from Joe that you were good in a scene perhaps months after it was shot. I hesitated before parading my own little doubts and anxieties in front of him. He was under so much pressure, surrounded by lounge-suited executives who would nervously clear their throats and adjust their ties if the shot was not in the can by the fourth take.

Filming *Accident*'s opening and closing sequences, the camera remained fixed for many expensive minutes on the exterior of the Surrey house we were using for Dirk's Oxford residence. Toward the end of the long take the owner's dog by chance ran out through the main gate. There was no second take and, ever since, learned cineastes have discussed the symbolism inherent in this image!

Gradually we pieced in the story. Until my parents bought me one,

one of my few lacks as a real Oxford student had been a dinner suit. I was forever borrowing and hoisting ill-fitting cuffs and sleeves. I made up for that now with a magnificent outfit of my own, beautifully tailored by Dougie Haywood, one of the new breed of trendy tailors then sending tremors down Savile Row. It was for a sequence to be filmed at Syon House, which was standing in for my own ancestral home. Here house guests were entertained with an alarming competition, half Eton wall game and half aristocratic high-jinks, invented on the spot. My jacket could be reversed to reveal a dazzling, appropriately royal blue lining, ensuring that, at least visually, I was outstanding in the film.

Another sporting sequence, similarly more a test of character than skill, was a tennis match completed in one strenuous afternoon. Finally there was a quick return to Oxford for more boating on the river —a flashback sequence to recent more languid times when we had drifted down to Parson's Pleasure, a wine bottle cooling in the wake.

Cornwall Gardens

CHAPTER ELEVEN

By the end of that uncertain summer of '66, I found myself, for the first time in my new career, in the condition afflicting the majority of my brethren—out of work. I had expected to rejoin the National Theatre but, for whatever reason, was not asked back. I set about exploring other prospects of work and meanwhile signed on at the Labour Exchange.

I received Her Majesty's hand-out for two weeks, the only time I have lived off state assistance. Later, when I had established a reputation and had started to earn significantly, I felt my own good fortune demanded that my unemployment pay be left in the government kitty whenever I found myself between jobs. I have abided by this resolution ever since, even though I know it is irrational and falsely philanthropic. I secretly admired the chutzpah of actors who ostentatiously left taxis with meters running while they lined up for their fare money. Being unemployed emphasized the job's harder reality. An actor who was not acting was, like a peacetime soldier, a contradiction in terms.

During the filming of *Accident* I had busied myself with domestic affairs, principally looking around for a flat of my own. Julia, needing a place where she could uninhibitedly practice the piano and sing, asked if she could take over the sharing arrangement with Adrian, whose work was still keeping him almost exclusively abroad. He readily agreed and much later wrote to me about the fate of this unlovely basement that had sheltered so many dreams and hopes:

> The Cromwell Road looks like wartime Warsaw now, Edwardian facades standing up against the sky and shielding burning rubble. Earls Court has become hotelsville and landlords are smoking everyone out. 26B was declared "unfit for human habitation" (though no worse than when we had lived there) and the fact came to light that it had been condemned in 1935!

Cornwall Gardens, Kensington, a leafy enclave of bedsitter land near the Gloucester Road, was where I eventually found a flat, in a building that was formerly the Imperial German embassy. "From the outside, it looks like some mad architect's dream of a camp church. Gothic spires and turrets. Lonely trees. Occasional windows gleaming mournfully," wrote one journalist. It also boasted large rooms with high, elaborately stuccoed ceilings. In the bedroom, French windows looked across a small paved terrace and garden to my neighbors, who included Ivy Compton-Burnett and Joan Sutherland. I moved in with just a bed bought from its previous owner and that most indispensable piece of furniture for an actor, a telephone.

Discovering a secondhand emporium near the Twickenham Studios, in scenes reminiscent of my BBC prop department days, I shifted home great thronelike couches, huge breakfront bookcases, hanging brass oil lamps and cases of stuffed birds. My favorite armchair I found abandoned on a rubbish dump. "The sitting room," as the journalist noted in one of my first interviews, "swallows mammoth furniture as an elephant might swallow oranges." This was all before the impending vogue for Victoriana had made such unfashionable stuff immensely popular and commensurately expensive. I was particularly pleased with a giant gilt-framed mirror that went wall-to-wall behind the bed, reflecting the ordered gardens without and the untidy life within. A mixture of modern oil paintings, Victorian watercolors and Gillray cartoons completed the eclectic decor.

For the moment it was pleasant to get off the treadmill. Under Julia's enthusiastic guidance I explored her world of live opera, discovering especially the incomparable artistry of Fischer-Dieskau. I was also lucky enough to see Maria Callas in her last Covent Garden performance as Tosca. Her cry of *"Mori mori"* still thrills, as does the memory of her *"Visi d'arte,"* prefiguring her own tragic death in the service of her Muse. The Royal Ballet's new production of *Romeo and Juliet* enchanted. I went to Antwerp to see Adrian at work. He was winning further awards in his Benelux base and would soon settle permanently in Amsterdam. I also saw Dirk socially in his beautiful old Sussex house, where, at long Sunday lunches like the one we had just filmed, Dom Pérignon and good fellowship flowed liberally. To get there he also sold me a little Renault Dauphine car, chic and most reliable.

There was one horrible black cloud that overshadowed all this brightness. My grandmother was dying of cancer. May told me that just after her visit to Rome, Nan had revealed she had a tumor in her breast; she had kept quiet about it, apparently not wishing to spoil Irene's long-awaited visit from Rhodesia. She had subsequently received treatment but was now paying exorbitantly for her typically self-sacrificing behavior. I found my grandfather in uncharacteristic tears when I visited him and wondered how he would cope with looking after himself. May insisted on nursing her mother at home with weekly professional assistance from Penny. But it was too late to save her. It was death's first sting to our immediate family and I was shocked at the speed and mercilessness of its victory. Before she died, I was glad at least that Nan had some small inkling of my achievements in the profession she had urged me to follow.

Later in the year, returning to the BBC Centre (this time through the front door), I made my television acting debut as young Jolly in the now celebrated dramatization of John Galsworthy's *The Forsyte Saga*. This was where the mini-series genre, so brilliantly suited to the medium, was born. The cold, electric smell of the studios still intoxicated and I enjoyed the new techniques of TV acting, a strange hybrid of film and theater. If freedom was limited by the lumbering cameras, there was compensation in being able to play entire scenes rather than having them fragmented into little cinematic moments.

There was a warm company camaraderie, presided over by my genial screen father, Kenneth More. The typical British film star of the fifties—easygoing and charming, like Bogarde in his *Doctor* films—he was also capable of heroic things, such as his portrayal of the legless fighter pilot Douglas Bader. His attitude on the set betrayed the same nonchalance he then showed leaping into a Spitfire and giving Jerry a drubbing. He made acting look easy—a sincere compliment—and enjoyable. Eric Porter was as funny and mischievous offstage as he was stiff and sepulchral on camera as the severe Soames Forsyte. He delighted me by writing a most flattering prognostication of my future on a canteen napkin that I have kept and still try to fulfill.

Further prognostications came from Zeffirelli, who wrote enthusiastically after seeing the first cut of *Shrew.* "Now perhaps begins for you the most exciting and difficult moment of your life. The only advice I can give you is never lose your confidence in your destiny which is to succeed fully and completely." He added, "I keep receiving good reports about your progress—I can't help feeling very proud about it."

He had obviously not heard about my next job in a small film called *Red and Blue* directed by Tony Richardson, who on the first day of shooting was divorced from his wife, Vanessa Redgrave. As she was playing the leading role of a cabaret artist reviewing her life in terms of song, it set the tone for an odd atmosphere. In unexpected homage to my Welsh ancestor, Ephraim, I played a circus performer, one of Vanessa's first screen amours, the setting for our tryst being a large tent pitched on the outskirts of London. Asking Tony on arrival where exactly he wanted me to go, I saw his eyes swivel upwards to the high wire overhead.

Sensing a certain Dexterian challenge, I climbed to the swaying top, even venturing out onto the wire as the cameras recorded my folly from way below. Pride came puffingly before my Icarus-like fall. The shot finished, it was time to return triumphantly to earth. In faithful imitation of other high-wire artists—and yielding fatally to that impulse to show off, which is fundamental to the actor's psyche—I leaped onto a rope and began my vertiginous descent. Halfway down I could detect the smell of burning flesh and by the time my feet hit the floor, my hands were done to a turn!

The rest of the time was spent less dangerously, producing doves out of the air for a delighted Miss Redgrave—an act taught to me on the spot by an imported magician. Like so many of the skills an actor has to acquire, I have never been asked to repeat it; it lies unused in my ragbag of talents and unlisted on my résumé.

Two Dutch directors, known collectively as Wim and Pim, requested me for their next film. Checking out their reputation with Adrian, I found they were noted for some interesting offbeat work. Moreover, their letter intrigued. "We shoot rather quick. We love actors, so we only give them a general idea of the scene, leaving much of the details and even often the lines to his or her common sense." The budget was infinitesimal. I was offered £15 a day plus meals and air fare ("unless you prefer that horrible boat-train").

Reporting for work in an Amsterdam cafe, I requested the script, and was handed an old envelope scribbled over with the outline of a possible scenario. It could barely contain the film's title, *Liefdesbekentenissen* or *Confessions of a Loving Couple*. Moments later, we started filming in a Chinese restaurant. As a conventional clapperboard wasted precious film stock, there was just a vague clap of the hands. I was given the extraordinary responsibility of taking the story in whatever direction I wanted—the lunatics truly in charge of the mad house. It was an exhilarating if unusual three days' work. Several weeks later back in London, there was a knock on my door. "Action!" Wim, or was it Pim, yelled as I opened it. There they all were on my doorstep to film an extra sequence. I improvised some more and they happily vanished as quickly as they had materialized.

Next year, 1967, my widely scattered dramatic seeds began to germinate. The harvest came together. *Shrew* and *Accident* appeared at the same time as my two episodes of *The Forsyte Saga,* followed closely by the Dutch film. *Shrew* was selected for the Royal Command Film Performance, and deserved to be. Disappointingly, my scenes had been trimmed, but at least I still introduced the film just as the film credits "introduced" me. It was my eye-opening introduction, too, to the whole heady hoopla involved in merchandising a film and manufacturing "celebrity."

Accident was even more successful. Gerry Fisher's magnificent photography—his debut as a lighting cameraman—totally belied its sunless origins. John Dankworth's delicate score matched the subtleties of the mood, as perfectly appropriate to the story as Nino Rota's rumbustious score for *Shrew* had been. *The Times*'s headline was unequivocal if ungrammatical: "The Joseph Losey film everyone has been waiting for." I received my first serious critical appraisal, thereby accelerating an ongoing process of hide-hardening. "An exuberant young animal, as attractive as a Yorkshire sheepdog, which he somewhat resembles," one critic pronounced. Dilys Powell, though, endeared herself to me forever: "The theme of defeat is made poignant in *Accident* by the performance of Michael York, a young actor with a presence and a resource which can stand up to formidable acting competition." However, as I could not believe the one without totally discrediting the other, I decided that critics were at best unhelpful and at worst destructive. "Everybody is happy about *Confessions* except for the critics," confided Wim, comfirming me in this conviction.

Peter Bayley wrote warmly from the Senior Common Room at University College, Oxford:

> I've now had the slightly shattering experience of seeing both my old tutor (Hugo Dyson, the literary cove in John Schlesinger's *Darling*), and a pupil dead on screen—very unpleasant, really. I'm afraid I wasn't convinced by the dons except the bespectacled one who never spoke—nor their standard of living; but I enjoyed the film very much. I'm sorry I never gave you as much sherry (or indeed, any whisky at all) as Dr. Dirk did!

I suddenly found myself a "personality"! Newspapers requested interviews and my opinions were solicited on the radio. There was comment about my shyness and about my "Brando-esque" nose, which was photographed by Lord Snowdon and others. "To straighten that nose," I was cautioned, "would be like putting arms on the Venus de Milo!" One also found that one was quoted about one's consistent use of the impersonal third person singular, which, a writer observed, one employed against this invasive onslaught of curiosity "as a jousting shield" to protect one.

Success, however, had its more tangible rewards. I was summoned to meet Laurence Olivier at his unpretentious office in the warren of prefabricated office buildings at the back of the National Theatre. It was odd to see him in his other working mode, jacket off, suspenders bared and behind a desk. He was still enthroned. He asked me to return to the company, this time to play some leading roles. I found myself committing the lèse-majesté of refusing his offer. "Nothing will come of nothing: speak again!" I swear I could hear him growl. But the Instincts had prompted unequivocally. I explained that I was now between two dramatic stools and would like to consolidate my apprentice work as a film actor. To my unbounded relief, he understood and even sympathized, saying that he would have liked to have stayed longer in Hollywood. I forbore to tell him that, had that happened, he would never have made the film of *Henry V* that changed my life, and that we wouldn't be speaking now.

His beloved colleague Sir Ralph Richardson also requested an audience and I went backstage to meet him at the Haymarket Theatre. With its crackling coal fire in a massive grate, its comfortable antique furniture and musty prints, his dressing room seemed more like a study in a country parsonage, the garish battery of lights on his dressing table a vulgar intrusion. Gas lamps would have been far more appropriate. "Ah lahked yah fillum," he intoned in that memorable voice redolent of favorite uncles and eccentric bishops, "especially thah cricket!" Reluctantly, I turned down an offer to join his company. The same inner voice insisted it would be easier to return to theater from films rather than the other way around. Besides, I had tasted the cinema's anarchic freewheeling unpredictability. It made the theater's regular repetitive routine seem as old-fashioned as the room I sat in.

My cricketing prowess, however, had fooled others as well. I was asked to record the hearty voice for a beer commercial! Life was now a ferment of new opportunities and pleasures. The costume designer Bumble Dawson invited me to dinner at her cat-haunted Bayswater basement flat where another feline creature, Vivien Leigh, was also a guest. I was enchanted by her presence, compounded not only of her immediately perceived personality but of overlying images of her screen persona as well. Most movie actors disappoint when encountered in real life as their own character and looks rarely live up to those artfully manufactured for them. Vivien Leigh, her beauty now fragile but still vibrant, was no letdown. She completed my evening by allowing me to drive her home.

I soon grew anxious to work again. After recording a television drama, I returned to the theater in a new play called *Any Just Cause* in which Jeremy Brett was my brother and Phyllis Calvert my mother. Reviews were excellent apart from a crucial one from the *Sunday Times*, ever in disagreement, whose critic, wielding almost the same fascist power as his New York cousin, effectively stopped our transfer to the West End. It was symptomatic of a trend I would eventually get used to: I seemed destined never to enjoy the long run of a play.

I celebrated my new freedom back at the Cannes Film Festival where *Accident* had been born, witnessing it being awarded the Special Jury Prize. This time cameras and microphones were turned on me. Publicity, I now realized, was a concomitant part of a job in which hiding lights under bushels was counterproductive. Although stopping short of hiring a publicist, believing, as I still do, that work is its own best advertisement, I subscribed to a clipping service and was inundated with reviews and remarks. "There's a Philip Sidney quote isn't there?" I was quoted as quoting. "Something like, 'If ye enter ye public life, ye private lie goes out of ye window.'"

Certainly my own private life, if not quite defenestrated, was not without turmoil. Julia and I found a growing incompatability in our lives and ambitions. She wanted a smaller, more intimate universe. I, on the other hand, had been given the world. We decided to part for a time in which both of us could determine our priorities for the future. Going off to Wales to walk and ruminate, I came to a decision temporarily to free myself of exclusive emotional attachments and concentrate on work. This soul-searching session was curtailed by an appointment back in London with an American journalist from *Glamour* magazine at 4:00 P.M. on Friday, April 4, 1967. He—or possibly she—was called Pat McCallum.

Before the appointed hour, I spruced up the flat and myself, unaware of the irony that I was about to let into it a creature who, though fastidiously clean, was ferociously untidy. I put on my new black corduroy suit, made a pot of tea and waited. The bell rang and the door opened to reveal a radiant blonde wearing an orange and white striped mini-dress, large sunglasses over huge green eyes, and a generous smile. I ushered her into my cavernous dwelling.

We drank tea and chatted. As Lear would have liked, her voice was soft and low. Assuaging my Henry Higgins–like curiosity over her unusual vowels, she explained that she was an American born in Jamaica, brought up in Germany and schooled in England at a French convent! After what I thought was an appropriate interval of small talk, I asked if she had any questions about my work. "No," came the firm reply. This must be some new American-style interview technique, I reasoned, where the interviewer turned on his subject, tapping a stream of consciousness like an analyst. I stammered along politely. Pat later confessed that her heart had sunk at that moment: "Not *another* boring self-centered actor!" she had inwardly groaned.

The situation then explained itself. In the gloom of my hallway, and dazzled by my guest's presence, I had failed to see her deposit a bag by the door. Retrieving her cameras from it, she went briskly to work both inside and out, using natural light and natural poses. She seemed to have an instinct for the exact moment to press the shutter. By a happy chance, I photographed her at one point, providing a mutual record of this fateful encounter. It was now late in the afternoon and the London light was its usual opalescent, shadowy gray. She asked if I would agree to another photo session earlier in the day, in brighter, more flattering conditions; also somewhere that, as her magazine insisted, would reflect the artistocratic setting of *Accident*. We arranged to meet the following Sunday.

That morning there was no sign of her. I waited. Outside, a fine day also waited to be enjoyed. But some instinct kept me at home. She finally arrived, furious and apologetic, and, as I would discover later, most uncharacteristically late. Her sister's housekeeper where she was staying had failed to wake her as arranged. Wearing no coat despite the spring chill, she looked half-dressed. She hated to be encumbered while working, she explained. This, the first of many endearing eccentricities I would come to love, was my first awareness that Pat was a beguiling mixture of seeming fragility and great strength.

Taking her to one of my favorite places, the Orangery in Kensington Gardens, I assumed "aristocratic" attitudes in its bright, classically elegant interior. At the end of the session, we were both reluctant to part. We lunched leisurely and then dined lengthily, conversing with an instant easy intimacy. Pat—she was never Patricia—had a refreshing openness and directness that America, and especially New York, had instilled in her. Her sophisticated chic fascinated me—the saloned hair, the discreet jewelry, the Chanel shoes, the ubiquitous sunglasses worn indoors and out, and the unself-conscious habit of reapplying lipstick after a meal.

We stayed talking in my flat until the early morning. When I asked her to stay the night it seemed the most natural and inevitable thing in the world. She demurred and, annoyed at myself for my insensitive presumption, I drove her home. A few moments after my return, the phone rang. It was Pat, asking me to collect her. From that night on, we were inseparable.

I learned more about her. She had come to Europe to work and also to put her young son, Rick—he was never Richard—in school in Switzerland. She had had assignments to photograph Raquel Welch in Spain, Francoise Dorléac in Finland and, in London, unknowns like myself and Albert Finney, who was now directing his first film. A former travel editor of *Glamour* magazine, Pat had whirled around the world in a first-class seat from Cuzco to Moscow, from Iran to the Ivory Coast. As a fashion editor she had gone on a world trip with David Bailey and Jean Shrimpton, the archetypal sixties artist and model. She had bought a Nikon camera in Japan and Bailey, the cockney maestro shutterbug, while cautioning her it was like learning to drive in a Ferrari, had taught her how to use it. Pat discovered an instant, instinctive talent for the medium, which her employers recognized and exploited to the extent that photography had now taken over from her writing.

When I probed further a steel barrier came thundering down to the sound of strident alarm bells. She was guarded and fiercely loyal about her past relationships. The facts only emerged as our own friendship grew in trust and intensity. Divorced from her first husband, whom she had married whilst still a teenager, she had just concluded a relationship—at the exact same moment that I had finished mine. In fact, informed that I was in Wales, she had asked to join me there—sensing either coincidentally or instinctively the very first moments of my new emotional freedom. She, too, had apparently determined to dispense with long-term romances but such logical decisions were powerless against the passion that had instantly inflamed us both.

A week after our first meeting, Pat moved in with me—for good. Fellow Arians, we shared many enthusiasms. I traded my interest in films and tea for her passion for newspapers and magazines, finding out that her broken engagement had in fact been to Si Newhouse of the American publishing dynasty. We both shared an impatience with cooking. I realized that a future of cozy domesticity was improbable when, at one point, Pat let slip a complaint about her son's cooking! Soon afterward I met Rick, who was thirteen years old and as handsomely dark as Pat was fair. They seemed very close.

Confirmation of Pat's gifts and our compatibility came in a telegram from America: PIX OF YORK SMASH SMASH SMASH SMASH SMASH SMASH SMASH SMASH SMASH. Appropriately my next film role was in *Smashing Time,* a comedy that paid homage to her mentor, David Bailey. I played a trendy cockney photographer mouthing such argot as " 'ere, I'm mad about yer boat race." Pat was employed, too—both to instruct me in the mysteries of her art and to photograph the adventures of my co-stars, Rita Tushingham and Lynn Redgrave. Rita with her gamine looks was a current darling of the comic cinema, although she could rise formidably to the dramatic occasion as in *Dr. Zhivago.* Lynn, a former National Theatre colleague and future California neighbor, was a blossoming branch of the famous Thespian tree.

Playing gauche provincial types come to "swinging" London to find fame, fortune, and me, Lynn wore the now statutory mini-skirt and Rita some fashionably disastrous hand-me-downs. I, for reasons best left unexplained, was wearing an attachable mustache and wig. It was all outrageously "mod" and "pacey" to use the current phraseology, a tribute to that extraordinary time when London shook off respectability, let down its hair and danced uninhibitedly to wild new rhythms. All roads led to Carnaby Street, down which marched the outlandish children of this strange new age, chanting aloud the prevailing gospel of youth, and pied-pipering their astonished elders.

A custard pie in the face of convention, the film is memorable for the real ones in it that, flying thick and fast, culminated in one of the longest, smelliest food fights in cinema history. As most eating scenes take hours to shoot, actual mastication has to be minimized to avoid overindulgence. This one lasted a week and the intensifying smell of rancid cream putrefying under the hot lights was not at all smashing!

What was enjoyable was working together with Pat and sharing the camaraderie of the set. When she went off for an inordinately long coffee break with a handsome fellow photographer I must confess to pangs of jealousy and possessiveness. At the first break in shooting, I whisked her up to the Lake District in my new Sunbeam Alpine roadster, a car that, like Pat, had a singular personality. One night we stopped at a beautiful secluded hotel only to find it was fully booked. Refusing to accept this refusal, however, the car refused absolutely to start, throwing us on the mercies of the hotel until mechanical help could be summoned next morning. Our involuntary hosts then escorted us to the most romantic lakeside cottage, apologizing for its unkempt condition as it had been closed up for the winter. Furniture was dusted, fires were lit and a bed was made—and deliciously slept in. In the morning, of course, the car started up at the first turn of the key. I could swear a headlight almost winked.

On other occasions it would balk against being driven down certain roads. Annoying as this was, invariably the rerouting would turn out to be more interesting and picturesque. Once it insisted on taking us to an obscure guesthouse where we shared a gooseberry pie and compliments with Joyce Grenfell. Her generosity, as the Michelin Guide puts it, *vaut le détour*.

Romeo and Juliet

CHAPTER TWELVE

The prospect of being in *Romeo and Juliet* was consistent with the romantic mood of the unfolding summer. Consistent, too, with the prevailing cult of youth, Zeffirelli had plans to film a version using very young actors, so that, unusually, his Juliet would approximate to her historical age of fourteen. He asked me to play either Paris or Tybalt. Sadly I had to decline as I was already contracted to make *The Strange Affair,* a film about another doomed young man, a corrupt policeman. Both films, however, were for the same company, Paramount. "So no problem," Franco shrugged. "You will only be needed in Italy for two weeks." I was there, of course, for over three months! Three magical, unforgettable months.

Pat and I shared the sweet sorrow of parting. While she snapped away on her five other film assignments, I flew back to Rome for my new assignment: Tybalt, the fiery young cousin of Juliet. It was bold and unobvious casting and I was grateful to Franco for this opportunity to lay the pallid ghost of Horatio to rest and play a character who was totally "passion's slave." In order to claim credible Capulet cousinage with the raven-tressed Olivia Hussey playing Juliet and Natasha Parry her mother, I submitted myself yet again to the hairdresser's skills, emerging from the dryer with black locks and looks. Franco's conception of Tybalt was of a golden boy, who did everything well, whether fighting or fornicating. In fact, my filmed introduction was never used. Discovered in the act of proving my reputation as the "King of Cats" between the thighs of a nubile young maiden, at the call to arms I leaped up, pulling on tights and another kind of rapier. Even in the edited version, I enter the film from the crotch upwards!

The relative youth and inexperience of our cast made me feel as veteran as the Panavision cameras, inscribed, as was then customary, with a roll of honor of the films they had photographed. The scenes they now recorded were extraordinarily beautiful. *Shrew* was all fabricated facade; this was the real thing. With the removal of a few modern signs and telephone wires, Romanesque churches and ancient towns became the exquisite background for a docudrama of *cinquecento* life, making Siena's Palio seem mere showbiz by comparison.

Again Zeffirelli handpicked his extras. Every one of them was photographed, including his international battalion of Botticelli hippies, and he arranged them within his film frame as meticulously as any Old Master would group his saints and angels. Far from remaining aloof behind his camera he loved to physically demonstrate his directions, often acting out whole scenes with all the overemphasis of a silent-movie star. His line readings had to be acknowledged and then unlearned as Franco could sometimes be, as our profession puts it, "a little over the top"!

Maintaining the pattern of synchronicity that was to become a feature of our lives, Pat was asked to photograph on the film, too. We were joyfully reunited in Pienza, a picture-postcard-perfect Tuscan hill town and former papal residence. Within days, one of her photos appeared in *The Times,* endearing her to Franco, who, despite his film's subject, was still Friar Laurence–like in his attitude toward romance and to ours in particular: "Therefore, love moderately; long love does so. Too swift arrives as tardy as too slow." We were all staying in a delightful little family pensione in Bagno Vignone, returning after work to suppers of fried zucchini flowers and other regional delights and soaking tired limbs in the local thermal mud baths. Huge harvest moons hung in the sky silhouetted against the cypress trees, while a million crickets made the darkness vibrant.

Much of my spare time I spent rehearsing duels with Leonard

Whiting, our Romeo, whom I had first met as a boy actor at the National. Instructed by an Olympic fencing master, after several weeks we were fit and proficient. The first fights were filmed in Gubbio, an extraordinary out-of-the-way Umbrian town seemingly cut off from the onward flow of history, where crossbow contests were still held in the main square. Franco decided to dispense with the authentic graceful foils of the period and use heavier weapons that registered more on film—and, as it turned out, on body. Moreover, on the day of shooting, he capriciously changed the sites and sequences of our patiently learned routines so that we now fought each other on a gravelly hill. This gave the duel its own mad momentum, provoking an alarming spontaneity and, especially as we were fighting with both sword and dagger, a real sense of danger. Our cameraman, Pasquale de Santis, followed every cut and thrust, at the same time crying *"basta!"* to stop an impending massacre as blood began to seep from superficial wounds. Heat hurt, light seared, sweat soaked and great clouds of swirling dust choked eyes and lungs. Stripping off sodden shirts and gulping down water between set-ups, we panted and foamed like mad dogs. "He that hath the steerage of my course," however, and our hours of training, preserved us.

It was an enchanting time. Pat and I were falling in love. "Ah then, I see Queen Mab hath been with you!" commented Franco on my obvious happiness. Insisting that Pat and I stay with him in his villa on the outskirts of Rome when the production moved to the Cinecittà Studios, he masked his generosity with characteristic dismissive bluff. "I plan to push you two together so that, by the end of the summer, you'll be sick of each other," he grinned mischievously. A man who didn't easily wear his heart on his sleeve, he was, deep down, as hopelessly romantic as his two classic lovers.

Franco's household reflected the manic vitality of the set. Droves of visitors dropped by and there were never less than twenty for meals. Olivia, still a bright-eyed teenager with a throaty giggle and a chaperon, was also a house guest. So, too, were Robert Stevens and a pregnant Maggie Smith, who had fallen in love while playing those other classic lovers in Franco's *Much Ado*. Ed Limato, now speeding up the agency ladder in New York, also came to stay. Peter and Natasha Brook were next-door neighbors.

After work and at weekends, there was a swimming pool of local mineral water to plunge into as well as the pasta of Vige, the ever-provident and patient cook, to plunder. Maggie taught Dorino,

Franco's tiny Sicilian butler, to speak some English and he would graciously serve at table, proudly enunciating the most purple obscenities! Sitting at the piano one afternoon, Nino Rota played his music for the film. For the first time we heard the haunting, sensuous melody that would enrapture the world. Pat later photographed him with Fellini in a joyous, jokey, day-long session.

The main square of Pienza with its cathedral towers and fountains was skillfully duplicated on the studio back lot so that, in the climactic fight with Romeo, we chased down a real stone street and, seconds later, burst into its painted replica. Also duplicated was the dust, now whirled by wind machines. It was at Cinecittà that the Capulet feast was filmed. A literally brilliant idea of Franco's was filling the air with gold dust that shimmered in the candlelight as the lovers came slowly, irresistibly, hand to hand. It got everywhere—in lungs and hair and also in Pat's cameras, but not before she had exultantly shot off roll after roll of film. It was all almost too photogenic. At least *Vogue* thought so—they published an unprecedented eight pages of her color photos.

But time, that old enemy of filmmaking, began to press. Our summer's lease had all too short a date. There were urgent calls from England to return. However, John McEnery, our Mercutio, had fallen ill, the probable result of his prolonged soaking in the fountain at the beginning of our duel. The crucial moment where he returns Tybalt's sword so that, moments later, he can be killed by it, had still not been shot. Necessity, as so often, bred brilliant cinematic invention. Donning Mercutio's doublet, Franco filmed his own shadow hurling the weapon at my feet, enabling the fight—and the story—to continue to its tragic conclusion.

As well as each other, Pat and I embraced the considerable pleasures of Rome. She was earning more money than I was and unlike me had even been assigned a car. I was indulged in such shameless luxuries as a blue suede jacket from Brioni. Pat introduced me to old friends of hers such as Gore Vidal and Howard Austen, who entertained us to pasta with white truffles and nourishing conversation at their local trattoria. A master communicator in all media, Gore passed on to me a useful tip about television interviews. If there is another guest, he instructed, always put your arm behind him. A disconnected limb looks odd on camera and a two-shot is almost guaranteed. Delighting in Gore's ironic, astute and often acerbic intelligence, at his suggestion I read his *Julian* and dreamed of bringing it to the screen.

Pat was also assigned to photograph Jane Fonda on the set of *Barbarella* at my old De Laurentiis Studios. This huge sci-fi epic was directed by her then husband, Roger Vadim, with Jane in her most rampant incarnation as a sex kitten. Pat's photos of her cooking her family lunchtime pasta clad in plastic breastplate and lace-up boots are both erotic and endearing. I was even offered a part but, as the project was already a month behind schedule after only two weeks of filming, felt I should decline as, at that rate, I would never have my *Strange Affair!*

Within days of returning home I was walking a London beat as Police Constable Peter Strange with Tybalt's sword traded for a truncheon and his black curly locks shorn to regulation length. Renaissance piazzas were exchanged for the concrete metropolis now transforming parts of London, where the work of Hitler's bombers was being finished off by developers whose brutal tower blocks thrust up where sedate, tree-shaded terraces once stood.

We were filming around the Harrow Road, an area in particularly violent upheaval because of a new overpass that raped its way across the cityscape. It was symbolic of the new Britain, where old values were being energetically discarded for new, with consequent moral and social unease. Our film even had modish crimes—drugs and pornography—and a Maharishi-type arriving by helicopter to be greeted by an adoring throng of white-garbed devotees. The idea was to get as far away as possible from the traditional cop shows with their formula plots and clichéd settings. Although successful in this respect, on reviewing it, *The Strange Affair* looks as curiously old-fashioned as the trilby hats that some of the detectives still wore. There isn't a single gun in view and even the car chases are done in a sedate old Rolls-Royce.

Trying for a modern look, it suffered from some of the worst excesses of sixties filmmaking, where unconventionality of style matched that of other media. Big-budget films were being handed to directors barely out of film school whose outstanding qualification was that they were young. Although technically circumscribed by a morals clause—its details as mysteriously vague as those of my university morals tutor—cinema reveled in the newly relaxed attitude to sex, exploiting the screen with long, often slow-motion scenes of lovemaking. Yet only ten years before, my screen goddess Simone Signoret tucked up in bed with Laurence Harvey in *Room at the Top* had been considered a daring breakthrough.

Stripping for the camera provoked a certain personal reluctance. It had obviously been a prerequisite of *The Strange Affair*'s script, but this discomfort, compounded of native reserve and alerted instincts, intensified as I sensed I was being exploited voyeuristically. It did not help that the character I was playing was unattractively weak, a quality barely redeemed by his woolly social conscience. Moreover, in the scene where he was compromisingly photographed, the setting, with its circular bed and bath and whip-wielding statuary, made his innocent incredulousness seem merely incredible. And very hard to play.

"Felt so sorry for you," Adrian commented after seeing the film. "The script didn't seem to give you any character at all! She said, "Oh go on, do!" And you said, "Oh, all right," and there you were corrupted. Really, you're much too good to accept films like that after the marvelous things you've done with Franco and Losey. . . . No wonder you broke your contract."

This last refers to my using a technicality to disentangle myself from further bondage—to Paramount. Once freed, I have remained so ever since.

But there were benefits, too. I made other technical improvements. Having forgotten that the eyes had it, I discovered I was still doing too much, and was trying to justify perfectly valid silences with active "acting." There was another positive outcome. Hal Prince told me later that he cast me in his first film, *Something for Everyone,* on the strength of a look I gave as, tieless and disgraced, I was led away to prison.

Life in London was fun and so was living together. I introduced Pat to my parents. We became regulars at Mara and Lorenzo's romantic little trattoria in Beauchamp Place. Sitting under the big tree in its tiny garden, it was hard to imagine then that San Lorenzo would spread over the years into a cherished London institution. Our social life was as active as film schedules allowed. This was not inconsiderable as, in that civilized era, filming stopped around five in the afternoon, allowing for a modicum of evening entertainment before the dawn summons back to work. Catching up with theater, there were special happy reunions with my former colleagues from the Waterloo Road.

There were also, thankfully, scripts to be read. I now had the satisfying intimation that I was getting the first offers and not just others' refusals. My Anglo-Saxon sensibilities were instantly aroused by one called *Alfred the Great* in which I was asked to play the Viking King Guthrum. As it required further work and revision I made a noncommittal commitment, a shrewd device that I have now finessed to a highly sophisticated degree.

The most exciting submission was the outline of a film called *The Guru* to be made in India by the team of James Ivory and Ismail Merchant. Their earlier film, *Shakespeare Wallah,* like *The Guru* about the inevitable clash between two disparate cultures, had seemed to me almost Chekhovian in its quiet observation and gentle, sad humor and its sense of inevitable, irreversible change as India found her new postcolonial identity. On the strength of this synopsis, their reputation and my gut feeling I agreed to do the film. Pat and I were thrilled, too, with the prospect of going to India, one of the few remaining places she had not visited. Curiously, in doing so we would be fulfilling the childhood prophecy of an old Gypsy fortune teller who, reading her palm, had marveled: "This is the most traveling hand I have ever seen, and anyone who comes into contact with you will travel too!" This seemed to include Rick, whom we invited to join us in India during his school holidays.

I was to play a pop singer called Tom Pickle, who, tired of the West's relentless materialism, goes east to learn spiritual values—and how to play the sitar—from a guru. It cleverly mirrored contemporary events in the pop world, particularly those associated with the Fab Four from Liverpool who had just started their much-publicized discipleship with the Maharishi. Assembling an appropriate wardrobe was no problem, London being the undisputed pop capital of the world. An empire of boutiques now centered on Chelsea's sedate King's Road, displacing the general stores and greengrocers and such long-term tenants as Thomas Crapper, whose plumbing genius had so fertilized our language. Even staid Simpson's in the West End now had a "Trend" department, which furnished my white cotton and red brocade suits, innumerable scarves and the pop artist's sine qua non, sunglasses.

Only my hair looked wrong: the policeman's cut was still too short. Ironically, while I was trying to grow mine, Pat's long blonde hair had been bobbed into the newly fashionable Peter Pan length. I considered boosting mine with a wig à la *Smashing Time,* which prompted the following letter from James Ivory in India, reflecting the contemporary obsession with hair:

> To wig—or not to wig? I got a telegram from Fox saying you're arriving with a wig. Before that I got another (the style was a bit

excited) saying you wanted a wig, but that wasn't in the budget, etc. I wrote to say you told me you didn't want a wig, that you'd have your own hair trimmed and shaped. So then I had visions of you coming to India with a shaved head, on orders of your last producer who was insisting on some last minute shot or something. Which worried me.

Ismail had appended to this, in equally characteristic ebullient style: "Have you received my card from Paradise? If not, we are waiting to receive you here. . . ." Little did we know that this garden of Eden we were about to enter would pose, as it had for its first innocent adventurous visitors, pleasures and dangers in equal measure.

I n d i a

C H A P T E R   T H I R T E E N

O ur flight prefigured the problems that lay ahead in India. In the first place, "flight" was a misnomer: we spent more time grounded in airport lounges than actually airborne. The two days it took to get there seemed to elongate the distance actually traveled. Stopping in freezing Frankfurt, we waited vainly for the promised Air India plane to arrive; lodged that first unscheduled night in frozen Wiesbaden, I had a hot taste of Pat's gloriously uninhibited temper. We had requested a double room.

"Not pozzible," the officious receptionist replied. "Your pazzports have not the same name."

"That's none of your business," we countered. "We happen to be traveling together."

Again our request was curtly refused in those cold *Ausweis, bitte* terms of countless screen Gestapo interrogators. By my side, a small blonde volcano then proceeded to erupt, spewing indignation over the man, who was told, in no uncertain terms, that we never stayed in anything less than the Presidential Suite, and that he must provide such accommodation *immediately!*

My grandparents Amos and Mabel.

Young brave, Yarnton.

Major Johnson and family.

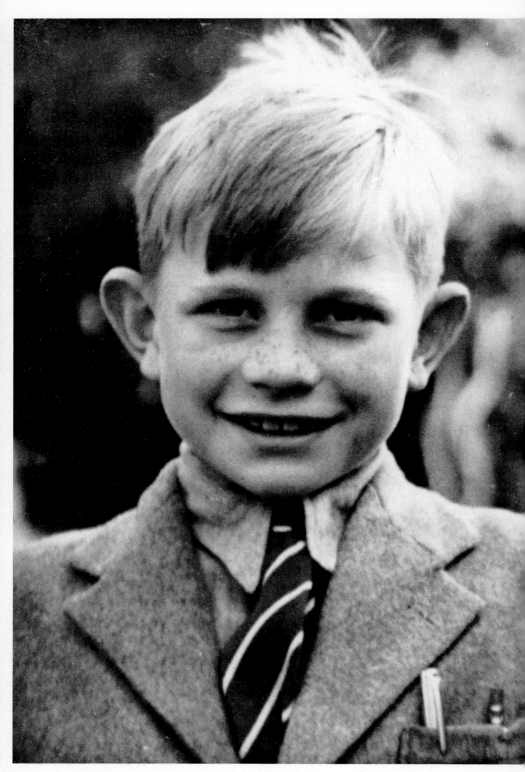

Daybug, Hurstpierpoint College, c. 1951.

"Watch!"

Gypsy and pirate, Burgess Hill.

Penny, Caroline, Michael.

At left, as Bassanio in *The Merchant of Venice,* Bromley Grammar School.

Romanoff in
Romanoff and Juliet.

Youth Theatre with Michael Croft *(at right),* myself next to him. *(Douglas Glass)*

Punting on the Cam with Lesley and actor Andrew Crawford.

Braham Murray *(far left, second row)*, Michael Emrys-Jones *(second from right, fourth row)* and I *(next to him)* as freshmen, University College, Oxford, 1961. *(Gillman & Soame)*

First professional photo, taken in my last year at Oxford. *(Mark Gudgeon)*

With Julia at the University
Commencement Ball.

Adrian Brine. *(Michael York)*

Oxford University Dramatic Society *Twelfth Night*, with
Annabel Leventon. *(Studio Edmark)*

Salad Days, Dundee Repertory Theatre, with Amanda Murray, 1964. *(John Leng & Co. Ltd)*

National Theatre Player—gentleman in Zeffirelli's *Much Ado,* 1965.

Lucentio in *The Taming of the Shrew* with Richard Burton, 1966.

Accident with Dirk Bogarde and Joseph Losey, Oxford, 1966.

With Ed Limato, Rome, 1966.

One of Pat McCallum's smash pix.

Pat McCallum by Michael York.

As Tybalt in *Romeo and Juliet,* 1967.

The duel with Leonard Whiting as Romeo. *(Pat York)*

Playing a pajama game with Rita Tushingham, India, 1967. *(Pat York)*

Tom Pickle in India, 1967. *(Pat York)*

Guthrum the Dane, summer of 1968. *(Pat York)*

"Oh, yes, that is pozzible," the man pleaded, squirming pleasurably under this tongue-lashing and producing keys—to *two* suites.

Installed in one of them, we heard a knock and, bowing and scraping, the victim of Pat's wrath obsequiously sidled in bearing a bedside gift of caviar and champagne. Mumbling denigrations of the rules that had obliged him to behave zo incorrectly, he craved acceptance of his abject apologies. It was a lesson that, alas, I have seen frequently repeated. Squeaking hinges tend to get oiled, especially in my profession, where decent, undemanding professionalism is misinterpreted as weakness. I admired Pat's spirit and that volatile Irish temper that some Cork ancestor had stamped into her genes. It was not the last time that I would see her stand up to institutionalized bullying, displaying that frank directness that was the badge of her borrowed Americanism.

Our plane finally catching up with us, we journeyed on. And on. It was my first long-distance flight and everything fascinated, including the little old lady in front who sat serenely all the way, limbs tucked under, in the lotus position. Yet another night rushed to meet our 707 out of the Arabian desert that flickered below with the lights of a thousand flaring oil wells.

We landed in Bombay and the plane door opened to allow an inrushing assault on the senses—smells of spice and cooking-fires, of dung and tuberoses. Our London clothes seemed suddenly burdensome in the sweltering heat. Jim and Ismail were there to welcome us with a little ceremony, garlanding our travel-weary shoulders with musky flowers while our foreheads were encrimsoned with the *kumkum,* the auspicious third eye. People were everywhere, dark eyes wide with patient curiosity, lips bright red with betel-nut juice. A beggar girl thrust a withered stump through the window of our car as we drove off to our hotel with its improbable name, the Sun 'n Sand. Overwhelmed with first impressions and fatigue, we fell gratefully into an exhausted sleep.

Another setting sun flashing gaudily off the Arabian Sea awoke us late the next afternoon. The hotel lived up to its name. Outside, palm trees nodded and swayed in the breeze along a fine beach. I got down to work immediately, meeting up with the scriptwriter, Ruth Jhabvala, a small, dark, saried lady of European extraction but who sounded and looked entirely Indian. Together we ran through the lines, she in her slightly singsong accent, me in my broadest cockney, and tried to give an authentic timbre to the pop singer who was about to take over our lives.

Life here, I soon discovered, was imitating art with a vengeance. Luminaries such as Mia Farrow were flying in daily in search of enlightenment, delighting us that our story was becoming so fortuitously topical. Utpal Dutt, a darkly handsome Bengali actor who had played the super-civilized Maharajah in *Shakespeare Wallah,* was our guru. But first a real guru, Ustad Vilayat Khan, a man whose boundless good humor matched his musical accomplishment, had to teach us to play the sitar convincingly. The only really hard part was the callused groove that had to be formed on the finger to allow it to run painlessly up and down the key string. I became quite proficient, even sitting down one day in a Bombay studio to improvise a tune with George Harrison, the Beatle who seemed most affected by the Indian experience.

Elsewhere, things were wildly discordant. The day before shooting was due to start, Utpal was arrested. Allegedly a communist sympathizer, he had inflamed the authorities with some Bengali agitprop theater. The emergency situation prompted by the recent flare-up with Pakistan was still in operation, breeding a nervy police-state atmosphere. Bundled off by plane to Calcutta, Utpal was released only after Ismail had personally sat on Mrs. Gandhi's front steps and requested her intervention, persuading her of the unflattering publicity that would ensue in the world press if he was denied. Ismail, I was to learn, had a way. And in this case, as in so many others, he got it, too. Plumply handsome and given to giggling laughter that could turn in a twinkling of a flashing eye into furious anger, he was a whirling Nataraj of energy.

He delighted in showing us his native city. We mingled with the crowd in the marbled cool beneath the Gate of India that, like a giant stone parasol, sheltered postcard hawkers and currency black marketeers and people awaiting the ferry across the harbor to the Elephanta Caves and their wondrous carvings. He fed us huge sticky sweets from an open market stall and I recall thinking that our days of robust health were numbered. He showed us the red-light district where cages of teenage prostitutes waited patiently for the religious fast to end so trade could return to normal. Paper kites darted through the endlessly azure sky, while birds of prey wheeled over the towered Parsee dead. We were overwhelmed with the sheer strange prodigality of it all.

Rita Tushingham was again my co-star, playing another young girl lured from home into an exotic environment. This time she was Jenny, a hippie drawn both to India and its simple spirituality, and to her complex, worldly guru. And yet again, of course, to me. But there was little of the Kamasutra in our relationship. *The Guru* was as chaste as the kind of Hindi romantic film lampooned in *Shakespeare Wallah,* whose luminous star, the enchanting Madhur Jaffrey, was now playing our guru's spoilt, jealous wife. The film lacked the blatant sexuality of the voluptuous nude on the gold cigarette case that Pat gave me for Christmas, no doubt cherished and fondled by some past maharajah. My present to her was an antique emerald necklace that lit up and complemented her glorious green eyes.

Christmas Day was spent with the Kendalls, that charming family of traveling players who had inspired *Shakespeare Wallah.* Another of its stars, the magnetically handsome Shashi Kapoor, who came from an equally distinguished acting dynasty, was now married to Jennifer, one of the talented Kendall daughters. We dined off traditional turkey and mince pies and other wintry Dickensian staples. Outside, gaudy Christmas paper stars illuminated even the meanest shack. That night we had gone to midnight Mass at a jam-packed sports stadium, but the good news had been drowned out by a joyful cacophony of firecrackers and motor horns and our drunken driver who, inflamed with a different spirit, had deposited us in a ditch.

Filming began with another little ceremony where the camera was garlanded and a coconut was cracked and solemnly shared. As it turned out, we were going to need every bit of help that the propitious deities could provide. We filmed all over Bombay—in planes and cars, in shrines and streets. This could be hazardous. The mere glimpse of a camera was sufficient to attract a seething crowd of curious faces. In a country that made national idols of their film stars, there was no difficulty in gathering a mob of fans to scream after Tom Pickle. These dizzying moments gave an imitation of the madness that George Harrison was trying to escape from here.

The upright *pukka sahibs* who founded the Raj would have been shocked at our display of contemporary decadence. Bombay was their mausoleum, their ghosts still haunting the shabby portals of the Yacht Club, ever a bastion of reaction. Queen Victoria continued to perch disapprovingly over her gothic temple of a railway station. There was still a *Times* newspaper, school uniforms and, of course, cricket, while the faded glory flickered alive again in "I say, old chap, first class," and other snatches of imperial parlance.

But the irresistible change that Jim and Ismail had memorialized in their earlier films was everywhere evident. Temples stood cheek by jowl with cinemas, skyscrapers were emerging from their flimsy bamboo cocoons while, at their feet, huddled crowded huts and squalid tenements. Savile Row suits and ties marched alongside saris and dazzling white dhotis. Fume-belching buses plied between ancient horse-drawn tongas while flower-decked funerals jostled through the jammed streets to sounds of bagpipes and fireworks.

I once saw a perfect illustration of our film's theme: a sacred cow left to wander the lively streets at will had collided head-on with a car. Two cultures in conflict—one spiritual, drawn from the immemorial pastoral past; the other driven by a fast-paced materialism that would soon cover the city with concrete hotels, supermarkets and crudely vivid cinema hoardings. In the late sixties, the balance between the two was more equipoised. Western consumerism was less evident. There were fewer luxuries to buy. It was even hard to find razor blades. The Indian makeup artist shocked our pampered sensibilities by working with his hands and was replaced by a London counterpart employing conventional sponges and brushes. Duty-free liquor was in great demand, as Bombay was a "dry" state. If you wanted a drink you had, quaintly, to register as an alcoholic.

Much of the filming took place in a lovely cool house by the seashore where a timeless Indian scene unfolded. Lines of fishing boats were revealed by the soupy dawns and later a dazzle of colored laundry would be beaten on the black rocks and laid out to recover in the bright sun. Women masked against the involuntary inhalation of innocent insects patiently removed stranded aquatic life from the tidepools and returned it to the ocean.

It was fun to be with Rita again. Her huge mascara'd eyes crammed into a pixie face, she had a comedian's gift for inspired improvisation and was endlessly entertaining, both on camera and in the long pauses in between. Our lighting cameraman was Subrata Mitra. Renoir's assistant on *The River,* he had also provided its sitar music score and had photographed all of Satyajit Ray's films. He also operated the camera, sitting cross-legged behind it like a benign Buddha. Not a little of a guru himself, he was a perfectionist and took his time. Unfortunately, time in India has a different value to its Western counterpart. It knows little of urgency. Why destroy one's inborn equilibrium by fighting against the odds in this life when there is always another in which Fate can deal a more auspicious hand?

In the film process, however, time was a measure of money, even if, as in this case, the cash came in the form of Fox's "frozen" rupees. As those pauses between takes became longer and more numerous, the laughs became fewer. Subrata and Rita started to feud. Becoming their unwilling go-between, I translated information to both incommunicado parties. Twice Pat and I had to stop Rita from going home. If this was spiritual enlightenment and wisdom, we seemed to have come to the wrong place!

Through all this Jim remained politely aloof. If Ismail was the extrovert hit man, then Jim was his shy, undemonstrative other half. Invariably with a wry secret smile playing on his lips, he looked in his checked shirts and chinos like a superannuated college graduate. He also had a way, but an understated one, achieved with a blend of sharp intelligence and good humor. He could be exasperating, too. I once played a complicated close-up scene and afterward, asking for his reaction, discovered his attention had been riveted by the flock of crows that had unexpectedly animated the background action! Of undoubted if unconventional talent, Jim would continue with Ismail and Ruth on their uncompromising way to commercial and artistic triumph with such films as *A Room with a View,* another telling portrait of the English abroad.

Meanwhile our hotel provided a refuge from the rigors of filming and the conflict of personalities, especially after long night shoots when, rising at orange dusk and retiring at roseate dawn, we returned gratefully to the pampered life of poolside afternoon tea. In many ways the Sun 'n Sand reflected the dichotomous sophistication and simplicity of the city. Parties were frequent and from our balcony fat munching ladies could be observed swooping on lavish displays of food like so many jeweled harpies. It was all a far cry from the distressing images of the Oxfam posters.

Indeed, in order to cope, one had to adopt a little of the Indian's own fatalism. I pitied those Western tourists who judged the country by their first horrified impressions—of whole families dwelling in concrete pipes by the roadside, of the legless beggar who hopped out of the darkness froglike on his torso, of the omnipresent pleading palms. The constant iteration of our enthusiasm later persuaded Hal Prince and his wife, Judy, to go and discover our India. They lasted one horrified night. After the initial shock, it took time for one's surprised eyes to adjust to the overwhelming beauty. It was impossible, though, to become totally inured to the patent inequalities of society and the concomitant dirt and ignorance. Officially banned, the caste system lingered on, seemingly as ineradicable as the British class system.

Sometimes I envied the real hippies recruited as extras in our film. With their beads and bedrolls, theirs was an experience that we in our first-class luxury hotel could never know. But Pat and I also appreciated the simpler pleasures of sun 'n sand. Juhu Beach had its own bazaarlike bustle of life. Of course there were beggars here, too. I even heard rumors of a beggars' supermarket and had strange visions of bowls and rags laid out in ordered rows. There were seashell sellers, snake charmers and even an old fakir who earned an honest rupee by burying himself in the sand. Beachcombing dogs chased crabs while ravens cawed at the waves like indignant Canutes. On Sundays promenading families filled out this idyllic scene, sampling the pyramids of food piled up enticingly on stalls that were lit at night with soft naphtha flares.

Once we were accidentally locked in our top-floor room. A bearer was sent up with a key but, without us being aware, climbed an outside drainpipe. His grinning face rising, Kilroy-like, into view collapsed us both into paralyzing laughter. The more we chuckled, the more he wagged his head from side to side like a genial metronome, and the more he grinned, the longer the comic stand-off lasted.

Our happiness was as unclouded as the weather. We were in love. In fact, I proposed to Pat on the moonlit beach on St. Valentine's Day, giving her a heart-shaped filigree box as a memento of my feelings. These centered around a growing conviction that a relationship came to a crucial point where either it was consolidated or terminated. I now knew unquestionably that I wanted to share my life with this extraordinary woman. To my intense joy my proposal was accepted and we immediately made plans to get married while still in India. Weddings here were especially celebratory, the festivities often extending over several days—a perfect expression of our mutual happiness.

Within days of this momentous decision we set off for location filming in Rajasthan. Flying north to Jaipur, we explored the famed pink city, riding up to the spectacular Amber Palace on elephant back, followed by a musician playing an insistent little tune. Contained within battlemented walls, its courtyards and shaded gardens seemed to compete in beauty with the hills and polished lakes of its setting. Inside, great gobs of jeweled light glinted in filigree windows and flashed from a myriad faceted mirrors—the temporal frozen into the eternal.

We were delighted to have Utpal as a guide in the long desert drive to the remote fortress town of Bikaner, set at the edge of the immense Thar wilderness separating India from Pakistan. Lodged at the Maharajah of Bikaner's Lallgarh Palace, we found our rooms were cheerfully enlivened by his Highness's surprisingly modern paintings and by the constant attendance of a diminutive servant in a khaki uniform set off by a brilliant orange turban almost half his size. After showing us the palace, Major Singh, the Maharajah's impeccably courteous manager, lent us bicycles to ride into town.

There was something strange and austere about the dusty landscape with its camels, thornbushes and flat, ochre buildings, making the brightly turbaned men and their bejeweled women seem excessively exotic. Even the palace had a foreboding fairy-tale quality. Peacocks screeched in the trees. Photographs of slaughtered game were everywhere, and the billiard room was hung with grotesque trophies of animals that were all in some way deformed.

At dinner that night the company was joined by the actress playing a courtesan who is horribly murdered in a flashback sequence. She introduced an immediate shrill, discordant note to the gathering. Up to then the production had had its problems but these had been largely resolved and working relationships had evolved. Now people were at each other's throats across the dinner table and, for the first time, real anger flared. It was as if she had tapped a wellspring of frustration, loosening the constraints of good humor and professionalism that bound the company into a functioning unit. She was like an evil fairy. At her arrival clouds gathered, an ominous and unusual event in the middle of the desert winter. It hadn't rained for six years.

After the meal of stomach-knotting tension and strained embarrassment, Pat and I retired gratefully to bed. A few hours later Pat woke me complaining of tummy pains. I naturally thought this a response to the recent tortured atmosphere or at least a reaction to the food. We had eaten fish, which, so far inland, had seemed strange. I was not unduly concerned, as "Delhi Belly" and other mild infections were common in this strong climate. A little later, however, the spasms turned into agonizing cramps and Pat's limbs started to constrict and become paralyzed. With growing alarm I woke Major Singh. A doctor was called for and arrived trailed by an anxious Jim and Ismail.

The next morning the schedule was hurriedly rearranged to allow me to be with Pat who was now seriously ill and getting worse. The clouds, in sympathy, had melded into a leaden sky and a thin miserable rain was falling. I stayed by her bedside anxiously watching her drift in and out of consciousness. At one point I momentarily left her sleeping and returned to an incredible sight. Two giant breasts were swinging back and forth in a "native" shirt above Pat's bed. They belonged to an American woman, also staying at the palace, who was massaging Pat's stomach while coaxing her to eat a Hershey bar. For an instant I watched mesmerized, appalled, then brusquely thanked her for her concern. I learned afterward that massage was the worst thing possible as Pat's intestines had apparently become blocked and were turning gangrenous.

I was also informed that an urgent operation was required. My shocked response was a request that Pat be removed from this obscure backwater to an established medical center. Some Indians have an endearing, infuriating habit of telling you what they think you might want to hear, rather than what is necessarily the case. Now there was no embroidery of the truth. A plane was out of the question, I was unequivocally told, as there was no airstrip. The train journey to the capital took thirteen hours along a line still periodically molested by marauding bandits.

"She cannot travel in any way," was the firm, quiet statement putting an end to further panicky speculation. "It will kill her. The infection is only being kept in check by the weakness of her pulse. We must operate right here. And right now."

I then recalled that we had recently filmed in the house of a Bombay doctor who knew how to cast horoscopes. "I see hospitals," he said reading mine, "sickness and many doctors." Assuming he was referring to my many medical relatives, I complimented him on his skill, little knowing how truly prophetic his prediction was and how imminent its realization.

At this fateful moment two separate strands of good fortune intertwined to produce what only can be called a miracle. That very day a surgeon who had trained in New York happened to be in Bikaner lecturing to the medical students. Someone was rushed to find him, discovering him at the railway station on the point of returning to Delhi. The other piece of luck was that the Maharajah—or Mr. Singh to give him the title to which he had recently been demoted—had just endowed the hospital with operating facilities.

The surgeon, however, was not sanguine about Pat's prospects. At the most optimistic her chances of surviving an operation were a mere five percent. Moreover, it seemed as if his intervention would be unnecessary. "It's so strange, I am dying," Pat whispered to me, and the doctor's grave expression was no contradiction. Most significant and strange of all, those lines on her palms that had augured a future of unlimited horizons had now practically disappeared, as if the slate had been wiped clean.

Pat's blood pressure was also almost nonexistent. Losing an alarming amount of weight through rapid dehydration, she became too weak even to be moved to hospital. She was at times delirious, the tiny turbaned servant turning into a terrifying creature of ill-omen that had to be banished from the room. Luckily, methadrine was available and managed to stabilize the condition. It had the odd side effect of making her suddenly euphoric and to my astonishment—and unbounded relief—Pat started animatedly making lists of all the presents she planned to buy for the people who were helping her.

I telephoned Pat's sister Bobby in London and cabled Rick at school in Switzerland to inform them of these developments. Bobby called back and—a third miracle—got through on an old handset fitted into the ancient wall of the fort. Shouting the sad news, I tried to reassure her—and myself—as best I could.

Pat could now be hospitalized and I accompanied her in the ambulance as it bumped over the now muddy roads, its floor covered in old feces, presenting a most uninspiring sight. Utpal's blood had been found compatible with Pat's fairly rare type and he selflessly donated a supply to the surgeons. I was asked to sign a paper permitting the operation, and another making me responsible for her life. Coming within days of our vows to commit our lives to each other, it seemed perfectly right to assume this authority. Gently kissing Pat goodbye, I slipped my hand out of hers.

"She is in God's hands now," the doctor said, with a fatalism and certainty that both impressed and relieved. Pat told me later that the last thing she saw before losing consciousness was a shaft of sunlight that suddenly pierced the gloom.

Walking around the hospital grounds daring not to think the worst, I was waylaid by our courtesan actress who tried to comfort me in her own style. Flirtatiously, she invited me to her room and, on being refused, attempted to feed me great gobs of charred goat meat from a barbecue. I found Ismail and we waited for news outside the operating theater. Eventually a doctor appeared with a large bowl in which was a section of Pat's intestine. The spreading gangrene was pointed out and, unlike the rotten ghoulish greenness I had expected, it seemed but a faint discoloration of the healthy tissue. It provoked in Ismail, however, another faint discoloration and no doubt I shared his anxious pallor.

Then the doors banged open and there was the rest of Pat, albeit supine and bandaged and prodded with tubes and plastic bags. I expected her to be immediately installed in an adjacent recovery room, but instead, our little procession trundled down the main corridor lined with people who squatted, coughing and spitting, with the same abject resignation shared by waiting hospital patients anywhere. Barging through some swing doors and out into the open, we crossed a courtyard and came to rest in a little outlying room euphemistically called the "cottage ward." It was almost bare. It was explained that the Indian system required the close cooperation of the patient's family, with relatives often moving in to cook and clean. There was a cot for me to sleep on and I arranged for linen and food to be sent from the palace. I soon realized how potentially positive this family proximity could be. Providing a direct continuity of care and affection, it lessened the trauma of recuperating in an alien environment.

But all I cared about then was the outcome of the operation, to see if Pat's intestine would function after a six-foot length of it had been removed. I watched her as she lay on the monogrammed linen sheets, frail, exhausted and heartbreakingly thin from the struggle to survive. I wondered what kind of future lay ahead. Would there indeed be one? I recalled those British gravestones I had seen in Indian cemeteries that recorded the appalling loss of young life to this harsh, demanding country.

At last there was positive proof that the repaired organ was functioning. Relief overwhelmed anxiety, filling me with a euphoria that no methedrine-induced high could match. I bought a Rajasthani flower ring and slipped it on Pat's thin finger. A few days later, when it was confirmed that she was out of immediate danger, I went back to work. Again Art imitated Life. We were filming the scene where Rita had fallen ill in the palace and was being attended by a local doctor. For me it required no acting. It went beyond the Method—for the experience was not so much recalled as instantly replayed. In retrospect I find those scenes in the film curiously moving. There is a quiet simplicity about my performance and an exhausted verisimilitude.

Ustad Vilayat Khan came to Bikaner to organize the concert scene in which Utpal and I exploited our newfound skills with the sitar. All night long the desert air resounded with our artistry, but the music to my soul was the daily improvement in Pat's condition. Although

gaunt and emaciated, she was regaining the vivacity that had first
enchanted me. There was even talk of plans for the future.

Telegrams and letters arrived from home full of concern for Pat and
congratulations on our proposed marriage. My mother also told me of
another illness—my father's. A dangerously high blood pressure had
caused him to collapse and lose his memory for twenty-four hours. It
had almost been a stroke and he was now determined to take the
weight off mind and body. My grandfather later reported on Joe's
improvement and his own well-being. Contrary to the pessimistic
prognostications, he was managing splendidly on his own and had
even discovered such unexpected skills as cake-baking.

The filming in Bikaner was eventually finished and we moved on,
appropriately, to a place where life—or the lack of it—was of extreme
significance. The holy city of Benares on the Ganges is where Hindus
aspire to depart this life, leaving their remains to be cremated on the
wide river's banks. As Pat was in no conceivable shape to come with
me, I had requested the British Embassy to send out a competent
nurse to look after her, arranging also for Pat to stay in Delhi as soon
as she was strong enough to travel. For the first time in months we
reluctantly parted.

The long, dirty railway journey to Benares was used to film a scene
in a confined carriage, bodies and lights adding extra heat to the
already torrid atmosphere, and provoking a mass exodus at every stop
for little earthenware cups of tea. Benares is probably the most remarkable location I have ever filmed in. The city feels irredeemably
ancient. Our main set was a house by the Ganges past which a daily
tide of mortality ebbed and flowed. There were dead bodies everywhere—borne along on the backs of bicycles and in funeral proces-
sions and being cremated on the burning ghats where their ashes
mingled with the water in which countless pilgrims joyfully bathed. It
was a beautiful, barbarous sight. Telephoning Pat and corresponding
daily, I was overjoyed to learn of her progress: she had even started
to take photographs again.

One day, filming on the broad ochre river itself, I was singing an
odd little song Tom Pickle had composed that perfectly expressed the
quiescent values India had impressed on both him and me:

> The temple bells over the water
> The cows and the holy men
> The sound of the sitar

> *The smell of incense*
> *Jasmine*
> *The dust and the flies*
> *I don't know why it is so*
> *But I feel*
> *It's strange but*
> *I feel*
> *Let me stay*
> *Let me learn*
> *Let me listen*
> *Meditate.*

A boat approached, remarkable for having at its prow a carved figure of a woman. Suddenly the wooden statue waved and in a heart-stopping instant I realized it was Pat. We embraced in the sacred city by the holy river that, in a change of tide, brought life, health and happiness flooding in.

Back at Clark's Hotel Pat recounted her adventures. She had departed Bikaner in fragile state but in great style, her doctors and nurses and most of the town having turned out with garlands and music to wish farewell to their miraculous memsahib. The train compartment had been transformed with flowers, linens and even a marble commode. At dawn she had woken up black with soot to the sight of rural India squatting in the endless fields and, as if in salutation to her operation, moving a communal bowel.

At Delhi, a Rolls-Royce had whisked her from all this to the cool refuge of the British Embassy. She had even ventured down to dinner, meeting a fellow guest, the English comedian Tony Hancock, who was on his way to Australia and to eventual suicide there. His unhappiness had struck her forcibly as did afterward the irony of this encounter between one man in despair of life and a woman desperate to cling on to it. Anxious to be with me and, disobeying my orders and those of her doctors and diplomat hosts, she had left a note of thanks and flown the coop. Fortunately, she had met a fellow photographer, the famed Rhaghubir Singh, who had also worked on our film. Barely disguising his shock at her changed appearance, he had aided and abetted her flight.

The whole company rejoiced at her return, though the effort took its toll and for several days Pat was confined to bed. Ustad Vilayat Khan came and, sitting at its foot, serenaded her on his sitar. Soon she

was well enough to venture downstairs. We even took a tonga to
Ruth Jhabvala's hotel for another script meeting but the bumpy ride
was uncomfortable, making me resentful of Ruth, who had been unwilling to come to me. It amazed me that a person could be so insightful on the page and so shortsighted in reality, especially as Ruth's
husband had also alarmed Pat by telling her she would never fully
recover from her illness. But even when Ismail exploded into our room
on Holi Day, gleefully showering us with colored powders and water,
it was impossible to feel too exasperated. We now had too much to
genuinely celebrate.

There was a problem, though. Our visas were about to expire and
we physically had to leave the country before they could be renewed.
Originally a trip to Nepal had been planned for this purpose but I now
decided to take Pat home to England and return alone for the balance
of the filming. We gave a farewell lunch for the whole company—
from producer to humble sweeper—and everyone came to see us off
at the airport.

Again, our plane was late in arriving. We waited. No one moved.
Everyone stayed to chat and reminisce about the events of the past
extraordinary weeks. As the long emotional day turned slowly into
night, Pat began to weaken under the stressful obligation of being
socially gracious for so long. By the time the plane eventually landed
she was almost totally exhausted.

At Delhi Airport we resumed our wait in the limbo of the departure
lounge, having officially checked out of the country. Pat was now
palpably ill. What to do? Should we abandon all plans of flying on to
London and seek refuge in a hotel or hospital? This seemed the obvious solution except it was the eleventh hour now both literally and
figuratively: our visas were due to expire at midnight. The example of
the film's Italian accountant was fresh in my mind. Suffering a heart
attack, this unfortunate man had neglected to attend to his papers
while in hospital. Happily he had survived but his visa had expired,
causing the whole weight of Indian bureaucracy to topple down on
his head. He was still having problems in fully extricating himself
from the bonds of red tape.

The risk of this now happening to Pat was unthinkable. I made her
as comfortable as I could in the stifling waiting room and called, yet
again, on the services of a doctor. Fortunately sympathetic to our
plight, he injected Pat with a shot to revive her, but refused to allow
her to take another faltering step.

Like birth and death, flights in India usually arrive and leave in the dead, vast middle of the night. For the third agonizing time, our plane was delayed, eventually arriving at three in the morning. I carried Pat to its door and explained to the BOAC crew the mitigating circumstances that hopefully would allow them to take this seriously ill person from my arms into theirs. To my intense relief they accepted us both. I continued to hold her as the jet screamed into the night.

The crew was most solicitous. So, too, were the other passengers, including Donovan, whose own experiences in India mirrored my fictional ones. The captain radioed ahead for medical assistance at the next stop, Tehran. We stayed on board while a doctor, wrapped in an overcoat against the dawn chill, examined his patient amidst the curious gaze of the cleaners. After another injection he pronounced Pat fit enough to endure another segment of the flight. At Tel Aviv and Athens the same procedure was repeated, so that by fits and starts we made it home.

At Heathrow a horribly officious nurse came aboard and tried to bully Pat into leaving in an ambulance along with her other charge, a dead body. The volcano, long dormant, erupted again. "You are the first rude and unfeeling person I have encountered in months," remonstrated Pat, with that flash of spirit that had fired her fight to live and that mercifully, thankfully and joyfully would guarantee her return to complete health.

Married Life

CHAPTER FOURTEEN

No sooner were our bags in the door than we called another doctor. Examining Pat, he pronounced that to function adequately, she would have to take massive doses of codeine for the rest of her life. He also confirmed that the incident had not been caused by the conditions in India, but by the pills prescribed by a Harley Street colleague to prevent her getting sick there. Unfortunately, they had contained sulphur to which Pat was violently allergic, and the resultant stress had targeted the intestine.

Our second priority was to get married without any additional delay and I approached a gentleman at the Kensington Registry Office to this end. Fixing me with a concerned stare, he said he had a word of caution to impart. "It's my duty to tell you this." My heart sank and a tide of worst-case scenarios flooded my imagination. Did the British marriage laws exclude American divorcees? Did the National Health object to unwell aliens? "You do realize don't you . . ." he continued worriedly. There was another pause. I waited for the hammer blow to shatter my hopes. ". . . this will cost you three pounds, nineteen shillings and sixpence." I could have kissed him!

He agreed to squeeze us into the usual spring pre–income tax nuptial rush. Pat bought a golden Dior outfit with a fashionable skirt length that, on reviewing today, strays just this side of decency. My purchase was a chalk-stripe gray suit and a purple Turnbull and Asser shirt with matching tie to enliven the ensemble as the occasion and current sartorial trends demanded. I also ordered another new name. A few days before it was to be inscribed in the register and assumed by Pat, I changed my legal name to Michael York-Johnson, dropping forever poor romantic but effete Hugh and formally acknowledging the ascendancy of my self-appointed stage name. It even had first billing.

I was outnumbered temporarily by McCallums, though, when my about-to-be stepson came to stay. His arrival was preceded by a letter that I still treasure:

Dear Michael,
It's so hard to tell you what I really feel, partly because I hardly know you at all . . .
    First of all I want to thank you for everything you did for Pat. She informed me of the decisions you had to make etc. For that, Michael, I will always be grateful. Pat means so much to me. I couldn't begin to tell you all the things she has done for me. Honestly I consider her my best friend. I can tell her what's on my mind, how I feel, which is sadly not the case with most people my age. She has always appeared to me dynamically humorous and of course sophisticated, but fundamentally serious. You know as well as I she's extraordinary and marvelous and to say the least, I have never seen her so happy as she is with you. I know if I understand the word love at all, I can safely say she has discovered it with you, more than anyone else. But I'm sure you know all this.
    I have tried to assimilate what you might be thinking about me. It's hard classifying people. Sometimes, I must warn you, I can be unsentimental, almost incapable of affection, even hopelessly selfish. Sometimes I doubt whether I have a definite abstract goodness. I try not to show all this though. I can't tell you much else about me. I'm not sure I know myself. What I'm trying to say is, that although our relationship can never be a father-son one, which seems completely ludicrous to me anyway, I'm sure we will get on fantastically. I only hope that we can be honest with each other and say whatever is on our mind. That, it seems to me, is the most important thing . . .
    As long as both of you are happy, that's all I really care about.

I'm longing to see both of you soon. The truth is: I've always been hoping you would get married since the first day I met you.

Always,
Rick

P.S. Congratulations.

On the morning of my twenty-sixth birthday, with bouquets and flowers in buttonholes, we set off in separate limousines for Kensington. At the Registry Office our families and a few friends were assembled, the women in unfamiliar hats. "You can't get married, you're not French!" my young nephew Paul solemnly informed us. Notwithstanding, the ceremony was brief but most moving. We signed the register and man and wife emerged into sunshine suddenly enhanced by the flashes from a phalanx of press photographers. We had told no one of our plans but the photographic record provided made their unexpected presence most welcome. Tennessee Williams told me later that, seeing the pictures in the American press and mistaking Pat's cropped head half-covered by my embrace, he had marveled at London's swinging liberality that would allow newspaper photographs of two men kissing!

On the way to the reception at the Connaught Hotel our limousine broke down in Hyde Park: a lucky omen, so we were reliably informed. Lord Birkett and his delicious first wife, Junia, had similarly refused our request for a quiet celebration and arranged—to our eternal gratitude—a memorable feast.

Our honeymoon was in Brighton at the Royal Crescent Hotel. Those radiant photographs with their captions about my "miracle bride" must have preceded us for, as we entered the hotel's dining room, its occupants rose to their feet with warm applause. The excitement inevitably took its toll and Mrs. York-Johnson kept to the bridal bed, gathering her returning strength. When not similarly ensconced I revisited familiar boyhood haunts. These solitary walks reminded me of recent lonely perambulations around the hospital as Pat's life hung in the balance. We had both had an insight into the vulnerability of humanity. And we vowed never knowingly to squander or abuse this precious gift.

Returning to India to finish the film, I remained in daily contact with my wife through what were still quaintly called trunk calls. It was now snowing in England, Pat told me, making our gilded wedding day seem even brighter and more fortuitous. Her returning vigor, it seemed, was matched by a growing allergy to sympathy, her intolerance even making her leap from a taxi she was sharing with my mother when May had quite naturally tried to commiserate with her. But when Pat begged me to come home by any other way than by air I sensed her recovery was still incomplete and assumed that, all alone, she was prey to anxiety and her own fragility.

My last moments as Tom Pickle were tense and lengthy, jet lag compounding the exhaustion. Suddenly it was over and, ignoring Pat's renewed pleas, I flew directly home. A week later the same flight crashed. My wonderful intuitive wife was there to greet me at the airport. Already in the act of transforming myself into a bearded Viking, I was unshaven, for, despite continuing reservations about its script, I had finally agreed to do *Alfred the Great*. But first I had another definite commitment—our interrupted honeymoon.

Fulfilling an ever-strengthening ambition to visit America, I took Pat "home" to New York. Those first impressions—driving in the cold spring night through Central Park and glimpsing amidst bare trees millions of lighted windows towering and twinkling above— were unforgettable. We stayed at the Hampshire House hotel in an unfamiliar world of walk-in closets, brunch, ice-water, nonstop television and that ultimate luxury, a telephone in the lavatory. Our duplex suite beetled precipitously over the south side of the oblong park that, walled in by manufactured Manhattan like a preserved amenity, is both the city's exercise yard and its parade ground. It was to become one of my favorite places, along with its neighbor, the Metropolitan Museum, an inexhaustible repository of artistic wealth brilliantly displayed to dazzle and enrapture the senses.

The polished chic of New York was a world away from hippie London and even farther from the dust and flies of the past few months. At the swank Le Pavillon Restaurant I met another pal, the writer Irwin Shaw, who had once dedicated a poem to Pat, entitled, "Where the Fuck Is Fourth." This recorded not only a gear-grinding drive made together but also some of Pat's essential traits: a hair-trigger impatience, a predilection for vivid language when this trigger is pulled, and an enduring inability to drive a nonautomatic vehicle. We were warmly congratulated. Not so flattering was the remark I also heard in this stuffy, conservative place: "He must be famous to be allowed in here," referring, I presumed, to my burgeoning hirsuteness. Outside, a taxi driver's sneers also confirmed just how far Fifth Avenue was at that time from Carnaby Street. American trousers—or rather, pants—were worn at half-mast, as if in mourning for the end of a sartorial era.

But, like it or not, I was "famous." I was stopped for my autograph and made increasingly aware of a curious phenomenon. People would talk to Pat about me as I stood beside her as if I were incapable of an answer or wasn't even there. I was turning into that strange creature, a "celebrity," a commodity ungoverned by normal human impulses. I had, in fact, just been voted a "Top Star of Tomorrow" in an American trade paper. The fact that this august elevation came with a demand for money to advertise my new status was something I would learn to accept about this newfound land where fame and fortune were often interrelated and frequently synonymous.

Urged to capitalize on my current "heat" with publicity, I declined, insisting it was incompatible with a true honeymoon. One famous female Hollywood columnist, latching on to us, contrived to be invited both to the cinema and afterward to dinner, where she refused to diverge from a tedious line of questioning centered principally on what it was like for me to make love to my co-stars on screen. After her preliminary polite warnings had been ignored, Pat quietly rose from the table in mid-meal, announcing to my inquisitor that we were taking her home. And despite her astonished protestations, that is exactly what we did. Pat was no masochist, nor did she suffer fools gladly.

We "did" the town from the top of the Empire State Building downwards, from my first taste of eggs benedict for breakfast to Bobby Short's midnight twinkling over the ivories at the Carlyle Hotel. Our week whirled by. Both of us felt energized, reputedly by the static electricity pulsing from the Manhattan rock, evident in tingling kisses and sparking handshakes. There was a warm reunion with Ed Limato in that showbiz temple, Sardi's. We gorged on theater: *Hello, Dolly* with a black cast and Ralph Hochhuth's controversial *The Soldiers,* which Britain's Lord Chamberlain, soon to abandon forever his duties as censor, had banned. It would be a good riddance. It seemed to me that the play presented Churchill not as a monster but as the savior of a generation—a man who could see through the private sorrow to the public good. We posed and paid for a street photographer to record our happiness, but regrettably never received the result. Anyway, photos fade. Memories don't.

And beards grow. I was astonished that mine, albeit gingery and whiskery, was very evident, making me grateful for the hours saved from the shaving mirror and makeup table. Returning to London, I bought a new MGC sports car to speed us to the west of Ireland, where *Alfred* was to be filmed. In this remote, unchanged spot, where Europe petered out in a mass of lakes and misty mountains, it seemed natural that castles should be available for rent. We leased Creggana Castle near Galway, an ancient turret set amidst green fields and their patchwork of gray stone walls, that had been restored by a French architect with modern comforts. Meals, however, were still spit-roasted over an open peat fire in the huge stone living room and were often more burned than King Alfred's legendary cakes! Nonetheless, we delighted in this first romantic "home."

David Hemmings, playing the English king, had rented the even more impressive Oranmore Castle and flew the banner of Wessex from its sea-girt battlements. Not to be outdone, I raised King Guthrum's Danish standard over mine. One night there was a furious pounding at our massive front door, which opened to reveal a posse of locals with faces and accents out of Synge and O'Casey. " 'T'woudn't be the English flag you're after flying there?" one gnarled countenance demanded querulously. Reassured, they shambled off into the moonlight, reminding me that the bigotry and hostility that had killed Behan's hostage were still very much alive.

And not just in Ireland. In Prague, the "spring" of freedom was being nipped in the bud by a reactionary freeze. Later came the heart-wrenching news of the assassination of Robert Kennedy, someone whom Pat had once photographed and, like most honest Americans, admired inordinately. Their last encounter had been both illuminating and endearing. Pat had been taking portraits of politicians for a *Glamour* article whose theme was that young people were more interested than ever in politics because of the new breed of young, dynamic politicians. After her session with Bobby they had stayed chatting on the steps of the Senate waiting for her car to arrive. Suddenly a little puppy dog ran out into the busy street. Bobby chased after it, holding up the traffic like a policeman to allow it to cross uninjured. "I hear you photographed my brother Teddy last week," Bobby said. "Did you like him?" At Pat's affirmative reply, he added, "But did you like him more than you like me?"

Alfred was filmed out of doors amidst the local bogs and hills and in a studio complex erected in a local field that looked like an Anglo-Saxon theme park with its ancient buildings and modern facilities. It was here that we raped, pillaged and plundered, carrying on exactly as those shocked chroniclers had described to me in the hushed quiet of an Oxford library. In one thrilling sequence we used the River Shannon as the Viking "swan-road" over which their longships came sweeping ashore. Exact replicas of the Gokkstadt ship, they were immensely seaworthy. Indeed, some hardy fool was planning to sail one to America as a publicity stunt—presumably using the Vinland map for guidance! We also employed a contingent of the Irish army as extras so that, in the quaint way of this singular nation, many had their first taste of warfare using spears and battleaxes. Most spent their time lolling on sword and sward, blond wigs outrageously askew, looking for all the world like drag queens on a day trip.

It was a magnificent summer, the best since 1922 according to the locals. So instead of the wild, windblown skies the filmmakers had anticipated, we had an uninterrupted Mediterranean blue. Later I was able to confirm a correlation between Pat's and my presence and the weather. I hardly dare tempt providence by saying so, but fine weather seems to follow us wherever we go. I even became an adept horseman, although my enthusiasm remained as skin-deep as the bruises sustained from being involuntarily catapulted over stone walls in mid-gallop.

Rick came to stay and I loved getting to know my new stepson. He was as powerfully built as his mother was delicately shaped. A natural athlete, he was, in particular, such a phenomenal swimmer that his American school had wanted to train him for the Olympics. But—like the lonely long-distance runner in the film—he had turned his broad back on sporting glory. I like to think that it was my introduction here to the world of filmmaking that set him on the road to a career as a most successful and respected film producer. Another great film aficionado was Grandad, who also made plans, alas unfulfilled, to come and stay. He was now the enthusiastic owner of a television set and I kept him in touch with the film scene, mine in particular, with press cuttings and movie magazines.

Much as I relished our rustic domestic life, I didn't really enjoy the work subtended from it. The director had taken it upon himself to play silly games in lieu of actually directing. As I was the ostensible villain of the piece, he tried both to provoke me into a "villainous" response by being unnecessarily rude, and to engender offstage hostility between David and myself in order to reinforce the on-screen antipathy. I thought wistfully of better times and directors, and especially of Zeffirelli, who exploited and enhanced the actor's own intrinsic qualities without resorting to demeaning tricks. He wrote from Moscow where *Romeo and Juliet* was enjoying the same acclaim it had received elsewhere in the world: "A great experience altogether but not much fun—nothing like camp London or sexy Rome. Nevertheless they adore the film—the way they all sob and cry at the end is quite embarrassing. Many think that Tybalt was played in the Russian manner. Perhaps your Mongolian cheekbones? Miss you and Pat. Hope you can come to Rome." I also had the London reviews to hand and was pleased with one that commented on my "suggesting a hot gallant rather than, like most English players of the role, a retchy neurotic."

The brilliance of *Romeo and Juliet* only served to underline one of the major shortcomings of my current epic—the script. While I was in India, a rewrite had been promised but, in the end, never delivered. I still had to mouth such banalities as, "You give your body to me but not your heart," and even that old chestnut, "How beautiful you are in anger!" Vivien Merchant, who was in the film as a kind of Saxon Maid Marian, had also been promised revisions. When hers were unforthcoming, she insisted on playing her role as a mute—perhaps the least that Mrs. Harold Pinter could do! I was taught a valuable lesson: the flimsy celluloid structure of a film must be based on solid textual bedrock. It was true that often unexpected things happened in the course of filming, sometimes as a direct result of the actor's input, that improved on the written page. But in general skating on thin verbal ice was a highly dangerous practice.

I was unhappy. And even more so now that the film's expanding schedule was threatening my chances of accepting an offer to play Darley in *Justine*, a proposed Twentieth Century-Fox film of Lawrence Durrell's *The Alexandria Quartet*. One thing for which I unashamedly envied Hemmings was his experience of filming in a great Hollywood studio. He would play tape recordings of L.A. radio programs that made life there seem fun, exotic and infinitely desirable.

Despite the director's backstage shenanigans, David and I found that we liked each other. I admired his ferocious energy manifest both on the set and in the intervening hours of "rest." One night he invited us to feast at his castle with friends who included David Bailey, there to photograph Penelope Tree and Cheryl Tiegs, also guests, for a fashion layout. Dared to climb the inside of the keep as a postprandial entertainment, David scrambled nimbly up while Bailey muttered gloomily, "If I had shares in the insurance company covering you, I would withdraw them immediately." These words coincided with David's final push to the top. But he missed his hold. To a chorus of horrified gasps, he plunged to the stone floor, breaking a chair with his face en route. I steeled myself to look at the crushed body of my adversary. Miraculously he seemed to have survived, though his sudden total loss of energy was truly alarming. Gayle Hunnicut, his intended bride, cradled him unconscious in her arms, her elegant gown bearing bloody witness to his wounds. A doctor was summoned who arrived completely "stoshers," to use the local term for the walking inebriate, but managed to patch up the fallen monarch.

The schedule was frantically rearranged to accommodate this turn of events. I held the fort, literally and figuratively, while David the demon King lay low. Eventually he returned, still bruised and battered but fit enough to finish off our few remaining scenes, making the prospect of trading Guthrum's sword for Darley's pen a certainty.

It was then that Pat, like Caesar's wife, started to have nightmares, dreaming that David was seriously ill and in need of urgent help. I was so disturbed by the intensity of her premonitions that I arranged, with David's consent, for Pat's London doctor to fly over and examine him. He discovered something that the X-rays had missed: a dislodged tooth had been pushed up into his sinuses, forming an abscess that was about to burst. "You may be interested to know that, had antibiotics not been administered when they were, I could in fact have died," David later wrote. "So there you are!"

A fellow cheater of death, Pat grew daily more robust. For one joyous moment she thought she was pregnant and Harold Pinter kindly took a specimen back to London for analysis. Now returned to work at the producer's request, her still-fragile frame seemed at times overwhelmed by her heavy cameras. I loved seeing her back on the set, not least because people would tell her all the gossip withheld from me. Indeed she had a remarkable capacity for eliciting confidence, a gift, at times onerous, she never abused. She even ventured to one of her former headquarters, Paris, to buy clothes. But there fate not fashion was the order of the day. At night Pat dined with revolutionaries who spent their days at the barricades. Everyone was on the streets taking part in *les événements* in which the old postwar Gaullist order was trampled under the protesting feet of student power. Youth was the thing. It showed in the clothes Pat bought in the deserted shops—astonishing new Courrèges creations with fantastic structural designs.

Life back in sleepy Ireland was a world away from all this ferment, the "An Tan Tan" war cries of the battling Danes being the only voices raised in anger. Married life in our ivory tower thrived. A local farmer's wife came over to clean and, especially, tidy up. "Ah, that Mrs. York," she would keen, "she hangs her clothes on the floor." After her ministrations, though, we would have to open every window to expel her pungent presence.

The smells and rush of Dublin came as a shock on occasional weekend visits after the tranquil grandeur of the West. There we met another of Pat's Hollywood friends, Rock Hudson, who was filming *Darling Lili*—Ireland seemed the breeding ground of film disasters that year! Tall and jovial, Rock took us on a tour of the Gresham Hotel's kitchen, pressing on us huge joints of meat to take back for our fireside spit.

Another of Pat's valued friends was John Huston, who entertained us in his beautiful house. Renowned for a streak of cruelty, he had always treated Pat impeccably—perhaps because of her own re-nowned intolerance of male chauvinism. Master of the Galway Blazers, with a roguish wit and a nimble tongue, he was more Irish than the Irish and, similarly, deliciously eccentric. I loved the fact that in this western wilderness where nothing grew as well as the local stone, he had imported rocks from Japan for his garden.

By the end of the summer, though, Pat and I confessed to each other a certain exasperation with the native Irish. The blarney that had seemed so enchanting in short holiday doses was now tedious on a daily basis. There seemed no excuse for the backwardness and pov-erty. Even the local salmon, though cheap and plentiful, grew weari-some. That old Aries signal, now with a double intensity, was flashing insistently. Time to move on.

London was a brief interlude. I met with Federico Fellini about ap-pearing in his forthcoming *Satyricon*. Told that I was pledged to *Justine*, he devastated me by saying, "Now I know you can't do the role, I know that no one else could possibly do it." Any preening ambitions, however, were ruthlessly crushed when we went to see my Tony Richardson circus film, *Red and Blue*, at the local Odeon. It was a scene of Fellini-esque exaggeration, and a sobering one. As we entered the cinema, a man was not only vociferously demanding his ticket money back but threatening the management with violence if the film was not taken off immediately! It was. As the *Variety* headline put it: RANK ORGANIZATION SINKS *RED AND BLUE* LIKE SUBMARINE. It was time to harden my sensibilities, like my sitarist's finger, so that I could carry on performing without undue pain.

Prospects for *Justine,* however, seemed more promising. It was one of my favorite books and even Durrell gave my casting authorial approval. "With his air of freshness and vulnerability he should do a fine job as Darley." I would also be reunited with Dirk Bogarde, playing Pursewarden. Anouk Aimée, whom I had so admired in Fellini's *8½,* was the mysterious Alexandrian siren. The director was Joseph Strick, who had successfully brought James Joyce's *Ulysses* to the screen. The film had been eight years in preparation, a reputed fortune having been spent on script development. It was to be filmed in North Africa and—mirabile dictu—in Hollywood.

Justine Does Hollywood

CHAPTER FIFTEEN

Tunisia was our stand-in for *Justine*'s Alexandria, the cut-off, sun-drenched, timeless place that Durrell portrayed in such unprosaic, pointillist language. This trip would be the first of many to the Maghreb, a world first glimpsed in a schoolboy *Merchant of Venice* when the Prince of Morocco's complexion—"the shadowed liv'ry of the burnished sun"—had been thickly laid on with makeup. At first glance it all seemed too clean, lacking India's chaotic confusion of color and life. Neither Pat nor I could get that country out of our minds—it lingered on, growing tenaciously more extraordinary in retrospect.

Our balcony at Tunis's Hilton Hotel overlooked a Cubist moonscape of flat white buildings and narrow streets. Where we were filming, I later learned, had been especially swept clean by the proud city authorities, making the true replication of teeming prewar Egypt even more problematic. Indeed, the lack of authenticity extended to clothes, hairdos and makeup as, inexplicably, the producers had resisted a "period" look. Sixties faces and fashions—long sideburns, Giacometti-thin ties and stovepipe trousers—abounded, making the accurate telling of a complex, historically based story dubious. If an actor senses that he looks wrong, this can subtly, even unconsciously, undermine confidence and reflect in the performance. As it did here.

Nervously charming, Strick was given to occasional hysterical outbursts that, unfortunately, were rarely focused where they could be beneficial. The producer was the veteran Pandro S. Berman, once the whiz kid of RKO Pictures. Both he and his wife were friendly and supportive on the set and afterward when we would dine in a local French bistro that had lingered on after independence.

The American crew was equally experienced. Some were as old as the Hollywood legend itself. Expansive of body and humor, yet quick-witted and incredibly energetic, these men had fashioned the industry. The lighting cameraman was the famed Leon Shamroy. Wizened and bowed like an old sage, with cigar clamped between teeth, he would stand in the sunlight trying to outshine it with a battery of arc lamps worked by an army of assistants. The camera operator was equally ancient, having started work in the silent era, the focus puller had sharpened the image of over seven hundred films and the Best Boy had seen his best years. All had wonderful stories to tell of their pioneer days, the flavor of which lingered on in certain phrases. Little platforms of whatever dimension, for example, were still called "apple boxes" in salutation to the industry's rustic origins. Old Hollywood also invaded in the form of press junkets with journalists dressed in fez hats and entertained by the inevitable belly dancers.

Although Strick's unorthodox, eccentric methods antagonized the old guard filmmakers, they seemed to suit the impressionist nature of the story. He let us develop our characters in an intuitive, unforced way. I was enjoying myself and the outcome seemed promising. Living in a hotel room full of cats away from everyone else, Anouk was friendly but distrait, perhaps because she was preoccupied with a real love affair with her future husband, Albert Finney. Dirk, as in *The Servant*, was especially adept at "seedy" roles and Pursewarden's "gravy on tie, booze on breath" diplomat appeared a natural for him.

We filmed amidst the painted blue doors of picturesque Sidi Bou Said with its cafes where one could drink mint tea, smoke hookahs and enjoy a fried *brique* exploding with hot runny egg. Most of the American crew were addicted to stomach medications and suffered more from overindulging in them than from the food itself.

Justine's house was an exquisite villa belonging to Baron d'Erlanger, which President Bourguiba had apparently threatened to confiscate unless it could be used for filming. But there were limits to coercion. Talking to the immaculately mannered Baron one day, I noticed the villa's magnificent doors were being dismantled. "Oh, yes," he said resignedly, "they are being shipped to Hollywood." I managed to persuade him that, film being the art of illusion, they could be copied and reproduced by studio craftsmen, thereby securing a tiny part of Tunisia's astonishing artistic patrimony.

I especially enjoyed the drives out from Tunis across the grain-filled hinterland, the breadbasket of the Roman Empire, to a Turkish fort on the sea where the fateful encounter between Justine and myself was filmed. "10 a.m. Michael York and Anouk Aimée commence seduction scene," read the call sheet for one day. "If not completed by noon, finish after lunch." Word of these sexual intrigues seemed to filter back to America, for *Cosmopolitan* magazine asked Pat to photograph me for their first nude centerfold spread. We declined, and Burt Reynolds, the eventual recipient of this honor, reclined.

We ransacked the souks for art-deco glassware left behind by French colonists, returning home with hand luggage bulging with Gallé and Daum treasures. After catching our breath in London, we flew on to Los Angeles for the continuation of filming at the Twentieth Century-Fox Studios.

It would seem a hard task to summon up exactly those first impressions of a city that has been my home for over fifteen years. But they are still as vivid as my preconceptions of the place. I had visualized a shining metropolis lit by a diurnal golden sun and by prancing searchlights at night where toothsome men in straw boaters danced to the beat of jazz bands down palm-lined avenues patrolled by Keystone cops and filled with miraculously speeding traffic. Locomotives whistled into the distant cactus-dotted desert where ululating redskins chased after stagecoaches. Homburged gangsters rubbed shoulders with Stetsoned cowpokes and every pleasing aspect was adorned with an exceptionally pretty girl. Reality shattered—perhaps not entirely —this illusory vision.

Viewed from the descending plane, Los Angeles seemed to have been dropped from a great height to splatter thinly over a huge horizon. Spilling from the desert into mountain canyons it stopped only at the farthest west, at the ocean's edge where the plane finally landed. It was even raining! But there *were* palms. We stayed at the Beverly

Hills Hotel with its palm-tree wallpaper and palm-decked garden on a palm-lined avenue where the wind dislodged dry branches like so much bosky dandruff. I was delighted to be assigned Bungalow 21 in the hotel's jungly grounds in which, I was assured, Sir John Gielgud had once lodged his eminence.

There was a short interval before work recommenced—time for instant tourism. Asked to take us to the center of town, the studio driver looked at me in complete bafflement. I now understand his reaction. Los Angeles and its hinterland—called in a rather Tolkienish way "The Southland"—is a collection of petty fiefdoms held together by a concrete network of freeways, making the use of a car a necessity not a luxury. Oil still bubbled up between the streets and one of them, Sepulveda Boulevard, was even reputed to be over seventy miles long. There were rumors that you could be arrested for walking. The driver offered to take us to Malibu, but I was disappointed to find that what should have been a grand marine drive was just another elongated suburb, the view of the Pacific being walled in by the unlovely backs of an almost continuous stretch of beach houses.

Driving through the gates of the studio for the fist time was especially thrilling. Illusion was instantaneously evident. This was Turn-of-the-Century-Fox, for the skyline was dominated by the gigantic New York set left over from *Hello, Dolly*. Administrative buildings, in real life squat and practical, were masked by porticoed pleasure gardens and the facades of plush hotels. A sign exhorting us to "Think Twentieth" was suspended, a trifle inappropriately, from the Victorian elevated railway. Reality, however, intruded almost immediately.

In the middle of our first rehearsal Joe Strick was called away to the phone. He returned smiling strangely to announce that he had been fired. Working away from the studio's immediate influence, Strick had obviously rubbed up against the Hollywood grain. Now, with all the interiors left to shoot, there were rumors that the film would be abandoned. The production was thrown into limbo.

While awaiting our fate, we gave ourselves unashamedly to the pleasures of this strange new place and in particular to the hospitality of Pat's old acquaintances. She had lived for a time in Beverly Hills and her return was celebrated with a rare generosity. I began slowly to piece together details of Pat's past and realized that some of them —racing cars and flying planes—were unconventional if not downright daredevilish.

A rumor began to circulate that our film was to be taken over by

the veteran director George Cukor. Optimism flooded in like a returning tide. He was one of the undisputed masters of his craft. Indeed, he
had helped to draft its language. He was also known as a woman's
director, which augured well for our wayward Justine. The appointment was confirmed. Thanksgivings were made as Thanksgiving was
celebrated—my first taste of this all-American pilgrim feast. Cukor,
formal in shirt, tie and waistcoat, had a perceptible air of authority,
and the company happily deferred to this white-haired, bespectacled
deus ex machina to put their stalled vehicle back on track again. He
had brief meetings with all of us, explaining his objective of recaptur-
ing, as much as possible, the flavor of the original *Quartet*. We were
back in business.

The studio turned out to be a township in itself with a hospital, a
barber shop and carefully laid-out streets patrolled by its own police
force. Painted for visual relief and identity in pastel colors, the huge
bunkerlike soundstages dwarfed tree-shaded cottage offices. Elaborate
sets littered the vast backlot from which the futuristic Century City
with its Avenue of the Stars and Constellation Boulevard would soon
rise. In the Café de Paris, the Patton Blood and Guts menu offered
such delicacies as Planet of the Apes Salad and Lady in Cement Tomato Juice. Despite the restaurant's name, however, alcohol, even
under a cheerful pseudonym, was banned. I remember Philippe
Noiret, my *sympathique* co-star, growing pink to the point of apoplexy
at being denied his God-given Gallic right—wine with lunch. Eating
was definitely business not pleasure.

My dressing room was in the Stars Block, which otherwise mas-
queraded as the Peyton Place Hospital. Of intimidating dimensions, it
was more like a luxurious hotel suite. Reminding me of the Burtons'
Roman folly, it came replete with everything to make the mere
thought of work unlikely, if not downright repellent. I preferred to
use my trailer on the stage itself. Reminiscent of a Victorian bathing
machine, it could be trundled wherever needed. Seated within, where
legions of artists had previously prepared for their brief moments of
celluloid celebrity, I found I could maintain concentration while still
keeping in touch with the life of the set with its bangs and buzzes,
smells and yells.

"You've worked in the theater, haven't you?" the property master
said one day. How could he tell, I asked. "Because at the end of every
take you hand the prop back to me or return it to the prop table."
This, I found out, was unusual. It would also amount to the only
positive praise that, from then onward, I would receive.

Cukor made his disapproval of some of his inherited cast quite unambiguous. At the mention of our leading lady his face would flush, his lower lip jutting and quivering angrily, especially after Anouk, detained in Europe by her real-life siren songs and the uncertainty enveloping the project, failed to return on time.

As for myself, the joy went out of work. This was symbolized by the tatty, characterful raincoat I had worn in Tunis that was delivered to me here, dry-cleaned and plastic-wrapped, its soul sucked out of it. Suddenly the smiles stopped as if so ordered on the daily call sheet. Dear companions from Tunis became strangers overnight. You could smell the fear stalking the corridors.

Cukor insisted that everything be played "at a clip," even the atmospheric scenes where, it seemed to me, what was being said between the lines was of greater import than the words themselves. I felt my precious instincts threatened. But they were up against a world-famous director who was "saving" our film, so I kept quiet, slavishly obeying his direction. Seeing the results I regretted such inhibition and vowed never again to compromise without good reason or argument.

I was now excluded from the coterie who saw rushes, and the conspiratorial silence about the results was unhelpful. And hurtful. Cukor once filmed over twenty tortuous takes of myself performing a ludicrously simple action—pulling a wallet from my pocket and putting it on a table. Elsewhere on the set other more demeaning things were happening. Mature dwarfs, masked in yashmaks, played child prostitutes. Saddest of all, I met up with my screen hero Marcel Dalio, the incomparable, unforgettable Baron of Renoir's *La Règle du Jeu,* who was reduced here to an undignified costume extra. Becoming oversensitive, I clashed with the film's publicist when production shots of Anna Karina and myself on a beach in Tunisia were published with a caption that insinuated an unprofessional liaison. I should have heeded Durrell's own observation that "Life's too short not to be taken lightly."

My misery on the set, however, was in startling contrast to life off it. Pat and I were determined to enjoy ourselves and extract every possible positive benefit from the experience. I failed to share the cynicism of my fellow bungalowed inmate, Dirk, whose Hollywood phobia would be confirmed in his later writing. Exploring our new milieu, we watched performances by killer whales at Marineland and by Zubin Mehta—another of Pat's old friends—at the new Music Center that crowned a downtown hill with theaters, opera house and concert hall. The cornerstone of a building spree that in a few decades would forest the city with thickets of skyscrapers, it was the first substantial oasis in a much-maligned cultural desert. The Roman villa'd Getty Museum by the Malibu ocean also gave the lie to this old slur, although having to reserve a parking space in its bowels before being allowed to enjoy its riches testified to its distinctive, unclassical L.A. nature.

Certainly the city had grown up too quickly and was now in earnest search of sophistication. But the hippie values and alternative attitudes enshrined in the new musical sensation, *Hair,* were also very much in evidence and Women's Lib and its bonfire of bras had added to the fashion and sociological ferment. Long-locked youth in ethnic garb drifted along Sunset Strip, thumbing for rides beneath huge panoramic billboards boasting the more conventional good life. Roadside benches advertised mortuaries and undertakers as if to warn off the citizens who resisted the city's restless momentum by sitting down on them. It was a disappointment to learn that the area known as Hollywood was as gimcrack and unsubtle as its famous sign.

We were invited to a surprise birthday party for Henry Miller. I shall never forget the look of horror he gave the assembled guests invading his home and I vowed never to personally perpetrate such an outrage. Miller recovered, allowing me to add my signature to his wall of fame situated, as befitted a sexual nonconformist, in his bathroom. At this time I also met another literary giant of diminutive size, Christopher Isherwood, whose work would influence my life so much. He shared a house with his longtime companion, the American artist Don Bachardy, in Santa Monica Canyon overlooking the wide sandy beach and bay. Bushy-browed, keen and alert like a superannuated choir boy, he was an interesting amalgam of his native and adoptive lands, as much at home in T-shirts as in ties, and peppering his speech with "Gee" as well as "Gosh."

We dined with Merle Oberon and the young Steve McQueen and met other denizens of Hollywood's stellar aristocracy, especially when imperially entertained by Doris and Jules Stein. The founder of MCA, who had started by booking dance bands in the speakeasy days, Jules amused Pat with tales of taking Mae West to black jazz clubs where her voluptuous white flesh seemed even more outstanding. Mrs. Virginia Robinson, the celebrated Beverly Hills hostess, invited us to lunch in her palatial estate where monkeys swung through the trees and grave butlers served guacamole and frozen daiquiris. Dining with my California agent, I discovered the mysteries of the "London broil" and "English muffin" that exist nowhere in their putative homeland. We met up with a newly dentured David Hemmings and witnessed his marriage to Gayle in a flower-decked arbor by a swimming pool on which floated bouquets of love birds and blossoms.

Pat and I jetted off to Las Vegas to be entertained by Marlene Dietrich, Frank Sinatra and a chorus of slot machines gobbling up coins. There were even bags of money on our pillows, but no visible clocks to officially divide day from night. This fantasy experience continued at Disneyland, where Jane Fonda had arranged for us to spend the night after witnessing her father officiate at the Christmas parade and, miraculously without lining up, sampling its head-spinning delights. Installed in a hotel suite with connecting bedrooms, we were invited to come on over in our bathrobes to play Scrabble with Jane and her husband, Roger Vadim. Knowing their reputations as Siren and Svengali, we wondered if the game might develop into a more dangerous liaison. But nothing untoward happened and—for a fleeting funny moment—we couldn't help but feel a certain sense of rejection.

Back in Beverly Hills we shopped for gifts on Rodeo Drive, then full of family grocery and hardware stores. On Christmas Day we were asked to Jane and Vadim's ever-open beach house for lunch. Also invited were our fellow hotel guests, Yves Montand and the lady for whom my teenage heart had throbbed, his wife, Simone Signoret. I drove us all out through Westwood, then a village centered around the sprawling UCLA campus, along San Vicente Boulevard, with its magnificent coral trees in seasonal flame, and in through the exclusive gated enclave of Malibu Colony. Although Deborah Kerr and Peter Viertel were also there, as was the quiet and dignified Henry Fonda, the star of the occasion was Jane and Vadim's new baby daughter, Vanessa. No one paid much attention to Peter Fonda when he talked about the new motorcycle movie he had just made, though they would later when *Easy Rider* changed the face of contemporary movies forever.

Usually Vadim himself would fish for meals in the pounding surf outside but, on this day, a delicious fondue was served. Yet, to my senses attuned to the traditional turkey and plum puddinged Yule, it seemed as inappropriate as the sleighs and snowy decorations twinkling in the relentless sun. Moreover, Rock Hudson, who had invited us to dinner, similarly failed to provide traditional fare. But custom was served when, just making it back to the hotel in time, we enjoyed a midnight turkey sandwich!

Another old friend of Pat's offered to rent us his beach house in Malibu, and so we joined the elite behind the wall-to-wall barricade that had so annoyed me before. This house was remarkable. Its windows served as walls with views of the surfy beach in front and soft, rain-greened hills behind. Inside, it was alive with plants and light and even on gloomy days one's spirits soared within its spaciousness. Gas logs blazed in a generous fireplace and there was a long bar with sink and ice-maker—a world away from the discreet British tray of drinks. A swimming pool fronted the shore that was now generally deserted apart from its colony of resident dogs and stoic gulls.

In this tranquil, healthy spot, Pat furthered the natural process of healing by finally assuming responsibility for her own body. Taking her off the codeine, a local doctor prescribed instead heavy doses of antibiotics. One day Pat swept out all these drugs and began to study how to get well—naturally. That time marked the beginning of a fruitful, unending quest.

It was now the rainy season and the West lived up to its wild epithet, with dank sea fogs and storms of biblical intensity. As if dress-rehearsing the impending apocalypse when, as predicted by scientist and seer, the City of Angels would return to its ocean birthplace, the rains fell hard and inexorably. The winter of early 1969 was the wettest so far this century. Slide areas slid. Rivers of mud and rock poured from the mountains, uprooting houses and trees, restoring highways to the semblance of frontier trails and turning the beach into a log-jammed mess. At night, Pat and I would imagine our bed smashing through the window and being swept out to sea on a torrential tidal wave.

One evening we were dining at a restaurant with the writer Sterling Silliphant when he was called to the phone. On his return he allowed the story being told at table to finish before informing his wife that their house had just burned to the ground. Once they had ascertained that their dogs were safe, however, they calmly finished their meal. I wondered if this was an example of the frontier spirit requisite for living on the knife-edge of an earthquake zone.

Despite the deluge we were able to entertain, to return the hospitality that had been lavished on us. Expansive Sunday lunches with English trifles and California wines were followed by walks on the rainswept sand. Jane Fonda, her mane of blonde hair chopped off for her role in *They Shoot Horses, Don't They?*, though, ate only celery—a foretaste of the extremism that would soon extend to her political and exercise regimes.

Before leaving this extraordinary town, I was astonished to be invited for a drink at George Cukor's elegant house. Whatever our differences on set, we were united in the face of the great unknown—the outcome of our joint venture. As it happened, it was to be greeted with a general downturning of thumbs, proving yet again that, whatever the pedigree, a project had to have that indefinable "it" to succeed. As I walked through his gate in a brick wall covered in antique ivy, I had no inkling that just five years later I would be George's neighbor and this pleasant street my home.

Year Out

One inevitable homecoming chore was a reunion with lawyers and accountants, in an attempt to plan a course in the uncharted waters of my future career. The consensus, based on previous years when my work seemed to be mostly abroad, was that I should temporarily abandon ship—spend a year out of England and benefit from the taxes thereby saved. Pat's Gypsy prophecy was proving accurate.

Taxes in Britain were then at their most confiscatory—83 percent on earned income and a vicious 98 percent on investments. In a job where there is no guarantee of income or security of tenure, it seemed almost irresponsible not to look to the future through the few remaining tax loopholes. A friend confirmed that his accountants had insisted his only sure course for financial survival was to kill himself. All these tedious meetings reminded me of the telling scene in Albert Finney's film *Charlie Bubbles* where he sat glazed-eyed before his advisers as they intoned his fiscal fate. My head reeled from all these dry yet life-affecting details, a giddiness enhanced by my ancient adversarial attitude toward mathematics.

Spending a year abroad was a prospect that filled us with enthusiasm. In fact, I proposed to call myself a tax "advantagee" rather than "exile," the yellower press's prevalent censorious designation. We decided to give up our rented flat so that, on our return, we could buy something of our own and, while packing it up, we took temporary refuge in a large suite at the Connaught Hotel. At £20 a day it seemed exorbitantly expensive.

The new tax year began on April 5, 1969, so, before leaving on business, there was a certain pressure to catch up with friends and family. Penny was pregnant again. Despairing of having another child, she and her husband, Marek, had adopted a baby daughter, Kate, whereupon she had immediately conceived another daughter, Lucy. May and Joe were considering moving again, this time to the mild shores of Devon.

Hal Prince, the distinguished Broadway director, was also in London at that time. He had sent me a script called *The Cook* with which he intended to make his debut as a film director. I had accepted immediately and learned that Angela Lansbury was to be my co-star. Hal turned out to be slim, with a graying beard, radiating a youthful enthusiasm and energy manifest in the frequent use of the adjective "swell!"

I heard from Adrian, who was hoping to make his film debut as an actor in *Waterloo* in Russia:

I'm in that stage you were in three years ago of waiting to hear something—that tingling masochistic feeling knowing you've been asked for and of no one yet having said no. The time when dreams run freest . . .

He confessed a certain disenchantment with the contemporary theater:

The words of Che and Marcuse have been spreading discord among actors—they're demanding more participation in the running of companies and even choice of director. Needless to say, it's usually the bad actors who have the biggest mouths. If it spreads too much I can see myself at the Labour Exchange!

Derek was experiencing a similar disenchantment with the National Theatre. Involvement in a film of Olivier's *Othello* and his production of *The Three Sisters* had made Derek revise his previous strictures about the medium. I urged him to leave and be missed. This film of *Othello*, incidentally, illustrates most powerfully the differences between stage and screen acting. In the theater, Olivier's titanic Moor had totally eclipsed Frank Finlay's low-keyed Iago. On screen, the emphasis is reversed. Olivier in close-up is almost too overpowering, whereas Finlay's confidential style is ideally suited to the camera's intimacy.

It was while eating ice cream with Derek in a West End cinema that Pat and I had the first queasy intimations of the illness that would significantly affect our livers if not our lives. The film was *Where Eagles Dare* but I felt more like Prometheus again, with vultures gnawing at my guts. We continued to feel out of sorts and energy. Surely jet lag could not last this long? Need every little chore be so exhausting? Pat instinctively insisted we had hepatitis. The day we moved our belongings into storage a doctor confirmed we were indeed both suffering from a mild case—almost certainly a little souvenir of a recent Mexican trip.

It had happened on our way back from California. We had visited another old friend of Pat's, Jimmy Wilson, a dazzling charismatic Mexican-American beloved of everyone who had the good fortune to encounter him, including me. He was the regional tomato czar, growing them at his jungly ranch in Sinaloa, Mexico, where we had stayed, and exporting them through Nogales, a desert town that straddled both sides of the border. There, he had invited us to his Versailles-like extravaganza of a house improbably situated on a nondescript back street in the Arizonan half of town. One night we had crossed back to Mexico for a dinner of raw clams and chicken in black chocolate—a meal fraught with fateful consequences.

We felt as empty and bereft as the flat, now transformed into a shabby, echoing, inhospitable box. Saying goodbye to it, a side effect of the illness was to make me as weepily emotional as Gayev in *The Cherry Orchard*. Fortunately, it did not dampen the old peripatetic lust. Deciding to exile ourselves in the nearest foreign land, we headed for that old haunt of the expatriate British, the South of France.

Putting up at the fateful rendezvous, the Colombe D'Or in St. Paul de Vence, revived memories of that magical blossom-filled morning of a few years ago. In the dining room Alexander Calder sat beneath one of his creations surrounded by other artistic treasures that had paid many an impoverished artist's bill. The choice of locale, however, was perhaps ill-judged. Restricted to a bland diet, we were tortured with the sight of fellow diners engorging crudités, tarte maison and other delicacies definitely *défendus*. For some reason, though, *mille-feuilles* had been left off our doctor's list of forbidden foods and, taking flagrant advantage of this error, we ate it—without apparent ill effect—at every opportunity.

We fed fully, too, on the extraordinary local landscapes that had seduced so many artists and other visitors. Sadly, they were soon to be marred by a rapacious overdevelopment that would replace rose gardens with swimming pools, populating Eden with squat *résidences secondaires*. Then, however, we seriously considered renting a house in the region as a base for the year, even though the notion of being in one fixed spot was as unwelcome as it was improbable. Reading the newspaper one day, I happened to notice an advertisement for a ship sailing from London to Australia. Here was the perfect temporary solution—a traveling base! A week later we were aboard the SS *Oriana* heading south with no fixed plan on the horizon until the summer shooting of Hal Prince's film in Germany.

Reality slipped effortlessly away. Ship time seemed to have twice its terrestrial value. We spent it happily resting and reading, our heartbeats slowed to counterpoint the steady throb of the engines. Pat had all-consuming powers of concentration. Once involved in a book, the real world became for her insubstantial and I often found myself fighting off the humiliating impulse to be jealous of an author. If she became involved in a subject—whether oriental porcelain or occidental medicine—it would always be extensively and zealously researched. Her mind was as curious as her interests were diverse, and I constantly benefited from her enthusiasms. Through all of this I was being made inexorably aware of that great nuptial conundrum: that two into one *does* go. This untypically inactive period anticipated a time when we would derive the greatest of pleasure from simply being together.

The ship's grillroom was available for a modest half-crown surcharge. As most passengers preferred the communal dining room, we had the place to ourselves. There was even a dinner dance where, entirely alone, we solemnly circled to the beat of a little band. The crew seemed as delighted with our unique patronage as we were with our made-to-order food. Approaching the tip of Africa, we both felt so recuperated by the effects of sea air and rest that we decided to disembark at Cape Town. As Table Mountain drew into view I wondered what emotions the same sight must have produced in the breast of some Queen's trooper sent young and green from England, shilling in hand, to relieve Mafeking and, by jingo, knock hell out of the beastly Boers.

There was a different war being waged now—a human rights campaign to discredit apartheid. I had no qualms about visiting South Africa, although it was considered unfashionable, even unethical, to do so. Politically I was a sort of liberal humanist, of no particular affiliation, loathing the blinkered absolutism of the party line. *Cry the Beloved Country* and left-wing *New Statesman* leaders had fueled my passionate antiapartheid arguments with my Rhodesian Aunt Irene. Now I simply wanted to see for myself at firsthand and make my own judgment. I couldn't understand the incuriosity of some of the British crew, many docking in South Africa for the first time, who preferred to stay on board to save their money for a huge pub crawl in Australia.

The reality was different from our expectations. It was much worse. The stench of politics hung as heavily in the air as the smell of land after so many pristine days at sea. At our hotel, the receptionist asked Pat not to carry her camera bag. "We have Kaffirs for that," he admonished. Pat refused to hand it over. I was recognized and, either voluntarily or otherwise, interviewed and photographed. "Tybalt's in town," proclaimed a local headline. I learned that the chaste nude scenes of *Romeo and Juliet* had here been censored, making me wonder if I would have been allowed to stay had my in flagrante delicto scenes been left intact.

Going to the cinema one evening I despised myself for not going to the assistance of a black man lying on the sidewalk. He was probably drunk, but that is only a comfortable assumption. The feeling of being isolated at the end of the world was emphasized by there being no television. People were cut off from a great liberalizing democratic force that, as recent events in Eastern Europe have shown, was capable of giving the lie to any political system where truth was state-owned.

Renting a car, we drove out from the suffocating city, leaving its mountainous setting behind and crossing deserts to the fertile Natal coast and Durban. Staying in every kind of accommodation, we met people at every social level. After reaching the Boer heartland, the Voortrekker territory, we explored the new black "homelands" of the Transkei, finishing up in Johannesburg. In the farms and game parks the dignity of the animals contrasted strongly with that of the urban jungle dwellers.

A paradox of South Africa was that, physically so beautiful and so richly endowed, a man-made ugliness spoiled everything. The whites had an almost caricature uniformity, the men sporting short trousers and shorter haircuts, their lives seemingly circumscribed by beer and rugby. Their wives tended to wear hats and gloves as if permanently at church. It would have been so much simpler if one could have disliked them outright, but many were charming and helpful. When our car slid off a dirt road in Zululand, every single passing white driver stopped in the mud to offer help, refreshment and, inevitably it seemed, political opinions. Sincere and quite unhypocritical in their advocacy of apartheid, they did not regard themselves as having a political problem. Although their doctors had just pioneered putting new hearts into old bodies, it would be a long time before vital new ideas would be transplanted into the ailing body politic.

Kenya, our next stop, gave the lie to the whole doomed system. At the airport the immigration officials were as courteous and efficient as the other blacks who ran the country with an enthusiasm that made one's jaded heart leap. Their crisp go-ahead self-confidence contrasted strongly with the tattered dejection of their South African cousins who, restricted in movement and education, were shambling on the spot, little more than slaves. In Kenya we could relax and enjoy the ubiquitous beauty. We could tip naturally and not guiltily out of a blackmailed philanthropy or a self-conscious display of solidarity. I only resented being pulled over, fascist style, by some terrifying motorcycle cop, siren screaming, to allow the presidential convoy to thunder past like a herd of charging rhino.

We confined ourselves to the cool highlands where remnants of a vanished species could still be glimpsed. The old white hunters were abandoning their settlements, though foxhounds could still be heard baying in the mists. There were still country clubs that served six-course meals including such imperial staples as queen of puddings and Scotch woodcock. We tasted further white mischief at the Nairobi racetrack and black magic at the local market, buying a charm from a witch doctor to protect us while traveling. At Treetops, where Princess Elizabeth had received word of her accession to the throne, we watched regal lions and majestic elephants while that cheeky commoner, the baboon, stole our teatime biscuits. There was a lake encrimsoned with flamingos and the parks teemed with game. There was no hint then in this hushed, unchanging primeval landscape of the impending lust for ivory and its resultant genocide of the herds.

After this enjoyable recuperative month our tourist extravaganza came to an end. It was time to return to work and we flew to Munich for costume fittings for *The Cook* and to approve the house reserved for us for the filming. It turned out to be a sinister appendage to a clinic, full of strange sinks and wheeled beds and was summarily rejected. It was also horribly expensive. All this revealed one of the pitfalls of our profession: people assumed we were overpaid, and overcharged accordingly. They never thought that actors, like everyone else, hated to be cheated, especially when uprooted from home. Pat was particularly sensitive to atmosphere and environment and it was not uncommon for her to sample several rooms in a hotel before finally settling in. I soon tuned into this wavelength and we would often enter a room or restaurant and simultaneously walk out again without exchanging a single word or glance.

Facing *Waterloo,* rejection was also the theme of Adrian's next letter.

I was very grand about it and turned it down! Suddenly a black thing came out of the mist and said, "Don't." It seemed a pity to spend three months hanging around for the privilege of saying, "What is it?" Paramount pointed out that Orson himself only had four speeches so I couldn't complain. Being a quarter of Orson Welles is, I suppose, quite something. Pity for my film career, which will now take another twenty years to get off the ground.

We had news, too, of Rick who, following in my footsteps to Oxford, was spending his sixteenth summer studying there. "Please don't worry about my taking drugs or indulging in communal orgies for the elite for I assure you I'm not. I have decided to travel around England visiting Stratford and whatever comes my way with a bag of apples and oranges, two loaves of bread, some beer and the *Shell Guide to Britain.*"

He was also pursuing my interest in the Drama, playing Sir Toby Belch in a recent school production of *Twelfth Night.* "I can't think of anything quite so disgusting as a Shakespeare play recited with a Kansas City accent," he added, highlighting an enduring American misconception about the Bard. The received wisdom was that Shakespearean performance was the exclusive property of the British, that the plays only sounded correct in the Queen's English. Despite the best efforts of Joe Papp and others, this attitude survives. I am forever trying to bolster confidence by pointing out that the present-day American accent is much closer to the speech of the first Queen Elizabeth than that of her current namesake. Rick's exuberant letters, though, were beginning to reflect a Shakespearean zest for language. He was president of the senior class and had thoughts of studying in Paris.

With time again on our hands, before the start of filming in Germany, we took refuge in another ship, the *QEII,* heading for New

York. One of the first crossings of this brand-new liner, its novelty had attracted a Bluebottle and a Beatle, for Peter Sellers and Ringo Starr were shipmates. The liner was as aggressively modern as Pat's new clothes and haircut. Plastics might have replaced the plush of the old *Queens* but their tradition lingered on in the staff who were neither new nor redesigned. Bald heads brilliantined, "a touch of the Cunards" in their swaying walk, they reminded me of Percy and kind at Oxford. Each day I spent an hour in the sauna sweating out such issues as the Vietnam War alongside portly American executives and German tourists. The war was polarizing opinion everywhere. Even respectable little Holland was in a ferment. "It's quite exciting the last few days," Adrian reported:

> Students occupied the university so the police cordoned off the middle of the town and stood outside looking aggressive in black helmets with batons, guns and shields. Naturally there were plenty of street scuffles, and little civil wars with huge crowds charging the police cordon and cops motorcycling about and hitting all and sundry. When I find this a bit barbaric, the Dutch explain that the English police are really a bit phenomenal in their stoicism. Perhaps they are. I remember that I'm writing to an ex-policeman!

The nightly cinema show only reminded me how anxious I was to get back to work on the film. This was the longest time I had been professionally inactive but I sensed that without good health, good work was impossible. Meanwhile I had word of recent activity. *Alfred the Great* had been selected for a Royal Command Performance, the third that I would have to miss, an almost treasonable situation. *The Guru* had opened to mostly enthusiastic notices. "A quiet comedy, it has a great deal to say about today and yesterday, about the fads of the young and the foolishness of their elders and about things of the spirit and of the moment." This was Judith Crist's comment. Another perceptive reviewer called the film "a souvenir of a time already in recession." Indeed, a subtle backlash had set in against the cultural hullabaloo, the gurus and mysticism of the previous year, a disenchantment reflected in the public reaction. No one came. Moreover, having spent untold millions on making and selling *Hello, Dolly,* Fox, no doubt "thinking Twentieth," were unwilling to spend real greenbacks promoting a product requiring delicate special handling. A film's marketing costs now almost equaled its production budget, so the sad outcome was inevitable.

My own reaction was mixed. Each frame of the film was like a diary entry redolent of those stirring times, making critical objectivity difficult. But I particularly missed one scene that had been edited out in which Tom Pickle, world-weary and wary, had poured out his heart to Jenny, explaining his reasons for being in India. Because I knew I had this crucial scene to play, up to that point I deliberately made Tom tight-lipped, enigmatic and, hopefully, intriguing. The outcome showed how dangerous it is to second-guess a director and reinforced the unglamorous truth that actors do little more than provide raw material for others to cut into shape. However, despite certain shortcomings, I believe *The Guru* is both an amusing and meaningful social document of a very special time.

New York was reached in the ideal old-fashioned way. We swept under the Narrows Bridge, past the welcoming lady with the torch, to see the towers of Manhattan rise like a mirage from the waves. Bunting flapped in the warm breeze, a Tissot marine painting come alive. It was a perfect May day. I met my future co-star Angela Lansbury, then the toast of Broadway in the musical *Dear World.* I soon found out that her warmth and friendliness were a genuine, not just Thespian, endowment. Looking sexual and predatory, as the film's story demanded, we posed together for Richard Avedon's publicity photos.

I rushed back to California for the weekend to dub *Justine* and add an extra narrative. As flattering as it was that Darley's presence should be reinforced, I was concerned that the story required external explanation. I was astonished, too, to find that this narrative footage was taken from a publicity film showing me strolling through Carthage in costume and vaguely in character. So much for the millions of dollars spent in scripts and preparation! But at least it provided the only contemplative moment in a film thick with plot played relentlessly "at a clip." Amidst the babble it was refreshing to hear Durrell's own ironic voice.

New York was "Fun City." This self-conscious designation was willed on it by Mayor John Lindsay, whose handsome campaign photograph, incidentally, Pat had taken. Its headquarters, in a society growing ever more unfunny, stressed and violent, was Central Park. On Sundays, when cars were banned, there was a general drift from the polluted streets into the greenery where concerts of improvised jazz and calypso competed with the merry warblings of an antique carousel. Shorn, saffron-robed monks, be-sneakered like the all-American kids they so recently used to be, chanted mantras while in the leafy shade couples lay stoned or love-locked amidst the stage-scenery rocks. The fashionable world would parade down an enormous flight of steps with an aplomb and éclat barely equaled on Broadway itself. I once saw a splendid black girl descending in a pompadour wig and crinoline escorted by two equally groomed and exotic Afghan hounds. In general, the Woodstock generation's hair and hippiness were now more in evidence than hats and suits. Even the police lost their usual Kafka-esque menace patrolling on horseback or silly little scooters past the bagel sellers and the benchfuls of prim English nannies.

"Gee, what a great vagina!" This remark came floating out one day from behind a bush and, on investigation, was found to emanate from a tiny child engrossed with friends in a copy of the salacious *Screw* magazine. Involuntarily shocked, Pat and I offered to buy it from them in the futile hope of protecting them from further corruption. They drove a hard bargain!

We went to see *Oh! Calcutta,* the scandalous apotheosis of this new freedom and the theatrical complement to all those bust and buttock cinematic orgies that, together, threatened to give sex a bad name. I can recall exactly how I felt about all this because it was all enshrined in an interview the *New York Times* did with me at the time:

> It's not the young people today who are hung up on nudity. They aren't queuing up to see porno films. Nowhere else does the generation gap show up so clearly. Young people make love when they want to make love. They don't pay money to watch others doing it.

Rising to my theme I continued,

> There are times when sensuality and sexuality are demanded and can be treated artistically without giving offense, but unless sex and love are allowed to retain their mystery and privacy . . . If one's capacity for being aroused by the human body should be alienated by over-exposure . . . If breasts and private parts should become as commonplace as neck and wrists . . .

At this point Pat mercifully intervened to stem the flood of rhetoric. " 'Hmmm, I'd better cover up,' purred Michael York's pretty photographer wife."

Something for Everyone

CHAPTER SEVENTEEN

Sex, however, was one of the main ingredients of our German film. Adapted by Hugh Wheeler from Harry Kressing's novel *The Cook,* it was sexual appetites rather than alimental ones that now animated the plot. They were stimulated by the mysterious Conrad, played by me, who, insinuating his way into the household of the Countess Ornstein, played by Angela, becomes king of the castle, played by Neuschwanstein, one of Ludwig's fantastic Bavarian follies.

This time there was no castle to rent. We found a little alpine refuge in the nearby village of Lechbruck where forests of firs swept down to aquamarine lakes and craggy mountains hovered in the haze above verdant meadows and fields straight out of Brueghel landscapes. The house had a certain overbearing rustic charm, but after clearing out the plethora of Bavariana and substituting a double bed for the Masoch-designed bunks, it became another welcoming little home.

Like all the best comedies, even black ones, the film had serious overtones. Conrad was the 1970s version of the New Man—greedy, opportunistic, materialistic and downright immoral. Against him, the old orders—aristocratic, political, moral, whatever—had no protection. Attila the Hun was come again as a nouveau riche, trailing the thundering war chariots of the present economic miracle. "Without money there is nothing. Nothing," says the Countess Ornstein intoning the new creed, with dirndl abandoned and skirts slashed sexily above the knees in the new style.

Yet this parable of lust was told in fable form as befitted its once-upon-a-time setting. Like a fairy story it would prove to be one of the most enjoyable films that I have ever had the pleasure to work on. The happy-ever-after part of it was that almost everyone involved remained friends. To this day the film remains a favorite of countless people.

Hal Prince proved to be an insightful and wonderfully enthusiastic novice director. He knew exactly what he wanted—recasting one key role after a few days when this was unforthcoming. He never dictated but his combination of passion, humor and intelligence proved irresistible. "Swell" indeed! Many of the colleagues with whom he was remolding the face of Broadway came to stay. There was Ron Field the choreographer, the expansive John Guare and the shy and fiercely talented Stephen Sondheim. Florence Klotz, another collaborator, did our costumes and John Kander provided the perfect score.

Hugh Wheeler, who wrote the screenplay, became an especially close chum. Graying and handsome, chain-smoking and short-sighted, he had a fey English self-effacement that matched his still English accent. He gave an endearing impression of helplessness, having to keep renting new typewriters as he couldn't change the ribbon of the old ones. Pat, when not working on the set, was unofficial chauffeuse, showing off local sights, such as those holy ballrooms, the rococo churches and, under ever-changing Wagnerian skies, driving up to Munich. There we would order Strawberries Walterspiel at the Four Seasons Hotel, analyze its contents and triumphantly reproduce it in our little *alpenhaus* where Hugh and others came to dine and stay for weekends.

Munich was a civilized urban refuge whenever rustic domesticity overwhelmed. Shopping at affluent Dalmayers made those postwar years of smuggled tea seem long, long, past! It was hard to imagine that so much of the immaculate city had been devastated and yet a new destructive war with explosive noise and craters was being waged all over again—the construction of a metro in time for the upcoming Olympic Games. Peace returned at night enabling open-air performances of Mozart operas at the Residenz Palace. We luxuriated in the city's other artistic wealth—its museums and galleries. Pat became particularly passionate about Franz Marc's paintings, going repeatedly to stare at his powerful expressionist tiger.

Visitors brought news of the real world—the grisly Charles Manson cult murders in Los Angeles and the other blood bath of the Vietnam War. Fortunately, one of the great events of the year—the manned landing on the moon on July 20, 1969—was broadcast worldwide on television. Hal invited us to watch the epochal event on his specially rented television. Unfortunately, we arrived too late to witness the actual landing itself and were treated to an evening of interviews with German scientists such as Werner von Braun who elaborated on their nation's contribution to the achievement. Infuriating at the time, it would be useful later when I was asked to incarnate just such a person in a television version of James Michener's *Space*.

The summer was golden, the weather unusually fine. The shooting went well and without hold-ups. For whenever it did rain, we retired immediately to our cover set inside an ingenious "airhall" inflated in a nearby meadow and looking for all the world like the monstrous breast that menaced Woody Allen in one of his films. For the most part, however, Bavaria itself was our set—beer halls, railway stations, mountain lakes and crags and especially the castles that Ludwig had dreamed up to present such a dazzling, dotty exception to the sober Teutonic rule.

Uprooted from home, we were especially sensitive about our hosts and it was interesting to see the German character in lengthy close-up. I remembered Jörg, Penny's amiable boyfriend, glittery-eyed with excess emotion, and I wondered in the hearts of how many other young Germans a similar torch shone—like the butler in our film, dismissed for turning his room into a secret Nazi shrine. They were an extraordinary, gifted people. But beneath the exterior civility and charm there seemed to be a core of ruthlessness mixed with unexpected hysteria. They were either screaming at you or being screamed at and I resented having to get heated and abusive in order to be emphatic.

It seemed to me no accident that Hitler had come to power in a Bavarian beer hall. We filmed all night in one. Sitting jam-packed in an assembly of local extras, who were singing and sinking stein after stein of beer, I witnessed a nightmarish transformation. Row upon swaying row of genial lederhosened rustics turned inexorably into slurred glazed-eyed monsters.

Perhaps all the madness was due to the Föhn, the strange depressing wind that blows over the Alps, driving the most rational in its path to irrational deeds. Then hospital operations are canceled and even murder is excused. Apart from these occasional irritabilities, however, we certainly felt the benefits of our magic mountain cure. Concentrated filming made for a monastic life and our livers responded to the discipline. We both began to put on weight, although the hepatitis had left us with a lean and hungry look well suited to my voracious Conrad and to Pat's pretty Pucci print dresses.

She was her old familiar self again; I loved the new unfamiliar feeling of being married to her. It was wonderful to have Rick to stay and to accelerate the process of getting to know him. He was becoming his own person—irresistible, if agreeably eccentric. An ancestor had once apparently committed suicide by thrusting his head in the ice of Lake Michigan and, performing a handstand, had frozen solid. The disturbing possibility of Rick serving in the Vietnam War loomed on the uneasy horizon. Closer at hand, though, were the first skirmishes in a war with drugs, soon to turn into a full-scale battle. Their use was now nationwide in America and demographically unlimited. But Rick never once gave cause for parental concern although I am sure that peer pressure made it impossible for him not to have experimented with them. Pat's love and respect were obviously strong factors in his life. Once he turned up looking positively dirty and unkempt. "I love you so much and would do anything for you," Pat gently cautioned, "but if you prefer to look like that then I would prefer not to see you." There was an uneasy standoff that must have required courage from both parties but they were soon back in each other's —very clean—arms!

Filming finished in appropriately fairy-tale Salzburg. By chance my parents were visiting Vienna where we joyfully exchanged our hoarded news and together feasted on Sacher torte, Hapsburg and Klimt treasures and very grand opera. Paris was next, yellow and misty in an autumn sunshine ideal for reading newspapers in cafes and watching *le monde* pass by. The high spot of our visit was dining opposite Jean-Paul Sartre and Simone de Beauvoir at La Coupole. They were quarreling fiercely. While his eyes swiveled furiously in all directions, she remained as tranquil as a nun. We were transfixed. For some reason, though, I felt like an exile in Paris—a psychic later gravely explained that I had been there in a previous life and had witnessed my fiancée being guillotined. Whatever, Pat and I decided to return to New York and, for the time being, use it as a base.

Asked to appear on a TV show there, we went by way of Dublin.

After the orderliness of Germany, the city seemed shabby and impoverished. Little grubby boys hawked newspapers at midnight and the taxi drivers consistently cheated. We saw *Juno and the Paycock* in a funereal production at the Abbey Theatre where, at the mention of the Troubles, the actors turned out front and keened their lines. One longed for a Brendan Behan to give them all a good salutary kick in the rear end. Where was the present-day O'Casey? Certainly the lack of a thrilling contemporary voice was felt elsewhere, too. "Away at last from all those hermetically sealed English plays all disguising the shipwreck of England as dramas about university lecturers, mental home patients and cancer sufferers," Adrian wrote, having just started his own young company in Holland:

> How old-fashioned the theatre begins to look, going round in circles round the same authors, the same plays being blown across the world like pollen. No wonder that the really creative people in the representative arts turn away and make films; the Ibsens and Strindbergs and Wedekinds of today are writing screen scenarios and directing them themselves.

In New York we rented an apartment from our former Kensington neighbor Hardy Amies on West 58th Street. As befitted a fashion tycoon, it was smart and modern and also tall enough to overlook adjacent buildings and command spectacular views of the city's concrete and steel stalagmites and now tawny park. On our second day there I was contacted by a producer who asked me to be in his next film, entitled *Love Story*.

Every time a new script is opened there is a feeling of excitement that the outcome of the reading could possibly be momentous, with life gallivanting off in a totally unpredictable direction. But I wasn't overly impressed with this one. It seemed an essentially American story in which one's tears, to my cooler British taste, were rather too forcefully jerked. Nevertheless, I lunched with the delightful Ali McGraw who was to co-star, and met with the then head of Paramount, Robert Evans, who informed me the story was to be serialized in the *Ladies' Home Journal* and issued as a book. I'm afraid I did him the injustice of interpreting all this as extravagant hype, although his offer of a generous gross percentage in addition to the modest fee did give me pause.

My agents counseled refusal and I felt the time had come to be more selective after serving an apprenticeship going from role to role for the acting experience afforded. I was now prepared to wait for something special. It was time, perhaps, for young wine to ferment.

The instincts, however, were sending contrary uncodable signals. It would be an interesting new challenge to play an American, they suggested. On the other hand, *Alfred the Great* turned out, as the instincts had initially warned, to be a disappointment. We were critically hacked to pieces with a positively Viking ferocity. I decided to play it safe. Thank you, but no thank you.

From that moment my career's career was arrested. It seemed that my rude stare in a gift horse's eye had stopped it dead in its tracks. For a time nothing bruited ever came to fruition and I soon suffered that common actor's malady—a desperation that I would never work again. Was I being shown something? Had I tempted fate by looking forward to a period of unemployment to soak up sensations other than professional ones?

I began to realize that I had made the right decision at the wrong time. With its people in ferment, American films were taking an intensely introspective turn—a process of self-examination that excluded foreign subjects. I had failed to see that the theme of *Love Story* anticipated and provided for a growing need. In a world overshadowed by a shameful war, it spoke of simple, necessary values. In short, of youth and love. It was no coincidence that the big Broadway success at the time was *Butterflies Are Free,* in which the young blind hero (a bodily affliction seemed an essential factor) fought off an authoritarian mother to find his way to romance with another quirky American girl.

The stupendous unexpected success of *Love Story* taught me a lesson. It was not to cleave to the old adage "Never ask for a job; never refuse one," for working on rubbish is both depressing and demeaning. Rather, to listen more astutely, not to one's advisers, but to one's own intuitions. As a result, I have subsequently tended to accept rather than refuse, and would now much rather regret the sins of commission than those of omission. Ironically, Pat had been asked to photograph on the film and I accompanied her to the Boston location. One positive outcome of this visit was an introduction to the film's publicist, Nicholas Meyer, a young man fresh from university who bubbled with intelligence and humor. He showed me some plays and scripts he had written. I was so impressed that I recommended him to my agent who signed him at once as a client.

It was odd to be unemployed in New York, an environment where work and industry are paramount. While I looked for a job, Pat went the rounds of specialists to try to ensure that, after the Indian experience, we could have children of our own. Together we launched on a minor social whirl that was highly enjoyable after the privations of the summer. I began to rationalize that I was in a profession from which there was no mandatory retirement—one could go on acting, given wits and health, until one dropped. So it was essential to use any involuntary free time with the same creative relish as if it were retirement time. Easier said than done!

We spent a great deal of pleasurable time educating eye and intellect in the art galleries of Madison Avenue and amidst the extraordinary treasures cramming New York's museums. We made our first art purchases, a passion that would grow by what it fed on. An early prized acquisition was an exquisite Klimt drawing of a female nude and, ever since, I have craved a Schiele counterpart.

For exercise we walked and I even indulged in the newly identified sport of jogging. Any self-satisfaction about my exertions, however, was instantly squashed by our doorman's pointing out that a fellow tenant, the astronaut John Glenn, habitually rose at dawn to orbit the park. My modest mid-morning circuit amidst the falling leaves and foraging squirrels seemed trifling in comparison.

A more serious workout was to be had at the park's open-air skating rink. I was first a casual, then a captive audience of its circling skaters, until an uncontrollable envy eventually drove me through the turnstile and on to the ice. With a growing confidence undiminished by impromptu plummeting falls, I graduated to a bravura circuit of the rink. My fellow skaters, mostly senior citizens, astonished me with the transformation that overtook so many of them. One old man—surely the original Hunchback in the Park—would hobble painfully to the ice and take off with the ease and grace of a spotlit ballerina. At weekends the kids invaded, exploding into the whirling confines like so many bladed dervishes.

Next door was the zoo. Smelly and cramped, it was a sad place and I tended to avoid it. There were too many other exiles like the buffalo and polar bears staring stonily across their shrunk, paved pasture. Only the sea lions sporting in their pool like velvet torpedoes seemed to obey Mr. Lindsay's dictum about having fun.

The cinema was a more congenial place. There was something deliciously indulgent about digesting lunch with a movie. We finally saw *Easy Rider,* but already it had been copied so many times that its acid-tripping scene was becoming as modish and clichéd as the now statutory nude romps and obligatory pot-smoking scenes. But Haskell Wexler's *Medium Cool,* with its scenes of police brutality at the Chicago Democratic Convention, demonstrated the violence that had overtaken the flower children everywhere. "Hell no, we won't go!" was chanted with growing vehemence.

"Students have formed a sort of terrorist group that bombards performances with tomatoes," Adrian wrote from Amsterdam.

> Not that they find the performances unacceptable, they want to break the system wide open, cause a revolution. The east wind is blowing. It has resulted in some strange goings-on: audiences sent home; actors jumping off the stage and laying about these self-appointed critics with their fists. Their criticism is all mixed up with a lot of half-hearted Marxism, about the theatre's place in society. They make me want to retire behind a protective cover of "old-pro-ism" and fight for the right to produce Noël Coward.

New York itself seemed to be in an equally constant state of revolutionary renewal. Outworn buildings met untimely ends in pulverized roars of protest. Scarcely before the dust settled a new upstart came howling into life rooted in the gaping hole. I remember watching mesmerized as a building opposite—destined to be the Park Lane Hotel—grew like a steel beanstalk at seemingly a floor a day. On the other side of the apartment a solid wall of buildings eclipsed the sun by day and replaced it with a thousand lights at night, with huge electric signs to distinguish the time and temperature. Noise was a constant factor: the rumble of subways, the officious sirens and the impatient snarls of trapped traffic. The warning whistles of the dynamite blasters would be followed by earthshaking booms and the thump of falling debris. We went to see *Oh! What a Lovely War* in a cinema situated next to an active building site and the bombardment outside marvelously enhanced that within.

It was hardly surprising that affluent New Yorkers should flee this inferno at weekends, commuting in lemminglike droves to rural and coastal retreats. But, as in London, I found the city was then at its best. Exploring it from the breezy Battery up through Wall Street, deserted on Sunday as if plague-struck, through the villages, ghettos and grand avenues, I began to share Pat's passion for this dynamic monster. The warmth of the New Yorkers was sufficient compensation for any environmental hardships although this was not immediately apparent. Communication had been conditioned to be direct, functional and fast. Little quarter was given to the obtuse or circumlocutory.

Taxi drivers were the chief exponents of this aggressive lingual shorthand and under their tutelage I became well qualified in the wit-sharpening skills of "answering back." The cab's caged grill may have protected the driver from being mugged but it afforded the passenger no protection against being assaulted with conversation. I learned more from these enforced tutorials than from any guidebook. America's very classlessness gave no limits to communication. The two Englishmen alone on a desert island who did not speak to each other because they had not been introduced would be inconceivable here. Anyway, to my astonishment I now found that I was saying "Hi!"

At Christmas the city wore a sentimental heart on its business sleeve, carols mingling with the tintinnabulation of tills. "There but for the grace of God go I," read the sign on the blind man blocking the Fifth Avenue flow of shoppers with his outstretched pencils. On Christmas Day it snowed and there was a "family" reunion of sorts —Franco Zeffirelli, Sheila his secretary and Ed Limato. But there were no jobs in my stocking. A proposed epic film about Benvenuto Cellini had been canceled four days before I was to depart for Italy. I had enjoyed researching the role—always an educative process—and the disappointment was keen. A request to be in a Broadway musical had similarly fallen through and I was secretly relieved: the thought of doing the same thing until June was still unattractive.

My mood, darkening with winter, was beginning to match the national malaise. Patience—like that emanating from Moondog, the famous Viking bum who stood all day on Seventh Avenue—was not my forte. That old restless urge to travel proving irresistible, we flew off to the Caribbean, meeting up again in Barbados with David Bailey and Penelope Tree, whose mother, Marietta, invited us to dine by candlelight in her beautiful beach house. Anthony Eden, that relic of a vanished, defeated Britain, was seen looking careworn in the garden of our hotel where clouds of little colored birds fought over the teatime sugar and biscuits. I learned to water ski and, in the teeming Technicolor reef of another hotel in Tobago, to scuba dive.

It was after spending an idyllic day here swimming and cooking fresh-caught fish on the deserted beaches with Norman and Wenda Parkinson that Pat received word that her sister Bobby was seriously ill. Rushing back to Europe, we were horrified to learn that her illness had been partly caused by pills prescribed by the same doctor who had almost killed Pat. The yoke of inauspicious stars clamped down harder with further bad news. Franco Zeffirelli had been smashed up in a car crash in Italy but, miraculously, had survived.

For the first time we began to feel like exiles shunting between hotel rooms in Paris, Amsterdam and Brussels, our lives confined to the dimension of suitcases. Joining us whenever school permitted, Rick lightened our spirits. Cut off from England, I valued my family even more. After sampling the melancholy beauties of Venice in winter, we moved down to Rome to visit Franco, who was recovering slowly from his injuries, and continued south to Morocco, staying in Winston Churchill's old winter haunt, the Mamounia Hotel at Marrakech. Its orange-blossomed gardens, silent except for the gurgle of water and the intrusive muezzin's calls, were a refuge from the great square that overwhelmed with a kinetic profusion of colors and cries.

We tasted *b'stilla,* the sweet pigeon pie, as well as bitter kif. Invited to a pot party, we were shown photographs of a group of young people, including the Rolling Stones' Brian Jones, on a drug trip. They are now all dead. It was not, as they say, my scene. Neither was it Pat's, although once in the innocent early sixties, while *Glamour*'s travel editor, she had taken LSD with Timothy Leary in order to write about the "ultimate trip." This disinclination was reinforced by her recent drug-induced brush with death. We both sought the high of good health.

On the drive north from Marrakech through snowy mountain passes and cedar forests, the highway was dominated by huge red trucks and buses that bore down on a certain collision course only to pull over at the last terrifying moment. Fez lay snug and compact in a hazy hollow, a homogeneous assembly of dazzling white buildings. All wheeled traffic stopped at its gates while within, the honeycomb of streets encompassed a hive of industry. Alongside the cacophony of hammering, beating and bartering, the mosques stood cool and dignified, their minarets guarded by solemn storks.

Tangier was like Justine's Alexandria, full of expatriates looking faintly ne'er-do-well with overt overtones of sexual promiscuity. We met the bejeweled and caftaned rulers of the mostly homosexual society centered on the casbah. Encounters with Kenneth Williams as well as the policemen, pubs and tommies in Gibraltar across the slender straits, gave a little nostalgic taste of home.

Our peregrination took us back to Rome, where Franco had asked us to stay with him, as in happier days, at his villa. Now, as then, he was, despite his weakness, host to a constant influx of guests who joined in endless games of canasta. For us the rootless joys of tourism were wearing thin. The winter seemed endless. I began to feel like the Anglo-Saxon Wanderer "crossing the watery ways and treading the tracks of exile." Pat continued to snap away but my employment prospects seemed ever elusive. I met with Sergio Leone about a film but the jinx persisted.

"You've been everywhere. We've been nowhere," Hal Prince wrote from New York. "Oh, yes, we did go to Eleuthera about the time you went to Barbados and I immediately was bitten by a swarm of bugs and had to return. The whole trip lasted less than 72 hours." He went on to say that the release date of our film was as uncertain as was its title. Hal's choice was *Fairy Tale,* others wanted *Nowhere in Particular,* which cruelly underlined our present status.

He was working on a new musical with Stephen Sondheim called *Company.* "I'm in rehearsal now. Have two more weeks to go until Boston. It's the goddamdest show. Funny and more than a little up-setting. It seems to get in all our craws—makes you re-examine so many things. All of this with the full knowledge that when it opens (if it 'works') they'll think it's this light comedy about nothing." I envied such industry and commitment.

Celebrating my twenty-eighth birthday in Rome, I felt far too young to be so professionally inactive and hors de combat like Gina Lollobrigida and Jane Russell, who shared Easter Day with us. It marked the end of our expatriate year, one rich in terrestrial journey-ing and, hopefully, in self-discovery as well. With eleven crammed suitcases and much emotional baggage, we finally returned home.

Eaton Terrace

CHAPTER EIGHTEEN

*W*e rented a flat amidst the generous gardens and exuberant trees of Eaton Square in Belgravia, a former swamp to which the Victorian master builder Mr. Cubitt had added stature. It was one of my favorite parts of London.

As if rewarded for returning to native soil, I found immediate employment in a film called *Zeppelin*. It wasn't a great role but a decent, workmanlike one, and after six months of inactivity, I felt a real need to exercise atrophying acting muscles and undergo that constant challenge to the confidence that is a stock-in-trade. I played a British officer in the First World War, gallantly fighting off the German threat in the form of a dirigible airship and Fraülein Elke Sommer, the film presenting a return to both aerial and Teutonic matters.

Being back at work was like taking a vacation. England was equally pleasurable, validating the old cliché about absence and fond hearts. Even after so short a time, things looked strangely unfamiliar and remarkable. Pat and I extended the German connection by buying a new Mercedes sports car—an automatic, my conversion a consequence of my American experience and Pat's poetic influence—which speeded the process of reacquaintance with country and countrymen. We drove down to genteel, cream-tea'd Devon where May and Joe now lived and swam in the arctic summer sea.

There was another encounter that would change our lives. In her continuing quest for perfect health, Pat was introduced to homeopathy by Hardy Amies, our New York landlord, himself a glowing advertisement for this branch of natural, drugless medicine. His physician was Dr. Chandra Sharma, a leading London exponent and, not uncoincidentally, an Indian. We had a guru again. Under Sharma's benign supervision we both began to practice this safe holistic regimen —learning the importance of considering the whole picture rather than localized symptoms and of the key principle of like treating like. We were also introduced to chiropractic, a twin weapon in the healer's armory. Ironically and tragically, it was during this time of enlightenment that Pat's sister Bobby died after her protracted illness primarily caused by chemical medicine. It made us even more determined to seek the alternative way.

During Bobby's long hospitalization, Rick came over from Paris and greatly comforted Pat and his young cousins. He had been working during the school holiday in a fragrance factory. Robbed of all his money and refusing to bother us for funds, he had been sleeping under a Parisian bridge with all the other vagrants. Ever selfless and generous, he manufactured for his mother a whole gallon jar of some extravagantly expensive perfume that was promptly confiscated at Heathrow. Having aroused suspicion, Rich was subjected to a humiliating body search and detectives were dispatched to Eaton Square to verify this young American's wild claim that we were his parents. Seeing Pat's youthful, sensual form wrapped alluringly in a nightgown, not to mention my own improbable paternal presence, they were hard put to disguise their incredulity. Complaining to the U.S. embassy, Pat was informed that harassment of young long-haired people here was widespread but nothing compared to that inflicted at home. "What's happening here you may well ask," Nick Meyer wrote from Los Angeles.

Well, for one thing, this country seems to be blowing itself apart at the seams. Nixon without telling anyone on the Hill (they had to read it in the paper the same as us poor slobs) invades Cambodia, even though his Secretaries of Defense and State are against it. Then all Hell broke loose on the campuses. And at Kent State,

Ohio, the National Guard blew its cool and shot into a crowd, killing four students. Positions here are being rapidly polarized; construction workers kick the shit out of demonstrators and shout USA—all the way quote unquote. The Nixon administration realizes it has gone too far. Would you believe me if I said I was cautiously optimistic about all this? We've been bumbling along in our unselfconsciously monstrous way, but I think the past ten days' shocks have really jolted us to the core. The thing has become a political issue at long last, and the kids are going to campaign for candidates who stand for getting out, etc. etc. Keep fingers crossed.

My battles at the time were fought from the air, heroically thwarting a dastardly German plot to capture Magna Carta in a Zeppelin raid. Most of the flying, though, was stage-bound apart from a spectacular headlong leap I made from the gondola of the crashing airship in Malta. We had gone there primarily to use its studio tank abutting the Mediterranean, giving the seamless illusion of being in mid-ocean. Its rocky shoreline also stood in, less successfully, for the muddy flats of Holland. Having been rowed out to the gondola suspended high above the tank I naturally thought that the water was deep enough to dive into. Foolish, nay, almost fatal, assumption! Seconds after hitting the water my head torpedoed into the tank's concrete bottom. Almost blacking out, I somehow managed to swim away sufficiently to complete the shot, despite the blood flowing into my eyes.

It rammed home a stern lesson and one often difficult to obey in the heat and excitement of shooting: stunts are for stuntmen. And even they are fallible. There was a near catastrophe on *Something for Everyone* when the stuntman doubling me—one of the best in his bizarre business—was dragged over a precipice in a plunging, crashed car. A simple stunt, he had shrugged, donning my chauffeur's uniform and boots. But as he tried to jump clear his leg became trapped in the door and only slipped out of his boot at the last terrifying moment. It instilled a healthy respect for this work and sympathy for the stories recounted about the legendary Victor Mature who, asked to climb a staircase, would meticulously check out each step.

While in Malta, we received a cable: "73 Eaton Terrace is available price subject to contract 31,500 pounds." This was a house we had looked at, loved, lost and lusted after with that heightened longing for the unobtainable. We cabled back a joyful "yes" and on our return it formally became ours. Like all those acquisitive characters whirling around me in *The Forsyte Saga*, I was now a man of property, feeling an instantaneous affection for this old place of which we had been granted temporary stewardship. It was a typical Regency terraced house with all the rooms piled on top of each other, an extraordinary feature of which was the garden room looking on to a rustic rectangle containing uninhibited shrubs, roses and a fish pond. Though just minutes from Piccadilly, we could have been in the depth of the shires. In my new cornfield there were many mansions.

Our terrace had a corner shop, pub and neighbors that included C. P. Snow, who could be seen plodding his corridor of power to post his letters. At one end was Pimlico with its village of bistros, antique shops and a house where Mozart had played. At the other was the house where Osborne and Pinter had played, that new home of British dramatic writing in Sloane Square, the Royal Court Theatre. Number 73, unlike its neighbors at the end where the new council flats stood, had survived the Blitz but had been left with a catalog of aches and pains and petty infirmities. We drew up plans to cure them.

Dwelling in every room and sleeping in every bedroom to get a feeling for how they should ideally be decorated, we made an early decision to restore the classic L-shaped drawing room previously chopped up into the master bedroom and bathroom. One entire wall became a bookshelf. There was ample room for his and her desks, Pat's being an extraordinary creation covered in her favorite tortoiseshell found in New York well before ecological awareness made such indulgence unthinkable. Between dealing with rising damp and bulging copings, I looked for the means to pay for it all.

The grapevine reported a film was to be made of Hal Prince's stage musical *Cabaret* and that they were looking for a "Michael York type" for the Isherwood role. I ventured to suggest that I might still possibly fit the bill. "I've now read the screenplay," my agent reported from New York, "and couldn't be more disappointed. He is straight, dull, square and boring as a character and has no songs. Really just support for Liza Minnelli so am proceeding cautiously." Putting this information in a mental pending file, I thought no more of it. Meanwhile Philippe de Broca invited me to return to Morocco later that year to be in his next film, a comedy adventure called *La Poudre d'Escampette*. The idea of working for the director of such distinctive comedies as *King of Hearts* and *That Man from Rio* was most appealing, but I was also eager to add another string to my professional bow—working in another language.

I was in my London agent's office discussing these plans when his phone rang. It was the new Thorndike Theatre requesting casting suggestions for their new production, *Hamlet*. Seizing the moment with a most un-Hamlet-like resolution, I proposed myself and was immediately accepted. In this year of renewal I was keen to tread neglected boards and give a taste of my quality and I was delighted that Joseph O'Conor, whose *The Iron Harp* had ignited my first professional ambitions, was announced as director. We were to rehearse for three weeks and play for another three in the smart new theater in Leatherhead on the outskirts of London named after that distinguished dramatic Dame, Sybil Thorndike. An octogenarian, she reputedly kept her memory fresh by learning a new poem every day. As well as I knew *Hamlet,* the tables of my memory were still dull with disuse. It had been a long time since I had embraced the disciplines of a major stage role.

Packing a text, I dashed back to New York for a screening of our Bavarian film, now finally entitled *Something for Everyone*—but, to keep the indecision alive, *Black Flowers for the Bride* for the British market. "Hal Prince, Angela Lansbury and Michael York have all made it together," winked the advertisement with just the right mixture of innuendo and amusement. It was strange to watch myself in a role that displayed attributes quite antipathetic to my own perceived personality, something akin to observing a total stranger. My portrayal of absolute unabashed amorality struck one reviewer as most credible and thus not a little frightening. Another painted a portrait that was equally—if disturbingly—arresting. "Nothing about him is conventionally cinematic: his nose is too large and spread, his lips too generously fleshy, one front tooth protuberant, his ears Gable-sized, his body muscled but thin and oddly proportioned." This depressing catalog was thankfully alleviated with the qualification, "But Michael York possesses other qualities that compel attention—his eye concentration, his control of gesture, his vocal inflections: and overall an aura."

The most arresting sight of all, however, was the line of moviegoers snaking round the block from the Paris Cinema (a lucky theater— *Romeo and Juliet* had triumphed there). It was gratifying to be a success in a country where this was both craved and rewarded. Reaction, consistent with the American character, was spontaneous and direct. I found myself referred to as a "star" and had no difficulty in obtaining good tables at restaurants and tickets for sold-out shows. Americans *liked* success. Zeffirelli once told me about the difference between failing artistically in the States compared to Britain. There people had bent over backward to acknowledge and appreciate his intentions, whereas his Broadway failure had been so complete that "even the dogs in the street refused to wag their tails at me!"

We commuted to Washington to spend a welcome day with Penny and Marek and their growing family. They were there for a year while Marek worked at a local hospital, and were loving the experience. Washington continued to focus the nation's tenseness, but the problems of rebellious youth gave an apt cue to my Hamlet, very much the student prince who grows into student activist.

Back in England, the play's limited rehearsal period should have benefited from my familiarity with the beloved words, words, words. But I often felt like Hamlet himself trying to recall Aeneas's tale to Dido, and like him experienced the same rush of excitement when, at last, they fell into place. They were now mine and each extraordinary thought would reverberate around the head, yielding new, unsuspected insights. For the first week of rehearsal, if not exactly "fat and scant of breath," I was catatonic with effort and jet lag. But as voice and body became accustomed to their new regimen the infinite pleasure of interpreting this most fascinating of roles took over.

O'Conor gave the production an updated setting of about 1520 so it was impregnated with the Spanish Catholicism then dominating Europe. This gave resonance to the play's religious overtones, its Christian bias exemplified by a huge Nordic cross that dominated the stage serving, with telling symbolic overtones, as altar, throne and bed. There was no possible way that this Hamlet could have killed a praying Claudius. The student aspect was suggested with an experiment, later abandoned, to play the "To be or not to be" speech as an exercise in academic logic, reflecting a contemporary passion for rhetoric and Shakespeare's own love of antithesis. Stating the basic argument to his fellow student Horatio, Hamlet proceeds to debate both sides of the issue: on the one hand suicide, on the other a means of enduring life, "being" as opposed to "seeming," two vital issues in the play.

Our efforts were warmly received. Both the local and the national press reflected approbation, apart from one, whose judgment and critical faculty seemed not to know hawk from a handsaw. The critic of the *Sunday Telegraph* took exceptional exception:

At Leicester, Leatherhead and Nottingham Hamlet will be played by respectively Messrs Peter McEnery, Michael York and Alan Bates. I shall neither see nor review these productions. What I object to strongly is the use of *Hamlet* as a kind of initiation rite: when used as a bait for film stars Hamlet is irresistible. No doubt the result is healthy for the box office and incredible though it seems, there must always be youngsters who have not seen the play previously. But the pretence at artistic significance must be shattered.

These wild and whirling words laid bare an arrogant absurdist assumption, a brainish apprehension, that these productions were for the exclusive edification of a tiny corps of critics. It ignored the fact that they were presented for a brief time in regional repertory theaters hundreds of miles apart, mostly for a local audience. "Film stars" we might have been but our financial compensation was hardly stellar. During rehearsals I was paid £6 a week, a fraction of my National Theatre salary and barely enough to provide petrol for the tiring daily journey to and from London. But it *was* healthy for the box office. Shakespeare and Co. proved a palpable hit, the entire run being sold out. Most of the ten-thousand-strong audience were schoolchildren seeing the play for the first time and hopefully sharing my Youth Theatre revelation, for many came back for more.

A few years ago I was delighted to come across an article in a theater program called "Everybody's Hamlet" by B. A. Young. After an examination of the multifaceted, multi-interpreted character of Hamlet he concluded,

This is no melancholy Dane, or existentialist undergraduate, or sensitive intellectual. This is a proud arrogant prince, longing for the chance to emulate his father and smite the sledded Polacks on the ice, perhaps kill Fortinbras in single combat. I have actually seen him in the person of Michael York at the Thorndike Theatre and very convincing he was.

Morocco Bound

CHAPTER NINETEEN

I cast my nighted colors off in the sun of Puerto Rico being photographed for an American magazine. The clothes provided were all for golf and this is the closest I have ventured to a sport that Mark Twain aptly described as "a good walk spoiled." It is a pastime I am saving for later, along with gardening and bridge. Any thoughts of dallying in the Caribbean were dashed by an urgent message from London that the director and producer of *Cabaret* were in town: could I absent myself from felicity a while and see them immediately? As it happened, I was still rather anxious to prove to the world that I was the quintessential Michael York type.

Returning via New York, we met up with Rick, who introduced his new girlfriend, a beautiful blonde Locust Valley aristocrat named Serena: our future daughter-in-law, although we—and, indeed, he—little realized it then. I went straight from London airport to the audition with Bob Fosse and Cy Fueur, who between them read all the roles including a gruff Sally Bowles. Auditions are a necessary evil but tolerable as both parties are mutually tested in this superficial encounter. Soon afterward I learned that Herr Issyvoo, now rather leadenly renamed Brian Roberts, was mine. But first in line was Ferguson, the comic British army officer I was to play in the French film starting the following week.

De Broca was short and wiry like a Gallic leprechaun and charged with a gleeful humor and energy. His only reason, he claimed, for making the film was a desire to winter in the sun. But one look at the natives wrapped from head to toe in thick wool made us realize that our suitcases full of summer clothes were hopelessly inappropriate. The climate, like the traditional stage Arab, was wily and treacherous. Costumes were hurriedly adapted and I went off to battle again, this time a Second World Warrior against Axis spies and the Afrika Korps.

Filming began in Rabat where Michel Piccoli, as an engaging black marketeer, and myself were chased by soldiers over the flat rooftops, only some miracle preventing us from literally dropping in for tea. As in India, the entire local population seemed to scrutinize our antics, refusing to *degager le champ,* despite entreaties yelled down "talkie walkies"—an odd Franglais inversion—by assistant directors. Their curiosity was justified: the usual absurdities were taking place.

While the sun blazed, we were drenched in artificial rain, only to pay for this willful manipulation of nature later by waiting half a precious day for an essential single sunny glimmer. Days off were spent by the sea where the cold, sardine-laden Atlantic sweeping down from the Pillars of Hercules pounded the rocky shore, filling the sky with thunderclouds of spray. Long walks along deserted beaches engendered appreciative appetites for the local specialities. The French might have departed but their cuisine lived on triumphantly, unlike in Malta where the British had bequeathed their enduring stodgy legacy of army grub.

This first experience of working with a French film unit was a revelation, especially their natural assumption that good food was as much a staple of life as breathing—or their universal Gauloise cigarettes, to which I became temporarily addicted. I was reminded of Rick's account of employment in his French factory where the early part of each morning was spent discussing the previous evening's meal. At mid-morning this switched to a contemplation of the forthcoming lunch, a critique of which occupied the afternoon until the approach of dinner enforced another conversational switch. Certainly a significant part of our morning was spent in the ritual shaking of hands with every member of the crew with an accompanying *"Ça va?"* Every weekend we took turns to offer the *"pot,"* the celebratory drink.

It is no accident that such words as joie de vivre, bonhomie and camaraderie have been borrowed from the French. They were omnipresent. This total immersion in French did wonders for the rest of my schoolboy vocabulary. I even began to have French *pensées,* although playing Ferguson with a deliberate, excruciatingly bad accent almost stopped my bilingual career in its infant tracks.

Freewheeling in our own car, Pat and I drove south to the Sahara through blossoming almond orchards, wild mountain passes, across even more parched plains and down into the valley of the river Ziz with its green flood of palms offset by battlemented casbahs. Here old men dozed against warm mud walls and the Berber women's jewelry and bright clothes seemed to compensate for the prevailing ochre tones. Here at last were Othello the Moor's mysterious "antres vast and desarts idle, / Rough quarries, rocks and hills whose heads touch heaven."

Erfoud was where the paved road stopped at the edge of the wilderness where a signpost read, "Timbuctou 36 days." The flat pink town was dominated by a fort on a rocky promontory and from its ramparts, a horizon in the welded emptiness of sky and sand could barely be discerned. Mellow sunshine alternated with howling sandstorms. Everyone took to wearing turbans, wrapping up the whole head and leaving a slit for the eyes that could be further protected— and embellished—with kohl. With our battered clothes and dusky eyes, Michel and I began to look like refugees from an Arab production of *Godot.*

Some film locations were so remote that we would fly there in a little plane that landed at random, creating a plume of dust and a nine-day wonder for any passing native. One set-up was so distant that the local Caid invited us to lodge overnight with his garrison soldiers in a desert fort. We dined splendidly on roast lamb and a couscous eaten by being hand rolled into little balls and flicked into the hovering mouth. Juliette Greco, then Michel's wife, was with us and added her celebrated voice to the chorus of songs around the fire. We slept on the floor and were woken to witness the fiery eruption of dawn—a sight more thrilling than anything our puny efforts could capture on film.

Mornings began with the essential sweet mint tea brewed by a small boy whose only job it was and who lugged around a huge kettle half his size. We also filmed amidst the great sand dunes for which the region is justly famed, whose shapes would be constantly rearranged by the shifting winds. The sun would chase out the long cold morning shadows, transforming the sand into a pink and purple ocean. By midday all was featureless in the fiery glare but at sunset when, as the French poetically put it, the light was "between dog and wolf," the chill beauty and mystery would return.

I was grateful to have Pat with me to share the unglamorous rough with the luxurious smooth. Having made a commitment early in our marriage to stay together, we had now established a pattern and I valued her unswerving support. Already I had seen too many relationships compromised by the demands of time and distance. Each movie was a little adventure and it was fun to evaluate it with such a compatible, life-enhancing sensibility. I knew now that if I told her, "We are going to China tomorrow," her response would probably be, "Why not today!" The endless ambient beauty drove Pat into paroxysms of photographic frenzy. With a young boy, Mahommed, as an assistant, she went everywhere in our faithful Renault 16. Following byways and tracks, and, as usual, never taking *non* for an answer, she ended up in spectacular places like the Glaoui's mountain fortress, delightedly recording the unself-conscious beauty of a people still in a natural rhythm with their environment.

Perhaps the strange biblical setting exaggerated the fervor with which Christmas was celebrated. There were tinseled trees, funny hats and whirling dances to jolly accordion music. Jojo, the amiable special effects man, made the night vivid with his pyrotechnical magic. Juliette dispensed manna in the desert, a huge pot of caviar being included in her baggage. We raided the souks for gifts, which were exchanged with as much excitement as if they had been Cartier bijoux. My childhood Christmas-stocking mandarin could be bought by the basketful. Selecting dates, however, we were advised to avoid the shiny ones, the delectable effect being achieved, it was rumored, by their vendors peeing on them! I went to buy Pat jewelry from an old lady immured within a catacomb of dwellings in a nearby ksar. Though veiled, she refused to do business in person, remaining doubly concealed on her roof terrace, displaying her wares through a hole and revealing the hard cleverness of a people who, though often illiterate, could use numbers like counters in a game. Pat was far more ruthless than me at bargaining. Having beaten down a price she would get justifiably annoyed when, feeling sorry and fortunate, I would spoil the game for both parties by paying the original sum demanded. She would later put her acumen to much more profitable use, supervising our business affairs.

Among my Christmas presents was an invaluable letter from Rick.

I've always wanted to write to you much earlier. Strangely enough, I couldn't quite rid the curtain that seemed to separate us. And yet now I no longer feel I'm obstructing or causing unnecessary conflict, I really enjoy seeing you both. I love the way you seem to pull me into your world. Through you I am able to see my dreams more clearly and, most important of all, I think I am finally able to speak of them. I loved your Hamlet because there was real feeling for us all to see. Your arrogance and cunning were superb. In fact there was no need to fulfill a conception of Hamlet because you were he. I see that as a match to your life as well as Pat's. I've seen her change so much for the better and happier with you, and it's just now I feel myself slowly moving ground. You never impose but, through your intensification I feel so much more together with you and Pat and with everything going on around me. Much much love.

Rick himself followed his letter after an epic two-day journey by bus. We had written to him that we were "12 hours" by road from Casablanca, which he had misread to mean between one and two hours and had casually caught a bus. After innumerable leisurely stops at every village, it halted for the night. Taking pity on Rick, the driver invited him to the local hotel, where communal hashish transformed the meager hostelry into some garden of Allah. My stepson, I was to learn, had a charmed habit of consistently falling on his feet. His infallible method of hitchhiking was to kneel and pray at the oncoming motorist. He once arrived in Paris at the wheel of a Ferrari with the owner dozing blissfully beside him, having handed over the keys that morning in the South of France. He turned up in Erfoud in lesser style, still reeling from the overnight hospitality. We were all thrilled to be *en famille* again, although Pat and I learned with a little parental dismay that the romance with the gorgeous Serena was already over.

The weeks elided into months, infecting us all with "desert fever" —the combined effects of a grueling schedule and close proximity. Taking me back again to those French youth hostels of yore, its main symptom was a predilection for practical jokes. There were silly schoolboy food fights. Hair disheveled, Philippe would pretend to sleepwalk through the long noisy *folklorique* evenings. Michel, dragged naked from bed into the crowded hotel bar, outfaced his giggling captors by refusing to turn a pubic hair, calmly remaining there to delight and shock tourists in equal measure. The pièce de résistance, however, was the spiriting of a baby camel up two flights of stairs and into the producer's bed. The joke was enjoyed by all but then began

to turn as sour as the droppings spraying liberally from the unfortunate animal as attempts were made to reverse the process. Impasse.
The hotel manager recommended butchering the beast on the spot,
resolving the problem and the week's menu at a blow. Western bleed-
ing-heart sentimentality prevailed, however, staying the execution,
and the stubborn beast was finally extricated from its malodorous
needle's eye.

The same soft sensibility motivated one of the camera crew to adopt
a scrawny dying puppy, which, pouched in a pocket of his overcoat,
he nursed back to health. But the joke was on him. When we met
months later, his life—and Paris flat—had been overwhelmed by a
now giant hairy canine the size of a small yak.

As we left Erfoud I took a long last look at the strange scene to
imprint it Isherwood-like on my mind since the odds of returning
seemed impossibly small. I should have known better than to challenge fate which, fifteen years later, brought us right back to the same
spot.

A postal strike in Britain emphasized the sense of isolation but
occasional letters would still get through the snows blocking passes
over the Atlas Mountains. Architects' plans for the house arrived for
approval. Every bedroom was to have a bathroom en suite with—yet
another American influence—showers. I heard from Hugh Wheeler,
who, to my delight, had been engaged to rework the *Cabaret* script: "I
have almost finished the script under incredible pressure. I *still* think I
like it. Ghastly pressures from ABC to bowdlerise it so far unsuccessful. *Love Story* has made them all convinced that all movies must now
be *Rebecca of Sunnybrook Farm.*" The Ophelia syndrome—"thought
and affliction, passion, hell itself, she turns to favour and to prettiness"
—seemed all-pervasive. Nick Meyer, now in Hollywood writing and
script-reading for a studio, wrote to me that he was planning a story
that would be inevitably successful. Called "Abraham Lincoln's Doctor's Boy's Dog," it incorporated every element dear to the sentimental American heart.

Ksar-es-Souk, a military town as unlovely as its name, was where
we made one of those cross-cultural gaffes born of equal ignorance
and politeness. The two of us were lodged with a local government
official whose hospitality was unstinted, his only demand in return
being a request not to smile at his servants. At the end of the day we
would return to a veritable mountain of food—everything it seemed
except sheep's eyes. And it was all to ourselves for our host was

conspicuously absent. Not wishing to offend, we tried desperately to do justice to this heavyweight banquet, forcing ourselves to feed like Strasbourg geese, little realizing that a whole hierarchic process was being thereby endangered. For our uneaten food fed our host, what he left nourished his family, the residue going to the unsmiled-upon servants and so on down the chain.

Our car was now an Aladdin's cave of bric-à-brac—candelabra, rugs, brass trays and rocks and fossils culled during those inevitable waits between camera set-ups. Driving down the spine of mountains through thickets of olive trees alive with nimble, Chagall-like goats climbing the branches to munch the oily fruit, we arrived at our final location, the Atlantic port of Essaouira. The location for Orson Welles's *Othello,* stern ramparts and towers thrown up by the Portuguese confined this dramatic town, the former Mogador, to a rocky promontory flanked by enormous beaches ringed with driftwood and mimosa.

It was now getting harder to see the schedule in any other terms than as a sentence to be patiently served. Civilization with a huge, gilded, flashing *C* began to call inexorably. We were out of touch. It was time to move on.

Life Is a Cabaret

Two weeks later we were back in Munich, our Mercedes greedily devouring the concreted kilometers spanning its motherland. Having bade a fond au revoir to raffish, endearing Ferguson, it was time to say *willkommen* to a total stranger, Herr Brian Roberts. Luxuriating in the confines of the Hotel Continental, I now gave my undivided attention to the screenplay of *Cabaret* . . . and was horrified.

Despite repeated, ever more desperate readings of the script, I could find no role to play. Isherwood had turned himself into a camera and his pallid screen doppelgänger, even though contemporary permissiveness now allowed his bisexuality to be overt, shared the same voyeuristic passivity. My American agent's warnings were amply fulfilled. I cursed myself for my arrogant pride in pursuing the role. Here was another introspective literate Englishman in the Darley mold, another dull foil to all the brilliant extrovert characters enlivening the story. I was furious with myself. Past experience had made me determined never to commit to a script about which I felt halfhearted, but somehow the difficulties of communication in Morocco and my usual obsessive involvement in the work at hand had botched this resolve. Reality now stared me rudely in the face.

That night I paced the damp city streets in panicky desperation wondering what to do. Besides being foreign to my nature to do so, it was too late to withdraw. I hardly knew Bob Fosse and, moreover, was reluctant to give him the impression of being a self-centered neurotic before filming had even started. I resolved to meet him and unburden myself of all these reservations.

To my relief and delight, Fosse—bearded, balding and blackly clad—agreed with me. He reassured me that he had intended to rehearse and review the dialogue during the two weeks scheduled for the song and dance rehearsals. Moreover, Hugh Wheeler would be there to supervise revisions. Relief blossomed into optimism. I met with my Sally Bowles, Liza Minnelli, and with Joel Grey who, small and dapper, was to re-create on film the role of the nightclub master of ceremonies he had famously played on stage. Then twenty-five, Liza was on the threshold of consolidating a multitalented career. Her huge eyes mascara'd into astonished spikes and framed by black hair bobbed in a Louise Brooks style, she was a compendium of high voltage energy and irrepressible spirits.

We set to rehearsing, embellishing and improvising. It was a happy time. Real characters slowly began to coalesce from their insubstantial textual and improvisational sources. Sally was now an American transplanted, like Louise Brooks, to Germany. My character was more recognizably English although I left unchallenged such distinct Americanisms as "horse's ass" for idiot, as this could be justified as coming from Sally's growing influence. In the same way when Bob later asked me to smoke a cigar when Sally announces she is to have a baby, it seemed churlish to argue that this was not an especially English way of celebrating.

We also used this time to assemble more authentic wardrobes for our now more authentic characters. My clothes seemed too stiffly tailored and unlived in. I asked if I could scavenge for some more appropriate things in the junk shops of London as I was briefly returning home while all musical numbers for the Kit Kat cabaret were being recorded. The King's Road provided rich trove—authentic old jackets and an ancient period raincoat. I also unearthed an old, worn camelhair dressing gown that had belonged to my father when a student in the 1930s, the same era as our film. Gwen Verdon, then Mrs. Fosse and Bob's unofficial muse and tireless helpmate, used her dancer's experience and instinct to help Liza assemble Sally's eclectic wardrobe.

Back in London, Pat and I saw twenty films and innumerable

friends. We attended the premiere of *Zeppelin,* which, to my relief, was
not shot down in flames. "What a gas!" was one enthusiastic reaction,
reminding me of "Me no Leica," the famously brief review of one of
Cabaret's sources, *I Am a Camera.* After supervising the initial building
work on the house, we returned for the start of filming which, appropriately enough, was in the Kit Kat Klub itself, re-created in Munich's Bavaria Studios. Pat delighted me by elaborating into a
tradition something begun with *Hamlet*—an apt and thoughtful
good luck present. For the gloomy Dane it had been an ivory skull
seal from the Danish Royal House. For the ingenuous Brian it
was a remarkable pen drawing of Christopher Isherwood by David
Hockney.

Looking more like George Grosz caricatures, the technicians quaff-
ing early morning steins of beer prepared my first scenes where, glass
of beer also in hand, I sat in the cabaret reacting to the songs that had
now been put on guide track. They included new ones such as "Maybe
This Time" and "Mein Herr," again with lyrics by Fred Ebb and music
by John Kander. Word of their brilliance had already got out and my
delighted response was totally unfeigned. Our extraordinary, unassuming cameraman, Geoffrey Unsworth, filled the set with his ravishing, subtle lighting, diffusing it with a thick fog of smoke. Outside,
the pristine May sun shone in a brochure-blue sky back-lighting the
fresh young greenery. It seemed almost irreligious to be shut up in
this choking, tawdry confine with its overpowering scent of cheap
perfume and old clothes.

There was also a heavy smell of Big Money. The contrast with our
freewheeling French film could not have been starker, although they
had similarly slim budgets. *Cabaret*'s was a modest $4 million, over a
quarter of which had already been spent on the rights to the story.
"Money, Money, Money"—another new song—supplied an appropriate leitmotif. The production was supervised by a legion of producers and assistant producers and innumerable assistants assisted by
their assistants.

Bob Fosse, I soon realized, was under a certain pressure to prove
himself. His earlier film musical, *Sweet Charity,* had failed—financially,
that is. He later admitted to me he had fallen in love with the zoom
lens, allowing his camera to dance too much. The lesson had been
learned. With viewfinder worn like a talisman he was a coiled dynamo
of charged energy. Lean and squintily watchful through the haze of
smoke from the permanent cigarette, dragged down to the butt that

tinged his mustache with a yellow aureole, he was the antithesis of the *danseur noble*. Yet his angular, sexy choreography matched the Brechtian mood of the cabaret, a perfect expression of a disjointed time epitomized to perfection by Joel Grey as the leering, omniscient MC. Indeed, Fosse's achievement was to make the sleaziness of the cabaret believable while at the same time showcasing the improbable brilliance of the performers in it. He put to good use his studies of Grosz and Otto Dix, who had similarly employed their genius to depict decadence with artistic élan.

Back in Munich, Pat and I had originally intended to rent accommodation in the city, reasoning that our recent Saharan stint and previous Bavarian idyll had exhausted all enthusiasm for rustic living. The city center, however, was still being noisily disemboweled for its Olympic duties and we fled to its forested fringes, to Isherwood's "millionaire's slum" of Grunwald close by the studio where owls hooted from the encircling firs.

Our new home came with a charming motherly housekeeper, a dog and a garden. At weekends there were long walks in the forest, museums, the occasional opera and more ambitious outings in the car. We went to visit Rick who was also in Germany, at university in Heidelberg. Compounding the coincidences that seemed to be rapidly becoming a feature of our lives, he was living in Bönnigheim, the village where an adolescent Penny and I had stayed.

The weather continued fine. This was fortunate as we were filming outside as well. These sequences included "Tomorrow Belongs to Me," the only musical number not confined to the cabaret itself, and which found me back in a Bavarian beer garden engulfed in emotional song. The young man who sang this rousing hymn to the fatherland almost missed the chance through great reluctance to have his dark hair cropped and dyed to an appropriate Aryan hue.

Watching this scene being filmed, I couldn't help wondering what the extras who had lived through this traumatic period must have been thinking. The young, I found, had few problems or guilt about the war. My German co-stars, Helmuth Griem and Fritz Wepper, for example, could discuss it objectively and unemotionally. But others who had actually tasted the triumph and tragedy were more equivocal. Fosse captured this ambivalence by sending his talented camera operator, Peter MacDonald, to roam around the set, quietly and unobtrusively in the Isherwood manner, with a handheld camera recording random reactions. The face of one old man in particular seemed to express a haunting mixture of disillusionment and reluctant pride. Like Mother Courage, he had seen it all.

I felt the same curiosity later in Lübeck, where morning commuters arrived to find the station, standing in for the Berlin Hauptbahnhof, filled anew with swastika'd Nazis. Filming there exemplified all the schizoid nature of the craft. One take had me arriving in Berlin fresh-faced and optimistic; in the very next I was leaving, head full of the experiences that would find initial immortality in print. I managed to work in the phrase "Goodbye, Berlin" in genuflection to Isherwood, but it got lost in the final edit.

Rapport with other actors was unusually close. Liza, a tireless perfectionist, was a constant joy to work with. She seemed to share much of the literary Sally's quixotic caprices. Like Herr Issyvoo before me, I tried to keep her earthbound. She was a real partner. Her off-screen lines were played with the same intensity as her on-camera ones, a by no means invariable situation. She was always open to the unexpected. Once, in the tea party scene, a sandwich I passed accidentally flew off the plate and into her lap. Staying in character, her reaction is a joy to behold.

When I first met Marisa Berenson she was wearing hot pants—what her grandmother, the couturière Schiaparelli, might well have described as "shocking"! In this latest fashion zenzation, the female glorification of lederhosen, it was hard to imagine her transformation into the virginal Natalie Landauer who would eventually find true love on her father's library sofa. Fritz Wepper had just started playing a young police officer in a TV cop show. He's still there today—promoted and popular—astonishing me with the inimical notion of an actor playing one role for his entire career. I wish I could have played more scenes with Joel who, offstage, was the antithesis of his grotesque on-screen persona.

Life in Grunwald soon settled down to regular suburban routine. Proximity to the studios had its rewards. My call sheet would read, "Pickup 8:20. Makeup 8:30." I often walked through the budding groves to work. Pat would bring me delicious homemade salad lunches in my dressing room. Studio food was stodgily functional at best and I enjoyed this quiet time. It was difficult to describe how tired one can get after a day of concentrated make-believe, and Brian and Berlin invariably made way for a more bourgeois litany of broth, bread, book and bed.

On set there was never any time for us actors to sit around idly while the technicians were busy. Fosse would use these moments to improvise around the scene about to be filmed, often coming up with invaluable new insights that gave further dimension to our characters. Invariably, by the time the set was ready he had brought us all to a creative boil. This process continued with the daily rushes. He encouraged us to view the results of our labors—again, a by no means automatic practice. Open to ideas, he often shot a scene according to the actors' suggestions, and then shot it his way. At the rushes he would select a preferred version. When the choice was not self-evident he often had the confidence to reject his own version and choose another's, always explaining his reason for doing so. It made everyone feel an essential part of a creative process rather than performing animals jumping through hoops at some ringmaster's command. Experiencing a rare rapport with him, I often anticipated his directions. I found myself smoking to please him. He seemed to identify with me more with a cigarette similarly stuck in my mouth. Pat told me she had never photographed anyone who had such complete concentration.

There was only one occasion when I saw him resort to subterfuge rather than inspired reason to get an effect. It was at the end of a long, exhausting night shoot when Marisa was reacting to the killing of her dog by Nazi thugs. She had painstakingly registered shock and horror in repeated takes but still Fosse wasn't satisfied. Without telling her, he sent for a bowl of butcher's offal and, placing it by the camera, provoked a reaction of spontaneous, genuine revulsion.

There was only one occasion, too, when I refused to obey Bob's direction. It was at the climactic moment where, warming to each other as people and not as sex objects, Sally and Brian make love for the first time. The script had us both looking down to register my tumescent member while I expressed my delighted surprise in a rousing Shakespearean quotation. Declining to do this, I felt intuitively that it cut across the real feeling that had been established on which the whole plot, with its ensuing plans for marriage, was predicated. In the film, Liza does look down, but this can be interpreted as a moment of rare and touching modesty! Later, I asked Christopher Isherwood if he had in fact gone to bed with Sally Bowles. Once, he had replied, when the flat had been overfilled with friends. But there had apparently been no accompanying shouts of triumph, Shakespearean or otherwise!

One other disobedience occurred after filming the difficult "screw

Max" scene when we were asked to provide a euphemistic alternative for television consumption. Outraged by this request, Liza and I determined to perform the bowdlerized version so badly it could never be used, forcing adherence to the original. Of course it *was* used and I still wince when I see it.

After the double incarceration of filming in a building within a building it was good to get out the suitcases and go off "on location," first to Schleswig-Holstein where Schloss Eutin was used as the baron's castle. We all stayed at a ponderously grand hotel whose vintage wines were suddenly and mysteriously unavailable after Liza had mischanced to order a Coca-Cola with dinner.

In the castle one of the film's most powerful moments was conceived. Unscripted, it occurred during the "divinely decadent" episode when Sally and Brian are the baron's guests. In the cold early morning we gathered to improvise in the main salon, a vast room with huge fireplaces at either end. As the fires began to blaze, so did the creative forces. In the course of that long, extraordinary day a whole sequence was invented that culminated in the three principals' faces interlocking in a revolving triangle with looks speaking more poignantly than any improvised words.

We also had a tart taste of contemporary German cabaret at one of the sleazy sex shows on Hamburg's neoned Reeperbahn. My encounter with Elke the transvestite in the men's lavatory was nothing compared with the Salambo Sex Show's extraordinary perversions. Pat and I sat there with Liza and her boyfriend in glum, disheartened silence especially after overhearing the manager berate a black American "artist" for failing to perform with his contractual frequency. Perhaps *he* should have tried some Shakespeare.

Filming was completed in Berlin itself. To my astonishment, there were still prewar buildings within the new glass and steel metropolis where, as Isherwood had described, "street led into street of houses like shabby monumental safes crammed with the tarnished valuables of a bankrupt middle class." Charlottenburg Castle, where we shot a scene, later cut, with a boys' choir, was still miraculously intact along with all its precious porcelains. Even more extraordinarily, we were able to capture some of the film's most rustic sequences amidst the lakes and tree-lined cornfields on the city's fenced-in outskirts. But when we saw the infamous wall for the first time, in appropriately dismal pouring rain, it was impossible not to shudder at this grotesque concrete slap in the face of freedom.

As usual the last scene in the can was one occurring early in the story where Brian, encouraged by Sally, abandons his inhibitions by joining her in screaming under a railway bridge. This time my yell was an unequivocal shout of exultant joy.

At a celebratory dinner, Bob Fosse let slip some of the devilish, driven quality that went hand in glove with his usual good nature. Going around the table, he asked the assembly for their opinion of him. It was like Lear asking which daughter loved him most. While some eulogized him fulsomely, the British contingent were as tongue-tied as Cordelia, and sat silent in stiff-backed embarrassment. I murmured some evasion, not wishing to spoil what had been a wonderfully enjoyable relationship and work experience. Fosse didn't press me and it merely confirmed my conviction that he possessed Cocteau's definition of genius, "the ability to know how far to go too far." We stayed friends, and he was constantly caring and supportive. I am only sorry that I was unable to fulfill his expressed desire to film me in the role of—to use his own ambiguous words—a "mean dick"!

We drove home by way of Nuremberg where the birth of its favorite son and one of Pat's favorite painters, Dürer, was being celebrated. There were other more infamous associations. The weed-strewn parade ground where the Nazi machine, in such discreet background in our film, had first menacingly stirred and then theatrically strutted, was also visited. Here in one town, where retribution for such corrupted ambition had been meted out, was an exposition of the twin poles of the German genius.

Two days after returning home we were off again, this time back to Italy, seduced anew by the telephonic siren song of that old tempter, Franco Zeffirelli. He poured out a story, claiming to have searched the world for a suitable actor for a crucial role in *Brother Sun, Sister Moon,* his forthcoming film about the life of St. Francis of Assisi, but in vain.

"All right, what is it?" I eagerly interrupted, swallowing the bait and wondering vaguely if tonsuring the head hurt.

"A leper."

Francis, it seems, had once demonstrated his saintliness by embracing a leper and this was the scene that, covered in filthy rags and sores, I found myself enacting in the grotto of a waterfall near Terni. To my surprise, the episode was most moving to play. Having completed it, I was summoned to Franco's hotel room, now transformed into a

Sicilian bandit's lair. A pile of glittering watches littered the bed and he asked me to pick out one in payment for my services. Knowing how slim the budget was, or perhaps influenced by Francis's precepts about worldly goods, I chose a modest one. Franco would have none of this. He insisted I take a slim, jewel-embedded watch, perhaps anticipating—correctly—that I would think of him whenever I donned it with black tie. There would be no other memorial to my labors for my scene was cut from the film's final version. "Heard melodies are sweet. Those unheard are sweeter," I hope.

Pat's Gypsy prophecy continued its furious fulfillment, her influence extending to May, Joe and Caroline, who made their first trips to the United States. The year also witnessed my grandfather's eightieth birthday. He had doubled his life expectancy on retirement and celebrated by returning to work part-time in the pathology laboratory of a Brighton hospital. The child is the father of the man, and like his infant grandson he also made a great bonfire of memorabilia. On a fleeting, fortunate visit, Pat and I managed to rescue some precious photo albums from this smoldering pyre of his past. Other family photos—particularly one of May and Irene in Japanese fancy dress that I remember enchanting me in my grandparents' bedroom—were destroyed. This rigid unsentimentality, however, had its limits. When they brought him a suicide's brain to examine in a biscuit tin he was uncharacteristically unnerved, and retired anew to the beauty of his roses.

"I hope your house isn't out of date by the time it's finished—like London airport," Adrian cautioned, referring to the slow work on No. 73. A possible reason for the delay was revealed when, returning from Germany, we surprised the Irish painters who had obviously discovered our cache of liquor. I have rarely witnessed such falling-down drunkenness—not even on stage! The real culprits, though, were ourselves: we were too seldom at home to check and supervise.

A few days after picking off my last leprous sore, we found ourselves in Russia at the Moscow Film Festival. Slumped in our shabby room, buried among three thousand others within that pentagon of a hotel, the Rossia, I paused to reflect what on earth—indeed what the hell—we were doing. True, the house was not yet fully habitable, but was it necessary to go so far to find alternative accommodation?

My natural curiosity and carpe diem enthusiasm, however, had been fanned by Pat's own ardor. She had gone to Russia in the mid-1960s to write a story for *Glamour* and on her first night there had met

Dominique Lapierre, then a correspondent for *Paris Match*. Few doors remained closed to his charm and tenacity. He took her everywhere and she met everyone, from Maia Plisetskaia to a surgeon who had grafted two heads onto a dog. Once she left something behind at the model apartment she had been inspecting and returned to find that several families had already moved back in.

At that time travelers had to use prepurchased coupons for meals, but having been so generously treated, Pat had been unable to spend a single one. So she expended her entire hoard on one spectacular party. A piano was installed in her room and, while prerevolutionary songs were sung until dawn, caviar was served alongside the latest culinary rage, Baked Alaska. The piano, we were recently reliably informed, is still there. Thanks to Dominique, her resultant story was so unusual, especially appearing at the stultified height of the Cold War, that *Newsweek* promptly offered her a job.

Both Pat and I loved Russian things. As a wedding present she had given me some exquisite Fabergé cuff links inset with the Romanov double-headed eagle. They were purchased from Wartski, where we used to go to marvel at their Russian stock over a glass of Mr. Snowman's best vodka. I myself felt immediately at home in Russia and, especially in the streets, had an extraordinary feeling of kinship. Years later Alan Bennett sent me a photograph of some Russian steel workers in Pittsburgh at the turn of the century. It provoked an involuntary double take, for there I was, eerily staring out of it.

The weather was spectacular—far too good to be incarcerated indoors in the dark looking at fabricated life when all Moscow waited to be discovered. We marveled at Fabergé eggs in the fabulous museums and ate chicken Kiev under the chandeliers of the National Hotel. We licked ice cream in the sunshine of Red Square and lined up for the main attraction—Lenin's mausoleum—still playing after all these years. It was here that the cult of personality really exerted itself: *I* was stopped for autographs.

It was the perfect illustration of the fruitful juxtaposition of timing and location. The BBC's epic tale of bourgeois capitalism, *The Forsyte Saga,* was playing back to back on Soviet TV with our visit coinciding precisely with the transmission of my brief episodes. I was suddenly another kind of Red Star, even being presented with little bouquets.

We tried to travel farther afield. A recent reading of Troyat's superb biography of Tolstoy—Tolstoyan in its drama and scope—still reverberated in our minds and we managed to pay homage to the great man at his country estate at Yasnaya Polyana. Donning huge felt overshoes we shuffled around the house, afterward murmuring a prayer at his grassy tomb.

Attempts to get even farther, to Leningrad, however, were repeatedly thwarted by immovable Intourist, making us thank providence for our ability to cross exterior frontiers at will. I was curious to go there, especially as one of my Higginbottom ancestors, James, a Derbyshire man, had worked there in the eighteenth century as a renowned engraver. But we left neither empty-headed nor empty-handed. A taxi driver who stopped for us in the rain—not because he had to, he told us, for he was paid the same whether or not he picked up fares, but "because I like your face"—offered to sell us an icon. We took a gamble, offering him my watch and all the money we were carrying. In best Le Carré style he drove into a darkened street and pulled out from under the taxi floor an exquisite enameled bronze crucifixion scene. Its beauty was only marginally enhanced when it was later authenticated as being genuine.

England Made Me

*A*s the summer progressed, our house bloomed with embellishment. It bristled throughout with smart coconut matting while the dining room's ugly wood floor had been painted to create a luxurious *faux-marbre* effect by an artist using a simple feather. Thick-piled carpets tranquilized the bedrooms. A dark stairwell was transformed into a romantic tent and in the garden room a bright jungly wallpaper and fabric, full of leafy greens and flowery pinks, competed with the tamer foliage outside. Antique pieces and traditional Lenygon and Morant sofas and armchairs—the overstuffed aristocrats of their breed —were mixed with the latest lucite, glass and chrome tables and Bauhaus chairs all set on a white fur rug.

But our sitting room was to provide little sitting. After so much disconnected dashing around we decided to take a conventional, restful holiday in Greece. This presumption of making long-range, offstage plans soon caught up with us. Just before leaving for Lemnos I was offered a role in a film of Graham Greene's novel *England Made Me*, which threw me into a dither of indecision. On the one hand I was work-weary, but on the other the project was an interesting one.

Moreover, the film was to be made in a country that neither Pat nor I had visited, Yugoslavia, although conditions there were such that an organization called Yugoslavs Anonymous was rumored to exist. If offered a film assignment there, you could contact them to be talked out of it! However, the screenplay concerned the adventures of a young Englishman in prewar Nazi Germany. This, I felt, was over-familiar territory and a change of—well, trains—was in order.

But turning down work was an increasingly cruel task. To be objective, I needed to get away. Agreeing to think about it on the flight, I resolved to call with a decision that evening. At the airport bookstall the very first volume my acquisitive eyes alighted on was a paperback version of *England Made Me,* its jacket staring challengingly back at me. I bought it—and sealed my fate—for, by the time the plane landed, Greene's narrative skills had me in their thrall. Cutting our holiday short, we returned home. Anyway, I have always preferred proscribed to unlimited leisure.

Learning that Peter Finch and Michael Hordern had joined the cast redoubled my new enthusiasm, and a funny exasperated letter from Hugh Wheeler, painting an ever more negative picture of States-side film production, made me doubly glad about my new employment:

I'm still piddling around with the television pilot which has now become the center of such farcical intrigue, counter-intrigue, power playism etc. that it is no longer relevant whether it is good or bad but merely contingent upon which warring cadre wins out in a struggle for precedence among vice-presidents in Hollywood. I have never before written for a medium in which writing has nothing to do with it. The paradoxes are staggering. They start off wanting an "original" idea—in this case an utterly unoriginal one but original in their minds—*then* should it be handled with any sort of freshness they become gibberingly panicked because all of their computers say it doesn't fit into any already petrified category. The next move is a desperate attempt to mold the "original" idea more closely into their formula. This still—to their amazement—doesn't pass the guardians of the pre-tested. The third attempt is not only virtually, but *exactly* similar to the "unoriginal" formula which they claimed they wanted broken. And over and above this basic theme are ten million overtones. Everyone makes ten thousand secret phone calls plotting, planning and interpreting. I could gladly forget the whole thing if it were not for the fact that the theatre and the movie-movie are rapidly disappearing and, more than possible, the future may involve television and television alone. And then where will one be?

America was also in sharp focus in letters from Rick, now in New York studying at Columbia University. To earn his keep there, he was also well on his way to earning a master's degree in the University of Life. At night he drove a cab and was also a patient in a laboratory monitoring dreams. As he was also a part-time sperm donor these should have been unusually vivid especially as, Rick informed us, every sort of literature was provided to give erotic stimulation—even the *Wall Street Journal!* His observations betrayed the sensibility of a born filmmaker:

> I live on the "fascinating, compelling, must-not-be-missed" image of N.Y. It's full of crazy things unique in their immediacy and scope. If you don't like what you see, you change the focus, write a different script, edit out the confusion and change the whole movement, the sounds you want to hear. I feel I've become a working zoom lens focusing in and out of every activity that comes my way. N.Y. will always be incomprehensible.

It was interesting to go from the divine decadence of Isherwood to the world-weary cynicism of Greene, both writers shrewdly portraying the disaffection that gripped the 1930s. Sweden had been the novel's original background but the film's German setting was justified by a comment Greene later made about this early work written in 1935 that it was "clouded by the Depression in England and by the rise of Hitler." It was also curious to return so soon to prewar Nazi Germany, a journey I would now continue to make on repeated occasions.

England Made Me was, like *Cabaret,* a story of a triangular relationship, this time between a feckless young Englishman, his authoritative sister and her industrialist lover. Tony sponged his way through life and around the world, outwardly affecting a phony Eton tie as a social passport, inwardly conscience-stricken by an unexpected streak of schoolboy decency that made inevitable his own prediction about himself: "I have no future." The ruthless new order that was sweeping the world left little place for moral scruples.

Filming began in President Tito's villa on Lake Bled in northern Slovenia, amidst golden autumnal trees and spiky mountains. The imposing marbled pile had been newly converted to a hotel so that

one could almost literally fall out of bed and onto the set. Apparently
Tito was a great movie buff—he had films screened every evening
after dinner—and allowed us also to use his magnificent 1928 Horch-
Auto Union parade car captured by partisans during the war. It had
been a gift from Goering to Rommel, the latter a character that I would
play some eighteen years later, back in Yugoslavia parading around
in the same car.

The years of Hapsburg rule in Yugoslavia had stamped this area of
alpine chalets, meadows and rococo churches with a distinct Teutonic
character that made it a creditable substitute for Germany. Moreover,
the Istrian town of Opatija stood in equally convincingly for an opening sequence in an as-then unravaged South of France. Days of sunny
weather assisted the illusion, the trompe l'oeil allowing for lazy summer beach scenes despite the lateness of the year. Winter caught up
with us in Belgrade. The gray city lowered under grayer skies.

Having again brought our own car, we used every spare moment
to explore, one weekend driving to Sarajevo, with its mosques and
minarets and ineradicable "Historical Significance." For the return
journey we decided to take a spectacular mountain road that squiggled
its way back across the map to Belgrade. An anticipated afternoon's
pleasant scenic drive turned into a nightmare switchback ride over
furiously undulating unpaved roads. Dusk fell like a thick blanket over
the bare mountains and the car's swiveling headlights would pick out
dizzying chasms and, once, an ancient stone bridge beautifully spanning some unnumbered torrent. We reeled back into Belgrade an
exhausted panicky instant before I was due on the set that morning.

Less ambitiously, we drove out for Sunday lunch at the national
monument perched on top of one of Belgrade's surrounding hills.
Snow was prettily falling as we corkscrewed our way up but, by the
time our meal was finished, the road had turned into a ski slope. As I
ventured gingerly downhill, the car took off like a bobsled skidding
sickeningly sideways and slaloming into a ditch. No sooner were we
pushed out and moving again than, to my growing embarrassment,
the same thing happened. An obliging Montenegran then offered to
help, claiming he knew these conditions well, and especially how to
drive an automatic down what was now rivaling the Cresta Run in
vertiginous iciness. Agreeing, I yielded up the useless steering wheel
whereupon he threw himself behind it and the car into gear, plunging
down the slope with Pat wide-eyed beside him. Eventually at the
bottom I saw no sign of either and, tales of ravishment fleeting alarm-

ingly through my imagination, I made my slow way back to town. To my relief both wife and car awaited my benighted return and seemed none the worse for the adventure, which Pat likened to being kidnapped by a maniac racing driver. A begrudged gratitude overwhelmed my outrage.

It was difficult not to like these people. They were strong and gutsy, hardened by conflict and dissension. In the whole history of their country there had been only eight years free from warfare. Indeed, their film industry seemed committed to an endless retelling of the story of the people's heroic struggle. I often wondered if some of the Yugoslav actors kept their own jackboots and Nazi uniforms at home, so often were they in demand. Anxious questions were now being asked as to what would happen when Tito finally went to the great projection room in the sky, and the threat from Russia—a great cohesive force on the disparate states—was removed.

Filming was much more enjoyable than anticipated, perhaps because of the resourcefulness of our director, Peter Duffel, who squeezed every iota of value from a minuscule budget of less than a million dollars. He could think on his feet and invent cinematically. Seeing Rijeka harbor full of ships he improvised an arrival for my character down the gangplank of a steamer—the perfect expression of Tony's rootless gadabout nature. Finding out that there were lumbering Russian biplanes still in use that resembled prewar transports, he immediately changed a scene from a railway station to an airport, a single flat propped up in a field ingeniously suggesting an entire waiting room.

He encouraged us to be inventive, too. It was always a pleasure to see a little bit of personally devised business being remarked on by critics, as in the moment when Tony leaves some coins for a phone call and seconds later furtively retrieves them. I also became involved with reworking the script, returning to the Greene original whenever possible.

I especially enjoyed filming with my old *Shrew* stepfather, Michael Hordern, who was in fine scene-stealing form as Minty the down-at-heel Old Etonian journalist who lives off the scraps of information he shamelessly scrounges. Offstage, I helped him learn his lines for Tom Stoppard's *Jumpers,* guiding him through the tortuous maze of choplogic and surreal philosophy that was to provide his next triumph at the National Theatre.

Peter Finch was also someone I admired. A performer on a world stage, he seemed, like Bogarde, to have matured into an actor whose fine-tuned talent and experience made what he did look easy. Working with him was also enjoyable. He had a fund of good-humored theatrical stories although I was most affected by his tales of life on walkabout in the Australian outback. At night some of this geniality would retreat under the assault of alcohol, especially when he was left defenselessly on his own. The naughty boy lurking beneath the leonine maturity would rudely poke out his tongue. Whenever his wife, Elitha, and their little daughter joined him, however, he became a model of paterfamilial sobriety and good behavior. A secret smile would play sphinxlike on his lips hinting at mischiefs past and present.

Often during the filming I had a déja vu sense of being back on the *Cabaret* set, especially during a street scene of a Nazi parade complete with marching band and banners. This was intensified when I dubbed *Cabaret* in a tedious session at a local film studio where the equipment had a similar period flavor.

This postsynchronization process is usually a most enjoyable one, providing an opportunity to alter, embellish and, hopefully, improve the performance. The strident can be softened and the unassertive emphasized. Extra dialogue can be sneaked in over long shots, and in close-ups, too, providing it matches the mouth's movements. "Yes" can virtually be turned into "no." I especially enjoyed the French system where some scribe painstakingly wrote out the dialogue by hand to run in a band under the screened picture like a demented subtitle. As long as each syllable was enunciated precisely as it coincided with a marker, perfect synchronization was guaranteed. *Voila!* This arcane skill reminded me of the essential contribution of those other unsung specialists who dub in footsteps to match footfalls.

The charms of London life agreeably reasserted themselves, in a house that was finally a home. We were now ready to entertain in our little marbled dining room hung with warm paisley fabric and a collection of Indian miniature paintings begun with a parting gift from Jim and Ismail. An octagonal Regency table, trove from a Sidmouth visit and Pat's especial dowry of Steuben glassware and Flora Danica porcelain —most of it looted in transit from New York—looked especially fine.

Downstairs a fire blazed in an open grate, while getting there from the bedrooms provided wonderful daily exercise. We unpacked and commingled our books. Some of Pat's had now cost a small fortune in their transatlantic shuttle but she, like me, had found it almost impossible to throw away a single one. A fourteenth-century carving of a Japanese monk enhanced the serenity of the library.

There was, inevitably, a new legacy and pattern of friendship. Physical separation had taken its toll, but also a certain healthy natural attrition had occurred. Hoops of steel, of course, bound many long-adopted friends. Zeffirelli was often in town but, true to directorial form, Franco was much better at being a host than a guest and loved to surround himself with friends for Chinese food in Limehouse. Adrian I saw too little of, but we corresponded regularly.

Among our new friends was a Chelsea neighbor, Ned Sherrin, whom I had first met at Oxford after a performance of *Prometheus*. At the cutting edge of contemporary gossip, he was now the undisputed emperor of TV satire. Hal Prince and Stephen Sondheim came by when they were astonishing London with the gritty sophistication of *Company,* the musical about the mating games of contemporary New York, that had succeeded in getting not only into Hal's but into everyone's craw. The adventures of its footloose hero hopping, heartstrings untied, from one relationship to another was a world away from Pat's and my experience. We were complete in ourselves, a functioning unit and permanent partners in the dance to the music of time. Although we enjoyed the company in the ballroom, we rarely sat out a dance.

While casting around for future employment I had word of past activity. In December, Hugh wrote after attending a screening of *Cabaret*:

> It is either terribly good—or not, if that expresses anything. I saw it with all the money people being imposing, neutral big-shots exuding as always that deadly "I'm not going to commit myself" aura which so chills in a projecting room. I just got nervous and non-reacting. Then I saw it alone again the next day and loved it.

This was to be exactly my own reaction when I saw the film in New York at its world premiere.

With nerves on edge, I was disappointed with the press show and feared the worst. But at the film's gala premiere I was enchanted. So, it turned out, was almost everyone else. We were that gratifying phenomenon, a smash hit. As far as I could be objective it seemed to me to be one of the best-edited films I had ever seen. Some cuts were almost subliminal and one was always left wanting more.

The publicity machine, humming in low gear on the film set, now roared into full action, affording glimpses of a bizarre promotional world through the darkened windows of intensely carpeted low-slung limousines complete with crystal-decantered bars and television sets. The most surreal atmosphere, though, was provided by the film's opening in Chicago where we filed up to the cinema between pha-lanxes of tough cops, arms linked to hold back a totally nonexistent crowd. I was asked repeatedly for my autograph. One fan, perhaps in belated punishment for my pubescent rejection of pure penmanship, even rejected my scrawl demanding that I write properly!

In these heady circumstances, talking about the film was a pleasure, although talking repeatedly about oneself became wearing. I remem-bered with wry envy David Hemmings telling me that he used to invent stories to entertain both himself and his interviewer. I soon learned that on talk shows, which in any event were more show than talk, it was of little use to be my normal reticent self. I was dressed and made up for a performance. This was once forcefully illustrated on the *David Frost Show*. Liza and Joel were with me to promote the film and they reprised on camera some of their musical numbers. When it was my turn David asked if I regretted my character was given no songs to sing. I mumbled some brief vacuity whereupon he rejoined in those inimitable eager-beaver tones: "Well, here's your chance to make up for that now!"

Behind me a curtain rose to reveal a full orchestra playing the opening bars of one of the songs from the theater show whose melody I could but vaguely hum. I was instantly back on stage at the Old Vic, in the dark and not knowing whether to fight or flee. The millions of eyes connected to the lens of the TV camera stared unblinkingly at me. Vainly protesting that I was a guest not a jest, I managed to rescue myself from this auto-da-fé of embarrassment by getting David to sing along with me. I have since learned that any person who agrees to improvise on television has—quite properly—been rehearsing their improvisation for weeks!

I received a letter from Penny saying how much she had enjoyed *Cabaret*. She added a postscript: "Kate was asking where heaven is and I said that I didn't know as I hadn't been there yet. She said, 'Has Uncle Michael, 'cos he's been everywhere!' " Indeed, our travels were not over. The film showed every sign of becoming an international zenzation. Everyone, it seemed, wanted to come to the cabaret.

Beyond the Lost Horizons

To my amazement, there followed a request to appear in another screen musical—a remake of *Lost Horizon,* the famous James Hilton story previously filmed in Frank Capra's memorable 1937 version with Ronald Colman. On paper it all looked promising—a splendid yarn with an excellent cast including Peter Finch, Liv Ullmann and, especially, another idol of mine, Sir John Gielgud. The team of Burt Bacharach and Hal David provided the music and lyrics and the whole confection was to be produced by the ebulliently successful Ross Hunter.

As usual I agonized over the decision even though I had now acquired a certain Yankee directness from Pat. When she had first heard me turning down work in my usual circumlocutory British way —being grateful for small mercies—she would think I was accepting. Even so, this offer was a tough one. Not only was the script undistinguished, but my character, the younger brother George, was only distinguished by his nonsinging status. Guided by my new principle of carpe diem, however, I decided to commit myself, trusting that a combination of luck, talent and timing would make it "all right on the night."

Returning to Los Angeles in April, I was just in time to be a presenter on the 1972 Academy Awards show. I now sported a carroty mustache, grown for the film, that Pat hated, pressing her case by claiming to feel less affection for me looking this way. I felt it made me look more mature, more plausibly Peter Finch's brother and, besides, mustaches along with bell-bottom trousers were back in vogue.

At the Oscar ceremony, having mouthed my stilted words—some cliché about the importance of sound in film—I envied a fellow presenter, Tennessee Williams, who, mischievously faking myopia and an inability to read the cue cards, made up his own inimitable little speech. The real hero of the hour, however, was Charles Chaplin, making a belated return to America and the city that had brought him international fame. The overdressed audience, perhaps expiating a nation's guilt, gave the little tramp a standing ovation. Humiliated and ostracized for so long, he was clasped greedily back into the bosom of the Great American Public, who especially loved their heroes to make a final-reel comeback. It was all intensely moving.

We settled in Beverly Hills, "the land of lotus, luaus and leased furs" as a new friend, Mart Crowley, described it. He was the author of the hit play *The Boys in the Band* that sounded the first outrageous voice of homosexual freedom. Our little rented house was on a hill and precious imported water, used then with flagrant abandon, had turned the scrubby decomposed granite landscape into a verdant paradise. Switched on with clockwork regularity, artificial rain inundated lawns and flower beds. Jacaranda trees flamed with a violent seasonal violet.

Attempting to return some of the hospitality enjoyed on previous trips, we gave a dinner party where the company included three of the greatest living practitioners of the English language—Sir John Gielgud, Tennessee Williams and Christopher Isherwood. They were all old friends—and a study in contrasts. Gielgud the mellifluent *grand seigneur;* Williams equally fastidiously dressed but given to cackling like a maniac; Isherwood calm-eyed and crop-headed like a monk. They wore their mantles of fame with distinctive style and disarming humor. All three were artists with decades of achievement behind them and yet they were active practitioners and constant perfecters of their craft.

We had hired a black cook and waiters for the evening. Tennessee accused one of them of being a Black Panther and of trying to convert him. We suddenly had a glimpse of his ever incipient paranoia—or was it his singular dark sense of humor? We urged on him a calming herb tea instead of coffee and, the next day, were delighted to have his astonished report that he had almost fallen asleep on the way home. Unassisted slumber, we learned, was not a luxury he often enjoyed. It was as if the somber side of his imagination infiltrated his dreams so that refuge from this nocturnal haunting had to be artificially induced. His "thank you" letter, dated April 15, 1972, was written from a beach house in "Malibrouhaha" and would be the first of a long, treasured correspondence.

> . . . It was a lovely evening despite the fright I received from the Black Panther. Since I love Black Panthers, the word fright is inaccurate. I meant to say the shock of. You two have a way, a grace that makes any occasion with you, even the Academy horror, a memorable light. I am bad at writing this morning as I have passed a totally sleepless night in a guest room obviously designed to prevent the overnight presence of a guest. I plan to do something about this, and although I trust you completely I know that you would not care to know who did what to whom when the flicks move in with their questions. It is a fiercely bright morning and there are no curtains or drapes against the Pacific blaze but I have a dark tie that I shall knot about my bruised eyes. Sunday evening— about six—two lovely actors are going to read (aloud, I trust) my last desperate (major) work for a theatre that I hope still exists and I doubt you're free to attend this occasion, but it would give me great comfort if you were and did.
>
> Because I love you,
> Tennessee

The play he was referring to would figure significantly in our subsequent relationship.

In a sense, Tennessee's paranoia with black sensibilities mirrored a wider concern. This was another summer of racial tension. L.A.'s black ghetto of Watts had burned. One dark night Pat and I were intercepted in our car by a black driver obviously intoxicated with something more potent than mere antiwhite rage. As he loomed menacingly toward us, swearing violently, Pat urged me to step on the gas and go. Instead, something made me roll down the window and in my politest voice ask him if I could possibly be of any assistance. This unexpected maneuver literally stopped him speechless in his tracks as we made our urbane exit.

The production of *Lost Horizon* was fanfared with a lavish party that must have cost the best part of the budget of *England Made Me*! There were elaborate costume tests and I found myself fitted out in some vaguely hippie caftans and sandals by the legendary designer Jean Louis. To Pat's delight, the carroty mustache was shaved off.

Filming began in Oregon, eleven thousand feet up in the snows of Mount Hood. We all stayed in a ski lodge and were hauled up to the mountaintop in helicopters and great caterpillar trucks. Some of the best snow sequences, though, were staged in the lodge's parking lot, a reminder that Capra had achieved brilliantly realistic effects—frozen breaths and frosty rime—filming in an L.A. ice house.

My partner in the story was my erstwhile Capulet cousin, Olivia Hussey. Now married, she was experiencing one aspect of passionate romantic love that Juliet had surely missed out on—pregnancy. It somewhat cramped our style as we staggered around in the deep drifts in elaborate fur hats and coats. It also made Olivia's exhaustion during the escape from Shangri-la quite genuine and her transformation into an ancient wizened crone even more bizarrely poignant.

For the long haul of the film we were based at the Burbank Studios in the smoggy San Fernando Valley, just about as far as it was possible to get from the reality and concept of Shangri-la. Amid the water towers and abandoned sets of the backlot, the fabled lamasery was constructed from the cannibalized remains of that other mythical haven, *Camelot*. Despite all the skillful art direction, the profusion of orchids, macramé and candles, the interiors reminded me of nothing more exciting than the James Hilton Hotel. I began to understand why Capra had destroyed the first two reels of his film containing his vision of Shangri-la. Utopia was best left to the imagination. Besides, the story's yearning for peace and harmony, which reflected the nation's own yearning for healing from war on the battlefield and in the ghettos, was trivialized by our updated band of crass Westerners who crash-land in paradise. Seeming to be more on a package tour than a spiritual quest, they indulged in an unthinking brand of cultural imperialism, teaching the Shangri-la children to sing—not about spiritual or racial harmony but about Babe Ruth's home runs.

Additional snow scenes were filmed in the sweltering heat of Bronson Canyon, a few yards from the distinctly unspiritual purlieus of Hollywood Boulevard. Blizzards of plastic snow and oily mist were whirled by noisy wind machines. Furs, if not spirits, weighed heavy. Hugh Wheeler wrote: "John G. calls me every now and then with hair-raising stories of climbing mountains involving practically every known natural hazard—except Abominable Snowmen—and usually any movie company is more than able to provide them. Can the movie be awful enough to be a smash hit? I don't see why not."

Nor did I. In America's present internecine state, an antimilitaristic story that preached a creed of brotherly love would seem to be welcome. The pacifist McGovern had just come wooing at the elections. Ecology was becoming an issue—the first intimation that we were polluting and destroying the Shangri-la within and without. Like mushrooms after rain, health food shops were springing up in a greasy wilderness of hamburger and taco joints. Pat pursued her quest for health in this land of opportunity and refreshing naïveté where any crackpot seed found fertile soil to flourish. Becoming a disciple of the great California nutritionist Dr. Henry Bieler, she served up at every possible opportunity his famous vegetable concoction, "green goo" soup. Brown rice bubbled in the kitchen and bowls of papayas decorated the dining table. Stimulants were banished, the replacement of Earl Grey by raspberry-leaf tea threatening to compromise my very essence as an Englishman.

We were happy in our adopted home, but at work the instincts were flashing caution. I became daily more incredulous of the wildly enthusiastic progress reports put out by our producers. The emperor, if not entirely naked, seemed to me to be most peculiarly garbed. Ross Hunter, however, positively glowed with approbation. In an interview he later disclosed that this was customary: "I had a habit of coming on the set every day in an up mood and my opening line was always 'The rushes are great.' "

The effect this had on me then was the decision to stop being a cynically sophisticated smart aleck. Instead of fighting the situation, like my character George, for whom heaven on earth was intolerable, I resolved to go with the friendly flow and enjoy myself. I was glad that, through George, I could at least sound discordant notes of pessimism and caution amidst the self-congratulatory hullabaloo.

Certainly Peter Finch appeared to mellow in our painted paradise and like me seemed to share the qualities of the character he was playing—or maybe it was the constant presence of his family that kept a benign smile on his face! Liv Ullmann was his leading lady and just riding to work in the same car as this most luminous of Bergman's many extraordinary actresses was for me a source of quiet but positive pleasure. I briefly met Charles Boyer who was playing the High Lama. Perhaps it was the probity of his present role that made him disclaim any reputation as a legendary screen lover. This illusion, he insisted, had been achieved by merely looking his partners directly in the eye.

It was John Gielgud, however, who became my special friend. I basked in his affection. Indeed, the privilege of getting to know him and Martin, his delightfully eccentric companion, was one of the great rewards of the film. John called me "the Juve," but I could have applied the same term to him for his mind and spirit were irrepressibly youthful. Besides his famous ability to complete *The Times* crossword with contemptuous ease, I discovered that he had also read all the latest books, seen all the newly released films and was *au fait* with all the current gossip.

Wreathed in scented smoke from his distinctive oval cigarettes, the eyes set far behind the noble nose would beam with wicked delight when struck by an amusing thought and the incomparable mechanics of diction would then smoothly engage to deliver it. He had an instinctive ability to turn a phrase, the elegance of which was doubly enhanced by his own stylish dress and demeanor. Even his laughter was finely wrought, being the essence of amusement taken to the highest degree. It was some measure of his charisma that he was able to remain noble and grandiloquent even when wearing an absurd tea-cozy hat as Chang the High Lama's major-domo.

Above all, John was an immensely *professional* actor. He rarely protested or procrastinated—he just did it. This set him apart from some of the indigenous cast members who typified the American way of acting. Though talented and likable, they turned their craft into a very self-conscious, highly wrought display of neuroses. During these endless moments, the British contingent merely stiffened upper lips, raised eyebrows and exchanged long-suffering looks. At times I reproached myself for not agonizing over my role more publicly. But then Coward's actor's imperative, "Speak up and don't fall over the furniture," would come winging back to mind, and I would save the angst for private rehearsals at home and in my trailer.

John and Martin became traveling companions. I saw the Grand Canyon for the first time alongside John, who gazed over its awesome dimensions like an omniscient Prospero reviewing his wild kingdom. We stopped in clockless Las Vegas and witnessed another extraordinary sight—the flashing fishnetted thighs of Debbie Reynolds dancing up from the stage and around the perimeter of the booth in which we were dining. John was about to direct her in a revival of the musical *Irene* and sat bemusedly unfazed by this delicious taste of her quality.

Debbie was appearing with her children and I had the first glimpse of a future admired actress and writer, Carrie Fisher, whom we later encountered backstage. We dabbled in Mexico and indulged in Martin's passion for animals at the San Diego Zoo where, it seemed, all the ugly, overweight humans should have been corraled in the enclosures and their beautiful occupants released.

We all saw more of Christopher Isherwood and Don Bachardy in their house hugging Santa Monica Canyon just before it spilled its tide of urban dwellings into the Pacific. It was there, in the bright living room hung with contemporary art and immortalized by their friend David Hockney's famous double portrait, that Chris and I together read the notices of *Cabaret*. To my undisguised relief he was complimentary about my performance, although less happy with the film's ambiguous sexuality. Pat took some wonderful portraits of him at this time—his eyes still clear, amused and youthful, only their pendant gray bushy eyebrows giving some hint of advancing years. Seeing the results Chris paid her the compliment of saying that now only she could claim, "I am a camera!"

I sat for Don who was an accomplished artist and younger than Chris by several decades. Their mannerisms and even their voices—especially on the phone—had over the years, however, become indistinguishable. Chris was then studying and writing about the Vedanta and the uncurtained room where he woke with the sun and their simple, wholesome hospitality had more in common with the rigors of monastic devotion than anything happening on our absurd film set.

My role and the shooting schedule being not exactly overdemanding, we continued to entertain in our little house. Twiggy, that sixties fashion icon turned seventies actress, came by for lunch and we attempted to repay Jimmy Wilson some of his lavish hospitality. It became very hot with temperatures in the hundreds, making our scenes in furs and plastic snow even more unbearable and moonlit concerts at the Hollywood Bowl especially enjoyable. There were nostalgic thoughts of moist Europe, of natural green lawns and gurgling gutters, and the before and after work plunge in the pool became an essential daily rite.

There was only one major irritation: a local dog barked relentlessly. To escape the nightly noise we moved from our king-sized bed to a queen-sized one in the guest room and by desperate declension to a single bed in the maid's room at the back of the house. To no avail. We discovered the howling monster belonged to a couple who were both well-known television stars. Well known, that is, except to me.

Something for Everyone with
Angela Lansbury.

Something for Everyone, Bavaria, 1969. Hal
Prince standing *at left* in dark glasses;
Hugh Wheeler and Rick sitting *at right.*
(Pat York)

Hamlet, 1970. *(Frank Page Studios)*

In the Sahara, 1970. *(Pat York)*

With Michel Piccoli in *La Poudre d'Escampette,* Morocco, 1970. *(Pat York)*

Cabaret, 1971, with Liza Minnelli. *(Pat York)*

Cabaret, Berlin, with Bob Fosse between takes. *(Pat York)*

D'Artagnan in action, Oliver Reed temporarily inactive in background.
(Pat York)

The Three Musketeers with Roy Kinnear, 1973. *(Pat York)*

With Raquel Welch in *The Four Musketeers,* 1973. *(Pat York)*

Out Cry with Tennessee
Williams and Cara Duff
McCormack, 1973.
(Pat York/Camera Press)

With Derek Jacobi
outside Eaton Terrace,
early 1970s. *(Pat York)*

Logan's Run, 1975: Saul David (producer), Logan, Michael Anderson, Peter Ustinov, Jenny Agutter. *(Pat York)*

With Richard Jordan on the *Logan* set. *(Pat York)*

Jesus of Nazareth, with Franco Zeffirelli, Tunisia, 1976. *(Pat York)*

The Last Remake of Beau Geste, 1976, as Marty Feldman's twin. *(Pat York)*

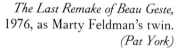

The Island of Dr. Moreau, St. Croix, 1976. Lunchtime swim with costar. *(Pat York)*

Broadway, 1980. *(Jody Caravaglia)*

Cyrano de Bergerac, Sante Fe, 1981. *(Pat York)*

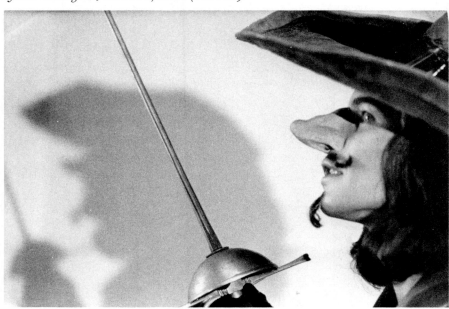

For Those I Loved with Martin Gray, 1982. *(Pat York)*

(left) As Robinson
Crusoe in *Vendredi,*
1981. *(Pat York)*

The Master of Ballantrae, 1983, with Timothy
Dalton, Sir John Gielgud, Richard Thomas and
Fiona Hughes. *(Pat York)*

Playing the Palace with Jeanne Moreau, New York, 1983.
(Robin Platzer)

*Success Is the Best
Revenge,* 1984, with my
son, Michael Lyndon.
(Pat York)

The Secret of the Sahara, 1987, with Andie McDowell. *(Pat York/ Intertopics)*

Filming *The Long Shadow* in Israel with Liv Ullmann and Vilmos Zsigmond, 1991. *(Pat York)*

Rick and Serena on their wedding day, August 1983. *(Pat York)*

Pat and Consuelo, 1987. *(Rick McCallum)*

Pat with Alexandra and Olivia in full makeup, 1990. *(Michael York)*

May and Joe with Henry, 1990. *(Michael York)*

With Pat. *(Nancy Ellison)*

We had once been briefly introduced but, not being familiar with American series television, I had failed to catch their names. Our exasperation and exhaustion combined to drive me to the composition of a letter that was polite except in one unfortunate detail. Unable to address them by name, I—unwisely, as it turned out—left a blank after the "Dear Mr. and Mrs.," explaining my predicament. This unwitting rudeness provoked a damburst of outrage and bruised self-esteem:

> We received your letter of complaint with regard to our dog. As to your concern with thinking of your response as neurotic, rest assured we don't. On the other hand to be assured rest is another thing altogether. I certainly can appreciate your problem. But sadly I must report there is no other place in which to kennel our dog. I would prefer that she recite Shakespeare's sonnets or sing *Aida* when aroused for I much prefer her sweetness, loyalty, albeit her noise to the stark rudeness I've experienced from near strangers I've encountered . . .

Here my crime for being unable to put a name to their famous faces was furiously rammed home:

> For say what you will, our canine companion is never rude . . . loud, yes, but never rude. Which permits me forgiving her for not knowing our names, even after all these years and so Mr. York, I don't know what else to do. I have read your letter aloud to her with every nasty intonation I could summon up, in my best contemptuous Oxford, I might add, but understanding letters is even more difficult for her than reciting or singing. Barking is her bent. Perhaps you will have more luck if you bark back at her, or have you tried talking to her civilly?

Here after much rattling and puffing the snake struck:

> Pollyana is her first name. Her last name, of course is the same as ours.
>
> > Sincerely,
> > Mr. and Mrs.—

The foibles, insecurities and childishness of some actors was further revealed in a letter of Adrian's from Turkey, his new holiday haven now that the colonels had crushed democracy under their jackboots in Greece.

We're here with a group of actors we know—who resemble every group of actors the world over. The director desperately searching for bigger and better parts for his wife (to get peace at home one supposes). The juve lead after two successes leaving to "start his own theatre," the small part actress flirting with me for some professional reason—and eating and drinking hilariously into the small hours after a performance.

The last description was one that I could not identify with. Despite the popular picture painted of my trade as one of uproarious debauchery, filming was an exacting, demanding and exhausting business— usually performed at hours that were small and unsociable. Midnight oil was only burned during night shooting, that abominable practice, that left the body feeling weirdly jet-lagged and made me echo Falstaff's fervent plea, "Would it were bedtime, Hal, and all's well!"

We used our free time for escapist travel—up the coastal highway to Hearst's architectural folly of a Shangri-la at San Simeon and on to a San Francisco pearly gray with summer fog, down through the wild expansive beauty of northern California with its rolling yellow hills studded with native oaks to Big Sur, Carmel and the other historic mission towns. Although my presence was only intermittently demanded on the set, there was insufficient time to return to England for Caroline's marriage. She sent me photographs of the day that was beset with unseasonable bad weather with ladies holding on to hats. This tempestuous start sadly augured the future of the nuptials.

We heard from Rick, who was suffering from hepatitis. He had been alerted to his illness by repeatedly breaking down into fits of uncontrollable weeping at the news of the death of the Duke of Windsor. It came as a relief to find out that it was his liver malfunctioning and not his mind.

I also received a letter from Tennessee containing the genesis of one of the most extraordinary and creative times I would ever enjoy. Since our earlier meeting we had discussed the possibility of working together—perhaps my recording some poems from his collection *In the Winter of Cities*. There was also the "major" work he had mentioned earlier. "This morning I continued working on the play for you. I will get off a first draft of it to you as soon as possible," he wrote.

My excitement that Tennessee was considering me for his latest work was quickened by a letter dated July 4, 1972, from his home in Key West that followed hard upon the other. Among other things, it confirmed that Tennessee, a fellow Arien, was also a fellow tourist, equally restless and curious:

My little recuperative vacation in New Orleans is over. Billy Barnes [his New York agent and at that time, mine, too] has summoned me back to NY for "conferences" with the added enticement of a party for Mick Jagger and the Rolling Stones. I must say I don't much mind interrupting my stay here. It is ninety degrees in the moonlight and none of the furniture I had ordered from New York has arrived. Bare rooms are more depressing than hotel rooms. My secretary, Victor, has gone into something called "lucite": it is a liquid that can be solidified into objects. The proliferation of these objects is alarming. He is intending to market them, and since in the States practically anything is marketable, the enterprise may work. But at the moment I find it an harassment.

On my bedside table are three lucite animals, a fox, a deer and a crocodile. For three such different creatures there is a remarkable similarity in their appearance in solidified lucite. At night I put them under the bed and try to forget their existence.

When I next see you all I hope to present you with a script, at least a holograph of the first draft. But I don't want you to ever to suspect, I mean to think, that I value you for professional or selfish reasons. You are simply two of my dearest and most quickly known friends in the world. *A bientôt.*

Two Characters Playing

CHAPTER TWENTY-THREE

With *Lost Horizon* finally finished we were able to attend a screening of *Cabaret* at the Venice Film Festival. Andy Warhol was also there with his gang, which included dapper Fred Hughes, his producer, and their latest minimalistic film offering, *Heat,* together with its stars, the ebullient Sylvia Miles and pony-tailed Joe D'Alessandro.

We spent an inordinate amount of time photographing each other. Warhol, deathly pale with hayrick hair, had a Polaroid camera that he used with the same prolific industry employed to turn out works of art, even signing the results. Almost monosyllabic, his invariable expression was "Great!" Firing back through the barrels of her Nikons, Pat took one memorable photograph of him photographing her while being photographed by the director Paul Morrisey. It was all as incestuous as Warhol's new magazine, *Interview,* in which the same five people seemed to interview the same five other people.

Tennessee was also there, together with Bill Barnes and Lady Maria St. Just, my Belgravia neighbor and his good friend and future literary executrix. As usual he was immaculately turned out in his clothes for

a summer hotel. A blue striped seersucker suit and white boots adding
flair and dimension to his height, the whole ensemble was rendered
curiously formal by a precisely knotted tie.

Over drinks on the Lido Hotel terrace he handed over, as promised,
the completed manuscript now entitled *The Two Character Play*. That
night, although not entirely understanding it, I spent an extraordinary
time reading the work. Trespassing into the dark, repressed confines
and the sunlit open spaces of his teeming imagination was fascinating.
There seemed to be a play within a play within a play. Felice and his
sister Clare, whose father has murdered their mother and then committed suicide, are left abandoned on tour in a cold, empty state theater
in a state unknown, deserted by their fellow actors who consider them
insane. Terrified and disoriented, their only recourse is to perform a
two-character play set in a small town in the American South. There
they are found, shut away from the world in a house surrounded by
real and metaphysical terrors. Weaving back and forth between actual
and assumed roles, they struggle against madness. Felice wants to risk
leaving the house; Clare is unwilling. At the end of the play reality
and illusion seem to become one, the writing suffused with extraordinary images both of stark terror and of great poetic beauty.

Tennessee and I met again the next day. I gave him my puzzled if
positive reaction, whereupon he asked if I would play Felice in a
Broadway production. It was a royal command—and unhesitatingly
obeyed. Refusal would have been unthinkable. Toasting our new collaboration, Tennessee spoke further about the piece, which was, in
fact, an integration of two earlier plays originally intended for two
much older actors.

Like much of Tennessee's most powerful writing, the play was
intensely autobiographical at heart, dealing with a time when, overwhelmed with personal torment, he had retreated from the world in a
kind of panic and had actually been locked up in a St. Louis psychiatric
hospital. He quite literally had not known where he was. Now sixty-
two years old, a survivor of heart attacks, heartbreaks, drugs and other
unmentionable terrors, he had returned shaken but resolute from his
stumbling journey through the valley of the shadow of death. His
writing was a means of exorcising his demons. Lear's crazed heath
now had boundaries and limitations. As Clare exclaims: "I never knew
the world had so many frontiers." But this demarcation line between
reason and madness in the play was left purposefully vague, just as its
dream world repeatedly elided with the "real" world.

At the end of our discussion Tennessee gave me his copy of the play to study. Next day, as Pat and I were about to embark at the Venice airport en route to Capri, there was an urgent message to contact him at once. My own paranoid fear that he had changed his mind turned to relief and then to a burning curiosity when I learned that the package containing the play also held the only existing type-script of his memoirs. Resisting the temptation to indulge in a glimpsed preview, I made sure that this treasure reached its author and posterity.

Staying with Jimmy Wilson in his rented villa on Capri, we found that everything now agreeably depended on the progress of feet or boats. Sitting under vines perched vertiginously above the sea in Tennessee's favorite part of the world, I tried to absorb more of his extraordinary Pirandellian exploration of the realms of the creative imagination. Pat and I lunched with Gore Vidal and Howard Austen at Ravello and together met the legendary Mona Bismarck, now in her latter years but still as vibrantly beautiful, elegant and coquettish as any of Tennessee's heroines. Entertained in her historic villa, we sipped the ambrosial wines grown on her land and wished all such beakers of the warm south could be as pure and untainted. We were also introduced to the very latest fashion—or "fayshon" as he pronounced it—the sleek designer Valentino, who roared us across the bay in his even sleeker motor boat to Ischia and then over to Zeffirelli's villa in Positano.

In slower style we saw the regatta in Venice—Guardi and Canaletto paintings come alive—from the balcony of the Volpi Palace. It was there in the men's lavatory of the Cipriani Hotel that I encountered Charlie Chaplin again. Side by side about our business, our eyes met by chance over the porcelain. Astonished and delighted to see the man who had astonished and delighted the world for so long, all I could do was murmur "good morning" even though it was then late in the evening. "Good morning," he gravely returned. I regret to this day that my confusion prevented me from saying something more complimentary. The moment, and soon after the little man himself, was gone, both victims of British reserve.

At St. Tropez, our next port of call, we stayed with Dominique Lapierre at the estate he shared with his writing and tennis partner, Larry Collins. Between generous bouts of beach, pool, and provençal cuisine, we discussed the possibility of my appearing in a film version of one of their earlier best-sellers, *Or I'll Dress You in Mourning*—the extraordinary life story of the Spanish matador El Córdobes. By some quirk, it seemed I had more than a passing resemblance to the book's charismatic hero. This had been recently borne out when, back in Hollywood, Jimmy Wilson had again invited us down to his Mexican ranch, requesting us to bring, as entertainment, any films we could find. All I could come up with was a BBC documentary about this bullfighter who, in hirsuteness, unconventionality and popularity, rivaled the Beatles. It was duly screened and the excited whisper then ran round the village that El Córdobes was there reviewing his taurean triumphs. Suddenly on all sides I was besieged by reverential looks and shy autograph seekers. I must confess that I maintained the illusion by signing the great man's name with a delighted—if wordless —flourish.

News of our plans somehow leaked out to the British press and on our return to London I was equally besieged by animal rightists begging me not to glamorize barbarity and determined to deny me my suit of lights. The project eventually fell into limbo where it still languishes, although I met a man in a bookshop the other day who claimed he was producing it.

In September we were back in New York, where I was asked to read *The Two Character Play* for its possible producer, the great impresario David Merrick, and its director, Peter Glenville. If it was an audition, it was the most civilized one I have endured. The actress playing my sister was a slight, fey, dreamy blonde girl called Cara Duff McCormack. With her unusual, otherworldly quality, she had attracted attention and awards the previous season in a play called *Moonchildren,* and had so impressed Peter Glenville with her instinctive reading of the Williams play that he was pressing for her to re-create it on Broadway.

While waiting for Merrick's crucial response I briefly became involved in another Williams project, an excerpt for a television program of *The Glass Menagerie.* Maureen Stapleton played Amanda and I was the Gentleman Caller in the scene where, dancing with Laura, he breaks her glass unicorn.

Encouragement arrived in the shape of a telegram Bill Barnes had received from Tennessee: "Please let me know as soon as possible Merrick's reaction to reading. If negative, think we should move immediately to another producer as you suggested stop." There then followed something that stopped me in my tracks: "No other English-speaking actor would match York in the role stop. We must remember Merrick belongs to the establishment to which I don't belong. My loyalty is to you, Michael and Glenville. Love. T. W." This extraordinary benediction made me determined, if approved, to redouble my efforts to be worthy of his confidence.

While I awaited my fate, however, Pat and I kept another karmic appointment, an unexpected invitation to return to India having proved impossible to refuse. We were both anxious to see if the life-shaping drama of our previous encounter had been illusory, the product of romantic and fevered imaginations.

Our dawn arrival in Delhi coincided with the time of that last frantic departure, triggering off an explosion of memories. There was the same thick light and pungent smell and, seeing a man cutting grass with a hand mower yoked to a bullock, the same extraordinary, picturesque cultural confusion. In Bombay, too, the venerable Taj Mahal Hotel was now yoked to an ultramodern tower block complete with boutiques and bone-chilling air-conditioning, and a spindly TV mast had joined the jostling skyline. India seemed bent on exchanging dhotis for Diner's Club, traditional values for international ones. Managing to slip away for sentimental old times' sake to Juhu Beach and the Sun 'n Sand Hotel, we were thankful to find that nothing much there seemed to have changed.

Retracing our fateful journey to Rajasthan, we stayed in Jaipur in yet another palace, the Rambagh, now newly converted to a hotel. Fortunately, the princely dimensions of its rooms had been retained and especially their bathroom fittings, a symphony of sculptured chrome with giant marble baths big enough to house whole cricket teams. No doubt all this has now gone, along with the aristocratic plumbing of other grand hotels across the five continents and drab, mean standardized fittings substituted.

We had a last glimpse of princely privilege when the Maharana of Udaipur, a gentle, unassuming man whose ancestry stretched back over thirteen hundred unbroken years, invited Pat and myself to stay in his private palace by the lake on which floated, like a fantastic mirage, his fabulous Lake Palace, now also a hotel. What had been a film set for *The Guru* was our new reality. We slept in a canopied, gilded bed awaking to the shriek of green parakeets as they streaked over the glazed azure water outside. Before the last world war, however, there had been two thousand servants; now there were only seventy-five. The whole feudal system was in retreat: and there was unemployment in the town.

The Taj Mahal stopped us in our tracks, the request to remove shoes before entering this cool, exquisite shrine seeming for once totally justified. Reality intruded jarringly with a shouted phone call from Bill Barnes in distant New York. The play was on! Cara—and myself—had been approved. Ah, India, place of destiny! Before returning home, delighted that our passion for the country had been confirmed, we both felt compelled to complete the journey we had promised ourselves before fate and events in Bikaner decided otherwise—a trip to the mountains of the north.

It was easy to understand why Kashmir was so hotly contested. It has the intense, undiffused beauty of a Pre-Raphaelite landscape. Fruit and nuts grow in abundance: the air is crisp and wholesome. We stayed in "New York," a houseboat built of sweet-smelling wood moored alongside a flotilla of similar craft on Dal Lake. They could have been mistaken for Oxford barges on the Isis were it not for the floating flower sellers plying their trade. Aboard, on the canopied top deck with its chintz-covered armchairs, strong tea from the neighboring hills was served in cozied pots with scones and jam. The tranquillity was unearthly. This is where *Lost Horizon* should have been filmed!

The present century caught up with us on our flight home. I had been allowed, in a practice now discouraged, to further boyhood dreams of flight by sitting in the cockpit of the huge new jumbo jet for its landing in Frankfurt. Once at the terminal, our craft was immediately surrounded by armed guards and the captain was asked if he had been hijacked by the long-haired, bearded man—me in my new dramatic guise—they had noticed sitting behind him. Sadly, this illustrated a new and terrifying development in international affairs, with aircraft and their innocent passengers becoming tools of the terrorist's deadly trade.

India was still very much with us in London. We were able to entertain our first guest, Dominique Lapierre, who came to work on *Freedom at Midnight,* a new book about the partition of India. Arriving at regular intervals for interrogation, there seemed to be an Indian waiting patiently in every room. When I later met Lord Mountbatten he claimed that partition was nothing compared to the hard work that Dominique had put him through recalling that epochal event.

Dominique's character possessed interwoven streaks of charm, intelligence and luck. Grandly announcing his plan to visit India for the first time by car, he suggested we go and look for a Rolls-Royce with left-hand drive and air-conditioning. Protesting that London was the last place to harbor such an exotic creature, I was prevailed on to accompany him around the corner to the local Rolls dealer in Sloane Square. And there, of course, it was. Just brought in from the French Embassy was a vehicle that fulfilled all his requirements, even down to the French number plates! His progress to the subcontinent, Dominique later related, had been positively regal. At his approach awe-struck crowds had parted and, if he was to be believed, almost genuflected, too. Encountering India would, of course, change Dominique's life just as much as it changed ours. His work with Mother Teresa and his literary highlighting of the plight of Calcutta's lepers would reflect the sublimation of all his curiosity and enthusiasm to a more spiritual end. Years later, I would be delighted to have the opportunity to record his words.

My mother was the next occupant of our guest room. Seeing her again, we had been shocked to find her looking gray with illness and had persuaded May to try the homeopathic alternative, conventional medicine having failed to diagnose her problem. Agreeing, she stayed with us for the weeks Dr. Sharma required to root out the viral flu he had immediately diagnosed. It was a profound pleasure to see May's color and vivacity gradually return. Now she and Joe have become devotees of homeopathy and their enduring good health is testament to its gentle efficacy.

Meanwhile we shopped for wholefoods and organic produce, a practice now commonplace but then considered eccentric. I remember one dinner guest was Carol Channing who went even further by bringing her own bear meat, which she proceeded to decant, before she could be stopped, into a used ashtray, mistaking it for a plate. Nonetheless, and none the wiser, she consumed it with relish.

Rick, now living in Paris in a romantic, soon to be bulldozed garret "under the audacious shadow of that high-rising, ugly, bourgeois, phallic Gare Montparnasse," was another welcome visitor, together with Maggie, his vivacious new girlfriend. A doting mother proceeded to dose her son with liver-quickening remedies, principally great quantities of the famous and effective "green goo" soup.

It was an extraordinary pleasure to have so many family members assembled under one roof. I was happy being married. I tried to explain why at the time to a journalist:

I think marriage works simply because it is indefinable. I believe in the validity of pledging a troth, making some kind of commitment, but I think the rest is best left indefinable. An individual human being is so extraordinary you cannot define it—least of all *two* people in some kind of formula. You have to make your own rules and find them out as you go along. I think marriage does keep people together longer, and that's good—I don't like playing games, least of all emotional games.

Pat was now strong and well and our personalities had meshed into a subtle duality. Each had positively influenced the other. She diminished my English reserve and I ameliorated some of her dynamic New York habits such as finishing off other people's sentences. Our timing was in sync.

An emotional game of a different sort was played on me just before we were due to leave London again for New York, illustrating the maddening feast or famine nature of the job. Richard Lester telephoned with an offer to play D'Artagnan in a film he proposed to make of Dumas's *The Three Musketeers*. Was I interested? Was I ever! I was a big fan of Lester's irreverent humor that had found perfect expression translating the Beatles' quirky appeal to the screen. Moreover, I welcomed a change of professional image, descriptions of myself as a "quintessential Englishman" having become worryingly familiar. At least playing an American on the Broadway stage would be different. And that reminded me, I had just signed a six-month contract for the play. I was not free!

Out Cry

CHAPTER TWENTY-FOUR

*T*he cold, echoing Longacre Theater in New York where rehearsals began had been long dark and unused. There is nothing
sadder, dustier or more depressing than an empty stage, lit by a raw
work light. It was, however, a perfect setting for the "mausoleum of a
theater" in which the two characters find themselves trapped. The
play, now finally retitled *Out Cry,* was, as Peter Glenville suggested in
a preliminary talk, perhaps tantamount to Tennessee's *De Profundis.*
As such there was no value in merely putting on a show. It had to be
an equally deeply felt personalized experience, demanding a departure
from the tight naturalistic plane of film of acting into another sphere
consonant with its stylized, poetic language.

We decided to rehearse without an intrusive lunchbreak, listening
to Messiaen records during pauses to capture their strange ecstatic
mood. I was elated and, after a few days of attempting to personalize
Tennessee's psychological conumdrum, utterly depleted, too. Olivier's
dictum about talent being an adjunct of stamina was ruefully remembered. Pacing myself, I began to enjoy the unfamiliar luxury of the
rehearsal process and the means it afforded, unlike in films where snap

instinctive judgments are generally made, to slowly flesh out the complex character. Fortunately, I found it no more of a problem to go from film to stage than to switch from right- to left-hand driving. The change, in fact, heightened perception. Nothing was routine.

Christmas Eve reunited us with Tennessee. He was now beardless but approved of mine, which was gradually reverting to Guthrum the Dane dimensions. Though warned not to let our fledgling performances reflect the author's presence, this was inescapable, as Tennessee's distinctive and uninhibited laugh erupted frequently. The playwright and his director presented two opposites—Peter, silkily urbane, was Apollo to Tennessee's unnerving Dionysus.

Surprisingly, Tennessee was somewhat shocked that Cara and I touched each other so much, claiming that his relationship with his sister had been unphysical. This revelation, though, gave instant insight into the play's intensely autobiographical nature. His sister, Rose, mentally incapacitated in controversial circumstances, had been institutionalized for years. By the end of rehearsals, however, Tennessee had come to accept Felice kissing Clare as an image of poetic, not sexual, intensity.

He was an immensely considerate if vulnerable man. "I simply cannot be alone," he said. On New Year's Eve, joining us in our apartment with his companion Robert, a young Vietnam veteran and promising poet, for a candlelit dinner that he himself cooked, he offset his immaculate black tie with a white surgical mask to prevent others catching his cold.

It was an unfailing fascination to glimpse daily into Tennessee's extraordinary mind, for he constantly revised and improved. Eventually that exciting moment occurred when confusions clarified and the play cut loose from its verbal moorings, sailing with wind and tide in an even more exciting direction.

During a final run-through, I felt incandescent with a strange energy, illuminating the "mad" elements of the play as never before, and almost collapsing on stage before all those "people stranger than strangers." But instead of the gods speaking through me it was a devilish attack of flu. What pained me most, though, was missing meeting Noël Coward, who was to have picked us up in a limousine with another legend, Marlene Dietrich, for a charity event.

Tennessee, ever compassionate, telephoned frequently and sent over books. Pat's researches into recherché health practices had come up with a shiatzu masseur, then uncommon in America. Prostrate and screaming on the floor under fingers that jabbed like cattle prods, I was kick-started back to life. As it was obscuring facial expression, I cut my hair and—again to Pat's unbounded relief—shaved off my mustache, leaving a strange Amish-like beard.

The world premiere of the play was at the Schubert Theater in New Haven. The out-of-town tryout—particularly in this traditional venue where urban brawn mixed with university brains—was the established way of "fixing" difficult shows. Audience reaction was an important factor and it was agreeable to again experience its immediacy. Sometimes it could be out of kilter, as when a black woman once laughed uproariously in all the quiet moments. But her outbursts were well matched by Tennessee's own stentorian bellowing that some members of the audience, sitting poker-faced in the presence of "art," found hard to accept or emulate. As he wrote in his memoirs, "Laughter has always been my substitute for lamentation." Certainly at this stage there was little to bewail. We were generously if guardedly received, with appreciative and encouraging notices.

We moved on to Philadelphia where John Gielgud came with Martin to see the play, as did Hugh Wheeler. Over postperformance Boston scrod at Bookbinders we discussed its merits and potential. "How interesting his employment of syllogistic rifts," Hugh claimed to have heard the young man sitting next to him exclaim to his companion. Further enlightenment came from Tennessee himself, who, in his own official postperformance symposium, declared that the play expressed a new intention to write in a less representational style, confirming that Felice and Clare were alter egos, the masculine-feminine, positive-negative, active-passive elements of one character. To people who objected to them being too young to be so emotionally damaged, he riposted: "Despair is not the sole prerogative of age."

Despite such insights the play seemed to be too special and personal for most audiences. Two girls stopped me in the street later that week and apologized for the lack of audience response. Brotherly love being apparently in short supply in this city, we were glad to move on to our next venue, the Kennedy Center in Washington. Tennessee referred to the impending critical reception as "the firing squad that waits in every city," ameliorating this on another occasion, however, by observing to Pat: "While there's a doubt, there's hope!" At other times, this paranoia could take on comic overtones. On a much later occasion we met him at a grand White House reception where, he complained, his wallet had been dipped.

A great aficionado of Japanese food, upon arrival at each location Tennessee would immediately comb the place in search of sushi. His other regime was swimming. Pat photographed him thrashing the length of the Yale pool and would later capture him emerging from the Malibu surf like a damp leprechaun. In many ways he was the most disciplined and organized person. Daily swimming—and daily writing. He had an almost Chekhovian appreciation of the value of work. In fact, the brother and sister's insistence that they put on a performance however terrible the circumstance was an affirmation of this principle. We are all locked up in the same theater, his play seemed to suggest, where life however threatening and unpromising, must be lived. Perhaps anticipating his own tragic, unnecessary death, Felice and Clare admit they had never finished their play. "There is no ending. It just stops."

Tennessee quickly grew to dote on Pat, and would never call on her without a bouquet or little gift. He was gallant in every sense of the word. Despite his professed sexual preferences, he adored the company of women and his writing displayed a warmth, a gentleness and a decency, all of which he lavished on those he loved.

Our Washington reviews were extraordinarily, disarmingly positive: *"Out Cry* is a beautiful haunting personal elegy to life with immensely tender visions of maturity not unlike the mellow wisdom of *The Tempest."* The effect of this approbation on Tennessee was most moving to witness. He even went so far as to interpret it as an authorization to continue writing.

Everything looked better in this new theater, especially the scenery, which had been cramped elsewhere. The designer Joe Mielziner perfectly captured both the brooding menace and the poetic fantasy of the play with a winding staircase leading nowhere and a huge brutal figure, manacled and chained, that dominated his set. There were also projections of prison bars and of a yellow flood of sunflowers. These watched over Felice and Clare like "the eyes of God," objects of beauty and at the same time Van Gogh–like symbols of deranged nature.

Tennessee's textual revisions continued on an almost daily basis even when, ever restless, he had flown off briefly to London and Key West. We learned them, and incorporated and evaluated them, this brain-teasing process only ceasing at Peter's insistence moments before the Broadway first night. I was now feeling constantly tired. Not a play that could be performed on automatic pilot, it demanded the total involvement of nerve and sinew. Cara confided that she, too, had to spend every spare moment resting. Washington mocked with its unvisited monuments and museums. However, an invitation from Frank Gannon, an old Oxford chum now working for President Nixon, to go on a personal tour of the White House proved irresistible.

A few days later, encountering Debbie Reynolds on the Metroliner to New York, we commiserated at the torment of touring shows. While she dozed I read the New York papers and, with a heart-thumping jolt, noticed photographs of us both as "coming attractions" on the arts page. Felice's panic at the monstrous inevitability of the impending performance in a theater that "sounds like a house of furious unfed apes" suddenly overwhelmed me.

That night we attended the premiere of Hal Prince's and Hugh's new music collaboration, *A Little Night Music,* with its overtones of our gemütlich sojourns in Mitteleuropa. I was unable to reconcile myself, however, with being on the other side of the curtain. My heart flooded with compassion for those about to be so cruelly exposed at its rise, all their hopes and ambitions at the mercy of the same small firing squad of critics. The cruelty of having to perform, that Tennessee had so brilliantly illustrated, suddenly unnerved me. Why should all that work, dedication and energy have to hang in such a capricious balance? Why were artists so desperately anxious to please in the first place? What was I doing here? What was I doing with my life! These and a babble of other panicked questions were allayed by the charm of the production and, at the intermission, I knew that one New York theater at least was going to have a hit.

The next day I saw my name up in lights, above the title at the producer's insistence, on Broadway's Lyceum Theater. I arranged my things in my "travesty of a dressing room." The backstage, too, was tatty and the theater itself in a less than salubrious part of town. Only at night, when hundreds of billboards lit up the buildings, banishing the filth and tawdriness, did Broadway's sobriquet "the Great White Way" and its pretensions toward any sort of glamour have the remotest validity.

On March 1, I woke with the immediate realization that tonight was The Night. Even without such an occasion a theater actor moves his slow way through a day overshadowed by the performance at its end that is its rationale, every intervening event being merely secondary. It was like playing Hamlet, where the actor knows he has to finish the arduous performance with a duel: reserve of energy was essential. "A performance seems an impossible nightmare, but we've got to give one and it's got to be good." This recently cut line came insistently back to mind, especially as, three days before, a doctor had diagnosed complete exhaustion. That morning I ritually shaved off what remained of my beard and felt a most un-Samson-like invigoration.

At the theater I methodically opened telegrams and notes, carefully arranging them amidst the plants and bouquets of flowers. Well before it was time I slowly made up and dressed as if for a "corrida," while all of Felice's paranoia and nerves as an actor became stomach-churningly real. My ancient dressing room was but a few steps from the stage where I joined Cara, who, for this instant, personified the quintessence of the word partner.

Houselights down. Curtain up. In the rake of the spotlights I felt supercharged from nerves and excitement. We began. Out of the corner of my eye I noticed something flash from Cara's eye: her contact lens! I felt a frisson of pure panic—perfectly in keeping with the performance, thank God—but she seemed composed and, though half blinded, managed beautifully. If anything, this fragile antithesis of my character, this gentle retiring fearful creature as delicate and evanescent as the soap bubbles she blew, seemed to soar to new heights of poetic intensity.

The final applause was sustained and carried over to the ritual supper at Sardi's afterward. Equally ritualistically, we went through that other masochistic custom of waiting for the first salvos to be fired by the press. In the upshot there was no massacre. Rather, guns were spiked with flowers, for the play met with general, if qualified, approval, as did, thankfully, Cara and myself. Clive Barnes was especially generous: "Michael York was making his Broadway debut. He should be made welcome any time he wants."

It seemed, however, that we were too fragile a sunflower to survive the withering blasts of Broadway commercialism. As a friend of mine perceptively noted, the New York critics had pronounced Tennessee Williams finished about five years ago and were chagrined that he had presumed to ignore their preliminary obituaries.

It soon became evident that the play was not going to run. I found out later that David Merrick had only agreed to mount this strange eclectic piece at Tennessee's insistence in order to obtain the performance rights to his more commercial *Red Devil Battery Sign*. His duty having been technically fulfilled, after three weeks Merrick posted the closing notice, sending a note thanking me for my performance and hoping that "we shall be associated together in some future production before long." I was both disappointed and—true to form—elated that I was now in a position to exchange Felice's magic shirt for D'Artagnan's tabard and plumes. I called Michael Anderson in London and secured my passage back to the seventeenth century. For the last time I repeated feelingly Felice's ultimate pronouncement: "Magic is the habit of our existence." The final curtain lowered. I was free.

Soon afterward, on March 11, a valedictory letter arrived from Tennessee:

> Now that it's over, I hope you don't look back on it as a bad dream. I'm sure there must be a sense of release in the end of such an unequal struggle: the fragility of the play against the obduracy of all but so small a percent of its audiences and critics.

Tennessee had confided that he considered *Out Cry* his most important work. How long, I wondered, before this was publicly confirmed and acknowledged?

Like him, Pat and I now felt the urge to flee the States as fast as possible but lingered on in New York for a few days. Feeling totally unable to summon up the artificial bonhomie required to join a glittering audience for the gala premiere of *Lost Horizon,* I stood in the crowd watching my co-stars emerge from the limousines like butterflies from cocoons to smile their way through fans and photographers in a blaze of flashbulbs. Huddled in the cold, emotionally drained, I was relieved not to have to put on another show.

I celebrated my thirty-first birthday with friends watching the Academy Awards on television. It was odd to be yet again observing colleagues from a distance, but this time my heart soared with pleasure and pride. I was given an unexpected, ideal present: *Cabaret* was awarded eight Oscars.

All for One

*T*he *Three Musketeers* presented certain pause-giving parallels with *Lost Horizon.* It was another popular story being colorfully retold for a new generation. Moreover, like Bob Fosse before *Cabaret,* Richard Lester was a director in search of a hit. He had pioneered an irreverent freewheeling style of screen humor, a cine-cynicism that had exactly caught the essence of the youthful sixties with its brash blowing of raspberries at convention and throwing of banana skins under establishment pomposities. Employing post–*Goon Show* absurdities with pre-Stoppardian glee, he had stood language, truth and logic on their bewildered heads. But since *The Bed Sitting Room,* Lester's films had been near misses or failures.

George MacDonald Fraser's script for the *Musketeers,* however, presented an amusing athletic springboard for graceful pirouettes and pratfalls alike while still adhering to the spirit of Dumas's original. Gags and jokes were precisely delineated yet they still provided room for Lester's trademark improvisations. I welcomed the opportunity to play in a comedy while knowing that, as with any other genre, the outcome was unpredictable. Films are like soufflés: sometimes they rise and often they don't. But the omens for this recipe looked promising.

Before that first call for "Action!" there was just enough time to get in some swordplay practice and, with the prospect of a horsebacked summer, some remedial riding. I still felt lean and fit from my recent *Out Cry*ing. Bill Hobbs, my old fencing teacher from National Theatre days, was the fight arranger and insisted that we would indeed be fighting. As speedy rapier play was difficult to capture on film, our swords would be heavy, and backed up by kicks and punches. The rules of civilized pugilism would definitely not apply. Christopher Lee, playing the villainous Rochefort, positively limped out of our initial encounter in a London gym.

Driving down to Madrid, Pat and I enjoyed a brief taste of the glories of France before the task of re-creating them. Our film locations were widely scattered all over Spain and, as before, our own car allowed us to explore this comparative terra incognita at will.

Arriving in the capital, I met my new companions with whom I was to spend the next twenty or so weeks in arms. Lester was lithe and balding—a psychology major let loose in a madhouse of his own invention. He seemed to be perpetually on the verge of making a funny remark, which he often did. Playing Athos was Oliver Reed, the dark horse of British films, scarred and saturnine with a dangerous, whispered delivery counterpointing his wild strength. Richard Chamberlain was Aramis and, friendly, handsome and with a rare ability among American actors to wear costume well, was very much in character. Frank Finlay, though puffed, padded and peruked, as Porthos was about to use all his early experience as a sports instructor to agile effect.

I made few concessions to conventional conceptions of D'Artagnan, even appearing without the traditional mustache and mini-beard that featured on my costume sketch. Luckily the play had left my hair long enough to be able to dispense with a wig or a fall, a benefit I cherished when the weather started to cook. Any nagging reservations that D'Artagnan should be dark and swarthy were put to rest when I later met the Duc de Montesquieu, a direct descendant of a noble Gascon family. He was as blond and blue-eyed as I was.

No sooner had I greeted my fellow actors than our hands were grasping swords. There were over a dozen major fight sequences to rehearse, the first being filmed only a few days later in Toledo, a city appropriately famous for its martial blades. We learned the hard way.

Disarmed in the melee, I dramatically yelled for a sword. One was duly thrown, and scythed its way across the courtyard. Momentarily sun-blinded, I missed hold if it and my poor, adventurous, put-upon nose took the brunt of its guillotine slash. This unkind cut was followed by the thrust of an antitetanus shot and a request that wooden swords in future be used in similar situations.

Lester encouraged impromptu happenings and liked to film rehearsals, working at a gallop both literal and otherwise. Stuntmen were allowed to substitute for principals, but only when absolutely necessary for he sometimes shot with up to five cameras at the same time, often in close-up. "There is a quality of excitement and tension when actors are not quite sure what they are doing," he told *Time* magazine. "That kind of thing was worth it to get the effect Dick wanted," Oliver Reed riposted, "but you could break your bloody back riding without stirrups or saddles as we often had to."

I remember leaping onto horses whose saddles were deliberately unfastened only to revolve instantly underneath amidst dust and prancing hooves. Setting off for Paris I bade farewell to my parents from the lofty heights of a huge horse. Its bulk, unfortunately, was partly due to pregnancy and the squeals of a piglet clasped in my mother's arms spooked it into charging around the courtyard scattering actors, film crew, camera equipment and—eventually—its horrified rider.

Ours was definitely a motion picture. We were in constant kinesis —whether jumping out of windows or off horses, slipping on laundry soap or paraffin-wax "ice" and sliding down shiny marble banisters. Few of us escaped injury. A sword ran through Oliver's hand, and Christopher Lee inflicted further unspeakable Hammer-worthy horrors on his knee. Raquel Welch sprained an arm in a set-to with Faye Dunaway. At one point, I even doubled for my injured double, finding myself resorting to that schoolboy ploy of stuffing the script down my trousers for protection from the beatings. The excitement of the moment suspended all rational judgment. I remember scrambling up the facade of a building—like Hemmings in his castle—only to reach the roof before the gut-wrenching realization of what I was actually doing hit home, instantly liquidizing limbs. I liked Lester and enjoyed his madcap, pell-mell style. We were his playthings. "I love toys," he would later remark, "I find them funnier than people."

Locked in a kind of time warp, Spain seemed a perfect choice of setting. Pat, too, was working on the film as a special photographer and exulted in the powerful beauty of our vast new horizons. Castile was not idly named. We filmed in splendid castles in Segovia, Rio Frio and La Granja. We even had permission to use Madrid's Royal Palace and the Escorial where Philip II had immured himself to rule his world with "two inches of paper"—about the same size as our double screenplay.

A fresh green spring gave way to burning summer. Ochre fields blazed scarlet with poppies under hot steel skies. Aranjuez, the Versailles of Spain and a verdant oasis in the scorched landscape, was where we filmed my investiture as a Musketeer. The ceremony took place in the vast marbled courtyard transformed by the combination of sun and arc lamps on reflective stone into a veritable crucible. At the best of times our costumes of tights, layered wool and leather, thick shirts, spurred boots, gloves and plumed felt hats were hot. That day a temperature of 122°F was recorded. Seven thousand bottles of water were reputedly consumed by the gasping ensemble. Ladies of the court lolled with jeweled skirts pulled up to their thighs. Makeup men mopped Niagaras from sopping brows. The sun was king at the Sun King's court.

Pat and I stayed for a time in the congested heart of old Madrid at the palatial apartment of a generous new friend, the gifted designer Duarte Pinto-Coehlo. As on our film set, we were surrounded by rare antiques, our every whim catered to by his five servants. At a leveelike beginning to each day they still assembled to dress Don Duarte, his housekeeper Amparo fondly tendering his underwear. Our long energetic day, however, began well before dawn and, often with drives of up to an hour to distant locations, finished late. A day spent exercising in the open air produced an unusual degree of hunger. Tempered with tapas, however, most Spaniards manage to postpone dinner until around midnight, putting insuperable demands on both patience and digestion. Despite repeated requests, we were unable to change this time-honored custom and as soon as it was belatedly served dinner was instantly and unceremoniously wolfed down.

In August we rented a spacious, modern house on the other side of the city's bosky lung, the Casa di Campo, away from the broiling heat and traffic now snarled in four daily rush hours due to a similar unshiftable adherence to custom—this time the siesta. In our tranquil, leafy suburb, the inherited Arab skill of manipulating water was everywhere evident, although paying for it turned out to be costlier than our food bill.

There were royal encounters of a genuine kind. Princess Anne came
from England on a prenuptial trip and we dined at the British Embassy
with much equine conversation interspersed with droll one-liners from
the Princess worthy of our script. At the same table was the Duchess
of Alba whose veins ran bluely with Stuart blood. Later, at her exquisite treasure-filled palace, the Duchess danced a wild flamenco for
Pat's camera and my admiration.

News from the outside world filtered through despite Franco's cen-
sorship that still left newspapers with gaping holes. I heard from Nick
Meyer about the gaping holes in my own penmanship:

Dear Prince Igor or Bridie Murphy, or Whatever,
I am answering one third of your very gratifying letter. This is
the third I was able to make out, or one word in three. Actually I
finally did decipher the whole thing. I took it round to a Cistercian
monk who is a friend of mine (I met him at the dog track painting
illuminations on a greyhound) and he told me what you were actually saying. So you're going to play a rabbi in a Yiddish version
of "The Comte De Monte Cristo Meets the Wolf Man." I'm so
happy for you.

He told me about his new screenplays and novel and particularly
about a Sherlock Holmes spoof called *The Seven Percent Solution*. He
later sent me the eminently readable manuscript. I made one or two
Anglicized emendations—"railway" for "railroad," "typist" for "ste-
nographer," etc.—and was convinced that this masterly pastiche
would intrigue and delight many other readers, as proved the case.
Later I was chagrined at having to turn down his offer to play Dr.
Watson in the film version.

Rick was still in the real Paris and beginning to fulfill his destiny by
working on a newsreel crew. Like my opportunistic Conrad, he was
also a part-time chauffeur—to the Aga Khan. The saddest news of all
was from May and Joe telling me that Grandad, having cheated his
fellow horticulturist, the Reaper, for over forty years, had finally died
in Devon, where he had gone to spend his last days living near his
daughter. Nipped in the bud, too, was a delightful May-December
relationship that Amos had described in one of his last letters:

It seems strange, an old man of 80 and a young attractive widow of
fifty. We first met just after her husband died. I gave her some

sympathy and encouragement and it was then that we became such friends. Of course, that is all there is in it. You will no doubt have a laugh . . .

Far from it: I still miss him.

Friends came to stay, such as Jimmy Wilson, who astonished us by getting straight off the plane from Los Angeles and breakfasting on Madrid's renowned tripe and suckling pig. Even the ever-restless Tennessee came to see "all those beautiful people on and off location. I love Faye Dunaway. Have great esteem for the talent of Richard Chamberlain. As for Miss Welch, she is said to have a lively tongue, and I mean in conversation."

Indeed, Raquel's considerable reputation noisily preceded her arrival. Apart from insisting on her own costume designer, her several representatives drew up and circulated a document giving exact instructions as to how their client was to be treated. The most weighty clause was the ban on any overt references to her mammary endowments, an outstanding display of which on countless European magazine covers had first brought Raquel fame. As the film was a duel of décolletés with many of the jokes—about melons and so forth—pointedly in this direction, it presented problems. Raquel seemed an unwelcome threat to the established camaraderie of the set. However, on her very first day at work, she gamely did a pratfall in the dust just like everyone else, proving instantly that she was "one for all and all for one."

I enjoyed our hilariously clumsy love affair and relished equally the comic improbability of her other amorous pairing with Spike Milligan, my schoolboy hero from *The Goon Show*. Working with Spike was a painful joy. The pleasure was derived from his constant barrage of gags and fertile verbal coinings—"They don't fall off trees chambers like these in Paris"—and the pain from the virtual impossibility of keeping a straight face. Totally incapacitated by laughter I remember being forced into that time-honored theatrical face-saver of turning my back to the audience.

Oliver Reed trailed a darker, different kind of fame. He seemed to be perfectly cast, especially when living up to Athos's dictum: "You will find the future looks rosier through the bottom of a glass." He indulged and was indulged in all manner of old-fashioned movie-star excesses. The press seemed to expect these of him, and he duly obliged. There was one irresistibly endearing prank, however. Oliver surreptitiously filled the ornamental pond in the lobby of his grand hotel with carrots and, before an audience of horrified tourists, grabbed and gobbled down these slippery live "fish." Adding another layer to his legend, he was thrown out.

It was an immensely physical summer. If not actually filming a fight, I was always rehearsing one. I watched in astonishment as my body began to bulge with musculature, and witnessed at firsthand the inextricable connection between physical fitness and well-being. Compensation for all the physical discomfort was the extraordinary variety and beauty of our locations, some fifty-five in all. We saw as much of Spain as we could. Toledo was still very much as El Greco depicted it and other places like the Conquistador's Trujillo seemed to be mere extensions of our set. Pat and I seriously entertained the idea of buying an ancient ruined church in Pedraza as a second home. This same pipe dream has since been conjured on other film sets. We have even contacted real estate agents for our castle in the air—and are *still* looking!

Driving to Pamplona one weekend to see the running of the bulls, we found Hemingway's macho celebration had gone to seed. The air was rancid with the stench of stale wine and urine. Not a blade of grass was visible, the ground being littered with booze-flattened bodies. French hippies—supra-conformist in the Gallic way—seemed to have colonized the place en masse.

As far as bulls were concerned, I had become the subject of a small scandal. Manuel Benitez, El Córdobes himself, had got wind of my plans to immortalize him on film and had protested—with some justification—that only one person could play him: himself! He had even started English language lessons in Folkestone—the first time he had been to school anywhere.

The delights of contemporary tourism were nothing compared to our long daily voyage through Dumas's world in which plebeian dirt and savagery contrasted with the fabulous excesses of court life. Slops flew from windows, teeth were pulled at the roadside, while gorgeously costumed aristocrats played chess with human pieces. I particularly liked the background shot of a tree being carted through the city streets, vividly illustrating the contemporary French passion for gardening.

At the end of the long adventure we left for a holiday in Greece, stopping en route in Rome to visit Rick who was now tangibly following in my filmic footsteps as an assistant director on a feature film.

Considering the coincidences that already bound our lives it came as no surprise that the star of his debut film was Elizabeth Taylor, too, or that he should be starting his career in Rome. Rick was to meet us on our arrival at Fiumecino but there was so sign of him—only a dark-haired gigolo sporting an apple-green cashmere sweater over a silk shirt festooned with gold chains loitered lasciviously and then glinted into the light. It was Rick. Elizabeth, like everyone else, had apparently taken a shine to him and, seeing his meager paycheck, the shine had taken this more lustrous form. Scandal magazines leaped wrong-headedly to the obvious conclusion and published pictures of Elizabeth and her new lover. For whatever reason he looked wonderful and was loving his new job and the extraordinary life subtended from it.

Our intended holiday was with friends on the far-flung island of Patmos, but just after our arrival Pat developed a raging toothache. This could have been a psychosomatic response to anther female houseguest. "Surely you don't consider acting man's work?" had been her opening conversational salvo to me, while to Pat she expressed disapproving astonishment that we planned to share the same bed. I had, in fact, often asked myself the same question about acting, but was reluctant to be reminded of it on a holiday from a film where I had almost emasculated myself with macho effort!

The local dentist, it turned out, also operated the village sweet shop. As if in a vignette from the film, this enterprising lady bludgeoned Pat's offending tooth with a rusty instrument to howls of agony, persuading us that we should hurry home for more sophisticated treatment. This was not easy as there was no ferry and, similar to another sequence in the film, we made a long, Byronic journey in an open caïque to distant Kos before fleeting back to London.

Returning to Madrid to pick up our car, we determined to convert the leisurely drive home into our frustrated holiday. After crossing the Pyrenees we called in one evening at a hostelry that furnished both a splendid dinner and a restful night. The next morning some instinct delayed us, insisting that we look around the town first before driving on north to the pleasures of the Dordogne. I was well rewarded. Quite by chance—or perhaps not—we were in Auch and, dominating the marketplace, was a huge statue of this Gascon town's most famous son—D'Artagnan!

A few weeks later I was back in New York thumping the publicity drum for *England Made Me* and enjoying Hal and Hugh's exuberant new collaboration on the musical *Candide*. Horizons of this best of all possible worlds were further enlarged with a visit to the Tehran Film Festival. Hindsight of subsequent events now makes me glad we went. I had been requested to attend a film opening in Beirut for example and, travel-weary, had declined, assuming, in flagrant disregard of our usual carpe diem dictum, that Beirut would always be there to be enjoyed. Now both cities have changed irreversibly.

Tehran was like Los Angeles—sunny, sprawling suburbs in search of a center, choked with traffic and often blanketed with a brown haze that blotted out the encircling snowcapped mountains. We were both impressed, in general by the Iranians' exquisite politeness and in particular by their treasure houses and not just of pearly black caviar. There was an ostentatious extravagance, symbolized by the fabulous crown jewels and the tented city erected for the Shah's lavish coronation, that made the escapist, Depression-era films of Frank Capra being showcased at the festival look especially decent and deserving. We met the great man himself, as modest, lively and entertaining as his work. Anne Miller was also there, immaculately made up no matter what hour of the day—even at dawn when she set off with us on those legendary legs to visit Shiraz with its honeycomb bazaar and nightingale-haunted gardens. We mused amidst the ruins of Persepolis with Helen and Trevor Howard, little realizing that this was but a preview of the fall of yet another Persian empire.

The Musketeers saluted the world later that year. Originally planned as a long, road-show presentation with an intermission, at some stage in its postproduction—or possibly during the filming itself —a decision was made to bisect the story and issue it as two films. In a hail of litigious indignation lawyers rushed back to their contracts only to find that the producers had scrupulously described the undertaking not as a film or films but as "our project."

The first part, *The Three Musketeers,* opened in Paris and, despite a certain chauvinist reserve, the French were enthusiastic. There were elaborate ceremonies where we screen swashbucklers were inducted into some mystic Gallic Order of Musketeers whose only raison d'être seemed to be the imbibing of unlimited quantities of Armagnac. I was presented with a giant bottle of the fiery liquor, its vintage the same as my own, and, as with the Queen's diamonds in the film's plot, managed to sneak it back across the Channel to England. It remains unfinished to this day.

The film was a crowd-pleaser. Reaction was often vocal with audiences cheering our antics. Lester had done his usual brilliant job of dubbing—witness the Velasquez-like dwarfs carrying Faye Dunaway's Milady in a sedan chair. Respectfully silent during the shooting, they now cheekily discussed their mistress's avoirdupois.

A few uninhibited laughs were dearly needed as the world situation grew daily more unfunny. Inflamed by war in the Middle East, the all-for-one attitude of the oil producers had spawned a global economic recession. In California, "No Gas—Bone Dry" was the sign greeting the long line of old-fashioned, fuel-guzzling automobiles, heralding the end of an era of cheap mobility. A period of political confusion continued as the Vietnam War ground unwinnably on. Civil strife also flared in Northern Ireland. Britain was beset with strikes, with some of the work force reduced to a three-day week. Prime Minister Edward Heath began his Pyrrhic battle with the miners' union.

In defiance of the gloom, unfamiliar lunches and dinners were enjoyed around our underused octagonal table. We also spent that Christmas with friends in St. Moritz, staying in a chalet that commanded Christmas-card views. It was our first visit to this cynosure of ski resorts and we relished the extraordinary well-being afforded by the delectable combination of sun, snow and pure mountain air. There were long walks and lengthier sleigh rides to little country inns where a now permanently peremptory appetite demanded constant, delicious appeasement. Rounding off an athletic year appropriately, we learned to ski, slipping and falling as frequently as D'Artagnan had. Our skills improved impressively if involuntarily when a jovial sadist lured us to the top of a mountain for lunch and insisted that we ski down. In general I found that the brief snow-borne sensation only just compensated for all the accompanying boredom of donning and hauling equipment. It was all too earthbound for an ethereal flyer.

We made new friends, especially among the family of Rick's Paris employer, the Aga Khan. St. Moritz was a holiday refuge for many celebrated talents. Herbert von Karajan, as mystic as a Wagnerian god amidst these misty peaks and pine forests, entertained us to dinner at his chalet. Sitting next to him, Pat was moved to learn that he was in almost constant physical pain, though his zeal for performing remained undimmed. Guenther Sachs personified the omnipresent jet set, with captains both of sport and industry at play. There were as many fortunes as fur coats on display, and much ritual kissing of hands and the ambient air around bronzed smiling faces and designer sunglasses. It was an interesting and novel milieu that provided a great deal of fun as well as glittering grist to my actor's omnivorous mill.

We found ourselves caught—not unwillingly—in the international social whirl and in the New Year in the company of some notables and many quotables, attended the opening of Beatrice and Atenor Patino's new luxury beach resort, Las Hadas, deep down in tropical Mexico. The event culminated in a White Ball giving an innocent seal to all the extravagant shenanigans. There was much media attention —the object of the exercise—and not a little carping at the sybaritic excesses. This was before a more materialist era had made hedonism acceptable in countless television showcasings of the life-styles of the rich and famous.

The Three Musketeers rode into London on my thirty-second birthday with a Royal Command Performance. For someone who had served the English Court so well it seemed only appropriate! We were a palpable hit—worldwide. Returning to America to publicize the film was an agreeable way of keeping in touch with events and friends there, despite the grueling, repetitive round of interviews and even requests to duel on television shows. The political ferment of the time had impregnated the film's advertisements. The public, reeling from the imbroglios of Watergate, were teased: "What famous trio hoodwinked the courts, embarrassed an empire while swashbuckling their way to fame and fortune? Hint: It's *not* Haldeman, Ehrlichman and Mitchell."

When I hung up my dusty plumed hat and sheathed my battered sword I had no inkling that, fifteen years later, they would be back in action again.

Made in England

*N*ineteen seventy-four was unusual. There were three films—all bearing the rare stamp "Made in England," and all boasting stellar casts. Consistent with our new mondaine life, the first was a glamorous ride aboard Agatha Christie's *Murder on the Orient Express*. This had been hard to refuse on several counts, not least because the story involved exotic foreign travel, incorporating a homage to the 1930s steam-train movie that the plane had made redundant and consequently ever more romantic. The invitation to join such an exceptional cast was, however, nearly impossible to decline. Indeed, playing the murder victim, Richard Widmark declared that he "signed on to meet the people."

And what a populace! Fellow passengers included the likes of Ingrid Bergman, Martin Balsam, Jacqueline Bisset, Sean Connery, Anthony Perkins, Wendy Hiller, Rachel Roberts as well as former colleagues such as Albert Finney, Jean-Pierre Cassel, Vanessa Redgrave and Colin Blakely. Sir John Gielgud, modifying his Chang, was also playing another in an idiosyncratic line of impeccable butlers. To hear him pronounce "Amber Moon" was worth the price of admission. A new

London neighbor, Lauren Bacall, was aboard, complete with her slow-burn eyes and throaty eruption of a laugh. Geoffrey Unsworth, magic light meter in hand, was also present to illuminate an even more confined set.

The director of this extravaganza was Sidney Lumet, who made films with the regularity and reliability of a railway timetable. Slight, bespectacled and disarming, he was given to jeans and sneakers and loud affectionate kisses. His enthusiasm and energy were infectious. Unusually, he rehearsed his talky stagebound epic—normally a process I dislike as it seems to have nothing in common with the creative ferment of film. But as a means of dispelling inhibiting shyness and getting to know such a distinguished cast, it was certainly no hardship. My own preparation for the role of the mysterious Count Andrenyi consisted of inviting the Hungarian emigré author George Mikes to tea where he gave me an amusing lesson in how to be an alien—or at least how to sound like one.

Actual filming began in Paris in a dingy train-repair depot in St. Denis. True to Gallic form, the caterer, or rather, *maître cuisinier,* produced miraculous manna in this bleak desert—*quenelles à la façon de Nantua* and other first-class fare. The station's platform was where the audience was introduced to the cast, including myself and my countess —an ostrich-plumed Jacqueline Bisset dressed way beyond the nines by designer Tony Walton. He was also responsible for the meticulous artwork and period detail, liberally interpreting an injunction in the script stating, "in brief our set dresser may go to town." Despite Pat's usual disapproval and my own discomfort, I sported a stick-on mustache and also luxuriated in curly locks and an enveloping camelhair coat that I adored. At the end of the production I dutifully, regretfully, returned this exquisitely cut garment only to be unexpectedly reunited with it a few years later on another film. It was a chance in a million. I bought it at once and we have been inseparable ever since.

The rest of the filming took place at Elstree Studios, and was at times as tedious as waiting for a real train. We sat for weeks within the exquisitely marquetried confines of a real railway carriage. Outside is windows an old-fashioned revolving drum of painted scenery gave the illusion of movement, an effect greatly enhanced on the finished result by Richard Rodney Bennett's splendid score. The train and the action then became bogged down in artificial snow—and, as the long inquiry and dénouement took place, in equally deep drifts of dialogue. Lumet, a graduate of live TV, was fast and inventive but even he could not disguise the fact that most of the cast were dress extras filling the scene while Albert, padded and brilliantined as Poirot, lengthily proved that this whodunit was an alldunit.

The great compensatory joy for this tedium was the company itself. Because several cast members were also in West End shows it was decided to dispense with a lunch hour and provide a buffet on set, so that we could all start later and finish earlier. Reservations at this "round table" were as highly prized as those on the famous train itself, the charisma of invited guests—such as Prince Charles—often matching that of the regulars. Only Vanessa Redgrave, true to her revolutionary political ideals, refused to join this bourgeois elitist assembly, insisting on eating with her fellow workers who dubbed her, either grudgingly or gratefully, the Shop Steward. Our other zealot was Ingrid Bergman, playing a drab Swedish missionary. I spent every morning alongside her under the hair dryer attempting to glamorize myself while she tried vainly to erase her pervasive star quality in what would be one of her last, and Oscar-winning, film performances.

It made a pleasant change to be operating from home. The garden bloomed, the fountain trilled and unwonted household instincts were fulfilled. We engaged in English pursuits. It was a time of consolidation, of feeling and feeding one's roots, perhaps because instinctively we sensed that, for the time being, this would be our last year as English residents. There were weekends in the country in the neighboring shires. We marveled at the great London exhibition of Turner paintings and, on a less elevated plane, I began a collection of Staffordshire earthenware portrait figures—concentrating on those from a theatrical background.

Reinforcing this mood, I added a very English portrait to my own gallery when cast as Pip in a new film version of Dickens's *Great Expectations*. In a sense there were parallels with my own life. Like Pip, the "common" boy from the forge who had acquired the accent and accoutrements of wealth, I had "growed and swelled and gentlefolked." Like him I prayed that in this process I had not become a snob and an ingrate. It was at this time that I started to research my ancestry at Somerset House, discovering I was mainly sprung from a long line of loamy Joe Gargerys. I revisited Yarnton and childhood, and in Oxford called on my aunt Edith, the last remaining member of her Higginbottom generation. Spry and upright and passionately respectful of the Royal Family, she still earned a modest living with her needle making stuffed toys. She shared her sister Mabel's stubborn streak. Pat and I arranged for a local taxi firm to transport her to wherever she required, but we never received a single bill.

As with the previous film, elegant clothes and coiffured hair were also a feature of *Great Expectations*. There was a similar heavyweight cast that included Sarah Miles, James Mason, Margaret Leighton, Robert Morley, Anthony Quayle and fellow Orient Express assassin, Rachel Roberts. Joss Ackland, my murderer in *England Made Me* and also my Musketeer father—in real life a paterfamilias extraordinary— was playing the honest blacksmith. With so many famous veterans of the British screen returning to the studios that had established their careers and made their fortune, the fate of these cavernous dream factories was especially poignant. Our native film industry was waning; this production was another example of American finance bolstering our declining output.

Our film was intended for television presentation in America, something problematic for my agent there. Actors of the smaller screen were then not entirely respectable, occupying an inferior niche in the pecking order to their stage and movie colleagues. In Britain, the generic crossover was natural and almost complete: actors acted in all media without hierarchical evaluation of their efforts. If anything there was a certain genuflection to the mother goddess of Theater and a concomitant insufferable insinuation that films were made "for the money." In America, it was like a terrible party, with the different actors confined to different corners of the room, eyeing each other contemptuously or covetously and only occasionally mixing. I don't think radio actors were even invited.

Questioning the advisability of my working on the smaller screen came as something of a shock. Television in America, it was joked, was a medium because it was neither rare nor well done. I listened politely but determined, as always, to follow my own instincts. The pill, however, was sweetened by the production's planned presentation as a cinema feature in certain markets—with great success as it turned out in China—even though a distributor was heard to complain it was "another of these movies where they sign their names with feathers." All this inhibiting nonsense was turned on its head in the late 1980s when, in the United States, feature films were cast specifically from a televisually approved pool of actors such as Robin Williams, Bruce Willis and the many alumni of *Saturday Night Live*.

Dickens seemed ideal for television, writing as he did in serial form for the penny press with a superabundance of personages and plots.

Indeed, the problem was that his characters were so compelling they were difficult to restrain or ignore. Our two-hour film was obliged to be just as much of a condensation and extrapolation as David Lean's celebrated earlier version had been. Ours concentrated on the Pip–Estella story and, by coincidence, was also photographed by Lean's ever-youthful colleague Freddy Young.

A major difference was that ours was also conceived as a musical: "Great Expectorations," as it was gleefully dubbed. I duly took singing lessons and even recorded such predictable ditties as "I Had Great Expecta-a-ations." Consistent with my reputation as the great non-singing star of the movie-musical, though, these songs went unfilmed. Instead of counterpointing, illuminating or ideally advancing the action, it was found that they stopped it dead. Such interior maunderings were ill-suited to Dickens's extrovert liveliness.

Sarah Miles was my co-star. Full of catlike unpredictability, alternately purring then pawing, she brought a vibrant, neurotic sexuality to Estella and a quirky offstage sense of fun. James Mason fulfilled all my great expectations of him. Intelligent, professional, if slightly distant, his presence was clouded by a strange melancholy shared by both actor and role, as if he had experienced Magwitch's own exile and accumulation of material fortune in distant lands. I was sincerely flattered when he told Pat over tea that we looked and sounded alike. Our producer was Robert Fryer and he and I made plans—happily fulfilled—to reunite with our gifted director, Joe Hardy, on a play at L.A.'s Ahmanson Theater, where the two had already presented a distinguished *Cyrano* with Richard Chamberlain.

The immersion in British culture reinforced in me a desire to see still more of my native land while opportunity existed and before the engulfing recession deepened the gloom. We delighted in the antiquities of the great country houses such as Wilton, where I posed for Cecil Beaton's camera on the Palladian bridge. I embarked on a series of poetry readings—Edward Thomas at Cambridge and Auden in London, to commemorate the latter's death. Pat and I drove north to Scotland in August, visiting en route other historic places and houses. A certain urgency inflamed this tourism. A recent exhibition at the Victoria and Albert Museum had cataloged the ongoing appalling pillage of our national heritage occasioned as much by apathy as by rapacious developers. The museum had resounded with a regular sickening crash, indicating the loss of yet another great house, and orchestrating the alarming rate of the destruction. At the Edinburgh

Festival I met some former National Theatre colleagues, Ian McKellen and Edward Petherbridge, who were presenting their self-governing Actors Company in a performance of *Tartuffe,* thereby disproving the conventional wisdom that lunatics are unable to successfully run their own madhouse. Sitting in the Assembly Hall, where ambition had earlier stirred and focused, revived a nostalgia that was further enhanced by a return to the Highlands, still redolent of Dundee salad days.

Invited to my Oxford college's St. Cuthbert's Dinner, I plunged further back into nostalgia, reentering the tight mandarin milieu of gowns and port, a bizarre world so brilliantly characterized by Pinter and Losey in the Common Room scene in *Accident.* Miraculously I found myself dining next to Stephen Spender and our flowing conversation inevitably turned to Isherwood and Berlin. He had known Jean Ross, the original "Sally Bowles," who, at one point married to Claud Cockburn, had lived quietly and respectfully in London until her death just before the release of the film she had inspired. Later he sent me some old snapshots of her, telling me he had just spoken to Isherwood who was writing about their life together in Berlin: "So we had better fasten our seat belts!"

It was at this time that another extraordinary person first embellished our lives. Michael McCready was a doctor practicing in pinstriped respectability in Belgravia. A brilliant homeopath, he was also one of only twenty doctors in Britain then employing radiesthesia, using the radionic "box." This, another branch of energetic medicine, represented an advanced, scientific formulation of the dowser's ancient art, relying on the basic concept that all life forms are connected by the same electromagnetic energy. It was a highly accurate means of both diagnosing and treating the patient. For our purposes it was ideal as, our being absent so often and traveling so much, Dr. McCready could both monitor and minister without our being present.

Over the years that he has safeguarded our health—and perhaps because of the unusually intimate psychological as well as physical details demanded by such an unorthodox medical practice—he has become a great friend. We learned that his mild, modest and unassuming mien masked an extraordinary personality. An Olympic fencing champion, he had also parachuted behind enemy lines during the last war, a homeopathic kit strapped to his leg. Joining up with the Maquis, one of his first patients had been a dying German soldier whom he successfully treated. In gratitude this enemy insisted on becoming his faithful assistant. Soon after we became his equally faithful, grateful patients, Dr. McCready moved to Dublin where, fortunately, he was never more than a phone call away.

It was as if the recent concentrated inoculation of British values as well as constitutional medicines made it permissible for us to travel abroad again. We stayed with friends on Cap Ferrat in their Venetian palazzo of a house. Terraced gardens ran leisurely down to the Mediterranean, one of the summer playgrounds of the St. Moritz crowd who brought the same effortless *savoir vivre* to their fun. Anchored in the lee of the Cap, their yachts bobbed in swelly symphony while liveried crews served lunch. Pat and I had started to discuss the possibility of living outside England. With a growing awareness that we might soon join their number, we met up with several expatriates. Dirk came down from his mountain fastness in Grasse to lunch with a tanned Rex Harrison, debonair even shirtless, in his ocean-embracing house full of sun, children and dogs.

On another occasion we stayed overnight in Tony Richardson's extraordinary village of an estate at La Garde Frenet where John Gielgud, Jack Nicholson, Anjelica Huston and Buck Henry were fellow guests. Curiously, many like us had just dropped by but, like the guests in Buñuel's *Exterminating Angel,* had been unable to leave the party and were still there weeks later. David Hockney was among them, immortalizing the pool and its underwater swimmer, an image destined to become as powerful an icon as his California pool paintings. We had become ardent collectors of his work—fortunately while it was still relatively affordable. The consummation of our Gallic *vie en rose* was the Rothschilds' garden party at their great country house at Ferrières. Watching the beau monde watching each other reminded me of a favorite scene in *Ashes and Diamonds* where the doomed aristocracy dance their last waltz. Harsher economic winds would soon be blowing.

A speedy trip to South Africa confirmed all our old prejudices about the place. These had been recently roused by Athol Fugard, whose plays such as *Sizwe Bansi Is Dead* had inflamed the Royal Court Theatre. Watching wild animals, whose freedom and integrity were totally accepted, did nothing to dispel the old nagging feeling that there was something rotten in the state, especially as the middle ground of opinion separating the factions from a potential apartheid bloodbath seemed to have eroded further. Again relieved to be homeward bound, we stopped in Mauritius, a jewel of a tropical island fringed by miraculous silver beaches. Even here, however, it was impossible to entirely escape business. A telex containing a whole film script arrived from Ridley Scott, a brilliantly promising commercials director who had asked me to star in his first feature film. This revised version unspooled lengthily around the restaurant like one of the Dead Sea scrolls, and like them was destined to dwell in darkness.

Rerooted in London, I made the last of the year's trio of films, a version of the stage success *Conduct Unbecoming,* set in a British military garrison on the Indian Frontier in 1878. Ismael Merchant had once talked of actually filming it there. Ours was a small-budget stage-bound version, however, produced by British Lion—in fact, its last toothless growl. A virtue had been made of necessity and most of the action was now concentrated on the trial scene—usually a guarantee of high drama. The screenplay had distilled a straightforward essence from its rather overwrought origins that one wag had dubbed, because of the pig-sticking sequence, "Back Passage to India." It was a story of honor and friendship, of the individual versus the institution. As the real world degenerated into economic chaos these traditional sterling values, though expressed through stiffened upper lips, seemed ever more relevant and appropriate. It was as close as I would get to actual military service, which was fine by me!

Like *Orient Express,* it was essentially a costumed whodunit, made entirely indoors apart from some brief authentic exterior scenes captured by a second unit. The budget was so tight that our director, Michael Anderson, was obliged to save time by keeping his cameras rolling from one angle on whole sequences before turning around, relighting and shooting them from another. I was playing another "young innocent" type to add to a growing gallery. But unlike some of these portrayals, the inexperienced, idealistic young subaltern Drake was a strong role, full of subtleties and opportunities.

I was given first billing, an unprecedented honor made even more prestigious by the luster of a cast that contained such distinguished actors as Trevor Howard and Richard Attenborough. Christopher Plummer and Stacy Keach, both managing impeccable pukka accents, advertised the vitality that can be achieved by casting against perceived type. Susannah York was the lady whose honor had been besmirched, igniting the drama and causing testosterone torment in the mess. Over lunch one day she and I discussed how many people assumed we were related. It was too boring, we agreed, to keep on denying this so we invented an entirely bogus lineage that united us, if I remember correctly, as the bastard offspring of the Archbishop of Warsaw. I, at least, have stuck faithfully to this story.

After five concentrated weeks it was all over, but for a long time afterward I continued to snap awake at 6:00 A.M. with that instant alertness born of the necessity to record some immortal scene some two hours later. There were no more furious rehearsals in the car going to work, when, between yawns, the reviving mind bred fertile ideas. It was enjoyable to come out of self-imposed purdah and to hear the chimes at midnight again.

The film did well on release. I saw it once on a plane whose confines added immeasurably to the claustrophobic nature of the piece. Viewing one's own films in such inescapable conditions is odd. But there are advantages. We were once flying back again to India, our government ticket seating us in the back of the plane where the film being shown was *The Three Musketeers.* An apologetic steward, however, came to us insisting it would be only appropriate if I watched my film in First Class. I did not demur—or move back!

Conduct Unbecoming also furnished the only professional award I have ever received—best actor in the Virgin Islands International Film Festival. However, over the years—and especially since becoming a member of the Hollywood-based Academy of Motion Picture Arts and Sciences—I have come to regard acting awards as pleasant but largely meaningless except as essential window dressing for the industry. They are frequently the fruits, not so much of popular choice, but of persistent, expensive promotion. It goes without saying, of course, that should I be offered another one, I would be more than hypocritically happy to accept! The whole honors system in America, however, is in danger of becoming devalued. Humanitarians there are two a penny, as omnipresent and unremarkable as the gourmet meal and the standing ovation. Soon everyone will receive an award for getting up in the morning.

I was pleased, however, that *Orient Express* was awarded the cachet of a Royal Command Performance with two queens in attendance— Queen Elizabeth and that Monarch of Mayhem, Agatha Christie. *Great Expectations* was also well received in the United States, perhaps because another half-hour of airtime had been purchased, preventing it from being slashed by the advertiser into little expectations. Thirty-eight million Americans, it was estimated, watched us, a respectable figure for a literary piece, but paltry compared with the 80 million who later tuned in to learn of J.R.'s shooting in *Dallas.*

Ring Around the World

The following year was marked by a strange cycle of accidents and almost ceaseless travel. An invitation to the Delhi festival proved predictably irresistible. My recent toil in the torrid frontier of Shepperton, however, had made me forget just how cold the real North India could be. We sought a warmer sun down in Goa, the Latin Quarter of India where, until recently, the Portuguese possessed a little enclave beloved of hippies and fishermen.

A luxury hotel had now sprung up within the confines of the doughty Fort Aguada. From its ramparts not a single protesting shot had been fired when the minuscule colony, a flea on an elephant's back, was incorporated into India, bringing with it as dowry an exotic cuisine and palm groves full of white cathedrals. Pat, ever adventurous, was ill again from eating something indeterminate at a Delhi cocktail party but somehow managed the flight down. Leaving her feverish in a darkened room, I took a walk along the magnificent beach where wooden fish boats were pulled up while their still lively catch was off-loaded and sold. A small boy tagged on beside me, full of wide-eyed conversation, and invited me back to his house. It was now my turn to be curious. After so many westernized hotel rooms, here was the perfect opportunity to see the real India, and I readily accepted. His mother was gracious and hospitable and I accepted her proffered drink—and with it the risk of gastric solidarity with Pat.

The boy was wearing a charming ring that I admired. "Oh, yes, it has touched the feet of St. Francis Xavier," he replied, explaining that every ten years the saint was displayed in the Cathedral of Bom Jesus. For some reason his body remained undecayed—cynics would say because he had died in China where the art of embalming had been perfected. "You must have this," my new friend insisted, removing his ring and overruling my repeated refusals to take so precious an object. Returning to Pat's sick bed I slipped it on her hot finger. Moments later—coincidence or miracle—she energetically jumped up, her fever having vanished.

We went to see her benefactor lying in state, tiny but uncorrupted, in a splendid robe. A fervent admirer had once bitten off a piece of his anatomy so we were kept at a respectful distance, but close enough to see the wisps of hair that still encircled his paper-thin ears. Pat wore her magic ring until it literally wore out. If ever there was a time that she would need divine protection it would be coming soon.

We started our journey back to England in a plane full of workers bound for the Gulf oilfields, landing at Muscat in Oman. A London friend who worked for the Omani government had urged us to visit and Pat to photograph, should we find ourselves in the area. He arranged for us to drive down to Nizwar, the old mud-brick former capital, stopping en route for a picnic in a gurgling date-palmed oasis. On arrival we were ushered into a large hall and escorted between ranks of wizened tribesmen who sprang to attention shouldering ancient Enfield rifles.

At the apex of their stiffened ranks, clad in a white robe with a great bejeweled dagger at his midriff, stood Othello. Gravely greeting us, he invited us to take coffee, served very thick in minute cups. Politeness toward him, and delight in this extraordinary thousand-and-one-night scenario, kept us constantly drinking. Etiquette, we learned later, required a firm shake of the cup to indicate refusal. As flattering as his reception was, it was obviously intended for someone else, as proved the case. Preceding the expected arrival of an official party—and triumphing in the beneficent coincidence of timing and place—we had been treated to a rare display of old-fashioned courtesy straight from the pages of Lesley Blanch or Richard Burton.

Elsewhere, Oman was in a state of future shock ever since the new ruler had replaced his father. For thousands of years nothing had happened: the population was still locked in the casbah at night. Then, in a few short years, all this changed radically. New roads, railways, factories, hospitals and the shiny black marbled airport where we landed had been constructed. And the people couldn't cope. The pace of change was now being deliberately decelerated and humanized. As our world continues to hurtle out of recognition I think that people long for a similar moratorium on change; hence the success of films and books that celebrate more secure and traditional life-styles rooted in the familiar past.

Back in London, Pat and I tried to cope with, and adjust to, our own changing realities, and to sense a pattern for the future. As the economy continued to flounder, England seemed a doubtful source of work. The only positive offers were from abroad—the most imminent being Bobby Fryer's promised invitation to perform at Los Angeles's Ahmanson Theater in Anouilh's *Ring Round the Moon*. It seemed to suit every contingency—personal, professional and financial—to spend another entire year out of the country and take advantage of the resulting tax benefits. In a job that had no guarantee of tenure, no retirement age or pension plan, this seemed not an indulgent, but a responsible move. Moreover, our family ties were close but unrestrictive. We were delighted to let our house to Gregory and Véronique Peck, who were in London for the filming of *The Omen*. I welcomed the prospect of attempting to establish myself, like him, as an international actor.

On a more frivolous note, we accepted an invitation from Norman and Wenda Parkinson to stop on our way to the States and play Mas with them at the Trinidad carnival and stay with them in their exquisite house in Tobago with its magical hill-perched pool overlooking the rainbowed coast. It was here that Parks returned from taking his "snaps" worldwide and raised the pigs that produced the now legendary "Porkinson's Banger" sausages.

From the moment we landed, a pounding, irresistible steel beat engulfed the island, sweeping us along its soulful syncopated path. Both Pat and I were still suffering from some minor skiing injuries—even our afflictions were now synchronous—and the doctor ordered absolute rest, but we literally could not keep still and sleep was a virtual impossibility.

We became "We Kind ah People," joining Parks and Wenda's

group and vying for carnival honors in the big parade that had preoccupied the island for the entire year and would do so for the next. It looked like a Las Vegas floor show run wild—a jumping, pounding, pulsating orgy of color and movement. Tall and immaculate, Parks rose above it all like a demented field marshal with his clipped military mustache, snowy dhoti and rolled umbrella. A rum bottle, cross-slung with his famous camera, hung from his Sam Browne belt. Everyone was out in the streets, from the Governor General downward, in a democratic display of spontaneous good fellowship. In the end, exhaustion reduced us to "chipping"—the almost imperceptible movement of one leaden foot in front of the other. Despite—or perhaps because of—our nonstop dance marathon, all our ailments vanished.

In Los Angeles we stayed in Jimmy Wilson's apartment in a building pretending to be a French château just below Sunset Boulevard. Jimmy also lent me his vintage Bentley to commute to rehearsals of *Ring Round the Moon* at the downtown Music Center. One evening after the first read-through where the director Joe Hardy introduced a talented cast that included Glynis Johns as Madame Desmortes, I drove home, stopping my splendid machine at a red light on a Hollywood freeway off-ramp. The rehearsal had gone well, the radio was playing some relaxing music. Suddenly there was a violent impact and this cozy world turned upside down. Fire flickered and someone was yelling "Get out!" The solidly crafted doors obligingly opened, depositing me on the sidewalk where—like an outtake from one of the current crop of disaster movies and the fulfillment of any childhood pyromaniac fantasy—I watched the exquisite car explode in flames. A newsreel crew taking a break at a nearby bar rushed out and filmed me standing in helpless horror before this conflagration—one of my most unforced and compelling performances.

I discovered that I had been rear-ended by an unlicensed drugged-out drunkard. The newly filled gas tank had ruptured and erupted. Apart from a whiplash blow to my neck, however, I seemed unscathed. On the principle of instantly mounting the horse that has thrown you, I rented a car to drive to the doctor for treatments.

In a curious way this accident was expected. While filming *Lost Horizon* I had returned home one day to find Pat being massaged. On seeing me her masseuse gasped involuntarily with shock. Recovering, she explained that she was psychic and had suddenly had a vivid image of me in a car engulfed in flames. She urged on us both the protective power of a special prayer that certainly proved puissant. The day after the accident there was a call from her. She had seen the incident on television and was delighted that it was now all over, with no real harm done. Except to the car, that is. But even this had a happy ending: Jimmy informed me that his insurance company compensated him with more than he had originally paid!

All these crude, material considerations were a world away from Anouilh's fey, gossamer comedy of manners, where the heroine's dress is described as "like the smoke of bonfires." In her own spangled midnight dress Glynis was a fairy godmother waving a magic wand over the proceedings in her hothouse of a château. I relished the acting opportunities provided by the twin roles of Hugo and Frederick, "so physically alike it's neither permissible nor possible," the one heartless and devilish, the other all heart and unambiguously nice. We were an instant crowd pleaser. It was gratifying to hear the massed roars of uninhibited laughter—surely one of the most irresistible sounds known to man. I was able to put into frequent practice all of Grace's early stage instructions about freezing to allow the audience to savor their pleasure.

Our evanescent moonbeam of a play was apparently one of the most popular ever presented at the Ahmanson. True to his word, David Merrick expressed interest in taking the production to Broadway, but I was already considering another film. Michael Anderson, my genial *Conduct Unbecoming* director, was at MGM setting up a futuristic film called *Logan's Run* and asked me to play its eponymous hero. Besides, the minimum contract for a play was usually four months and I could stay in America only for a limited time. Even though it seemed ludicrous to organize one's life around fiscal considerations, the prospect of paying excessive taxes was rather more unfunny.

Logan's Run was based on a popular best-seller, but on reading the script, I was disappointed. Pat, though, urged me to do it, as did my driver who, ever since the accident, had been deputized to take me to work. It was an interesting change of pace, they urged; a strong American hero. Enough of those earnest introspective Englishmen! Furthermore it would tap into that vast audience of Trekkies and sci-fi buffs who had been weaned on this material.

They were of course right. Adults still accost me and tell me that this film was their favorite when growing up. I was flattered to read afterward that had I refused it, the film would probably not have been made. Having secured its future I flew up to San Francisco to have myself photographed in a tiny lab where a new laser holographic process had been invented. It was for an interrogation scene in the film and the system, making its cinematic debut, was sufficiently revolutionary to fit into the twenty-third-century setting.

It was enjoyable being in a spotlight in L.A., a town that appreciates tangible success and prefers its laurels to be young, fresh, and un-rested-upon. I enjoyed getting to know some of the movers and shakers of L.A. society—notably the redoubtable Mrs. Dorothy Chandler and her Blue-Ribbon ladies—themselves fairy godmothers to the cultural life of the city. As well as the play, *The Four Musketeers* had opened to the same acclaim as its predecessor even though its darker tone warranted a more protective rating from the censors.

We felt happy and at home and started to entertain thoughts of permanently settling here. A local journalist, Aljean Harmetz, sketched a telling portrait of us both at that time:

> They have been married for eight years. Living as they have chosen to live—from airplane to airplane, and rented villa in Spain to ski lodge in Switzerland—they rely solely on each other. "Pat is my retinue, my only assistant," York says. "I would not accept a role without her consent, because where we go and what we do is Pat's life too." "It must be a good marriage," says a friend, "or they'd go crazy stuck in all these strange places alone together for nearly half the year." Bob Fosse, who considers himself an "interested spectator of marriages" has the same opinion. "Watch married people at parties. You see them head for the opposite ends of the room. Michael and Pat sit together. They listen to each other, corroborate each other. It is obvious they are important to each other."

Rick came to stay and also investigated the possibility of moving to L.A. as a student at the American Film Institute. I now had time at last to renew old friendships.

I heard from Frank Gannon, my old Oxford chum who had given us the tour of the White House. He was still in the disgraced President's employ, having fled west with him into political exile on that last emotional flight out, and was now assisting Nixon with his memoirs. We arranged to meet down in San Clemente, the seaside site of the former Western White House. There Frank introduced us to Diane Sawyer, who had also been on the team and who was now his girlfriend. As a media star she would achieve a fame and charisma that would almost rival that of her former boss. But then, for some reason, she was not invited along with Frank and ourselves to cocktails that evening with the President and Mrs. Nixon.

Indeed, there they were standing on the threshold of the Casa Pacifica when the three of us drove up at the appointed hour. I shall never forget the look that Nixon first gave me—like that in the eyes of a beaten dog about to be kicked again—which vanished as soon as he perceived that we were not a threat. He went on to say that he was a fan and I wished that I had been able to reply in kind.

Both the President and his wife were most cordial and hospitable. They invited us to look over the house, "so you can see that so much of the press's unflattering reports are exaggerations." We were indeed struck by its unpretentious modesty—especially the picture window in the library, puffed in the press as the last word in extravagance. Tricia's bedroom, where Brezhnev had stayed, was similarly unremarkable and was certainly in startling contrast to the photographs they showed us of the prerevolutionary splendor they had enjoyed in Moscow. Walking around the garden, I saw the President put his arm around my Pat. He told her how serious his last illness had been and Pat said what a shock this must have been. "That wasn't the shock," he countered. "From there to here. What did I say? What did I do?" The appalling stress of the past year was still evident, although we were both struck by Mrs. Nixon's composure. She was so much more natural than her stilted press image, uninhibitedly embracing Pat in her bedroom.

Inevitably the conversation turned to politics, and the President, previously idling in neutral, slipped forcibly into high gear. He spoke lengthily about his foreign policy, the cornerstone of his reputation, although Watergate would remain his tombstone. He elaborated on his celebrated overtures to China and Russia, the first thin edge of the Western wedge that would undermine the whole top-heavy unworkable Communist structure. Afterward Frank showed us a letter from the archive material in which the young schoolboy Nixon vowed that all he wanted to do with his life was to serve his country. Yet I found it hard to like him, much as I wanted, out of politeness, to approve. Perhaps it was Nixon's unfortunate smile—a feral flash that the encompassing lips failed to transform into warmth. Returning home, Pat and I were both emotionally drained, overwhelmed by conflicting sympathies.

The successful run of the play concluded, we flew back to renewed exile in Paris where I even had a summit meeting with my English lawyer and agent at the top of the Eiffel Tower. Pat and I reappeared in the South of France where, black-tied, we attended the Cannes Film Festival and, blue-jeaned, explored the sumptuous gorges and valleys of the hinterland. After a visit to Monaco, the idea began to germinate of using this odd pocket-handkerchief of a principality as a European base. We inspected some of the intrusive concrete high-rise apartment buildings that were rudely shouldering their way into the skyline, pushing aside their delicate *belle-époque* forebears. These monstrous "alphavilles" were reminiscent of some of the structures about to be used as sets for *Logan's Run* back in America and on location in the Dallas/Fort Worth area. Their confident futuristic styles were perfect for our story.

The film was about a youthful, monitored society three centuries hence that lived in a self-contained pleasure dome of a sealed city where everyone is programmed to die at thirty. Logan was one of the policemen—euphemistically called "Sandmen"—who ensure that this process of elimination takes place on Last Day at the Mass-like Carousel ceremonies. Sent to track down the Runners—the refuseniks living in an alternate aging society in a subterranean refuge, like early Christians in their catacombs—Logan becomes one of them and, Moses-like, leads the children out of blissful bondage to a real world of mothers and fathers where real emotions and even cats are novelties. Unlike my previous exit from that other Shangri-la, this one had a happy ending.

In the city where Kennedy's Camelot had seen its own Last Day, we attempted to re-create another idealized society. Dallas's giant apparel markets housed huge public concourses, while the Water Garden in Fort Worth served as the conduit to this domed, doomed city. The local youth were conscripted as extras. There seemed to have been a ban on bras and beards, giving the citizenry, intensely blond and comely in their diaphanous robes, the appearance of cheerleaders at a WASP convention. This contrasted with other youth we witnessed at a Rolling Stones concert—doped from the humid heat and other stronger factors—and I was at odds to ascertain which was more representative of the times.

In many ways the film was a telling metaphor of contemporary society with its enormous youthful population and a growing insistence on hedonistic values. Aldous Huxley's claim that, in the future, man would be governed not by Orwellian political imperatives but by his senses alone, by his pleasures and fears, seemed more and more plausible. Perhaps the appeal of the film lay in its positing of the startling theory that, without parental or marital pressures, there was no anxiety. Its description of an uninhibited sexual paradise complete with "Love Shops" was, of course, even in this age of pre-AIDS innocence, a recipe for a Faustian hell.

In many respects, though, it was on target, seeming to anticipate some significant trends. It illustrated the dubious luxury of the computerized society, where, for example, cosmetic surgery (from the "New You" shops) was freely available and socially acceptable. It depicted monstrous ghettos of urban violence, electric transportation and even, perhaps, predicted the elephantine shopping malls that were about to transform consumerism and city architecture.

Our director, Michael Anderson, ever good-natured and enthusiastic, set the tone of the production. Among the cast was Jenny Agutter, now transformed from the schoolgirl heroine of *Walkabout* into a mature leading lady. The extraordinary Capo of this Mafia of British talent was Peter Ustinov, playing the last old man left alive and improvising much of his dialogue—including snatches of T. S. Eliot's poems of cats a decade before a certain other Englishman made it world famous—in a marvelous swampy Southern accent. If he represented the future of normal Homo sapiens, then mankind had nothing to fear! Paradoxically shy and unassuming like so many brilliant men, he seemed to excel in everything he did. While filming he was at work on his next play, *Beethoven's Tenth,* and, as a vivid raconteur, was a constant source of genial entertainment. Not the least of my achievements on this film, however, was talent-spotting Farrah Fawcett. I saw her playing tennis on a friend's court one weekend, a vision of blonde perfection like her Dallas counterparts, and suggested her for the role of Holly, the laser cosmetician. I take full claim, of course, for all her subsequent amazing career developments.

Though our film had undoubted merits, its special effects, apart from the holograms, were not especially special. We suffered from being in the van of a sci-fi trend that Spielberg and Lucas would transform with their electronic wizardry. I was happy to be back working in the hallowed cathedrals of another major studio, especially as their value as real estate and the increase in location filming threatened their very existence. Some of our locations—in particular the sewage works directly under the L.A. airport flight path—were distinctly unglamorous, but a letter from Adrian describing his Dutch friend Hans Kemna's adventures while filming in Indonesia made me realize just how civilized our enterprise was:

> A book could be written to rival MacLiammoir's on *Othello,* full of Indonesians knifing each other for money, and co-producers ending up in prison, and threatening to hire killers to murder the Dutch director, and bribery and corruption going up the whole social scale there via the Chief of Police to the government itself.

My own built-in time crystal was, like Logan's, beginning to blink ominously. My days in the United States were numbered and to save them, we would flee south of the border at weekends, to Acapulco and Ensenada, returning in the small hours. At the end of the last lengthy day of shooting, I suggested to Pat that we go for an ice cream in Beverly Hills in lieu of dinner to make time for packing and sleep as we were leaving the next morning for a new film in Japan.

Crunching into hers, Pat complained it was full of ice. She had ordered vanilla and yet her lips were a vivid blood red. She then spat out shards of broken glass. "What do you do in a situation like this?" I asked the proprietor. "Faint dead away!" he whispered. We called a hospital for more helpful advice. Should Pat eat porridge or bread or try to vomit? "There's nothing you can do," stated the chilling voice of authority, "except wait for twenty-four hours—to see if an organ ruptures." "Then what happens?" Pat asked. "You die," came the cryptic reply.

The next day we left the United States with two days in hand, taxwise, and for Pat, an unknown number, lifewise. All the way to Japan I kept watching her for signs of imminent demise, but mercifully nothing happened. This was but round one in the coming year's pitched battle with glass.

Landing in Tokyo, I made the instant transition from ultramodern cop to modern prince. The story of *Seven Nights in Japan*—for such was our film's leadenly literal title—centered around a Prince George who, not unlike a certain other European prince, was a naval officer and also heir to the throne. His ship docks in Japan for a courtesy visit and, tired of the pressures—social, diplomatic and even romantic— that are thrust on him, escapes with a beautiful young Japanese tour guide for an unscheduled romantic leave.

This *Roman Holiday of Madame Butterfly* scenario shocked certain British sensibilities when the film was announced. Newspapers who keep their circulations going with lurid royal reportage muttered about a "right royal coincidence," and thundered it was a "cheap and sordid insult." Questions would even be asked in the House about the national disgrace of the heir to the throne being portrayed as a sexual athlete with a girl in every port. The chances of a Royal Command Performance seemed slim. Yet Prince Charles himself—whom everyone insisted I was impersonating—while not confessing the same irresponsible wish-fulfillment as George, confided that our portrayal of the rigors that face a modern prince was, in some respects, accurate. It was certainly not my intention to reflect unflatteringly on a man I admired.

Dropping anchor in oriental waters for the first time, I shared my mythical prince's own astonishment and pleasure at the simple beauties of Japanese life, especially away from the seething city centers. Pat had made several previous visits and, modifying the images culled from a thousand stereotyped war films, prepared me for my first impression of spotless cleanliness, efficiency and boundless energy. One immediate refreshing attraction was the lack of tipping. It was not that I begrudged this crude, feudal holdover. It was more the means than the amounts that bothered. Condemned to enjoy a life of hotels and restaurants, I loathed the whole condescending business of handing out banknotes and knowing who to tip, when, and how much.

Everywhere was a study in contrasts—beautifully expressed by the ultramodern Bullet train that sped us to Nagoya past the iconic, timeless beauty of Mount Fuji. We filmed in warm, blossom-treed sunshine in a region of lakes and country villages, staying in a *ryokan* and enjoying communal hot baths, having, as custom demanded, washed ourselves thoroughly beforehand. Wrapped in kimonos, we sat on the tatami floor to eat, and slept there, too—extremely soundly.

This first happy embrace of the Japanese experience stopped short, however, at the fish soup breakfast. Pat and I requested fruit, little realizing that our morning melon slice would cut a sizable chunk from our living allowance. Later, Hanae Mori, the brilliant designer, rescued us from the endless round of room service and crowded restaurants with the privilege of a dinner at her house that was as exquisitely tasteful and decorative as her clothes.

In Kyoto we found life was still very much as depicted on scrolls and screens. Its ancient tranquil buildings and gardens engulfed in an industrial metropolis, it reminded me of Oxford and soon familiar Michaelmas tints emblazoned the trees and Buddha'd temples. Abundant rain kept the moss gardens jewel-bright. We were entertained by a geisha, her powdered face as white as a clown's and about as sexy.

We returned to Tokyo, the nerve center of the emerging national powerhouse, where the upwardly mobile executive paid a fortune for his status symbols, thinking nothing of driving a hundred miles for a game of golf, or risking bankruptcy for a steak. What impressed us in this most modern of cities, however, were its immemorial aspects. At dawn we shared the coarse, unrehearsed drama of the fishmarket and stayed, spellbound, at the kabuki theater until late at night. The recognition of their great actors as "national treasures" reminded me of our comparative official disregard of our own talent apart from a knighthood here and a medal there. Greatness asserted itself through sheer force of talent, assisted, as always, by opportunity. When this happened, especially within the confines of the commercial theater, it was a landmark event.

"Have just got back from London—a journey made worthwhile by seeing the Knights in *No Man's Land,*" Adrian enthused.

It was like finally being in the presence of Michelangelo's David . . . so that's the work of art I've heard so much about! It sticks in your mind and doesn't leave you. I felt very happy for Gielgud and Richardson: how fantastic it must be after fifty years of acting, and crowns full of pearls, to have such a work delivered into one's hands and still to have one's talents unimpaired to be able to do it justice! Especially when both must have thought that modern theatre was leaving them on the shelf.

The most powerful—and bloody—piece of drama though happened offstage. Coming through the automatic glass doors of the hotel, Pat's attention was momentarily diverted by a bellboy asking to carry her camera bags. The doors continued to close on her, striking her forehead with all the force of an executioner's sword. Henry Kissinger was due to arrive at any moment and the hotel staff, anxious not to offend him with a lobby awash with blood like a crazed Japanese horror movie, spirited Pat away to a hospital. She refused to take penicillin and, holding her wound together, went from one emergency room to another until she found a doctor willing to sew it together without administering drugs. The hotel admitted liability but deliberated our claim before settling it by sending to our suite a whole boardroom of inscrutable executives, presumably to intimidate us.

With so many people crammed into so small a space, manners in Japan are of fundamental significance, the code of conduct having evolved to the point where, in department stores, an unfortunate female employee is obliged to bow in greeting, like a white-gloved automaton, to every entering customer. Individuality seems to be discouraged: there are legions of identikit businessmen and cloned uniformed schoolchildren. This artificial code, combined with an innate shyness, made it difficult to really get to know my co-star Hidemi Aoki, although before the filming my father had written enthusiastically about meeting her over a British tea ceremony when she had gone there to learn English. Tall and curvaceous, she was typical of the new generation of Japanese girls brought up on the Western diet left behind by their victors along with the baseball and chewing gum. But a typical reflex action—the hand covering the face—reminded one how close beneath the cosmetically finished skin and designer-labeled fashions lay the timeless mores of her kimono-clad ancestors.

Here, the Musketeer films had been perceived as Samurai epics, so it was gratifying to find myself fairly popular and my indecipherable autograph—even more inexcusable in this land of exquisite calligraphy—in demand. As a prince, it was interesting, too, to be the center of attention and to sample vicariously the royal routine. There were embassy functions where I was the inevitable Beau of the Ball and formal factory visits with hands behind back and detached, professional curiosity. And everywhere a laserlike concentration of attention a thousand times more intense than that for a mere movie star.

Our film unit settled into the usual easy international compromise with only the odd incident reinforcing the truth of Kipling's old saw about East and West. Our lunches, served on set in exquisite lacquer boxes, enraged some of the British crew. It was bad enough that the tea was green but serving rice with fish was positively unpatriotic. Soaking the grains with condensed milk and sugar, however, restored sweet contentment and validated our long-suffering hosts' long-held view of us as barbarians.

News of Rick's adventures on his film front filtered through: "School has started with a bang with hardly a moment to think. I really love it. I have already a project to film, ten minutes long, and am searching desperately for a subject." (This would turn out, quite by chance, to be *Sammy,* the play with which I made my debut as ASM at Oxford.) "AFI has one purpose—to professionalize. It believes in art but, more importantly, in work. Their policy is completely centered on finding a job." This last consideration was again upper-most in my mind as our film's final clapper board was struck in late November. Traveling slowly and making further Pacific overtures, we set off for Europe.

Like Prince George on royal tour we progressed to Okinawa, a remote war-blasted island to the south. Joining a new invasion wave of tourists, we visited the Expo whose somewhat coy theme, "The Sea We Would Like to See," was one of the growing number of early warning signs that the earth's fragile ecology was imperiled. Displayed underwater in a futuristic self-contained city, it looked like an off-shoot of the *Logan's Run* set.

Hong Kong followed, a monument to the untrammeled consumer-ism that is fueling the planet's demise. On a guided tour, where every building was described in terms of its cost and every person his in-come, it seemed inconceivable that communism could ever have flour-ished across the frontier that Nixon's Ping-Pong diplomacy had recently breached. Gazing wistfully at Moy Fah Loy's homeland, Pat and I determined to visit it one day. As a travel writer, Pat had earlier been denied a visa, the Chinese embassy in Paris arguing with Con-fucian logic that she could hardly presume to visit a country that for the United States did not exist.

This odyssey of the Englishman Abroad was further emphasized by an encounter with Sri Lanka, a country that, despite its new name, remained time-warped in a Victorian twilight. The aura of an imperial coaling station still haunted the tropic air, although the endless sandy beaches were now filled with pink, jolly Russians. There were marbled palaces masquerading as hotels, full of ancient bearers and bygone memories, and old-fashioned emporia with gothic cash registers and parcels still tied with string. We bought tea and uncut rubies.

Across the strait where the Indian Ocean, the Bay of Bengal and the Arabian Sea flood together lay our beloved India. There at a beach resort we studied yoga before heading north to Madras, visiting jug-gernauted temples and the placid seashore shrine of Mahabalipuram. The accompanying constant priestly whine for money, though, was reminiscent more of Hong Kong than of the Kingdom of Heaven. In our Madras hotel room I noticed the usual sign disclaiming responsi-bility for valuables and recommending their deposit in the hotel safe. Traveling for months now, we had accumulated sundry expensive items. These I obediently put into our trusty leather travel bag and requested the boy at reception to lock it in the safe.

It wasn't there when, checking out and already late for the plane, I asked for the bag back. Also missing was the receptionist I had dealt with. Roused rudely from his bed, the boy eventually cycled over, and countered our frantic looks and demands by calmly going to an unlocked cupboard that was in full view of the hotel lobby's daily traffic. With an air of some indignation he pushed aside some brooms and mops and proffered our bag. Things in India *were* different!

Bombay appeared ever more prosperous with a positive reek of money, much of it on ostentatious display as it was in staid, sterile St. Moritz, where we happily spent yet another Christmas. Cards and letters brought news from family and friends. The Cwynarskis presented us with a new niece, Emma. Caroline was now divorced and living with a publisher. She had become an equally successful one herself, often traveling as far afield as Japan and Brazil on business.

In the New Year of 1976 the United States celebrated its bicentennial, which found us appropriately back in the States—and, moreover, thinking American thoughts. Pat had gone to inspect a house for sale in Los Angeles and had fallen instantly in love. Irrationally so, it could be said, for she insisted that we purchase it. Calling me in the studio where I was revoicing Logan, she urged me, the moment I was finished, to run up and see it too.

The house turned out to be a single-level construction on its own little private promontory at the end of a quiet cul-de-sac. Deceptively modest from the outside, it was generous and welcoming within. Arranged at unusual angles with warm tile floors and high, sky-lit ceilings, the rooms had picture windows with panoramic views of the city that lay below that night like a shimmering electric ocean.

Our return the next morning only confirmed this initial approval. The house was alive with light. Sun glinted off the Hockneyesque pool and a distant silver sliver of the Pacific. Birds sang with equal delight in the shady Brazilian pepper trees and amidst the ferns and oleanders—a patterned jungle that our London living room had tried so hard to emulate. Even though Sunset Boulevard lay busy below, the house had a potent and perceptible tranquillity. Normally cautious, I shared Pat's enthusiasm. Having had no intention of buying a house, we *had* to have this one. The next day it was ours. With a providential synchronicity, I received shortly afterward notification that I had been officially deemed a nonresident of England.

Whirligig

*C*alifornia was full of friends. John Schlesinger was filming *Marathon Man* with Laurence Olivier, then in the middle of his own race against the effects of a crippling disease. We met again on the set.

This actor, who had been the supreme embodiment of dramatic vigor and physicality, was now so fragile that even shaking hands was difficult. Through sheer courageous force of will he was refusing to accept his fate, embellishing his legend with a continuing portrait gallery of roles. I wrote to him recommending a new therapy obtainable in Mexico. "I am terribly touched to receive your very sweet letter," he replied. "I am not honestly in physical pain, except that which comes with the feeling of frustration brought about by limited (and it sometimes seems to be increasingly so) physical activity. I will most firmly carry the information about the therapy in what I suppose you could call my mind."

We were reunited, too, with another battling genius in a setting that would not have been out of place in one of his works. Tennessee was staying at the Hotel del Coronado in San Diego and we brunched amidst its gingerbread eccentricities. We had just attended the premiere of his new play, *This Is (An Entertainment),* in San Francisco, which the local firing squad had predictably shot down in a hail of hostile words. Walking along the beach where Billy Wilder, a new friend, had filmed *Some Like It Hot,* Tennessee was again faultlessly, if incongruously, dressed in a gray flannel three-piece suit and tie. The image of his dapper departing figure, his arm linked affectionately with Pat's as they walked into the sunset was, sadly, one of the last I would have of him.

Rick had now left AFI and was a full-fledged professional assistant director. It had all come about by chance when John Frankenheimer had invited Pat and me to lunch in Malibu. As Rick was joining us for dinner elsewhere at the beach that evening, John had made an extra place for him and had proceeded to spend the whole meal talking almost exclusively to him. Such was their instant affinity he insisted that Rick leave school immediately and become his personal assistant. Rick, now working on *Black Sunday,* was apparently proving invaluable. It was not without pride that we visited him on *his* set.

In April I was back once more on my own film set—again working for Zeffirelli and again in Tunisia which, this time, was standing in for the Holy Land, the setting for Franco's epic *Jesus of Nazareth.* Here there were many reminders of the Romans, the power that tried to crush an obscure Jewish revolt and in doing so had given the world one of its most enduring symbols. His near-fatal car crash had apparently shaken Franco's soul and reordered his priorities so that, like Pat after India, he felt he had been allowed to survive in order to do something important with his life. This enormous project was it. I gratefully accepted Franco's offer to play John the Baptist, especially as, even more than Tybalt, it was an extraordinarily charismatic role.

The rest of the cast was a veritable bible of the industry—Olivier, Richardson, Ustinov, Steiger, Quinn, Mason, Bancroft. Olivia Hussey, now a mother herself, was incarnating the mother of God. Jesus, played by Robert Powell, had an unenviable task. While images of the Baptist might be vague, everyone had a positive personal concept of Christ. The task of reconciling expectations is perhaps easier in a silent film, for, once a character opens his mouth, he is immediately grounded in a specific milieu by accent and intonation. Robert's beautiful voice, however, matched the eloquence of his eyes and with beard, oiled hair and homespun robes, he was the very image of the Redeemer beloved of the collective consciousness.

We met on the banks of the Jordan—a dammed-up stream in the oasis of Gabes—where I baptized him in typical North African weather, sunny but cold. The water was gelid and, shivering in my designer rags, I was glad both that I was doing the inundating and that our crew was Italian, so there was an abundance of hot, steaming pasta—a distinct improvement on locusts and honey.

I, too, had grown my beard and hair to approximate the portraits of John I had studied for inspiration. As with most roles, I soon realized that gut instinct would be the prime motivation to re-create the extraordinariness that had obliged the Baptist to discourage belief in him as the promised Messiah. Much of my declamatory dialogue was left unspecific and Franco literally threw the Book at me, scattering gratefully borrowed golden words from Elijah. Chained half-naked in an ancient waterlogged dungeon, surrounded by a ski-suited crew, I had the fire of rhetoric to keep me warm.

Indeed, there was much crying in the wilderness, a great deal of it in close-up, and so I used a cosmetic paint to cover dental fillings. When Clive James met Pat for the first time he astonished her by asking: "Does your husband have capped teeth?" Apparently he had just filed a review remarking on the Baptist's film-star dentistry but his editor had insisted this be dropped unless it could be confirmed. Ironically this would be the last time that my teeth would be so intact.

As I had an appointment in Rome, we decided to cross over to Italy and drive up, converting the journey into our usual touring vacation. Sicily was an agreeable revelation—pasta with sardines and honey-stoned Greek temples and theaters nestling amidst wild spring flowers. After safely crossing between Scylla and Charybdis, real peril threatened as, traveling up through Calabria, we came head on with a truck loaded with oranges that blocked the entire road. Unconcerned, I had time and distance to brake. To my horror there was no response. It had just started to rain and we skidded helplessly over the slippery surface, smashing into the truck with a force that hurled us forward. I hit the windshield, my gloriously uncapped upper teeth slicing through my lip. Pat, who had been looking down at a guidebook, was bleeding profusely and quite silent. Somehow we both managed to crawl through a broken window of the crumpled wreckage and, even more miraculously, there was another car passing on this isolated mountain road. The driver let us bleed over his backseat like stricken game while he ferried us to the nearest hospital in a town ominously called Lagonegro.

Only Dickens at his most indignant describing a rotting prison hulk could have done justice to this dismal place full of bewildered patients. Pat was put in a mildewed room where an indifferent cigarette-smoking nurse tried to stick an old-fashioned syringe full of morphine into her. As in Japan, Pat resisted vehemently. As dangerous as it was to move her, she begged me to take her out of this bedlam. Someone stitched up my gaping lip and I asked to use the phone. *"Impossibile,"* came the suspicious response. "It is for emergencies only." Protests that we surely qualified for this status were met with peasant obduracy, so, still spattered with blood, I attempted to summon help at a nearby cafe. Rome proved unreachable but I managed to get through to the agency in London and in a hail of metallic, thudding tokens, stammered out our sorry story. I obtained details of a private clinic in Rome and, again miraculously as it seemed, found a private ambulance willing to drive us there.

Pat was gently laid in the vehicle and its door was firmly slammed —on her foot. Hurting now from top to bottom she accepted a mild sleeping pill and we set off into the night in the now pouring rain. Somewhere near Naples—unbelievably—the ambulance skidded off the road into a ditch. Our guardian angel, however, who had been so distracted earlier that day, at least ensured that our strange little odyssey continued. At dawn we entered Rome—our driver for the first time as it turned out—and wandered aimlessly around the empty streets in search of the clinic. In desperation I stopped a passing police car, which, with siren operatically blazing, escorted us to it. The door was locked and its bell went unanswered. Despite protests hurled from neighboring windows, our policeman trumpeted on his horn until the door opened and my darling battered wife was received into the clean and caring arms of the appropriately named Mater Dei. I collapsed into a bath and bed at the Grand Hotel and gratefully exchanged this nightmare for less substantial ones.

As well as facial cuts, Pat was discovered to have three broken ribs and, more seriously, a fractured sternum. Persistent dark circles under her eyes also betrayed a new, unexpected and endearing solidarity with me—a broken nose.

After leaving hospital she still felt dizzy and a misalignment of the cranial bones was diagnosed by Dr. Daniel Reeves. He was a remarkable healer in California who had recently come into our lives. While

Pat lay in Rome he "tuned" into her and in a letter from Los Angeles described precisely the injuries that the clinic's X-ray machine had missed. Like Dr. McCready with his radionic box he continued to heal us both from afar. Working with a surrogate, he was able to transfer the benefits. Chiropractic manipulation was especially effective. Later, he often treated me this way. I would feel my body suddenly unkink itself and know that, often thousands of miles away, he was at work on me.

As soon as Pat had healed sufficiently we flew gingerly to Nice, continuing her convalescence at a hotel on the rocky Cap Estel just outside Monaco. As unrelenting fate would have it, yet again she had been victimized by shards of glass. This time embedded in her face, they would take over two years to fully emerge. My front tooth, I discovered, had been cracked and displaced. Though I am still daily waiting for it to turn black it has fortunately so far remained crookedly intact and—leaving Clive James's cheeky insinuation unfulfilled—uncapped.

Sitting in the warm spring sunshine on our balcony overlooking the gentle Mediterranean there was time to ponder the recent upheavals. Why was my silver spoon reversed and reflecting such distorted images? Were all these accidents accidental? For what reason had we been permitted to survive? Where do we go from here?

The picture, however, was not entirely without humor. I had been sent a script written by the zany English comedian Marty Feldman—he of the eye-catching eyes—with which he planned to make his film directing debut. Called *The Last Remake of Beau Geste,* it was extremely funny—painfully so for Pat, who had to give up reading it when it proved to be literally rib-tickling. I happily accepted the role of Beau, his twin brother, and a cable duly arrived:

> Delighted that we are going to be together again, at last, for the first time as never before. Hope you don't mind having your nose and eye fixed. Ever thine, Your identical twin. P.S. I know you drive, so empty bottle of champagne is following.

The fortuitous proximity of Monaco and our unusual enforced idleness brought into sudden sharper focus the plan that had been slowly shaping for some time—that of using the principality as a European base. After meeting with local lawyers we decided to go ahead and obtain residency. Completing the paperwork, we found a charming apartment in an old villa on the Boulevard Princesse Charlotte. Its shuttered windows led to a balcony that overlooked a Matisse-like garden containing orange and lemon trees and four massive palms. After a fourteen-month absence, we returned to England at the end of May to pull up roots.

M . C . / L . A .

CHAPTER TWENTY-NINE

*R*eunions were now necessarily brief. Family and friends were embraced with that particular fondness engendered by absence and the prospect of further separation. Up close, the economic face of Britain looked even grimmer. The prevailing fiscal lunacy of taxing penally those with portable talents and potential earnings in foreign currencies remained, moreover, unchanged.

The long-empty house was made even emptier, its contents again packed and removed. We could have rented it out for a long period and still remained within the stricture of the tax law, but neither Pat nor I had any desire to be absentee landlords. Fortunately we both shared the same trait—a predilection for cutting off dead branches rather than propping them up. With the window boxes still bravely blooming, we left.

Pat's convalescence continued in France, breathing in D'Artagnan's good Gascon air at Eugénie les Bains. We put up at Michel Guérard's idyllic spa where the new minimalist gastronomic discipline of nouvelle cuisine was practiced to mouth-watering perfection. The spa's hydrotherapy also invigorated us, and we found ourselves in the same hot water as a brilliant Swiss financier who, from that moment, helped to guide our fiscal fortunes.

With *Logan's Run* now poised to open in the States, I flew back to the publicist's exigent arms in the newly operating Concorde which, in the futuristic circumstances, seemed the only appropriate way to go. Hurtling westward at twice the speed of sound brought patriotic pride—and childhood fantasies—rushing to the surface. The windows were hot enough to melt Icarus's wings. This was flying! America had tried to commercially kill off this marvel—cynically and hypocritically as their own skies were already streaked with supersonic military planes like the Blackbird, which only recently boomed from coast to coast in sixty-eight minutes. The Concorde was already a commuters' favorite. I noticed Leonard Bernstein lying there ashen with fatigue, his podium now extended to two hemispheres simultaneously.

Hugh Wheeler, I discovered, was returning to the States at the same time. His progress was similarly spectacular but for a different reason. He had been in Vienna filming *A Little Night Music* with Elizabeth Taylor, and they returned home together. Unfortunately, both had bad backs, which meant that neither could lift anything heavy, prompting this description of their odyssey:

> It was really a nightmare with me carrying almost two million dollars worth of jewelry in a flight bag, with one Shitzu, one Siamese cat in a carrier and six other pieces of hand luggage (over and above the trunks).
>
> How we got through beggars description. At one point we were driven through the Frankfurt airport on a golf cart stacked with bags and animals and Elizabeth facing rear, her legs dangling. At another point two wheelchairs were laid on for us. When we finally learned in mid air that we had to go through customs in New York rather than Washington where her betrothed had a fleet of lawyers and what have you to clear us, there were panicked visions (at least in my head) of thousands of dollars to be paid out in customs (let alone the million and a half in diamonds). What made it worse is that Elizabeth has never travelled with any money and didn't have a cent on her. What made it worse again was that, on the back of the customs card where you are supposed to list objects acquired abroad and the value, she wrote: 'Personal belongings acquired in Vienna during a three month stay' and then added, 'Value: No idea!' I knew we were going to rot in jail forever. But ... wouldn't you know the name is like magic. The steward on the plane called ahead

to New York and we were met by officials, rushed into a VIP room and never went near customs. All that was asked in return was a signed photograph of Elizabeth who, of course, said: 'Oh no, I never give out signed photographs.' I had to hiss in her ear this was the requested payment for breaking every known law, so we said she would send one and accepted a scrap of paper with the official's address. He'll never get it.

Logan's Run appeared to be a runaway success, racing for a box office of some $50 million, and seeming to touch an unexpected youthful nerve. Devotees saw it dozens of times and pestered the studios for information about souvenirs and fan clubs where they could discuss and replay—often in imitation costume—the minutiae of the film. There was even talk of a CBS television series. All this prompted reflection on the soundness of my own professional judgment and taste: the script of *Logan's Run* had so nearly joined that of *Love Story* in my wastepaper basket.

So an extra celebratory bicentennial Fourth of July was enjoyed on the beach at Malibu, amidst myriad flags waving patriotically in the balmy marine air like so many Impressionist paintings. The Nixons had kindly invited us, too, but with Rick with us we preferred to be *en famille*. Not for long, though. After choosing a decoration scheme for the house we were off again.

In our sunny new home in Monaco our London furniture looked remarkably well, especially displayed on a new, locally handwoven Cogolin carpet. The principality was at the height of its summer season with cafe society back in residence. A gold-plated facade hid this improbable little city's old-fashioned heart. Jewelers' boutiques were gilded cheek-by-peasant-jowl with street markets where peaches and other glowing produce were piled beneath large umbrellas. The harbor was crammed with yachts of every dimension. Fireworks blazed at night above the floodlit Royal Palace where, at an open-air concert, we met our ruling sovereigns. Princess Grace was gracious and welcoming, thoroughly deserving her "serene" title. Regine, the nightclub queen and unofficial mistress of the revels, also became a friend. Her realm, however, was not for us. We much preferred the diurnal pleasures of reading on our sunlit balcony and walking up and down Monaco's steep slopes or along the serpentine coast guard path around its rocky coast.

Prince Amyn Aga Khan invited us across the water to stay with him in his rustic house on the Costa Smeralda, the impressive picturesque resort created by his brother the Aga Khan amidst the rocks and goat tracks of this increasingly less remote corner of Sardinia. Hotels and villas—all built to coordinate with the landscape—dotted a wild terrain lapped by limpid water that made the crowded Mediterranean shore we had left behind look like the dead sea it had indeed become.

It was a pleasure to get to know better the unofficial ruling family of this unspoiled kingdom. Amyn was generous of both wit and hospitality. K, as his brother was familiarly known, imposed a dynamic presence, revealing a certain James Bondery at the helm of his high-powered yachts and souped-up Volkswagen Beetle. The Begum Sally was befittingly beautiful, as was Princess Yasmin, betraying her mother's film-star genes and looking as stunning in a bikini as she had in St. Moritz cashmeres. The whole family had an extraordinary ability to communicate fluently and privately in a mirror language where every word was pronounced backward. We swam and picnicked and dined as the locals love to do—en masse. After the traumas of that other Italian adventure earlier in the year and the subsequent domestic upheavals, it was delicious to feel the tiredness and tension being leeched from libido and limb. We even ate ice cream!

Costume fittings for the impending production of *The Last Remake of Beau Geste* required a brief return to a London transformed into Foreign Legion territory. The unending unseasonable sunshine had scorched the greenness from the dusty parks and trees and the many exotic tourists and Arabic graffiti on walls bolstered the illusion of oriental strangeness. This odd, involuntary sense of being sightseers was reinforced by our new London reality—hotel life. We sweltered in stifling suites. We joined the foreign invasion at the theaters, which were similarly insufferably hot, apart from the newly opened National. Here, in its eager and nipping acclimatized air, we saw Albert Finney and Angela Lansbury in *Hamlet,* a performance delayed as much by the theater's constructional problems as the Prince had been by indecision. Elsewhere the drama was like an old lady living off her memories—even *Salad Days* was playing! I invited May and Joe to a screening of the Japanese film, which, old-fashioned or not, proved royally entertaining. I also had word of Derek Jacobi, who was about to enjoy his share of international fame for a majestic performance in the television epic *I, Claudius.*

Beau Geste began his last remake in Dublin, where we rented a fine old Georgian house, complete with maid, dog and parrot. This was essentially a preparatory period for me. I was glad when we transferred to Ireland's west coast, staying yet again in a castle, this time one converted into a hotel, as was eventually Adare Manor, a flamboyant Pugin-inspired mansion set in fine grounds where I finally filmed. In the village junk shop I was amused to find a medallion bearing a likeness of Ireland's ancient enemy, Oliver Cromwell. It cost little and years later intrigued a friend working for Sotheby's, who suggested I send it for auction. Surprised to see it cataloged with a whole page of scholarly annotation, I was even more astonished when it sold for incalculably more than I had paid for it. So much, of course, that I wished I had kept it.

Beau Geste continued the Musketeers' lampooning of precious institutions, this time old-fashioned military heroism. Reinforcing this, the cast contained those two veteran scene-stealers Spike Milligan and Roy Kinnear. They were joined by a third, Peter Ustinov, his beneficent bearded old man now transformed into the brutal wooden-legged Sergeant Markov astride a wooden-legged horse and with a scar that wandered daily around his face. Trevor Howard reappeared, fulminating in identical mutton-chop whiskers, a zany version of his *Conduct* colonel. To proclaim our twinship, Marty and I appeared with hair identically peroxided and permed. Ann-Margret was our glamorous stepmother, and not the least pleasure this film provided was friendship with this multitalented entertainer and her husband, Roger. My nephew Paul, now an Elvis Presley fanatic, was also pleased. "Anyone who has worked with the King can't be bad!"

There were further Musketeer comparisons with our move to Spain, although actual progress was hampered by two unforeseen events. Marty, who was proving a quiet, grateful director, was felled with chicken pox which, for a vegetarian, was to add insult to injury. In addition, the Spanish rain fell torrentially on the freezing plain. Madrid was reportedly colder than London or Paris. The exceptional summer seemed to have used up the year's supply of sun, for it rarely broke through. For a comedy set in the Sahara this was as bizarre as its other elements. Peter withdrew to his damp trailer to correct the proofs of his memoirs, issuing at intervals funny cartoons commenting on the increasingly unfunny situation.

Barry Norman joined us to do a piece for the *Guardian* and wrote of the Quixotic craziness of it all, in particular lunch in the dining tent.

The wind came in at one end and blew the water out of the other. It was so enthralling to watch this plucky waiter approach, laden plates in each hand, only to be hurtled back whence he had come as the tornado struck him, that we almost forgot the rain dripping into the wine and the small river that roared and bubbled beneath the table. Occasionally the canvas above us would bulge dangerously under the tonnage of water and then Mr. Michael York, a man of action as befits one playing Beau Geste, would spring up and give the roof a shove and we'd all listen delightedly to the howl of rage as the water poured into the tent next door. A notable absentee from this sodden meal was Mr. Feldman himself but he, as the director, was in his trailer praying for the rain to stop. Besides, he never eats lunch, although, as Mr. Ustinov pointed out, "On a day such as this even Marty will need at least two helpings of nothing to sustain him."

On the plus side, with eyes and teeth outglinting each other, I at last got to sing on camera. It was a heroic number—later predictably cut —that, "aspiring to reach the impossible note," mocked every cliché in the genre. Soon afterward I was able to put all this macho nonsense to the test when one of Spain's foremost bullfighters, Palomo Linares, invited us to his hacienda. We all sat in a small bullring watching him go about his matadorial business. Suddenly he looked up, pointed at me, and beckoned me to his side. My limbs froze but somehow they escorted my reluctant body down to the arena where, in a haze of enveloping horror and disbelief, I saw him hand me his red cape. This was it. I was on the mythical, much-quoted spot. The honor of my country—nay, my manhood—was at stake.

A gate opposite then swung open admitting a very angry young bull who instantly thundered directly at me. *The moment of truth!* Was I really the stuff that El Córdobes was made of? There was no way that I could break ground and run, much as good sense overwhelmingly prompted this. I made a pass. It worked, thank God. The speeding horns veered way followed closely by the snorting, smelly bulk they were attached to. "Olé!" I croaked in astonished relief. It was only a small bull, but even so it—and its owner—owe me at least two months of my life. The Foreign Legion was far less fraught with danger. We withdrew to our Sahara—some scrubby coastal dunes near Seville—to continue the good fight against desert dogs and the atrocious weather.

As soon as *Beau Geste* was finished, Pat and I hotfooted it to the long-lost sun of the U.S. Virgin Islands—for another remake. Burt Lancaster was playing the title role in a new version of H. G. Wells's

The Island of Dr. Moreau. I had to join him, if only for the opportunity it provided of having York and Lancaster on the same bill, if not in that order! Besides, the role of Braddock, the mariner shipwrecked "one thousand miles from nowhere," was worth taking for the acting challenge of a single scene—where, resisting Moreau's diabolical efforts to turn him into an animal, Braddock fights desperately to remain human. Originally I had turned the film down, but fortunately the producer had turned down my refusal. This resonated well with my new-found work practice of positive, adventurous action rather than safe inaction.

Filming in the tropics was as languid and laid back as the weather. On the first day my driver failed to show up, an event that would elsewhere have thrown me into paroxysms of anxiety. Here I merely drove myself over the unfamiliar island of St. Croix until I found our location in a distant beach-fronted rainforest. Even the working hours seemed agreeable despite often starting at four in the morning to out-Moreau the evil doctor with our animal transformations. I tried to minimize the actual makeup, finding to my surprise that simply stuffing nostrils and cheeks produced a truly beastly effect. As with all the best characterizations, however, the disguise had to come principally from within.

When the now uninhibited midday sun stood hotly overhead there would be another break until the brutal light became beautiful again. This was when I delighted in taking the bears and tigers swimming— or rather, they would take me, dragging behind their leashes. Our resident menagerie was a constant source of fascination, especially when two coal-black panther cubs were born. We heard word, too, of a tiger abandoned on a neighboring, needless to say, not British, island. Its much vaunted fight to death with a human—a parody of central events in our own film—had been canceled. We plotted a rescue mission, and sent a small plane to kidnap the poor beast. Mangy and malnourished, it delighted us all by responding to all-around kindness and square meals and transforming itself—as the mad Moreau would have wished of me—into a magnificent animal specimen.

Even in the tropics where mangoes and coconuts fell obligingly off trees, food was a priority—especially for our British crew. Like their colleagues in Japan who had transformed prized delicacies into nursery puddings, they insisted on British location grub, even going so far as to open an al fresco cafe. Called The House of Pain after the ghastly refuge where Moreau's wretched tribe of humanoids was denied the taste of blood, here bacon, sausages and other parts of their slaughtered cousins were gleefully cremated and consumed.

Again we were lucky enough to rent a sea-viewed house that soon filled up with guests, including my parents. The greens where Joe played golf could rarely have been greener and we all enjoyed the weekend pleasures of picnics on Buck Island with its signposted underwater trail and sea-planing or sailing to the adjacent islands. After what had been a bruising year, Pat and I returned to L.A. as tanned and blonded as Beau had been and in good spirits and health.

In St. Croix I had met John Wayne, who ably practiced the acting dictum he preached: "Speak low, speak slow and don't say too much." Now, as the newest residents in Film Town, we were privileged to meet others of its most distinguished denizens from the Golden Age of moviemaking. Moreover, Billy Wilder expressed interest in my being in *Fedora,* his forthcoming film about a legendary film star. Someone who embodied this description was Bette Davis, whom I found myself seated next to one night at a dinner. Fixing me with those two interrogative headlights of eyes, the scarlet bows of her mouth quivered to issue the most irresistible opening gambit: "The only reason I'm here tonight is to meet you." I was unnaturally pleased and uncharacteristically speechless. Fastening my seat belt, I enjoyed every minute of the subsequent ride.

Other legends came in and out of focus. Pat danced one unforgettable night with Gene Kelly. We met Vladimir Horowitz in his hotel suite, where he treated us to a two-hour impromptu concert. The secret of success, he assured us, was to eat asparagus every day. We certainly devoured every last word and morsel of the fabulous Chinese meal that Danny Kaye cooked for us in his state-of-the-art kitchen. Finally, there was a rapprochement with my neighbor George Cukor, whom I would see outside his high-walled house—once with Katharine Hepburn. Showing bygones were finally gone, I drove him home from a party.

Back in Monaco, Princess Grace invited us to lunch at the palace with two former co-stars of hers whose friendship we would thereafter value and enjoy. Cary Grant, wearing a bright yellow tie, tripped on the carpet and literally fell into Pat's arms. "There's no place else I would rather be," he improvised with instinctive gallantry, while, with equal charm, David Niven lived up to his newly published reputation as a raconteur. Grace asked me to be a judge at the Flower Show. Her floral passion was genuine and she arranged the event so that there was a good chance of the local baker's wife winning a trophy and not being blasted into insignificance by the big guns of international floristry.

Next door was the Riviera dei Fiori and we drove along its blooming length to Ventimiglia for market shopping and seaside pasta. Italy was our new playground. Retracing the sprightly romantic footsteps of *Romeo and Juliet* to Pienza, we visited Florence, Siena and San Gimignano before roving farther to Venice, Ravenna and Portofino. We stopped one evening at Felliniesque Montecatini to take the waters. Next morning we returned for more, reasoning that, as one glass had made us feel so good, then several would make us feel extraordinary. They did—extraordinarily ill! Until then I was unaware that spa waters could be so powerful, some even requiring the drinker to lie down after ingestion. Ironically it was around this time that Pat and I gave up alcohol for good, apart from an occasional rum punch and slug of vodka, which conveniently and convincingly confirmed the grounds for our abstention. I also stubbed out my last cigarette. Under a homeopathic medical regime we found that our systems had become increasingly sensitive and intolerant of alien intrusion.

Visits to London became more valuable as their frequency diminished. Now conditioned to the opportunistic mores of a freewheeling society, we found the still-rigid English class system with its held-over talk of "rising above one's station" as quaint as the prevailing obsessive interest in the Royal Family. Our expectations and sensibilities were slowly being transformed: we were now tourists with a concomitant carpe diem philosophy put into overdrive. Patronizing its great hotels, we realized why so many foreigners cherished London as their favorite city. Sybaritically installed in the Savoy suite where Charles Chaplin used to reside, his view of the city lights was incomparable.

Staying with friends, too, gave a keener pleasure. Being John Schlesinger's guest in his smart Kensington house was especially enjoyable. Breakfast in bathrobes, with newspapers and mail piled amidst the toast and marmalade was a ritual. Small talk was impossible: John's film-director curiosity was irrepressible and he never let an idle remark remain inactive. Though white-bearded like an Old Testament prophet, an eternally youthful spirit graced his personality and ensured that an impish grin and saucy remark put paid to any encroaching pretentiousness. Friendship had recently taken on a new poignancy with the shocking premature death of Jimmy Wilson. He had been the extraordinary factor binding together the most disparate group of people. After his hasty burial service in Nogales, held, as local custom demanded, the day after his death, we all disbanded. The center no longer held.

Pat and I weekended in the English countryside, forgetting how damnably cold the climate could be, especially now that our blood had been thinned by living in the sun. I remember Pat retiring to bed in one house clad in every single item of clothing she had brought—including boots and raincoat! We dined with John Gielgud in his beautiful Queen Anne house, decorated inside and out by Capability Martin, and also stayed in cossetted comfort with Fleur Cowles and her husband, Tom Meyer, in the bracing Sussex Weald. Fleur had an enviable ability to perform several functions simultaneously—painting and conversing while at the same time supervising food and politics. Harold Macmillan, a neighbor, joined us for lunch, still looking like the Supermac of Vicky's cartoons. The country was in need of an extraordinary leader of his caliber. In fact, in a television interview, Macmillan had opined that a coalition government was inevitable as no single political party could risk the stigma attached to putting through the necessary unpopular measures to reverse Britain's current decline.

A fellow houseguest was Dr. Bernard Lown, the famed Boston heart specialist. Instantly taking a liking to each other, he and Pat locked horns, devil's advocates both, to argue the case of homeopathic versus allopathic medicine. Later, on a tour of the garden, Bernard slipped heavily on a waterfall, shaking himself up considerably. Pat insisted on administering arnica. Bernard was so impressed with this basic remedy for shock that he thereafter prescribed a preoperative course for all his heart patients—a splendid example of cooperation between two medical modalities and of open-mindedness in a practice addicted to blindfolds and blinkers.

My own heart had recently missed a beat when a routine insurance examination in Monaco revealed a murmur. A Texan friend urged me to come by Houston for a check-up on my return to America. On the plane Pat and I couldn't understand why so many passengers looked so waxy and ill until it dawned that we were all heading for hospital. At dinner that night in Houston, Pat found herself sitting next to another famous heart surgeon. Seeing him gorge uninhibitedly on things heart specialists were supposed to forbid, she was somewhat disconcerted to learn he was due to perform twenty-eight operations the following day.

After my check-up—and reassuring report card—I went to watch a few of them through a window in the ceiling of the operating theater, a scene reminiscent of Moreau's clinic at its most ghoulish. As if on a conveyor belt, bodies were systematically deveined, hacked open, and stitched up again to a rock beat as regular as the one to which their renovated hearts now throbbed. To compound all this, my Texan host swore that, should his own prove faulty, he had arranged with the local sheriff to obtain a new heart by "accident." As he kept an arsenal of weapons beneath his bed—including a machine gun—I was not inclined to disbelieve him.

Back in Monaco life was rendered inaudible by the Grand Prix, so, revving up our own car, we raced off down the *autoroute* to Nimes to join Dominique Lapierre at the Whitsun bullfight. After entrancing the crowd in the Roman arena with his elegant passes and immaculate kills the noble matador was suddenly caught and tossed out of the ring. A young urchin jumped in and took on his bull. In Spain he would have been arrested—as El Córdobes had been—but here the holiday crowd let him have his fine few minutes, afterward insisting he join the President in his box. It gave me hope for our own *Rocky*-type bullfight story. The timing was fortuitous. Franco was now dead and Spain was transforming itself. Even the great El Córdobes had given his approval—for a huge percentage of the profits.

We drifted to Paris, enjoying being swept along in its "season"—a pleasant round of cliquish lunches and dinners where manners were as refined as the clothes and matched by the excellence of the food and conversation. It was here that the full significance of *placement* was encountered—even at a round table, friendship and fortune were contingent on the trivial circumstance of seating. Intrigued just to be there, I happily measured out my life in tiny coffee spoons. We dined at the most exquisite house I have ever set foot in—Guy and Marie-Hélène de Rothschild's Hôtel Lambert, decorated by Renzo Mongiardino with the same sumptuous, faultless taste he had brought to his designs for our Roman *Shrew*. There was, however, a curious fin-de-siecle sense of impermanence and impending change. Many a party was announced as being the last of its kind.

At fashion shows we crammed into small hot rooms on small gilt chairs. We lunched at the home of Yves Saint-Laurent, who, gentle and shy as his clothes were bold and extrovert, was responsible for much of my wardrobe and for an unforeseen and surely undeserved accolade—a place in New York's Fashion Hall of Fame. In a year when not one wealthy sportsman or playboy made this international best-dressed list, the movie star was apparently making a resurgence as a fashion influence, exemplified by Diane Keaton whose kooky *Annie Hall* look swept the world. I'm still waiting for my contribution to be identified.

It was work that brought us back to reality—and to London. Or as one newspaper chose to put it, "After ten years in the lush wilderness of movie stardom Michael York has finally been lured to make a TV play." Reentering the Television Centre's familiar circle also represented a return both to Nazi Germany and to playing a man who, like John the Baptist, was an earthly spokesman for God.

Called *True Patriot,* the play was about Dietrich Bonhoeffer, a Lutheran pastor and theologian who, witnessing the rise of Nazism, had at first ignored its significance, claiming an interest only in heavenly kingdoms. When the swastika became more dominant than the cross in the all-Aryan churches, struggling with his Christian conscience, he realized that wishful thinking was insufficient—evil had to be actively opposed. Becoming associated with all four major attempts on Hitler's life, he was eventually arrested. Although his exceptional spirituality impressed even his jailers, he was executed two days before the end of the war he had fought so gallantly to curtail.

True Patriot seemed to touch a nerve and I was happy to be associated with the portrayal of an unstereotypical "good" German. The play presented a timely warning. The anarchist Baader-Meinhof gang was menacing contemporary Germany and fascist thugs of the National Front were fomenting hatred in Britain. There was a cynicism and despair abroad. The malaise in America was reflected on the covers of *Time* magazine. Before the President's disgrace heroes and leaders had been featured. Now any rogue or vagabond could be found staring from them.

In the face of this, the London theater continued to indulge in an orgy of rose-tinted retrospection. Three plays by William Douglas Home, and others by Barrie, Coward, Maugham, Travers, Rattigan and Agatha Christie set an escapist scene further emphasized by the ongoing celebrations of the Queen's Jubilee.

Fleeing from reality ourselves, we resumed our mondaine life in Greece. Though many new friends were shipowners, the preferred mode of transport was the private helicopter. We whirled over to Stavros Niarchos's private island and to Scorpios, Christina Onassis's domain, which, as well as a perfect beach, also had a little farm like Marie Antoinette's. We took a sunset boat ride—something Christina's father had encouraged but which she had always refused. Sadly, since his death it had become one of her greatest pleasures. There was a tangible air of melancholy. Both her father and brother lay nearby in a mausoleum. The great yacht *Christina* that had witnessed more elaborate festivities now swung empty and unused at anchor in the clear water, a mausoleum itself to former times.

Between bouts of hedonism, I returned to Munich and Paris to film *Fedora* for Billy Wilder. "If all the year were playing holidays, to sport would be as tedious as to work." I was happy to have a job to go to. Moreover, it was an offer I could not refuse, Billy had said. Indeed, the role was an intriguing but difficult one: myself. This was a unique instance, I had replied, where an actor could legitimately claim, as they so frequently and tiresomely do, that his character would not have spoken the scripted words. These, in this case, were by A. L. Diamond, Billy's long-standing collaborator, and were based on a novella by Tom Tryon, coincidentally the previous owner of our California house.

The piece concerned a *monstre sacré*, a faded movie star of the old school who, among the plot's other rather *Grand Guignol* developments, conceives a fatal passion for Michael York. As flattering as this scenario sounds, though, it is also peculiar to bear the responsibility for the death of a fictional character! I nonetheless supplied the brilliant Alex Trauner, who had designed my *Cabaret* boardinghouse from his own Berlin experience, with photographs and cuttings to adorn a York shrine, the ultimate accolade in fandom.

The film was resolutely old-fashioned. It even had as its chief protagonist William Holden, providing a link to *Sunset Boulevard,* Billy's earlier film about Hollywood's obsession with self, youth and stardom. Like its legendary predecessor, *Fedora* also dealt with those ladies of the screen who find themselves unable to manage that difficult final act. Furthermore, the film enshrined Billy's own exasperation with the contemporary studio set-up and an implicit statement that, in a town where old age was increasingly a taboo, the old school could still teach the new a few tricks. "The kids with beards have taken over," he said in an interview. "I learned how to make polkas: I don't know how to make rock and roll." This from a man who was as colorful and contemporary as the great art he collected. Humor, though, was never far away. "No one says, 'Boy, I must see that film—I hear it came in under budget,'" he reminded us. His mischievous pink face crowned by a signature hat, he was a constant fount of ironic wit.

For my part, it felt good to be in harness again and, moreover, back
in Munich, my good-luck city, where I was strangely at home playing
yet another prince whirling round a rococo ballroom set. For the Paris
filming later, I felt honored just to drive out together with William
Holden to the studio to attend Fedora's funeral. "Ah, this is living,"
murmured Billy wickedly, arranging the mountain of wreaths on that
other film star's shrine. Among other admirers sending tributes were
Moshe Dayan and also Fred Astaire, who, as irrepressibly youthful as
Billy, had just broken an elegant limb skateboarding in his driveway.
A reviewer later justified all of Billy's Herculean efforts to bring this
story to the screen: "If this is Wilder's final statement, he could hardly
have signed off with more elegance, grace and beauty." Another,
writing with the hindsight of this present decade, was even more
emphatic: "Quite simply a masterpiece."

Afterward we feasted on other films, sometimes seeing four a day
at the Deauville Film Festival, and set off for more nourishment at its
Cairo counterpart. It seemed totally consistent with fate that our first
visit to the Pyramids should coincide with its use as a film set. As the
ancient stones swam into focus through the shimmering desert air, so
did a frieze of familiar faces—a British crew filming *Death on the Nile*,
a sequel to Poirot's earlier Orient Express adventure. Life, it could be
said, was a movie set.

The long-haul jaunt to America never failed to provoke a surge of
excitement. It was an agreeable era of monopolistic plenty in air transportation, before deregulation and cutthroat competition turned aircraft into flying sardine cans. Then there were expansive piano bars
and even restaurant-style dining rooms. I always took a window seat
and would invariably be rewarded with astonishing vistas, such as a
sunlit Greenland shining icily through the clouds in a silver sea. Nothing, however, seemed to diminish the stress of flying huge distances,
especially across multiple time zones. I remember my astonished reaction on casually asking a chirpy, smiling stewardess how on earth
she coped, only to witness her break down in tears before me, confessing that her body's biological rhythms had been thrown completely out of sync.

Back in California, I lunched with my reputed alter ego, Prince
Charles, at a reception at the Fox Studios. This was distinctly more
glamorous than one given at the Carter White House, where attempts

to be modest and unpretentious were inappropriate in such a hugely symbolic place. Like Number 10 Downing Street, the White House is much more than a residence. As Jimmy Carter's successor, trained in these arts, was to prove, image was important. Photographs that flashed around the world showing an exhausted Carter collapsed from jogging were not conducive to Uncle Sam's upright global standing.

We spent another year end in St. Moritz, but our Christmas present was certainly not just what we wanted. We were robbed. The famous, much traveled ostrich-leather bag purchased at the beginning of our marriage to secure our valuables had taken on a talismanic quality.

Its charmed life ended, however, on Christmas Day when it was stolen by a Raffles-type thief from our bedroom while we enjoyed a black-tie dinner below. The irony was that kings' ransoms hung on the bejeweled ears, necks and bosoms of some of our fellow guests. Over the years, though, we had collected some charming pieces, including our wedding gifts to each other that had accumulated in value —and not just intrinsically. The sense of loss was somewhat accentuated by the fact that this same year, the private Swiss bank in which we had—entirely legally—deposited some of our riches had crashed, its directors depositing themselves in the bottom of Lake Geneva.

Pat showed remarkable grace in the circumstances. She insisted that such episodes, unfortunate as they were, reinforced priorities: baubles, however precious in monetary or sentimental terms, were nothing compared to the really important values. In these terms we were immeasurably wealthy. We had each other, love, families, friends, work and an unquenchable passion for life.

That Christmas, people gave us their support and friendship— invaluable assets. Harold Lever, then Chancellor of the Duchy of Lancaster, even presented me with a letter written on Cabinet note-paper, in which he pledged to "take full personal responsibility to any carrier or other person for accepting Mr. York for travel to the UK without passport." And so we came down to earth, and to London.

Excursions and Alarums

*B*ack in Britain, I televised *Much Ado* for the BBC, this time promoted to Benedick. Confirming my next film project, a version of Erskine Childers's *The Riddle of the Sands,* set a pattern for 1978, a year to be distinguished by British roles.

The moment the television recording was finished, we took the late-afternoon Concorde from Heathrow to be in time for a press conference in New York early the next morning for the American promotion of the Shakespeare series. When we were halfway across, a blizzard shut down JFK, diverting us to Washington where we just managed to land before its own runways met a similar fate. The only transport willing to attempt the terrestrial journey to New York through mounting ice and snow was a Greyhound bus. Having flashed across the Atlantic in some three hours it now took what seemed ten times that to crawl to the Big frozen Apple.

Deciding to return to Europe by an equally circuitous but warmer route, we went the wrong way round. Tahiti was the first soft, sensual landfall followed by stepping stones of other South Sea islands all the way across to Java. Then, weaving through towering tropical clouds, we landed in Bali. The whole island seemed assembled to welcome us with enchanting ceremonies, all performed in an untouristy, unselfconscious way—the exact reverse of our vulgar Shangri-la capers. By a serendipitous chance, our arrival had coincided with the day the old Balinese year ended and, along with the new year, we were joyfully and elaborately greeted.

An exquisite Hindu pearl set in a Muslim sea, Bali's ancient, unchanging culture was menaced with commercial development and exploitation—the classic contemporary threat in a furiously changing world. Would the cherry orchard be cut down, a native culture trivialized into *son et lumière* entertainment? Adrian reported sadly from Turkey the transformations overwhelming Side, where he and Hans habitually stayed:

> Ex-aristocrats, cultured and penniless, run an inefficient and broken-down hotel, while the boy they used in the village as a carpenter, who can't read or write, is now running a rival tourist "motel" which is expanding all the time—and when he tries to help them by sending overflow guests they, however penniless, say, "No, we're full," which they're not.

We stayed on the beach, soothed by the lap of warm waves and the sunset chimes of a gamelan band, and later with friends in the cool hills of Ubud. We feasted on an aromatic, gooey black rice—ambrosial food that would have surely fomented instant revolution on a British film set! Pat, a recent partner in an L.A. antiques business, gleefully bartered and traded, dispatching home Chinese porcelain and decorated martovans. Our perfect harmony was disrupted only when she tried to make me carry a very ancient—and very heavy—door onto the Singapore flight as hand luggage. However, amidst the faded charms of Raffles Hotel, it was soon restored. Pat later abandoned the business when—much to the benefit of our home and my back—she found herself reluctant to resell her treasures!

Returning to Thailand, we saw working in the jungle the originals of the mud elephants I had modeled as a boy. Preferring to avoid the well-beaten track, we were fortunate to get at the last moment visas for Burma. Insurrection there had flared anew, prompting a French couple to lose both their nerve and their seats on an overbooked flight to Rangoon. In Bangkok, people used to call our room directly for a chat, this annoyance being marginally outweighed by the pleasurable realization that I had Asian fans. However, once aboard the flight to Burma (which, chillingly in this era of accidents, crashed a week later), Pat commented that now at least, away from Western commercial pressures, I would be little, if at all, known.

Ancient British bureaucracy coupled with modern Marxism ensured that, at Rangoon airport, immigration form-filling was seemingly in quintuplet. Except for me! Smiles flashed from every quarter, propelling us through barriers, officials parting to allow my unchecked progress. A short drive through the city revealed the reason for this fervent favoritism. Vast poster images of myself were everywhere. Prince George had returned! Our little Japanese love story, which had fared respectably in the West, was here a smash hit, playing for over a year. I was reminded of Adrian's description of *Cabaret* in Java. "I can't go shopping without seeing garish hoardings where they depict you nose to nose with Liza M. and glaring at her with frightening and nearly uncontrollable lust. Apparently they don't dub it, that would be too macabre, they simply keep the dialogue low and turn music and FX up to full volume."

Word of my—or rather the royal—arrival spread and, like the screen prince, I, too, became a prisoner. Unable to walk the streets without being mobbed, I had to leap into a minibus for refuge and, for a bewildering instant, had an alarming intimation of what it must be like to be a real celebrity—a prince or pop star, or even a cult object like the Burtons. All this gave cause for reflection and a growing realization that success should be defined in global terms, not just by what found occidental favor.

Anxious to avoid the city and its veneer of Westernism, we escaped from our crumbling Russian-built hotel with its gray towels and smiling gentle staff. The panorama of temples at Pagan was unforgettable but, with our discovery that the mythical Road to Mandalay was unpaved and full of potholes, the barrenness of the prevailing socialist faith was never more shabbily demonstrated. A footnote to this episode was added much later when, running into the writer of our Japanese film, Pat warmly congratulated him on being the hit of downtown Rangoon. Until the circumstances could be explained he took this as the ultimate in put-downs!

On *The Riddle of the Sands*'s first day of shooting in April it snowed— a chilly reminder that we were now back in a particularly draughty corner of northern Europe. The story's setting was Germany but we were in Holland first to film on the landlocked Zuider Zee, unrestricted by unsociable tides. Erskine Childers's novel, written in 1903, was now a classic of its genre: indeed, he could be said to have invented the spy story. Captivated by it as a boy, after seeing it listed in a *Sunday Times* poll of all-time favorite books, I had been involved in earlier unsuccessful attempts to film it. Now, with a minuscule budget of a million pounds, Rank was backing a modest effort written and directed by Tony Maylam—one of the last bangs on their famous gong.

Staying close to the original, this version made no concessions to a transatlantic audience by introducing American characters—as was almost standard practice at the time. Its strength lay in its very by-jingo ethnicity, a quality that had been the bedrock of success of so many vintage British films. However, such was the current state of the British cinema that an American executive seriously suggested we might have to re-voice our film for the U.S. market.

This was at violent odds with the story about two quintessential Englishmen, from impeccable universities and establishment backgrounds, named Carruthers and Davies. On a sailing holiday in the Baltic, they discover a German plot to invade England with bargeloads of troops towed across the North Sea to land on its then undefended east coast. Britain's historic enemy had been France and so her main defenses pointed south. Hitherto uncoordinated, the German giant was now united and rattling his new-forged sword. The novel had actual historic consequences, alerting the Admiralty to a real potential danger. To confront the Kaiser's growing naval power, three new strategic bases were established. History, of course, confirmed the prescience of Childers's scenario.

I found I was perfectly cast as Charles Carruthers, the Foreign Office clerk who, in "an act of obscure penance," accepts an invitation aboard Davies's yacht *Dulcibella* to help elucidate the riddle. I entered the story in a close-up—of my beautifully polished brown shoes that, moments later, were symbolically mired in the omnipresent mud. I was carrying far too much luggage, still a personal peccadillo. Like Carruthers, I too preferred to stay on dry land in a well-appointed hotel rather than in the film crew's hotel ship moored nearby. I loved my fellow workers, but to be shipmates with them by day and night was too much. As usual I had brought our car and preferred to commute from Amsterdam.

This watery city was always a pleasant place to be, despite its continuing overtones of sixties hippiness and concomitant drug problem. After decades of correspondence there were happy reunions with Adrian and Hans. Our first visit to the Anne Frank house, however, saddened us—not just because of her tragic fate but for an entry we saw being made ahead of ours in the visitors' book by a young American girl. She wrote that she felt unable to share Anne Frank's confidence in the fundamental goodness of human nature—a reflection of the nihilism of her own dispirited, unheroic times.

Filming continued in our beloved Germany, in the Frisian Islands themselves, where the unfamiliar landscape of flat muddy estuaries and fog-shrouded fields had its own desolate beauty. The tide would recede to reveal a horizon-filling ocean of ribbed mud, as mournful as a seabird's cry. One of the novel's key passages, though, was the epic trip by rowboat through disorienting thick fog where our heroes put the kibosh on the Kaiser. The sea makes a notoriously difficult film set and this entire sequence was shot with smoke machines in a small pond near London!

Our *Dulcibella* had been found in Chichester and, by an extraordinary coincidence, turned out to have been built in the same yard as Childers's own *Vixen*, the model for his fictional craft. Similarly a converted lifeboat, it was small and distinctly unluxurious. I had been curious to see if the sailing in the film would awaken a latent unsuspected passion, turning me instantly from landlubber into old salt. Having spent lazy summers aboard well-staffed expensive yachts I discovered, however, that I shared Carruthers's own shock at the cramped wretchedness of our boat and an exasperation for all the accompanying nautical jargon. "Jibed all standing" is still meaningless to me. However, I admit to experiencing an occasional perceptible exhilaration whenever the canvas billowed under a sunny breeze, although the constant stabbing spring cold provoked nostalgic memories of sailing shirtless in shorts in the Caribbean.

Simon McCorkindale, our Arthur Davies, proved on the other hand to be a most able seaman, as did Jenny Agutter, the woman in our story, here transformed from futuristic rebel to bygone Gibson Girl. Her character had been introduced at the insistence, not of our transatlantic executive, but of Childers's publisher. As always, it was good to have a woman aboard, toning down all the pipe-smoking, clubby masculinity.

As successful and as well received as the film was, it made me wonder if a real thriller can ever be made of pre–World War I events. With their glamorous yet archaic military uniforms and weapons, there is a Ruritanian remoteness about these times. Ours was a gently told story faithful to the upright decency and stiff-upper-lippery of the long Edwardian twilight. "People don't behave like that—not even Germans," protests Carruthers. He and the rest of the world were soon to discover otherwise when the tank, submarine, airplane and my former co-star, the zeppelin, changed the nature of warfare forever. Incidentally, Childers's own life story is an adventure worthy of his own pen and one that I am still trying to bring to the screen.

Back in L.A., we watched other sailboats flock home at sunset to the Marina. At Malibu beach parties we caught up with such legendary residents as Merle Oberon, looking like Cathy again on the windswept moors as she walked the misty beach with hair and gown breeze-blown. Pat photographed Barbra Streisand back-lit in the flaming orange of the sinking sun. She was endlessly curious, questioning Pat about photography and seeming to file the information away in her avid mind. We roller-skated in raffish beach-bummed Venice. Our pool was warm and inviting, any guilt about self-indulgence dissipated along with the chill by a solar heater that I had installed to mitigate the continuing energy crunch.

It was at this time that Pat started to get actively involved in my business dealings and to manage our finances. "All professions are conspiracies against the laity," G.B.S. had remarked, and in Los Angeles, especially, there was a cabal of lawyers and managers encouraging people to abrogate responsibility for their affairs, just as many were encouraged to devolve all health care to their doctors. Idly glancing through a contract one day, Pat noticed a discrepancy. Following it up, she saved me a huge sum of money. Her fiscal instincts and business acuity were such that our lawyer eventually even asked her to join his firm. I realized that I was hopelessly out of step when I scoured Monaco in search of a bank that refused to use computers! My contribution was the name of our company—Pith and Moment Enterprises. Though taken from one of Hamlet's most famous speeches, it has provoked the most strange, diverse and inventive misquotations!

Our tenure of the domestic hearth was typically fleeting. In a Carruthers wish-fulfillment we reexperienced the pampered joys of sea-borne life in Sardinia aboard Lord Camrose's *Tartar* with its deep-cushioned, roomy cabins and afternoon tea on the poop. Staying with other friends in Normandy, we mingled with the polo and racetrack crowds—couture dresses clashing with jockey silks, hats with horses, like animated Dufy paintings.

We also visited the invasion beaches, for my next project was a television film of another great spy story. *A Man Called Intrepid* told the extraordinary tale of Sir William Stephenson, who had been responsible for breaking the Nazi communication code, thereby persuading the United States out of its isolationism and making possible the Allied landings. "It was the greatest Anglo-American intelligence enterprise in history. Stephenson's personal contacts were such that he got the willing services of talented men and women from every field of human endeavour, of every nationality," wrote Noël Coward, implying that he himself might well have been among that number. Evan Michaelian, whom I played, certainly was. Although a fictional character, in the story he was trained in the arts of code breaking and deception at Bletchley Park by the great spymaster himself, portrayed by the equally legendary David Niven.

Niven had served with distinction in the real life Second World War, which gave an implicit authenticity to our reenactment of historic events. He diligently rewrote his lines—and frequently cut them —giving his dialogue a pithy punch. With mischievous face and naughty eyes, he was stimulating company. As with Ustinov, I wanted to be his Boswell, capturing and preserving the effortless flow of stories. If not entirely sharing, I certainly respected, his actor's code for the selection of roles: "Where?" was the first demand followed by "Who with?" and "How much?" Curiously, Pat found it difficult to photograph David. Her camera and intuition perceived the fact—soon to be tragically confirmed—that he was not well.

Filming once more in Britain was a pleasurable experience, especially in the Cotswolds, where the mellow stone villages of my early boyhood stood in for France. Although all the cowslips seemed to have disappeared from the hedgerows, the woods were still immodestly carpeted with bluebells. We even spotted a nursery rhyme–quick brown fox and her russet cubs crossing a dewy morning field. A local wartime RAF airfield was also used and a vintage Mosquito bomber circling and landing on its grass runway provided an infinitely stirring sight. It was good to have an important story to tell—again one that had materially affected the course of history.

After taking us briefly to Rjukan in Norway where the heavy water crucial to atomic fission had been manufactured by the Germans, the filming ended in Montreal. Here, in the incomprehensible ways of our business, most of the London interiors were shot just as many of the Canadian exteriors had been filmed in England.

Celebrating Thanksgiving Day with Rick in New York, we were all invited to dinner with Princess Yasmin. Before our meal Rick insisted on taking us on a short drive. "We're only going twenty blocks from the Plaza Hotel," he said enigmatically. We finished up in the South East Bronx, an area of such physical desolation it resembled newsreels of postwar Berlin or contemporary Beirut. After witnessing the crowds lining up for their charity handout, our festive fare was even more gratefully received. Incidentally, the other side of the Bronx is still home to Justine Banevicius, a remarkable lady who, for the past ten years, has organized a Michael York Fan Club. It is gratifying to learn that she now handles our international correspondence. I even had a letter from a young girl who assured me that her parrot was a fan. Apparently my photo in its cage would calm the perceptive bird and its removal would produce protesting shrieks!

Returning to Switzerland for a holiday, we found its charms had palled and not entirely as a result of last year's débâcle. The beautiful people no longer looked so beautiful. A certain disenchantment had already set in with this other *huis clos,* where the same isolated elitist group insulated themselves from contact with those outside their charmed circle, the concomitant snobbish implication being that there were only certain people worth knowing. Tired of constant incommunicado communal meals, I was reminded of the definition of a free man as being one who can refuse a dinner invitation without giving an excuse.

I knew that basically our malaise stemmed from our birth sign: belonging to no group, we craved change. The conspicuous consumption, however, had begun to irritate, and it became less easy to condone the private jet dispatched to London for Fortnum and Mason marmalade or to laugh at the sight of costly ballgowns doused in champagne and willfully destroyed. Like Taki, one of the chroniclers of all this heady high life, I had become increasingly beady-eyed, though I hated intemperately gnawing the hand that so bountifully fed me. "They are as sick that surfeit with too much, as they that starve with nothing," Shakespeare again murmured in my ear.

Back in California, where purifying snows encircled the mountains, we sought spiritual sustenance at the San Francisco ashram of Baba Muktananda, a guru especially popularized by the actress Marsha Mason. As with his Bombay forebear, I found it hard to concentrate on the experience, my attention being constantly diverted by intrusive temporal thoughts mostly provoked by the holy man's woolly tea-cozy hat and the Almond Roca he liberally dispensed. As he flicked us with a kind of wand, I little realized that this would in fact awaken in me a spiritual reexamination of which these words, I suppose, are part.

I went to Atlanta to record *Mere Christianity,* a book compiled from broadcast talks made by C. S. Lewis around the time of my birth. This wartime "positive restatement of the Christian doctrines in lay language" had earned Lewis, who never even owned a radio, a reputation as a broadcaster second only to Churchill himself. Sharing a university staircase, and having a student of his as a tutor as well as similarly having an American wife, I sensed a certain kinship with this extraordinary ordinary man. But much as I appreciated the plausibility of his marvelously argued text I still found a reluctance to make it central to my own life. Like politics, religion seemed to me only as good as its individual believers, as manifest by acts, rather than words. Instinctively I sided with the undecided and noncommitted, avoiding the absolutism of certainty. "We are united by our doubts," Peter Ustinov had once perceptively remarked to me, "and divided by our convictions." At times I felt like that student of comparative religion in Shaw's *Major Barbara:* "And the problem is, I believe every one of them!" A year later I returned to Atlanta to put on tape Lewis's magnificent wartime sermons, *The Weight of Glory.* It seemed appropriate to be wielding these mighty words in the Bible-belted South for, in general, America's pompous boast of "In God We Trust" seemed to me mostly wishful thinking.

Our usual self-indulgent materialist summer was the immediate aftermath, spent exploring the byways of our new Mediterranean playground. We returned to Portugal to stay with the Patinos in their extraordinary house filled with exquisite blue-and-white tile paneling that would inspire the decoration of our own home. However, beyond the elaborate wrought-iron gates of this fantasy world where the maids changed uniform three times a day, the fires of revolution were smouldering menacingly.

The continuing fuel crisis, too, prompted poignant thoughts that magnificent private yachts such as *Tartar* were perhaps a dying breed. Sailing in the wake of Venetian triremes to Dubrovnik, we were grateful to again be aboard before its glorious day was done and inglorious little windblown *Dulcibella*s took over. Again I took this pampered time to prepare for another film role. It would turn out to be one of the unhappiest experiences of my career, and would validate the truth of Bruce Chatwin's observation that such luxury was only truly luxurious under adverse conditions.

The film's original screenplay, though, had been unusually intelligent and ambitious. A contemporary political thriller, it concerned a woman television journalist sent to Russia, then still in the frigid grip of the political dinosaurs, where she experiences the distinctly warmer grip of a Soviet press attaché, played by myself. The affair, however, is compromised by her involvement in a scheme to get a desperately ill child to the West for treatment. A Canadian production, it was made at a time when tax-shelter money there was flooding films indiscriminately onto a saturated market, squeezing the pool of talent that produced them and turning Toronto and Montreal into Hollywood North.

The warning signs were unmistakable from our first hours in Montreal. After the long transatlantic flight, Pat and I had gone to bed early so that I could be fresh and forthcoming at rehearsals and production meetings the next day. A phone call jarred us from sleep: it was the director inviting us to come on over and turn on with the leading lady. Drugs, it turned out, were to be an important feature of the film—and not of its plot, although their usage ensured that only a pale, disorganized approximation of the script was being captured on film.

Someone found the competence to fire our "director" and then the rush of lunatics to take over his madhouse turned into a positive stampede. A hack Hollywood writer, brought in to doctor the ailing project, produced a new script of dazzling banality in which all my dialogue was left blank. "You're being paid enough money to provide your own," I was informed. As the producer was daily laying out lines of cocaine for himself and my misleading lady, there was no court of appeal apart from my own outraged instincts.

Increasingly over the anemic, slipshod seventies, I had come to loathe the drug scene, especially when it trespassed beyond the confines of private use. Both Pat and I were allergic to marijuana smoke and hip dinner parties where unmeaty joints were served posed an especial dilemma. Should one leap up and flee in antisocial self-preservation or sit like Patience on a monument, smiling at grief? I now

repeatedly asked myself this same question and decided, for the first
time in my career, to leave unless the film returned to its original
structure and seriousness. In response I was chastised for my rudeness
in failing to attend a dinner party given in honor of the caterers! I
watched incredulously as the camera operator took over the film's
direction. I am not by nature a quitter and did everything in my power
to sail this storm-tossed leaking barque to safe harbor. But at times it
made me hate my job. That Patmos pronouncement about acting "not
being man's work" rang tauntingly in my ears.

Unfairly, I grew to loathe Montreal, although its Quebecois men-
tality did seem to combine the worst of French and American excesses
in a certain lunatic lingual fascism. "Perchman" becoming "Perchiste"
was perhaps forgivable in an age where "Chairman" was suspect. But,
name of a dog, why did they insist on "Arrêt" on traffic signs when
the universal word—even in chauvinist France—was "Stop"? Fears
of independence and secession had sent investment money rushing
westward to the booming prairie towns, devitalizing the old gray city.

We saved our sanity by fleeing periodically south of the border.
New York was itself too crazy for comfort as it slithered into bankruptcy. The city now had its "fun" in hellish, cavernous discos, insisting on metamorphosing the graffiti that vandalized every vista into
"art." The new cable T.V. channels featured self-conscious nudist
shows with advertisements for brothels, and establishments where
sexual behavior could be uninhibitedly and indiscriminately indulged.
Gravity in New York seemed to exert twice its force elsewhere, dragging down people's faces to their boots as they scuffed along at the
bottom of their concrete canyons.

Yet a strange artificial reflexive politeness was abroad to combat the
growing malaise. Calling on the telephone, for example, you would
be elaborately and time-consumingly thanked for having put through
the call in the first place. We found it more restful motoring down to
sample the neat, sensible virtues of the New England states where the
fall foliage was now at its glorious best. But even here were hidden
dangers.

The first storm of winter accosted us, coating the russet leaves with
a spectacular frosting of snow—and the road with a lethal sheen of
ice. As out of control as our film, we were horrified to find ourselves
skidding yet again into oncoming traffic, missing trees and telegraph
poles and other slaloming vehicles by hairs' breadths. Yet again ending up in a ditch, we were helped by a man in a nearby house who,

ironically in the face of my own current ridiculous employment, was out of work. He impressed us with his dignity.

"To live a life is not as easy as to cross a field," a Russian character in our film lugubriously observed and I was tempted to agree. Why were we being so frequently reminded of our own mortality? At least it put the agonies of our working life into proper perspective, reducing them by comparison to eccentric insignificance. The experience only confirmed a conviction that I had to respect my own slowly consolidating standards. I reasoned that if I invested a project with one hundred percent of my talent and enthusiasm then, whatever its outcome, I could live with it. Eventually the film was finished and released. Incredibly, it even received reasonable reviews—and I didn't have to write them myself!

Back in Monaco I became involved in other Russian maneuvers with the Ballets Russes, having been invited to join a committee planning to make a permanent museum of ballet in a place that had witnessed some of its greatest triumphs, a tradition continued by Princess Grace with her local ballet school. As its centerpiece it was proposed to purchase Serge Lifar's great collection of costume designs. Sadly, nothing came of this—a great loss for the principality. We became friends with another Monaco resident, Picasso expert Douglas Cooper. Invited to dinner at his appropriately Cubist apartment in a new concrete block, we had the opportunity to enjoy both his treasures and his wicked stories. Our own collection of stage designs continued to flourish, and our walls now hung with Bakst, Exter, Tchelitchew, Benois and Léger as well as Bibiena and other renaissance masters.

There was also a portrait of Diaghilev by Larionov done in Monte Carlo. Diaghilev was certainly the man of the hour but what his achievement would have been without the enormous contemporary buildup of musical, pictorial and balletic talent inside Russia pressing at the sluice-gates and demanding to flood Europe makes interesting speculation. Without babies, a midwife is irrelevant. In Paris we saw a splendid Diaghilev show but somehow the funereal atmosphere ill-served the creator of such ethereal art. "It's nice to see Serge de D's cuff links," Adrian remarked in confirmation, "but they don't really give you an idea of what the Ballets Russes was like as an experience. Ballet is music and movement—how can this be shown by motionless costume designs in the silence of a museum? It's Fokine nonsense!"

As befitted a ruling house called Grimaldi, a more successful local show was the Monaco Circus Festival, where one year I was delighted to find myself serving on a jury that included Cary Grant. It made me feel that maybe a permanent museum was the wrong place to honor the ballet—a killing jar for a butterfly art. It was better served when the ghosts of legend were reincarnated every time the house lights lowered and the curtain rose on another live performance. Exhibitions betrayed little of the passion, temperament and joy that went into the work's creation just as my Canadian film, when finished, revealed little of the agony that went into its birth. Magic was indeed the habit of our existence.

Lookaut Long Puk Puk

CHAPTER THIRTY-ONE

*R*eturning to California just before the decade's end, we enjoyed the unfamiliar sensation of being rooted for a relatively lengthy time. Another novelty was that Pat was now temporarily, if not temperamentally, a redhead, and yet another was her astonishing everyone by cooking Christmas dinner complete with all the trimmings.

The holiday was spent in the tinseled sunshine with Rick—and with Serena, the blonde beauty he had loved and lost when they were both teenagers. Meeting her again at an L.A. film premiere, we learned she was now a divorcee. Asked for news of Rick we gave Serena his number, thereby provoking lightning to strike twice, this time with redoubled intensity. They were now living together with Consuelo, Serena's young daughter, whose name bore the proud stamp of her Vanderbilt lineage.

In Los Angeles, seasonal hillside fires burned with an apocalyptic fury, prefiguring the changes that would transform the next tumultuous decade. Back in Britain, the first rays of Margaret Thatcher's rising sun, however, were thawing a land hardened by freezing weather and wornout work practices. Even the country's culture seemed embattled, the theaters being full of documentary plays by Howard Brenton, David Hare, David Edgar and Stephen Poliakoff all dealing with recent history and reflecting a society in ferment.

Our life, in contrast, was relatively undisturbed. I struggled with guilt feelings about not being more actively employed when in fact a time to ponder and ruminate was the most valuable Christmas present I could have had. In its tranquil setting, and full of beautiful things, the house was a joy to inhabit. Antique Portuguese tile panels and an ancient fireplace, brought stone by stone from France, dramatized the dining room while, in the living room, sunlight filtered through indoor ficus trees and a hand-carved balsa-wood banana tree from Bali. The bedroom featured twin Japanese screens blooming with exquisite flowers, and a carpet woven with oriental symbols of good fortune. The house reflected our travels while providing refuge from them. Perfect for entertainment, it seemed to cast a kind of Odyssean spell. No one wanted to leave it and, situated as it was in the land of uninhibited opportunity, everyone wanted to buy it. "But you're never here," one famous movie agent remonstrated with us petulantly.

Tearing ourselves away reluctantly from the unwonted pleasures of domesticity, we patronized some of the local restaurants, including Ma Maison, L.A.'s answer to New York's Russian Tea Room, where the meals were of less consequence than the deals. Some restaurants, especially those with Gallic aspirations, were insufferably snobbish, as if trying to make up for their cheek-by-jowl placement amidst their Mexican and oriental cousins.

Dining at one of these haughty hostelries one evening, our guests included David Hockney, who turned up in a silk shirt and tie worn with an immaculate Saint-Laurent cardigan. Addressing him as "Mr. Warhol," the Maître d' pompously denied him entrance unless clad in a "jacket," offering David the opportunity to atone for his gaffe by wearing the house Ted Lapidus garment. Outraged, Pat asked for the phone on this dictator's desk, using it to book a table at another restaurant. As we filed out, David turned on his inquisitor, whose pomposity was now visibly deflating like a leaking balloon, and in slow, deliberate Bradford tones advised him: "It's one thing for you to humiliate me in public but if you are to use sartorial discrimination, I insist you do it with aesthetic judgment." Chris Isherwood, who was also in our company, his Hitler Youth haircut positively bristling with indignation, fired the parting shot: "You have turned away the only living English artist exhibited in the Louvre and you call yourself a *French* restaurant. Goodnight!"

I used the time in L.A. to search for film properties to develop and to pursue plans for the actor's ideal vade mecum, a one man show. On the cinema front I was looking for an up-to-date comedy, but, as well as the Erskine Childers project, I harbored ambitions of making a film about those other English adventurers, the White Rajahs of Sarawak —the Brooke family who ruled the tribes like native potentates. Thoughts were obviously turning travelwards again, and we seized on an invitation to an awards ceremony in Melbourne to venture down under for the first time.

Heading as usual for Birmingham by way of Beachy Head, we called in at Tahiti, Bora Bora and New Zealand en route. The latter was like an antipodean version of England in the thirties, complete with cream teas and lawn bowls and fewer people. Our only entertainment was a show where varieties of groomed sheep paraded on stage like pampered beauty queens. Crossing the Tasman Sea to Australia, I returned to the world of my infant-school project, with the cut-out maps now reality beneath the descending plane. Joe had once been offered an important job with an Australian department store, so it was fascinating to speculate that this land, at once familiar and strange, could have been my home.

Both at the festival and at private screenings we saw many examples of the talented new school of Australian filmmaking—such as the first exhilarating *Mad Max,* made for $400,000. We discovered a whole new breed of native cameramen, adept at capturing the rich, hard-edged Pre-Raphaelite beauty of the local light. What was lacking in budgets seemed to be compensated by sheer talent and improvisational skill. I met up with Bruce Beresford, a director I admired, on the set of his latest film, *The Club.* He had in fact offered me a role that I had turned down, reasoning that an authentic ensemble—and a stronger personal interest—was essential for a story about one of Australia's greatest passions, football.

The besetting problem with the local film industry was a persistent, pervasive Australian inferiority complex—the cultural cringe. In an egalitarian society that preferred its superstars to come from abroad, the tall poppies were ruthlessly mown down. But there was a sense of a country on the move, forging synthesis between the best of the old maternal, and the new adolescent, worlds and expressing its delighted self-awareness in an exciting, individual voice.

We spent two days in Adelaide sampling its wine and arts festival and sensing what California might have been like before fermenting its own pernicious brand of smog. The center of the country was our next stop. In Alice Springs, a handful of streets flung down at random on the red soil, the gray-greens of the gum trees juxtaposed violently with the flaming earth and pop-art blue sky. This was still new terri-tory, dramatic and spectacularly empty and, strewth, fart a crowbar, mate, was it ever bloody hot! Flying to the dirt airstrip of Ayers Rock, we explored the extraordinary chameleon of a mountaintop peeking out of the encircling nothingness. The dry air and two-hundred-foot elevation made us both feel ludicrously well, although the 100°F heat demanded endless battles with marauding flies. Now there is appar-ently a jet airport and ritzy hotel resort at Ayers Rock—another pow-erful incentive for never postponing travel opportunities or ambitions.

We headed north to Papua New Guinea and from Port Moresby, a city full of neat white men in shorts and long white socks, we flew out to the Sepik River. Beneath us a huge primeval landscape of forests was bisected by serpentine cocoa-colored rivers, the odd mountain piercing the purple horizon. The plane had a noble lineage going back to pioneer days when New Guinea's uncompromising terrain made it a world leader in air freight operations, transforming the cargo plane into a cult object and uniting a nation that babbled over seven hundred languages.

Our destination was a jungle lodge perched on a ridge above the great river where flowers flamed in the forest gloom, white egrets flashed through the heavy air and a sign, *"Lookaut Long Puk Puk,"* warned of submerged crocodiles. Here our first tribal encounter was suitably strange and impressive. A spindly ladder led up to a large, thatched ancestral hut where, in the smoky half-light, some fantasti-cally accoutered forms were just visible. The eye adjusted to take in other whites of eyes, painted forms, bone jewelry and paradisiacal birds' feathers. Then someone was pounding a wooden drum, voices joined in a rhythmic chorus and the floor began swaying to the beat of the dance. It was all so unexpected and unfamiliar that our applause was genuine and unfeigned—and politely returned. The sensation of having slipped back into another time only disappeared when tourist and prey emerged into the sunshine for that twentieth-century head-hunting rite—the group photograph.

Modern paraphernalia intruded elsewhere: stone-age dugout canoes were powered by outboard motors. Solar heating panels protruded from sago-thatched huts beside which churches now smugly stood. Sports jackets were worn with native "arse-grass" and tribal warfare was a tourist charade, albeit enacted with hair-raising authenticity by a rep company of mud men called, with echoes of cozy village hall dramatics, the Chimbu Players. The influx of tourists seemed unaccompanied by the corruption evident along more well-trodden paths. Occasionally, though, witnessing a particular insensitivity, I longed for these complaisant people to turn on the camera-snapping hordes, chop them to pieces and devour them for everyone's edification.

Reality intruded with a phone call at five forty-five one morning in a town with the improbable *Goon Show* name of Minj. Equally improbably, it was my American agent. Would I care to take over in the Broadway production of *Bent?* The yawning desk clerk eyed me with a professional indifference masking a curiosity that I now shared. Well, would I? My immediate instinct was to turn it down: why return so soon to the world of Nazi horrors and to Isherwood's homosexual Berlin? But, as with *England Made Me,* I found it difficult to rest on my decision. Had I known that I had just made contact with a whole new tribe of cannibals I would have fallen instantly back to sleep.

In Singapore I read the play, which seemed to be a powerful dramatic metaphor for many things but fundamentally about the redeeming power of love. My agent got through again to say the play's management had refused to take no for an answer. He added that, bolstered by a tourist invasion bred by a low-valued dollar, the New York theater "season" now extended through the hot, humid summer months and that, after Richard Burton's taking over in *Equus,* there was little stigma attached to one actor replacing another. Would I reconsider? I did, agreeing to a three-month contract.

Back in London a friend, dubious of my apostasy, persisted in questioning the wisdom of my choice, pointing to a copy of *Variety* which revealed that *Bent* was hardly doing "boffo" business. I should have read the omens better, for, besides problems with visas and Equity permits, there were other signs. On our arrival in New York in early June I was asked to agree to three instead of four weeks of rehearsal as Richard Gere was anxious to hand over the role of Max. I soon found out why.

Bent was indeed in trouble. Apparently it had been so ever since it opened, despite good notices, and, after its Tony nomination, had been struggling along in the vain hope an award might boost its commercial potential. The immediate result was that I found no one to work with as my new co-star, Jeffrey De Munn, had not even been given a contract. Then, just two and a half weeks before we were due to open, rehearsals were authorized—with the stage manager redirecting from the prompt book.

It was another ludicrous, irresistible challenge. De Munn, a gifted, darkly humorous New York actor, and I threw ourselves into the work, our labors almost matching those of our characters—two homosexuals imprisoned in a concentration camp—in brutal intensity. We rehearsed night and day, perfecting the timing of the crucial rock-shifting sequences that allowed the two prisoners precious moments to communicate. Anyone eavesdropping at the door of our hotel suite would have been astonished to hear men making love to each other in terms of graphic explicitness. Our hands were bleeding, our heads were shorn, and events offstage continued to rival in horror those onstage.

As a proper dress rehearsal would have cost a measly $1,000, we were given one miserable technical run-through. Our first time in front of an audience was our first night. My Old Vic ordeal flashed back again. There was that same panicky sensation of having absolutely no idea what came next. Moment was played by moment. Miraculously, moves and words welled up into the void. Something worked. There was a favorable reaction. A New Jersey housewife wrote: "Yesterday when I saw the play for the third time it was as if I never saw Max or Horst before. I cried again but with different tears." One critic even went so far as to comment: "A compelling performance can turn a weak play into a theatrical event."

But the Kafka-esque nightmare continued. At the end of that first week the management informed us they were closing us down. We felt betrayed and abandoned. The challenge redoubled. Offering to waive my salary, I went into battle and, hiring a publicist, shamelessly whored myself on the airwaves, appearing on every TV and radio show available and gabbling incessantly to the press. Pat and Rick were splendidly supportive, distributing flyers and enthusiasm to positive effect. At the end of four weeks we were sold out and the announcement was made that the play was to run indefinitely.

It didn't, of course, but its benefits were numerous. Not least, I was honored with a much-coveted Hirschfeld cartoon to add to our collection. Playing Max was a stretch both of mind and muscle. The real reward, however, was a sense of having done something of value. One particular night, after the performance, there was a young girl at the stage door asking for me. Her mother, she told me, had just seen the play. Like the young girl in it she, too, had been raped as a child and interned in a concentration camp. There was an awkward silence. I expected the girl to censure me, a comfortably off actor, for trivializing her mother's agony into an entertainment. Instead she thanked me. Hitherto, apparently, her mother had been unable to speak of her experience, but the performance had been a catalyst, purging years of pent-up grief and unspoken horror. For a profound moment I sensed how powerful and useful my job could be.

Eventually exchanging muggy N.Y. for smoggy L.A. for an equally brief time, Pat and I doubled back to Europe via New Mexico. Seeing a performance of *Eugene Onegin* at Santa Fe's open-air opera revived a long-standing ambition to use my unexpected professional freedom to attend the Wagner Festival at Bayreuth and, after so much horror, to celebrate the more glorious aspects of Teutonic culture. Tickets, though, were as rare as Rhine gold, especially for Patrice Chereau's once controversial, now acclaimed, production of *The Ring*. Around this time, however, I had been approached by French television to play in *Vendredi*, Michel Tournier's post-Freudian version of *Robinson Crusoe*, later in the year. Its director was spending the summer in St. Tropez preparing his film and, the very same day of my fruitless dealing with the Bayreuth box office, he invited me over from Monaco for discussions. There, sunning on his lawn, was Chereau and I knew instantly that providence had secured our seats. Patrice indeed invited us to the very last performance of the Cycle after its celebrated five-year run.

The experience of Wagner at his shrine was a revelation—and a total commitment. We set about our initiation rites as complete Wagnerians by studying operas. The Cycle had a cumulative, mesmerizing power, stimulating anew the "imaginary forces," returning me to that old Anglo-Saxon realm of the spear-wielding Wanderer and his symbolic world of dwarfs, giants and gods. Sitting inside the unadorned wooden musical instrument of a theater, we were filled with vibrations that resonated days after the performances.

At the end of this incomparable week, the applause lasted for an hour and a half. I have rarely witnessed so ecstatic a reception. It ended only in deference to the exhausted singers who, on top of singing for hours on end, were being summoned back for over one hundred curtain calls.

This pilgrimage was the source of my Least Favorite Story. Married couples are remarkable for the stoic tolerance with which one spouse has to endure the inevitable repeated retelling of stories from the other. Pat and I once mutually confessed which was the one story that set the other's teeth on edge or induced pangs of insuperable boredom. Mine was of her orgasmic deflowering by Richard Wagner. Hers was my stolid account of why we were nondrinkers, something already stolidly recorded here—but hopefully with a now self-conscious brevity!

Back in England we visited my parents who had just moved into a cottage in the middle of Sidmouth. The change was good for them as it helped them resist the temptation in that mild benign climate to slip irresistibly into that last Shakespearean age. Their first grandchild, Paul, no longer a shining morning-faced schoolboy, was about to join the work force at a time when Britain's unemployment figures were the highest since the war. Penny, now a guiding force behind the foundation of a hospice in Faversham, was devoting her energies to this caring, demanding work. We again stayed with John Schlesinger, this time in his Sussex oasthouse, where Paul and Linda McCartney were dinner guests. They invited us back for tea in their rustic retreat where we happened to talk about alternative medicine. Years later, when we met them again after their concert in Los Angeles, Linda confirmed that this discussion had set her family on a path to homeopathy. We have yet to reciprocate entirely, however, their energetic espousal of vegetarianism, much as I would like to.

Not long after our first encounter with the McCartneys, John Lennon was shot in New York. With him the decade seemed to die. After the uncertain seventies, new brooms swept away old orders. In America, Reagan's folksy optimism replaced Carter's virtuous vacuity. With the rise of Solidarity in Poland, the world waited to see if their Russian masters would behave with the usual arthritic, knee-jerk reflex and ring up the curtain on a political *Götterdämmerung*.

Panache

My Gallic Robinson Crusoe set the tone for a year characterized by an almost total immersion in French culture. An international best-seller, translated into seventeen languages, Tournier's *Friday* was not so well known in the English-speaking world as Defoe's story. In it Friday turns the tables on Crusoe, literally blowing up his master's attempts to re-create "civilization" on their desert island and leads him back to more natural values, including the discovery of the sexual libido lurking within the stern Quaker body.

It was that body that suddenly assumed significance. Going native, Crusoe had to shed prudish garments as well as preconceptions, and a certain self-conscious vanity intruded on my part. I have always had a slight horror of the sweaty narcissism of gyms, preferring brisk walks and the lone pursuits of the pool to keep fit. For this special case, however, I entrusted myself to the legendary Mike Abrums, who had shaped the physique of countless Hollywood leading men, including that of the new President. While December sweltered in the eighties—a taste of the heat to come—I sweated it out under Mike's encouraging eye, pressing and pumping with gratifying results.

This regimen continued under leaden Paris skies early in the New Year. We were there for a month of preparation and filming in a freezing concrete bunker of a studio made bearable by the prospect of six months in Tunisia and the Caribbean that lay ahead and by presently putting up at the Ritz Hotel, where just walking outside into the Place Vendôme each morning set the pulse pleasurably racing.

It also made for a schizoid life. A tattered castaway by day and confined in this sybaritic temple of hotelierdom by night, I was reminded of a Parisian encounter we had at this time with the extremely wealthy Norton Simon and his beautiful wife, the former actress Jennifer Jones. Over an elegant dinner, they explained that they deliberately spent time riding the Métro in order to meet "real people."

While in Paris there was a reunion with Adrian, who had agreed to provide the English-language version of the script, which was to be shot simultaneously with the French. He also co-authored the words to a song from the film's theme tune, composed by Maurice Jarre, and had brief and, alas, unrealized ambitions of becoming a pop zillionaire!

Our Tunisian location was the southerly island of Djerba close to the Libyan border. Again we drove there, landing by ferry from Genoa straight back into my cinema past. From Justine's city of Tunis we went down by John the Baptist's riverside to the island which, in fact, contained the ancient Jewish settlement and synagogue of Hara Sagira, from which Zeffirelli had recruited extras for his *Jesus*. The putative land of Ulysses's lotus-eaters, Djerba seemed little more than a sparse sandbank dotted with palms, its beaches littered with Roman mosaics and barracklike hotels where *"Bitte schön"* was on every lip.

For the first few weeks I filmed on my own, a novel but useful experience as my isolated condition perfectly matched Crusoe's shipwrecked state. Any tentativeness at having to speak French again merely reflected Crusoe's own difficulty reusing language. Shooting one take in one language and immediately duplicating it in the other was not always easy, the internal rhythms of each language being so different. The French version, however, seemed to reveal hidden insights into the English and vice versa.

Here on my own I colonized my island, building a series of structures that became ever more useless and grandiose. There was a church in which I gave solitary sermons and I thundered out public edicts into an echoing, empty cobbled square lined with fully-stocked shops, museums, banks and even my Governor's mansion. In the course of this I added to my actor's repertoire of abstruse skills—how to milk goats and make cheese, plait fiber into ropes, plow and harvest fields and build a boat.

My days of going solo finally ended when I was joined by my Friday, the American actor Gene Anthony Ray, who had enjoyed a measure of fame as the street-smart black dancer in *Fame*. A native of Harlem, he had hitherto traveled little beyond his urban confines. When we first met I had asked him what his father did. "Time," he unself-consciously replied. I took him under my wing in Crusoe-like fashion, teaching him some French as Robinson had taught his Friday English, and initiating him into some of the mysteries of European culture. His delight at the new horizons opening up for him was infectious.

What I couldn't teach him, though, was a basic discipline that is fundamental to our craft. I found myself sharing Crusoe's exasperation when Gene, seduced by the holiday atmosphere of the island, would spend all night dancing in impromptu cabarets and turn up late and exhausted for work. But he had youth on his side—time enough to realize that fame was fleeting and only hard-crafted talent endured.

Pat was then exploring macrobiotics and, in contrast, was all discipline. A diet of mostly rice and aduki beans seemed to have the combined effect of adding energy and, not that she needed to, shedding weight. Besides photographing on the set every day—her work would eventually appear in a beautiful illustrated edition of the book —she was writing a film script based on Rick's more printable New York adventures.

I admired her dedication. As well as fleshing out many scripts I have also attempted to write my own and, together, the experience has given me an insight into how difficult this is. I am now aware, too, of certain basic rules. Most notably, each scene has to count for something and advance the action in some way. As a rule, less is more.

A sense of isolation persisted, reinforced by an at times welcome lack of mail and phone calls. At weekends we explored our surroundings, setting off across a landscape of empty deserts, and vast gleaming salt flats interspersed with puddles of green oases that had been the recent *Star Wars* set. Staying in the same hotel in Nefta was President Bourguiba and so we had the unexpected pleasure of sharing a vivid *folklorique* evening with the man who had created present-day Tunisia. Poets loudly honored their Habib and children sang his praises. The surrounding oasis also paid homage, being at its most flamboyant and paradisiacal. The air was cool and sweet and secret waters coaxed a dazzle of blossoms from a thousand flowers and fruit trees.

Celebrating our thirteenth wedding anniversary, as we had our engagement, by a palm-fringed beach, Pat and I then flew off into a virtual kaleidoscope of sunlit strands. Filming in the Caribbean for a few months should have been an actor's ideal dream. There was the added attraction for us of not being confined to any particular island for, after a spell of conventional hotel life on Martinique and Guadeloupe, the entire film company put to sea. Yet again I found myself involuntarily crewing a sailing boat, this time down through the necklace of islands that stretched out to the south. It was a novel and, I must confess, in the tropical warmth, an enjoyable experience to be furling sails alongside a terrified wardrobe mistress at some unsocial hour of the night.

Films certainly provided an unconventional existence and drifting through the Antilles made me muse on the vagaries of the professional actor's life. The succeeding islands, some close together, others far apart, seemed to represent the series of disconnected jobs that coalesced into a career. As André Gide observed, there was no way of discovering new lands "without consenting to lose sight of the shore for a very long time." Sometimes the wind and current were strong, making interisland sailing quick and straightforward; at others, you could be becalmed, and then suddenly storm-tossed with no friendly port in view. Some islands were merely for provisioning; others provided unlimited riches and you anchored there a long time or returned frequently for bounty. There were those that were surrounded by dangerous shoals that sometimes damaged but rarely wrecked. Often fog descended and, disoriented, you could find yourself sailing in the wrong direction. But when the sun shone and the fair wind followed there was no more exhilarating way of exploring this extraordinary world.

Each real island in whose reef we dropped anchor provided its own special feature—hills like breasts and vegetal pubic hair—that together made up the anthropomorphic shape of Crusoe's island of Speranza. One boasted the best volcano, some other the ideal waterfall, yet another a settlement of indigenous Arawak Indians and everywhere limpid water and thirst-quenching fruit. When filming the scenes where, under Friday's tutelage and courtesy of Mike Abrums, Crusoe goes native, clad only in a loin cloth, I shared his sense of release. It was fun to turn savage—to hunt and swim and paddle a canoe through mangrove-lined rivers under mango-colored skies and feel the constant caress of warm sun and water. In Djerba the wicked sun had been the gleam on a knife edge. When we filmed the naked Crusoe lying in a bog and intoxicating himself with its fetid fumes, the water in our artificial swamp was so icily cold that the pigs, meant to be wallowing pleasurably alongside me, had to be forcibly tied in place and outdid me in squealing and shivering.

However, there was a darker side to the real Caribbean paradise. We all began to get sick: wounds refused to heal, ugly sores started to appear and infections persisted. Eventually a doctor was flown in to treat us. A short holiday here, it seemed, was ideal. The unstressed immune system preserved good health and the body benefited from sun, rest and exercise. A lengthy exposure, however, taxed this natural resistance, and may have explained why so many white residents seemed to end up permanently pickled in alcohol. A more sinister threat came after filming an idyllic sequence in a freshwater river later revealed to be a breeding ground of such tropical diseases as bilharzia. Panicked blood tests in St. Lucia, however, revealed no damage. In the end, like Crusoe, we longed to be home. Our floating digs had turned into an unendurable *huis clos*. Hell was other people. Paradise was for the birds.

One morning submerged in a reef, that same evening I was high in the mountains of New Mexico rehearsing *Cyrano de Bergerac,* having been invited to play the title role in what would be the inaugural production of the Sante Fe Festival Theater. Instantly exhausted, I couldn't understand why until told that racehorses sent to compete there require weeks of acclimatization to the seven-thousand-foot altitude. Our dressing rooms were even provided with oxygen. I had just three weeks to rehearse this epic play. The great bravura speeches were already under my swashbuckled belt, but now there was a mass of other details to attend to—not least, of course, a fitting for that famous nose.

Cyrano is one of those roles in the canon that provides that much-sought-after "stretch," demanding both vocal and physical dexterity. A dreamer of flying machines and as gallant as D'Artagnan, Cyrano was a man after my own heart. Anthony Burgess's pithy translation, moreover, added outrageous rhyming wit to his wisdom. In short, he had panache.

The play's original success in 1897 had been attributed to audiences' surfeit of socialists, feminists and Scandinavians. The same disenchantment could be applied to modern audiences who had just weathered a jaded decade. Cyrano offered the kind of escapist romance then reaching its zenith in the storybook wedding saga of Prince Charles and his fair lady Diana. Watching the ceremony on television I was curiously depressed, seemingly witnessing the last waltz of an outmoded institution. It was as if Britain had channeled all her competence and energy into laying on this elaborately archaic show. I little realized that the bridegroom would soon step out of conventional line to use his royal position as a catalyst for an urgent and invigorating self-examination of the very society he would one day rule.

For the first few performances of my own little costume drama I was continuously tired, almost drowning in the perspiration swilling around in my elongated plastic proboscis. I had to gather my strength for the impending ordeal by, unprecedentedly, resting in the afternoon. Santa Fe, reputedly full of cosmic energy, was famous for its healers, especially of the alternative, holistic kind, and I put my overtaxed body in their competent hands, trying acupressure and Chinese herbs to great effect.

Once the play had opened to gratifying acclaim, Pat and I took stock of our surroundings. We had rented a house in rural Tesuque commanding views of the magnificent skies towering over the red rock formations so beloved of the area's most famous resident artist, Georgia O'Keeffe. A highlight of our visit was an encounter with her. She was still beautiful, her presence inevitably overlaid with those glorious earlier Steiglitz studies of her sculptural nudity. She admired a bright red cashmere shawl worn by Pat who immediately tried to give it to her as a present. "Thank you, my dear," came the gracious reply, "but at my age I'm trying to give up possessions." Pat, of course, was anxious for an opportunity to photograph her and was about to ask permission from O'Keeffe's companion and associate, Juan Hamilton, with whom we had become friendly. A noteworthy sculptor, he was sixty years younger than the great painter and had taught her his craft when her eyesight had begun to fail. "You know, everyone wants something from her," he happened to remark to Pat, instantly dooming her request to remain unspoken.

Santa Fe had been founded before the Pilgrims and the Spanish missionary presence mingled powerfully with that of the native Indians who still filled the main plaza selling turquoise jewelry and other traditional wares. We were invited to their Santo Domingo pueblo to witness a rain dance that made our nightly dramatics look pallid in comparison. Here indeed the gods spoke. Seeing the feathered and beaded rows of rapt participants it was hard to realize that this scene of pagan power was taking place in space-age America, especially as robed and sandaled monks could be seen among them ministering to their flocks. Whatever deity was responsible, the skies repeatedly flashed with electric fire—it seemed no coincidence that the atomic bomb had been created here.

Reviews for *Cyrano* were positive but again it was an unsolicited letter from a member of the public that most satisfied. After a flattering appreciation of the performance it continued:

> . . . Finally what I liked most was that you took on a character upon which you could not depend on your looks to pull off—it took pure raw talent. I like seeing that kind of discipline, energy and risk-taking in a person. I can see you still performing superbly at the age of 80.

In what medium, I was moved to muse? Though I had enjoyed myself, theater was beginning to look, in some respects, as curiously old-fashioned as the actor's formal bows at the end of a performance. It reminded me of what people used to say about National Service—that somehow all the repetitive, tedious routines were good for you and character-forming. The theater's chemistry seemed to lack the volatile combustibility of the cinema. Its flare-ups were localized, whereas a movie explosion could be heard round the world.

Just before filming in the Caribbean I had been approached about starring in a stage musical based on Antoine de Saint-Exupéry's *The Little Prince*. Its pedigree was most promising—book by dear Hugh Wheeler and music and lyrics by John Barry and Don Black. A musical was still one of the few professional undertakings that had eluded me and I was keen to accept. Even so, I had insisted on auditioning for it and, on holiday weekend, left my desert island duties to dash up to New York and give the assembled talent a quick taste of my quality. Eyes and teeth agleam à la *Beau Geste*, I belted out "Off We Go into the Wide Blue Yonder," and, to my delight, the existing approval was endorsed.

Later that year I made greater expectorations with a round of singing lessons, relishing the daily improvements until rehearsals started in New York. Earlier I had been shipwrecked in the real Sahara. Now, as a bold French Saint-Exupéry-type mail pilot singing exuberantly of "wind, sand and stars," I crash-landed in its stage approximation. The company, which included Ellen Greene with her ghetto-blasting voice, and several children, was full of youthful enthusiasm. Everyone about me in the daily dance class seemed capable of tying themselves comfortably into knots and, with muscles screaming in protest, I at first despaired. As with the singing, though, there was perceptible progress, and I particularly enjoyed finally getting to emulate Nureyev in a poor man's pas de deux.

A decision was made—fatally, as it turned out—to dispense with the traditional out-of-town tryout and open cold after three weeks of previews. Hal Prince had recently attempted the same procedure with *Merrily We Roll Along*. Despite his usual collaboration with the infallible Stephen Sondheim, however, the show folded after a few performances, the whole town having been privy to its problems. Although this freed a theater for us to play in, we, too, were duly punished for similarly tempting providence.

Two weeks before the first preview scheduled for New Year's Eve, the director was fired, leaving the show in a shambles. As in the famous drawing of the boa constrictor swallowing an elephant, the production had become immovably stuck fast with no time for proper digestion. Yet again I was asked if I would attempt the improbable and open as contracted. I should have turned them down. Once a show goes into a tailspin, Mike Nichols advised, it is best to bail out. But, as with *Bent*, the situation posed an irresistible challenge. Discarding the offered parachute, I free-fell back into the work.

The show was broken apart and reassembled. But as Saint-Exupéry had sagely noted: "Success is finally attained, not when there is no longer anything to add but when there is no longer anything to take away." With too many old concepts still clinging to its wreckage, our crashed vehicle required the magical intercession of a real-life Little Prince to get airborne. Help came from every quarter. Hal gave advice and the talented Way Bandy devised a cheerful cosmetic cover-up for my exhausted pallor. Pat brought macrobiotic food to supplement the stodgy sandwiches fueling the endless days. As with *Bent*, I turned myself into a publicity machine. And we almost made it.

The new year began on a note of hysterical jubilation. For we managed to open as scheduled. Playing Wagner in my dressing room, I went on stage supercharged with the massive vibrations, if perhaps inappropriate theme, of Siegfried's funeral music. New revisions were added at each performance, none of which was the same. Every time I came offstage, my dresser met me with a check list of the current running order. By the last few performances there was a tantalizing inkling of how good the show could have been given more time and money. As it was, both ran out on us and the producer was unable to find an angel to rescue his Little Prince. I thought ruefully of the French system that guaranteed a play ran for as long as it had been rehearsed and remembered that London's monumental *Mousetrap* had almost been taken off at the beginning of its decades-long run. However, my brave company had already vindicated themselves entirely. I am prouder of this "failure" than of many so-called successes.

Above all, this experience convinced me that the Little Prince's planet belonged in the unlimited universe of the imagination. Any attempt to realize it in concrete terms was perhaps inevitably doomed to failure. Moreover, I can now understand the truth behind that old adage that if Hitler is still alive he is engaged in the tryout of a musical!

Forty

CHAPTER THIRTY-THREE

Three Broadway outings and three aborted runs. Was someone sending a message? Was my choice of work misguided? I examined the fresh-killed entrails of my immediate career for guidance. Perhaps I was better suited to the hit-and-run method of the movies. Maybe I should return to my roots. "Will you try another play or go back to TV and films like me?!" a letter from John Gielgud echoed my thoughts.

Europe was still in the freezing grip of winter—but, not wishing to provide nourishment for schadenfreude enthusiasts, we had to get out of New York. Where to go? With my usual reflex when underemployed I accepted an invitation to a film festival, this time Manila's, and emerged into the tropical sun like one of the prisoners in *Fidelio* coming out of his dark cell into the light. But the visit was hardly an ode to joy. The film palace constructed especially for the festivities was strangely depressing. Later we found out why. It had been built so quickly to meet a deadline that some workers who had fallen into the wet cement were left entombed.

There was a ludicrously lavish and pretentious awards ceremony replete with sycophantic speeches, a symphony orchestra and opera divas, at which food was so long in coming that we were treated to the unedifying spectacle of our fellow diners falling upon and gobbling up the floral table decorations.

The next morning one of the formidable Blue Ladies who ran Filipino society called with an invitation to dine at the presidential palace. We had in fact already accepted dinner at the apartment of a young man we had befriended. Having fulfilled my obligations as a festival guest I felt I was now free to do what I wanted. The palace proceeded to barrage us with renewed requests, one minister even telephoning at seven in the morning, but our stubbornness grew in proportion to their coercion. When our young host heard about these maneuvers he nervously begged us not to reveal his identity, claiming that "they" might go so far as to arrest him to free us for the evening. Our enjoyment of his hospitality was enhanced when we later heard from someone who had attended the palace dinner that the postprandial entertainment had consisted of watching videos of George Hamilton movies!

We hoped that, outside Manila, our feelings of depression would lift. But the beauty of the famed rice terraces in the north was inevitably spoiled when, turning a corner, we passed a newly machine-gunned jeep. The country seemed to provoke violence. We lunched in a hotel by the waterfalls where the *Apocalypse Now* crew had stayed. Its proprietor proudly told us that he had periodically allowed them to smash the place to pieces, illustrating both the frustrations to which film crews are subject and the novel commercial enterprise of Third World countries.

My fortieth birthday, I felt, should be celebrated with a radical change of life-style. Giving up Monaco and becoming an American resident was an option discussed with increasing frequency and seriousness, even though "home" now seemed to be defined as the place where we kept suitcases and passports. But, wherever based, for the immediate future the most meaningful gift I could wish for myself was the continued practice of my craft. Theater work having yet again been mysteriously aborted, I looked around for employment in my preferred medium, the movies.

Sergio Leone, with whom I had almost worked over a decade before, was in L.A. preparing his gangster epic, *Once Upon a Time in America*. He happened to mention to a friend of mine that physically I looked perfect for one of the leading roles and that it was a pity I was English. Hearing this, his shortsightedness infuriated me.

It was Rick who suggested that I make a test to attempt to prove that actors are supposed to act. He had just finished producing a sumptuous musical of Dennis Potter's *Pennies from Heaven* at MGM— the beginning of a long-term, fruitful relationship with this brilliant, uncompromising English writer—and had no difficulty in persuading the studio to allow their Logan to run back and reuse their facilities.

Rick's persuasive genius as a producer was further revealed by his involving a trio of Grade A talents: John Schlesinger to direct, Conrad Hall to photograph, and Richard Marks to edit the results. I was coached in a Bronx accent—"Fordy thousan' dahlahs ya dumb schmuck!," etc.—and a scene between two hoodlums was improvised, then immortalized on 35mm stock and dispatched to Leone.

It was an act that could only be described as chutzpah, a showbiz commodity admired and despised in equal measure. But to my astonishment, far from being out of the question, I was now being seriously considered for the role—in fact, right down to the final casting. As hard as it was to overcome English reticence, this proved that conventional attitudes and images have to be constantly challenged. Working with John Schlesinger had long been an ambition. Our secret little film is one of my favorites and, I hope, but a taste of grander things to come.

The Phantom of the Opera provided a welcome return to the worlds of theater, film, television and travel—and, above all, to gainful employment. It was a CBS-TV production with Jane Seymour and Maximilian Schell that anticipated the extraordinary revival of interest in this old story. In this case the first of David Niven's criteria— "Where?"—proved instantly seductive. The film was to be made in Hungary, the cradle of so much Hollywood talent—Michael Curtiz, Leslie Howard, Ernst Lubitsch, lots of Gabors and Kordas, and even my neighbor, George Cukor.

Our arrival was memorable. Driving up through Yugoslavia, we had stopped in Opatija for old times' sake and had run into Tom Selleck. He was making his debut as a film star in an epic inevitably involving war, but miraculously this time, no Nazis. Learning of our destination over dinner, he pressed packets of food and even an electric kettle on us as if we were setting off into the uncharted wilds like some foolhardy explorers.

The Hungarian border bristled with an iron curtain of barbed wire interspersed with watch towers. Demanding our papers, a greatcoated guard looked at them intently then called over his comrades one by one until the car was surrounded by armed men, suffusing me with an irrational and involuntary guilt. What had I done or failed to do? Could I be punished for smuggling in food? A tea kettle? The chief guard then pulled out a piece of paper—surely my arrest warrant— and asked for my autograph, adding, "Welcome to Hungary, Mr. York!" From that moment I knew I would love this country, as proved to be the case. Admiring her proud, resourceful people who had pushed "the system" just about as far as it could go, we went every- where and made many new friends, including the brilliant director Istvan Szabo. The film was nothing much to speak of artistically, but, in terms of life experience, worth at least four stars in any critic's guide.

Back in Monaco, there was a chance to relax on our bowery terrace and exchange scripts for books. Princess Caroline came one afternoon for tea, inadvertently trapping our concierge in the bedroom where she had been tidying up. This old lady's shyness, loyalty and disincli- nation to disturb took such a tortuous, self-denying form that she refused to leave through the living room. Out of the corner of my eye, her own wide with terror, I saw her shakily climbing out of the window and down a rose-encrusted trellis to the ground!

Rick came to stay and our favorite pastime was to drive around the corner to the Plage de la Mala on Cap d'Ail for a swim and a simple *salade niçoise* lunch. The beach and its bistro were at the foot of a precipitous staircase that tended to restrict patrons to the young and lively. The three of us used to sit there admiring the beauty of a succession of topless girls—lunchtime fugitives from offices and fac- tories—as they unself-consciously showered and toweled in the sun- shine. Rick became besotted with an exquisite Danish girl—a vision of budding youth—who would sport provocatively before him. We reminded him of Dirk Bogarde's similar intimations of mortality in *Death in Venice,* which somewhat moderated his transports!

The last of 1982's trio of Gallic projects involved a return to both Hungary and Canada and yet again to that twilit shadowy world of the Holocaust. It would be especially successful in French-speaking countries—enabling me to enter France without showing a passport and be greeted with an enthusiastic, *"Bonjour, M. l'Acteur!"* followed by an intense discussion of the film.

The story was Martin Gray's extraordinary epic of survival, *For Those I Loved* which, like *Friday,* had been an international best-seller. Gray, a Polish Jew, was fourteen when the Nazis—or butchers, as he unequivocally called them—occupied Warsaw. Witnessing the isolation of the ghetto, he was instrumental in organizing its food supplies. His father, whom he idolized, gave him the commandment that still inspires his life: "Survive, Martin. Survive."

Somehow he did, though over a hundred of his relatives were killed and he himself lost an eye to a German rifle butt. Incredibly, he even managed to escape from the death camp of Treblinka, where his mother and brothers were taken from him. Joining the resistance, he went to Berlin as one of the youngest and most decorated officers in the liberating Russian army.

After the war Martin emigrated to the States, where his only known surviving relative resided. He lived the American dream, becoming a millionaire antique dealer by the age of thirty-five. He married a beautiful woman called Dina and they settled down to an idyllic life in the South of France, raising a family and embracing wholeheartedly the harmony and beauty hitherto so absent from his life.

But then on October 3, 1970, the horror returned when a forest fire duplicated the work of the concentration camp gas ovens. Dina and his children perished while attempting to escape to safety by car, leaving him yet again the lone survivor. Instead of killing himself as he was momentarily tempted to do, he took his father's advice and poured out his grief in the book that was to become a worldwide source of inspiration.

It provided the basis of a massive undertaking—a two-and-a-half-hour film as well as an eight-hour mini-series shot in what was fast becoming a specialty of mine, both English and French, on locations in Europe and Canada over the course of the next three months. At first I had resisted this return to the revulsions of war. But Ephraim Palfrey's blood must have called me to witness.

After Canada we moved to the South of France, where shooting resumed at Tanneron, a village perched on the hills behind Cannes where the tragic events had occurred. We even filmed in the house where, incredibly, Martin Gray was still living, having remarried and re-created a family of bonny children who roamed naked as wood nymphs in the grounds where Mozart minuets played amidst mimosa-strewn lawns. The house had survived the fire, as it had other conflagrations over the centuries. In fact, had Dina and the children stayed inside, they would have lived. It was to disseminate this and other life-saving knowledge that Martin Gray set up a foundation named after his wife.

The fire was restaged with an eerie, sickening verisimilitude. A mistral even blew up to exactly duplicate conditions. On being introduced to Martin Gray, I noted that there was a superficial resemblance between us. His handshake was firm, but his remaining eye spoke of the horrors he had witnessed with an eloquence that mere words were inadequate to match. Meeting Elie Wiesel later, I would see the same incomparably moving expression in his haunted eyes. For many, however, the enormity of Gray's experience beggared belief and, finding denial the easiest reaction, dismissed his story as fictitious. Certainly everyone involved with the project had a sense of working on something special.

The last part of the filming in Hungary was in many ways the hardest. It was now winter and, although we were staying in a comfortable hotel on the gray Danube overlooking the castle and the Buda Hills, the subject matter struck an uncomfortable, somber note as melancholy as the plaintive sounds of the local Gypsy musicians. Budapest was standing in for Warsaw with an area destined for redevelopment substituting for the ghetto. The authorities allowed us to fill it with tanks and firebombs during the climactic scenes of the uprising and literally blow it apart.

Although only make-believe, it was emotionally demanding to recreate scenes of daily life as the monstrous crime began to be perpetrated on the Jewish population, scenes so dreadfully familiar from contemporaneous newsreels. The Umschlagplatz where the butchers rounded up their victims for transportation in cattle trucks to the death camps was particularly disturbing. Pat was unable to photograph for tears and I saw them pour from the eyes of every crew member. Certainly its verisimilitude was powerfully confirmed when a Canadian tourist, a survivor of the Warsaw ghetto, happened to wander onto our set. His bewilderment and shocked disbelief at finding himself transported back to his horrific past was most moving to behold.

All this reinforced the fact that, as actors, we were responsible to history and—as with *Bent*—were articulating unspeakable events by reliving them. As Martin Gray's father insisted, life must go on. "I have a message to give the world," Martin himself asserted, "and I have a need to deliver it. It's very simple. No matter what happens to you, you must go beyond. You must not give up. One can rebuild even on ruins. Life can go on no matter what happens to you."

. . .

Early the next year, when I was toiling on the long postproduction tasks of re-voicing *For Those I Loved* in both languages, Pat called me in the studio with news of two we especially loved. Rick and Serena had suddenly decided to get married the next day. Everything was arranged overnight and, as with the simplicity of our own fuss-free nuptials, could not have been more pleasing. We welcomed our loving new daughter-in-law whose glamorous looks were now helping to support the family budget with modeling jobs.

We all laid back into the California life-style. Professionally, I set about telling the town I was back and available for work—especially in American roles. I was well aware of my perceived image—that of a European gadabout who was quite happily and frequently employed abroad. Hollywood films were not exactly thick upon the ground. At one point each studio had produced two a week. Now they were lucky if their output was as much as two films a year. Nevertheless I went about trying to integrate myself into the American mainstream.

However, this was to be the beginning of my British Year, inaugurated by the timely visit to Southern California, in unremitting torrential rain, of Queen Elizabeth. To my astonishment I found myself at the head table at the gala given in her honor, seated between Greer Garson and Elton John, and surrounded by such fellow British courtiers as James Mason, Victoria Tennant, Michael Caine, Joan Collins, the present reigning Queen of television, and Hollywood's favorite Joker, Dudley Moore. It was held on a vast soundstage packed elsewhere with major stars, the Elizabeths and Essexes, Richard Lionhearts and Queen Victorias of screen legend. Not holding British passports, however, they were banished from the royal presence and sat like dress extras among the hoi polloi.

I was introduced to Her Majesty, who asked the one question expressly forbidden in this otherwise insensitive town: "What are you doing at the moment?" I mumbled something vague and the Queen, the consummate professional, deferring to the hordes of performers before her, moved on to read her speech, somewhat spoiling the dazzle of her radiant presence with her severe schoolmarm spectacles. Surely the props department could have come up with a jeweled lorgnette?

A few months later, running into Sam Wanamaker by chance in New York, I had been invited to take part in a fund-raising tour on behalf of the Shakespeare Globe Centre—the fulfillment of his extraordinary dream to build a replica of the original Wooden O as a permanent London memorial to the supreme genius of our language.

We assembled a small group of traveling players, including Nicol Williamson and Cleo Laine and, in this updated version of the old bus 'n' truck tour, went from coast to coast visiting twelve cities in almost as many days with our Shakespeare show.

Starting in Washington, we encountered two remarkable people, Sir Oliver and Lady Marjorie Wright, the incumbent British Ambassador and his wife, and both passionate aficionados of the drama. We performed in the ballroom of the magnificent Lutyens embassy that, after our friendship was cemented, would become a cherished place to stay. It was good to sense the muse of fire breathing into my lungs again as we journeyed on to Denver, Dallas, San Francisco, and then full circle back to Pittsburgh and New York. "Put money in thy purse," was our principal intention and it was interesting to witness at firsthand the social and cultural strata that made up this rich and generous land, from the older, almost aristocratic, East Coast money to the newer fortunes of the Texas oil and the California gold fields.

Soon afterward we returned to Washington for an evening of unparalleled pleasures. It started at the White House where President Reagan gave a small dinner in honor of Laurence Olivier, whose film of *King Lear* was presented in a screening room replete with popcorn in silver Paul Revere bowls.

The Oliviers were also staying at the embassy. The gravitas of "Larry's" reputation, his latest role and our surroundings notwithstanding, his disarming good humor remained undimmed. Emerging in his dressing gown to find Pat taking photographs, he "camped" outrageously in the background, finally dropping a regal curtsy. This was, sadly, the last time we would see him alive. Back in New York I mingled with other showbiz royalty, joining in a salute to the Palace Theatre's seventieth birthday, where I was honored to share billing with that original vaudevillian George Burns, and, in a sort of swansong to my "French" years, to play a scene from *Phèdre* with an actress I had long admired, Jeanne Moreau.

Not long afterward, I was playing other scenes of doomed love in a film of Rosamond Lehmann's novel *The Weather in the Streets*. This was the quintessential story of the "other woman," a celebration of love by stealth, which, written in 1936, had shocked contemporary readers by dealing with adultery and abortion. It was as close as I ever wanted to get to the furtive fervor of an extramarital love affair. The film was made by the BBC, who still quaintly called their products "plays." My involvement all happened by chance. In a twist on the

Sergio Leone conversation, someone happened to mention that I would be perfect for the role of the antihero Rollo, but "of course he would never do it." "Why don't you ask him?" rejoined my benefactor, proffering my telephone number and thus ensuring our return a few weeks later to the heart of the Shires engulfed, in scenes reminiscent of photographs from my grandfather's albums, in an orgy of Englishness.

My native land seemed to welcome me back by enhancing the beauty of her landscapes with unendingly fine weather. At the wheel of an antique motor car we swept along its hedgerows and byways. I even met up again with my Herefordshire cousins who supplied the water tanker for the artificial rain—our only bad weather. We filmed in noble country houses with silk-stockinged extras and equally old-fashioned cakes for tea, in unspoiled country pubs, and on the banks of the Windrush River in the Cotswolds where a herd of curious horses came down to watch and swans pirouetted in the shallows. Cheltenham provided the civilized strains of festival music and we returned to the land of my fathers at Lake Vyrnwy in Wales, here transformed into the Austria where Rollo and Olivia consummate their illicit affair.

The film's principal love affair, however, was my reawakened one with England. There was a new spirit abroad: a growing self-confidence that the recent victory in the Falklands War had intensified. The remarkable Mrs. Thatcher, just like her great friend and admirer across the Atlantic, was making it permissible to be patriotic again.

We went to Buckingham Palace for a reception for the Globe, where I witnessed one rich American benefactor threatening to withdraw her donation unless the Duke of Edinburgh gave her an autograph. It never ceased to astonish me that these scribbles should provide such importance and pleasure. Contacting the old school, I inaugurated a prize intended to reward character rather than scholastic achievement, and returned to speak at the Union in an Oxford seemingly entirely scrubbed clean and bereft of every single teashop. After lunch at a London club, I celebrated that very English rite of passage —recording my *Desert Island Discs* with Roy Plomley. I had the unusual benefit of actually having experienced the castaway condition, and one of Crusoe's vellum volumes washed clean by the sea was my book request, so that I could write my own story. This book is partly the result.

We escaped temporarily from this deluge of Englishness to Taormina in Sicily, where I had been invited to serve on the jury of its film festival, the competition being held in the vast Greco-Roman theater. Staying at Tennessee Williams's favorite hotel, the Villa San Andrea, brought home the poignancy of his untimely death in February 1983 in a New York hotel room. "I think I just want to be not alone: just that," he had written to me in June 1972 from that same hotel, the Elysee. Yet it was a message from the Plaza Hotel that fluttered from my script of *Out Cry* when I reopened it on hearing that his unique voice had been stilled. "Mr. T. Williams called—'Sorry I'm leaving earlier than expected. Will have champagne another time.' "

Our British love affair continued with mounting intensity, a television film of Robert Louis Stevenson's *The Master of Ballantrae,* returning us to an England still golden with late summer glory. Again the countryside conspired to look its irresistible best. We were in the west this time, celebrating that great glory of English civilization, the country house, by staying in several that had recently been converted into hotels. It was like being guests in a magnificent private home but with none of the social pressures involved.

Not the least of the film's pleasures was a reunion with Sir John Gielgud, both of us sporting heavy plaid and even heavier accents. Richard Thomas, an actor and a man of great integrity, played the "good" brother, our fates decided, as capriciously as so much of our working life seemed to be, by the toss of a coin. Timothy Dalton, a fellow Youth Theatre graduate, was my comrade-in-arms, displaying all the tongue-in-cheek humor and physical dexterity so ideal for his impending James Bondage.

Playing an approximation of the "mean dick" that Bob Fosse had advocated, I had a showy, enjoyable role. Villainy is always more impressive than piety, and filming was fun, apart from a love scene with an actress who, unfortunately, possessed a black belt in judo. Our innocent roll in the hay turned into a punishing near knockout, far more perilous than our other exploits, like capsizing canoes in white-water rapids along a stretch of river notorious for drowning people or an all-night duel in which Richard and I cut and thrust by the fickle flicker of torchlight!

A seal on this English year was set with the British Film Academy's grand dinner at the Guildhall, where Orson Welles was the principal guest. I had often noticed his somber bulk lurking in the back room of his favorite Hollywood hostelry, Ma Maison. As pleasant and appropriate as it was to see him honored that night, it seemed the only meaningful award that could be made to this misfit genius was, as with Billy Wilder, the means to carry on directing.

As with *Weather in the Streets,* fate again stepped in as casting director, for also at the dinner was Jerzy Skolimowski, the Polish émigré filmmaker. Assessing me through narrowed Slavic eyes, at once amused and calculating, wide-set in a pasty face, Jerzy asked me if I was interested in working with him: "If you are, I'll start the script tomorrow. If not, let's forget about it." Unwilling to abort the birth of a project from a director whose quirky but genuine talent I admired, I found myself not only agreeing but committing myself to a film based not even on a synopsis but on a vague idea.

I met up with Jerzy again in London at the very beginning of that year of Orwellian apocalyptic doom, 1984. In it I would extend an ever-lengthening line of accented Eastern European roles by playing two different foreigners stranded in alien cultures. In Jerzy's film, entitled *Success Is the Best Revenge,* a companion piece to his earlier success, *Moonlighting,* I soon discovered that I was playing Jerzy himself in the guise of Alex Rodak, an equally opportunistic expatriate Polish theater director working in London and anxious to do something to assist the present Polish revolution by staging a happening, a special theatrical show. The film's intensely autobiographical nature was reinforced by the fact that Jerzy's own family—his long-suffering actress wife, Joanna Szcerbic, and their two tow-haired sons, Michael and George—became my own screen family and their Kensington house our film set. The project was in fact a filmmaker father's gift to his son, rather like John Huston's launching of Anjelica in *A Walk with Love and Death* and Coppola's recent bouquet to his daughter Sophia in the last *Godfather* film.

Despite having grown a beard for the role, I decided to embrace this illusion and try to emulate Jerzy as much as possible by wearing spectacles and clothes I normally avoided—T-shirts, scarves and boots. Adding a definitive personal flourish to this signature, Jerzy handed over a pair of stiff, authentic Warsaw-tailored trousers. I also wrapped myself in his own particular Polish brand of charming irresponsibility. The irony, of course, was that the drama erupting at home—both scripted and actual—threatened to overshadow even that happening in the homeland. Jerzy, like Rodak, could deal in great concepts but, faced with everyday issues, was powerless to direct them into a cohesive shape. As one critic observed, the film was "chaos raised to art form."

Much of the story's energy derived from the kind of father-son rivalry I had myself experienced to a much less volatile degree. There was a football match played in the soggy mud of a rain-swept Hyde Park where the pair skirmished in the ongoing macho trench warfare. It would reach its fullest expression with young Michael turning his back on his father and on England and flying off to Poland to show real, and not just ideological, solidarity.

Not having played soccer since school, this sequence came as something of a shock to the system, making me thankful that each spool of film in the camera lasted for only ten or so huffing and panting minutes. A reluctant athlete, I was constantly being driven on to sporting exploits. With fencing, riding and yachting under my belt, as well as brushes with cricket that left me convinced that a test match was a test of boredom, I anticipated other enforced cinematic encounters with golf, polo and perhaps even the unfathomable mysteries of American football.

The film had a paltry budget, the efforts of Rodak to raise funds for his show being reflected in Jerzy's own real-life battles with bureaucracy and defaulting financiers to keep our imperiled enterprise afloat. Being the Polish underdog, using wit and cunning in a guerrilla war with life was probably his chosen modus operandi. If you gave Jerzy $25 million to make one film he would probably spend it making twenty-five. He, himself, had surely played out the scene of Rodak's grilling by a censorious Thatcherite bank manager, played by Jane Asher, many times. However, Rodak's encounter with the strange underworld showbiz impresario had, I hope, no off-screen counterpart. This role was cast at the last moment—indeed, if John Hurt had left his house just two minutes earlier the night before he would have escaped Jerzy's irresistible clutches!

Like Rodak, Jerzy thought furiously on his feet: little escaped his omnivorous eye. When Jane breast-fed her baby on the set during breaks, I felt sure that, had Jerzy witnessed this, it would have appeared in the film. Much of the direction seemed to validate Brine's Law that Adrian had recently formulated: "The more visually imaginative a director is, the less he should be encouraged to write his own script." However, I liked Jerzy's insistence on an unshowy minimalistic style of acting. It was good to have something positive—if unusual and indirect—to say and I am convinced that *Success* will be fully appreciated when there is a chance to set it in the ampler context of historical events that are still transforming the face of Eastern Europe.

I enjoyed filming in London again and finally having my family to the set and to a gargantuan British location lunch and a feast of news. Caroline had just married Christopher, her pipe-smoking publisher. Paul had briefly considered becoming an actor, applying to Dundee where he fell foul of a ridiculous Catch-22 ruling. He could only become an actor if he had an Equity card, which was only obtainable if he was actually acting! I felt grateful for my own easy access to this profession, which, dealing with an indefinable commodity like talent, was best left open and unrestricted.

Success was later described as "a Godard movie edited by Spike Milligan." Days after finishing it I was plunged into a Marx Brothers farce edited by Gunga Din. We were back in India—a clue to reasons why I had been seduced into a farrago of intrigue and treachery worthy of the sudsiest soap opera. Calling in to see Ismael on a brief Christmas trip to Bombay and Goa, I had met a young English director who was finalizing production for an epic film about the Bengal Lancers. A change of schedule had just cost him his leading man when, like a deus ex machina, I walked in. Fate seemed to insist on casting a hat trick of roles.

Perhaps because David Lean was now filming my beloved *A Passage to India,* I wanted to be there, too. Again the script was imperfect but the setting, in that ever fateful venue, Rajasthan, set my gambler's blood racing. As usual I should have read the warning signs, especially when, back in London, one of the producers actually advised me not to fly out to Jodhpur for the filming! I had given my word, I smugly, stupidly replied, and was plunged into a celebratory Orwellian madness that made the Canadian misadventure seem almost mundane in comparison. Instead of the creaky plot, we should have filmed the imbroglios surrounding the production, especially the moment when its shadowy London financier asked for the script to be changed so that in the final reel he could literally ride in to the rescue on a white horse!

Having got me into another fine mess, fate kindly got me out again. Fortunately, there were mechanical as well as financial problems—all the footage we filmed was supposedly out of focus. Shooting was mercifully halted and remains unfinished. My contract had a stop-date, which, gracefully and gratefully, I was able to exercise. I was not the only fly caught in this absurd web. Trevor Howard had been persuaded to give his crusty old Indian army colonel yet another outing. My last sight of him was of a wild-haired Lear garbed in long khaki shorts, more sinned against than sinning, bewailing his unkind fate before the astonished tourists in the hotel lobby.

On the long homeward journey I was able to experiment with a cure for jet lag passed on by an L.A. doctor. As we had crossed the Atlantic eight times by May alone that year, we had already put its effectiveness severely to the test. It consisted of cutting out paper soles from a supermarket shopping bag and wearing them next to the skin during flight. Either this stimulated the body's acupressure points or some chemical in the brown paper was activated. Or perhaps it was just the placebo effect. No matter, it worked. I in turn later passed on this tip while chatting on a TV show and ever afterward grateful long-distance flyers have come up and thanked me for my philanthropy.

The unexpected change—or rather lack—of work plans exerted a usual reflex: the opportune acceptance of an invitation to a film festival. This time Cognac enticed with an unusual bouquet. Not having conventional hotels, guests were lodged either chez Martell, Camus or Hennessy. Together with the guest of honor, Lauren Bacall, we stayed with the Hennessys, whose unstinted hospitality included brushing the cobwebs in their cave from a barrel of 1812 cognac, one sip of which set off veritable explosions of Napoleonic canonry.

Back in Los Angeles our suitcases, bulging, battered and belabeled, were unpacked and, along with their accumulation of memories and memorabilia, stored away. They had provided for us on recent journeys rich not so much in artistic success but in personal growth. Keeping the machinery ticking over in good working order, we had drifted along some picturesque tributaries. Now, ever impatient with the status quo, I sensed it was time to steer back into stronger mainstream currents.

New Frontiers

*T*he bulk of the summer was spent—as hoped—sweeping along from coast to coast and continent to continent on that tide. Our vehicle was *Space,* a thirteen-hour television mini-series for CBS based on James Michener's monumental account of the United States's exploration of that open frontier. Again I brushed up my accent to play another alien, someone like myself transplanted from an older culture to root in a rich new soil. Dieter Kolff was a Werner von Braun doppelgänger, a rocket scientist conscripted at the end of the war to turn Hitler's secret weapons into American technical know-how.

My fascination with the role was genuine. Two years before, Pat and I had gone down to Cape Canaveral to watch the third launch of the shuttle *Columbia.* NASA, anxious to popularize their activities, especially with the announcement of President Reagan's Star Wars defense initiative, had afforded full VIP treatment, allowing us to witness the spectacle from as close as was deemed safe.

It was unforgettable. The countdown had its own built-in drama, but the violent reality of the takeoff—even though familiar from television reportage—was totally unexpected. The ground and air shook with the fury of the squat shuttle's effort to defy gravity, as a shaft of fire and smoke slowly inched its earthbound dead weight aloft, the brightness of the rocket blast outshining the Florida sun. Someone had left a tape running close to us and later sent us a recording of Pat's ecstatic cries that, amidst the background thundering, had an almost orgasmic intensity.

Space brought us back to England where we filmed Kolff's escape with his precious secrets from the devastation of war. Our romance with the country-house hotel continued, enabling us to enjoyably entertain friends. The christening of my new godson Henry, Caroline and Christopher's first child, also provided a welcome family get-together. My sister told me that, with his birth, the loneliness of being a half-twin disappeared, making her accept the possibility of reincarnation.

The United States was the film's major location—an America portrayed from a postwar time when, successful, competent and the unquestioned world leader, it could look forward to a future of unlimited prosperity, to a time when this dream had begun to sour. We filmed in Cape Canaveral itself, working alongside the men who had accepted Kennedy's lunar challenge. With over 400,000 people engaged on the program at its height, they had combined ingenuity with engineering to put astronauts such as Richard Gordon, another of our advisers, on the moon.

We filmed on the massive launch platforms whose concrete was extremely thick in places. Asking the reason for so much protection, I was sobered to learn that if a rocket exploded on takeoff, it was with a force equal to four-fifths of an atom bomb. My admiration for the heroes riding that tin can to the heavens increased proportionally. It was also, of course, the countless little backstage acts of unsung courage that together made this giant leap for mankind possible. I copied the engineers' habit of wearing shirt pockets bristling with pens. Thickening my accent for those sequences filmed outside Germany, I couldn't resist throwing in an exultant, unscripted "hot diggety!" when one of my creations lifted off.

Playing Kolff I found I could put my own sense of isolation as a foreigner, and experience of Americanization, to good use, a feeling enhanced by having a German actress, Barbara Sukowa, as my wife. The star of Fassbinder's *Lulu,* she came up as strongly against the prevailing American mores as had her fictional character. Her astonishment at being requested to shave her armpits for a bedroom scene taking place in Germany in 1945 was particularly memorable. One of the attractions of the role for me—and I know for Barbara, too—was the opportunity it provided to age over thirty years. Lined, gray-haired and bowed with experience, we were both surprised to find that many of our American colleagues had resisted the makeup artist's truth-telling and, living out the Hollywood dream, remained remarkably and unnaturally youthful.

We also filmed in Houston's Mission Control, a building that will surely rank one day with the Parthenon in terms of historical significance. It was there that Pat and I encountered a literally wonderful piece of luck. Asked if we would like to visit the building where the shuttle simulators were housed, an extraordinarily secure facility, we eagerly agreed. Permission was eventually granted and, badged with approval, we broached the sacred precincts. Again fortune conspired to perfectly match location with timing. Just as we reached the simulator, two astronauts were strapping themselves in for a space mission. We were introduced and, indicating the rear seats, they invited us to come with them. Our guide paled, telling us afterward that he himself had never taken a trip and that it was the one thing that visiting multistarred military brass and politicians wanted to do, although the privilege was rarely accorded.

Lying on our backs, we listened to the familiar litany: "Three, two, one. Ignition. We have lift-off." There was noise and vibration and we watched incredulously as the launch tower flashed past by the porthole and the curve of the earth came into view as the booster rockets and tank separated. The astronauts smoothly guided our craft under its own power into orbit. But ours was a mission fraught with crises, the red emergency lights flashing continuously. Every problem, though, was solved with a panic-free precision that was as profoundly impressive as it was reassuring. Suddenly there was a major emergency. Something went irreparably wrong, forcing us to abort our mission. Returning to earth, we hardly dared breathe. Soon the distant coast of Florida was in sight and then the landing strip at Cape Canaveral came hurtling toward us. Financial stringencies had reduced the shuttle's sophistication from a Cadillac to a Chevrolet, giving it no capacity for circling and just this one white-knuckled chance to land. Streaking in like a thunderbolt, its wheels came down and there was a jolt as we hit the runway accompanied by a long exultant exhalation as we careened to a halt. Only when the spacecraft's door was re-opened did the reality of the illusion hit home. Leonardo would surely have approved of his ex-assistant's adventure!

In the adjacent simulator we met other astronauts including Sally

Ride, whose vacuum-packaged lunch I still have as a souvenir, and Kathryn Sullivan, the first woman to walk in space. It was genuinely thrilling—one of those rare and privileged experiences that are the spoils of a spoiled profession for which I am profoundly grateful. Sadly, the person responsible for arranging this trip and for coordinating our work in Houston was Mike Smith, the modest, unassuming commander of the ill-fated *Challenger*. Two years later we were unable to accept his invitation to return to Florida to watch his takeoff when all the make-believe emergencies we had experienced metamorphosed into chilling reality. After the tragedy I received a note from a colleague of his: "We are slowly recovering from the accident. In the control center it was not unlike the scene in *Space* where we lost the crew, only this time it was for real. . . ."

Nineteen hundred eighty-four was also the year that Los Angeles hosted the Olympic Games. Doomsayers predicted apocalyptic happenings—monstrous smogs, marathon traffic jams and the freeways turning into interlocking Olympic rings with the traffic going around in helpless circles. In the upshot, the event was successful on every level—and not least the sporting. It gave the upstart city a boost of self-confidence that remained with it long after the flags were furled and the crowds and competitors dispersed. Moreover, an arts festival was organized alongside the athletic events, its oversold popularity manifesting a hungering for cultural maturity by the half-starved citizenry. There was a subsequent Renaissance-like flowering of museums, opera and other performing arts companies making it no longer necessary to trek to New York or London for good theater, to hear an aria or to be challenged by contemporary art. In short, L.A. grew up.

Finding myself working in the city at Games time, we paid scalper's prices to attend the spectacular opening and closing events, notable as much for their showbiz thrills as for their sporting triumphs. California's penchant for fun and informality seemed infectious. The Chinese contingent, for example, entered the arena in a formal, faceless phalanx and then, catching the mood, broke out of rank and into smiles.

With daytime traffic and deliveries restricted, we were able to travel on roads controlled for once by rationality, not self-indulgence—a reassuring pattern for the future where hell-for-leather development threatens to overwhelm the overfilled urban basin. Weeks of summer smog and arc-lamp heat drove us out to the cool refuge of Yosemite, amidst the soaring majesty so celebrated in Ansel Adams's photography. Here, too, there were traffic jams, prompting the reflection that perhaps ours was the last generation to be able to contemplate nature in all its untamed wildness. Would it soon have to be simulated too, in a state-of-the-art ecological Disneyland?

Lying on a beach in the Galapagos Islands surrounded by a bevy of lolling lady sea lions reinforced this speculation. We were there because an airline had offered free and fairly irresistible round-trip tickets to South America to its frequent flyers. Opening an atlas, I had scanned from Argentina to Venezuela until I lit upon the Galapagos. Since schoolboy days around Darwin's Down House I had longed to go there and the Old Vic's *Royal Hunt of the Sun* had planted a similar urge to follow the tracks of the real Incas. So we found ourselves in Ecuador, crossing the Andes in an ancient train from Guayaquil to the cold, gold-hoarding, god-haunted city of Quito before flying out to the scattered islands where man's understanding of his adaptive evolution had first been conceptualized.

Having to wear bags around our necks as receptacles for the detritus considered indispensable for our "civilized" life only underscored the awareness that *we* were the unnatural intruders. Shooting being confined to cameras, the creatures here were still unafraid, and tolerant of our clumsy presence. We walked amidst colonies of curious birds and wary iguanas, and outpaced the ancient tortoises. When swimming, sea lion cubs would playfully bite our toes. At one point an orphaned cub was seen trying to inveigle its plaintive way into the affections of an adoptive mother and we watched horrified as one female after another hurled it away to eventual certain death. Some of our party, overreacting sentimentally, had to be restrained from rushing in and "doing something about it." This, our guide reminded us, though red in tooth and claw, was the inexorable, ancient law of natural selection at work. This deliberate destruction of weaker life made man's hegemony over the defenseless animal world seem even more depraved and inexcusable. The islands had as profound an effect on me as they had on the other earlier British visitor. In such a fragile ecological framework privileged tourists are necessarily restricted, but I wish that everyone could share the spirit of this Galapagos experience.

Certainly the same inexorable laws seemed to apply to my own profession. Its dog-eat-dog mores tended, like capitalism in industry, to provoke both vitality and productivity. I had known of a situation in Holland where there were more jobs than actors, making for a bureaucratic laissez-faire attitude devoid of the kind of supercharged energetic lust that, for example, had galvanized the principal players in the musical *A Chorus Line,* that prime exposé of the process where talent and ambition are catalyzed into success.

Further exploration that year was mostly interior. We were treated by an American psychic surgeon who had trained in the Philippines, where charlatans exploited and discredited the honorable work of many of her colleagues. To have someone reach inside your body while you are fully conscious and, totally painlessly, remove its tissue, wiping away the blood and leaving not a trace of a scar or blemish is, of course, disturbing—especially for those raised within the inflexible parameters of orthodox medicine. Certainly, with one pull, the rug of scientific materialism was unceremoniously yanked from under me. There were suddenly many more things in heaven and earth than in my wildest philosophical dream. The sack of bones and blood that was our earthly habitat seemed even more extraordinary.

After this and another subsequent treatment Pat and I were transfused with energy to the point of feeling about to levitate. It made me speculate that any body having the ability to build itself from the interaction of two cells at conception into a complex machine should be capable of equally complex and unfathomable procedures. The arrogance of modern medicine was breathtaking—that, after being around for only a mere handful of decades, it could provide mechanistic answers for any dysfunction of a system that had managed to self-regulate itself into modernity. We were more and more convinced of the wisdom of homeopathy and of its basic tenet of encouraging the body to effect its own cure. Swift's observation, "The best doctors in the world are Doctor Diet, Doctor Quiet and Doctor Merryman," made more and more sense.

It was with regard to the first gentleman that we went on to experience the benefits of the fast at the Buchinger Clinic on Lake Constance in Germany. Suddenly I understood why fasting is at the basis of all the world's leading religions. Thirty percent of one's energy is expended in digesting food. Removing this obligation produces a concomitant increase in energy, spirituality and mental acuity. I realized how appallingly ignorant I had been of the body entrusted to my care. If it missed a meal I was convinced I had to compensate by overfeeding at other times. It came as a revelation to realize that once mastication stops, the whole system happily shuts down without a pang of hunger or discomfort, the body happily burning up its store of excess fat and later, the wastes deposited deeper in the tissues. Pat and I were overwhelmed with our bonus of vitality, going for long walks and swims, reading abtruse books and putting thoughts effortlessly on paper. We painted ceramics and views of the encircling panorama of mountains and trees mirrored in the wintry lake. Solemn and—regrettably—soon broken vows were made to treat ourselves and our bodies to this vital vacation on a regular basis.

The experience served as a sort of ritual cleansing, a new rite of passage before my next departure: becoming a United States resident. We had now resolved to give up Monaco, a pragmatic decision based on a newly evolved reality. Wanting to make a greater commitment to the country where I found myself spending more and more time, I made the appropriate applications and President Reagan's Inauguration in January 1985 initiated these American years. We were invited to the Washington ceremony which took place in freezing weather shared equally by a Europe which was suffering the worst winter since 1962. It was colder in Monaco than it was in Iceland. California beckoned with its bright reliable warmth.

Here I busied myself with American things, steeping myself in its most popular culture by reuniting with Raquel Welch to co-host the Golden Globe Awards, a widely televised show that presents the interim handicappers' odds for the upcoming Oscar sweepstakes. I did other more menial American things like obtaining bank accounts and a driver's license. Typically my examiner grilled me more about show-biz than road safety, but I proudly lined up for my license with the other new immigrants, now predominantly Hispanic and Asian. I even took part in an American soap opera—a pilot for yet another of those dynastic television sagas. This time we were a Seattle shipping family with Joan Fontaine as its matriarch.

After filming amidst the salt-sprayed glories of the rocky Mendocino coast of northern California and up in Seattle, it was agreeable to work at last from home. I could even walk down the hill to our set, the nearby Doheny mansion. However, once having committed myself to a long and lucrative contract and to the strange prospect of being settled, I found myself praying with increasing fervor for the pilot show to be rejected and for my freedom to be restored. It was—but it was a close-run thing.

One reason for accepting the role and the risk of imprisonment in a restricted genre was that the character was an American, seeming to provide a good opportunity of confusing, in the most public way possible, my accepted "British" image. It was hard to avoid this label, however many hoops of versatility I jumped through. As Thomas Huxley observed, "One of the unpardonable sins in the eyes of most people is for a man to go about unlabeled. The world regards such a person as the police do an unmuzzled dog."

It was time for a certain stocktaking to summarize what I was doing and why. As an actor I still felt enormously ambitious, an absolute prerequisite for the courage required to keep hacking through the jungle. Even if its end was not in sight the path was now becoming more direct, and the sunlit clearings more numerous. I had a certain name, reputation and "bankability." But, most importantly, I had a sort of self-confidence. Though the craft never seemed to grow easier, its basic tenet of balancing the pragmatic and the visionary gave me constant enjoyment. There was so much to look forward to, especially as maturity brought a whole new range of possibilities. Although I seemed to lack both the business acumen and the enthusiasm to produce films, at least I actively sought the chance of wearing a director's hat as well as the actor's cap and bells. It was a question of making, rather than waiting for, that opportunity. Above all, I think I now understood that talent was not enough. A spotlight could shrivel as well as illuminate. You were in command, but not entirely in control, of your destiny. As Ruth Gordon put it, "You have to have a talent for having talent."

I was reminded of earlier childish ambitions with news of the death of Grace Collett-Franklin, my schoolmarm muse. "A solo performance is harder after more than fifty years as a part of a double act," wrote Digby, her husband, with whom I had often shared a Little Theatre dressing room. My own double act was maturing, too. Pat and I wanted less, and enjoyed more. We had reconciled ourselves to the fact that we were unlikely to have children of our own. With them our life would inevitably have been different and, given the recurring pattern of our professional circumstances, it is by no means certain that it would have been better. Different, certainly.

Michael Croft also came back into my life. Careworn but still wryly amusing, he was in Los Angeles searching for $200,000 for a linkup between his British National Youth Theatre, now an organization of some sophistication and renown, and the fledgling California Youth Theater. Sadly, this initial attempt came to nothing, although it instigated my involvement in the CYT of whose board I am now happy to be chairman. We try to encourage the same important values as our British cousin, work that seems increasingly more important now that arts budgets are being cut and the school stage and concert platform —not to mention library—are accorded less importance than the playing field. I wanted, too, to try giving something back in return for the good fortune that continued to pile up in silver spoonfuls.

I developed projects of my own, "doing lunch," "taking meetings," and employing such local patois as "pitching," "greenlighting" and "the bottom line." My job seemed to me to be no more secure than those of studio executives whose offices seemed to have revolving doors. Even their memos were styled "From the desk of . . ." as this piece of furniture remained the only permanent fixture. It was fun to be part of a company town that, in screening rooms large and small, provided a year-round unofficial festival of films. These provided the glittering icing on the dull cake, for under Hollywood's starry facade was a totally unglamorous factory industry with unsocial hours of sweated labor.

I loved the elegant and always welcoming house we now called home and the life-style it afforded. The "Armed Response" security notice at its gate no longer elicited an involuntary shock at this Wild West holdover. I had grown used to the frisky helicopters and slow jumbos winging in to land at distant LAX. Only the occasional skywriting graffiti artist and the perambulating Goodyear blimp with its flashy advertisements, attracted passing attention.

Tuning out the subdued city buzz, I enjoyed the jazz of blue jays squawking and doves cooing as they lined up on the telephone wires. It no longer felt odd to drive everywhere, especially as this time could be converted to pleasure, listening to music or recorded books. The latter provided yet another professional departure and a welcome chance to keep the machinery active and to show off in tongues. Every morning Pat and I would walk in the hills in the fresh scented air listening to tapes or to each other or to the sounds of the city coming alive. I had watched the downtown skyline grow from a few tentative stumps to a forest of self-important towers. This, the first decentralized urban center, was the fastest growing megacity on the planet, its ethnic mixture seeming to present a pilot program for the future.

The only elements that displeased me derived from America's relative inexperience, which at least presented a refreshing contrast to Europe, where cynicism was as pervasive as the tobacco smoke now so rarely seen and tolerated in California. It was this residual naïveté that counterbalanced the absurdity of hotel doormen dressed as Beefeaters and which made people want to shake others' hands and clap their own whenever anything or anyone pleased them. At times, I would pine for a good old British fug when trapped in the Arctic wastes of an air-conditioned room, assaulted by music designed to suppress the slightest hint of conversation.

We made many new friends, including the oil-rich connoisseur Armand Hammer and his wife, around whom revolved a whole real-life saga of power and influence. On one occasion, he flew us to Phoenix to inspect his stable of Arabian horses that paraded sleekly before us like so many hoofed superstars. Returning, there was a delay before the Hammers joined their guests on their private jet. Eventually their limousine turned up loaded with boxes of their favorite food— Kentucky Fried Chicken, the entire stock of a local franchise having been bought out at a stroke. Years later, Pat photographed this extraordinary man whose generous ego insisted that, even at the age of ninety-three, he be captured from his best side and in front of his best painting.

Our farewell summer in Europe was centered around a brief appearance in a film that united two great sensibilities—its director, the great Hungarian cineaste, Miklos Jancso, and Elie Wiesel, on whose novel *Dawn* it was based. Set in Palestine in 1946, a young Jewish freedom fighter is sent to execute a British army officer, John Dawson, held hostage against the imminent hanging of other resistance fighters. Executioner and victim meet in the condemned man's cell and in the long wait till dawn come to realize that beneath their respective uniforms, as with Behan's *The Hostage,* were hearts that beat more in sympathy than cold-blooded enmity.

This fateful encounter, witnessed by a silent chorus of spectral characters from the past, was memorably staged by Jancso. In one uninterrupted ten-minute take his camera relentlessly roamed the confines of the cell, actors and scenery moving in and out of shot and focus, until the thousand feet of film was exhausted. The required concentration and resulting tension was almost unbearable, energizing a scene already fraught with intrinsic drama. In the end it was the focus puller who broke down, claiming there was no way he could guarantee the visual integrity of this elongated image.

It was perhaps fitting that so elaborate and sophisticated a shot should be created in the cradle of French cinema, for we were filming in La Ciotat, a tiny port near Marseilles where the Lumière brothers had so vividly captured the image of a steam train thundering into the local station, it had sent terrified patrons fleeing from cinemas. Compensation for my services reflected the modest budget. Returning to Monaco, however, I saw in a gallery two exquisite Renoir drawings of actors whose price approximated my fee. For that reason alone it is a very special piece of film.

Back in England, Caroline and Christopher retired from the publishing ratrace to a beautiful Georgian house under the Sussex Downs near Glyndebourne, joining the Cwynarskis as country dwellers, Penny and Marek having long since moved to a Georgian house of their own in Faversham. Going into the family business, my niece Kate became a student doctor at King's College Hospital. The Mc-Callums were also living in London now, Rick's association with Dennis Potter having matured into a mutual production company. After the extravagant Hollywood cataracts, he was enjoying dipping a toe in the perhaps deeper and certainly more rarefied waters of British culture. Pat's symbiotic relationship with her beloved son continued. She was always there for him when needed, and never more so than when we happened to return to London a few days after Rick had been seriously burned on one of his film sets. A special effect had misfired and, as producer, Rick had stayed within the blazing confines to ensure everyone's safety, escaping himself only at the very last moment. A few minutes longer, he was told, and this heroism would have cost him his life. Pat immediately set to work contacting Dr. McCready in Dublin who transmitted blue light, a potent healer, with his radionic "box." Dr. Reeves in California also assisted with surrogate treatments, all with astonishing results. Today there is almost no trace of this accident, something for which more conventional doctors are unable to account.

I myself spent the remainder of the year playing a most unconventional doctor. It was in Australia, the *Far Country* of Nevil Shute's novel that I had gone down under to film. Again I was an Eastern European, this time a Czech immigrant called Carl Zlinter, yet another stranger in a strange land. I had met the film's producer earlier in the year on a trip to the Sydney Film Festival for a screening of *Success Is the Best Revenge,* that earlier portrait of a displaced foreigner. I had started to read the script on the plane and, by the time it landed in Cairns en route to Hawaii and home, the Instincts were adamant that I accept.

Cairns, incidentally, was also where Pat faced up to her own irrational instincts—a recurring dream, suffered ever since childhood, that she would drown on the Great Barrier Reef. By coincidence, or as I have come increasingly to accept, by some greater design, a psychiatrist was on hand to counsel her the night before she confronted her fear. We were staying with Diane Cilento out in the bush, at the center she ran for the study of Sufi. One of the disciples had been a friend and student of Jung and, as if prearranged, Pat immediately sought her out, talking intensely and intensively. In the morning, Pat and I set off for the reef, swam and dived pleasurably all day, and vanquished forever her fearsome marine monster.

Carl Zlinter had to battle another kind of monster—the xenophobia that faced immigrants to Australia just after the Second World War. I myself came up against the same shortsighted attitude when Australian Equity, the actors' union, made hostile but ineffectual noises about foreign actors taking their jobs. Again I thanked the providence that had allowed me to work uninhibitedly worldwide since my earliest days. Even my Cyrano had been a lucky exception—I was one of the few aliens allowed to work in regional theater. Again my "foreignness" counterpointed the story and, hopefully, benefited it. Shute's charming tale with its central love affair and story of buried gold amidst the ferny gum forests was given a darker setting, and the fact of Carl's having served in the German army, a more prominent significance. Even on the other side of the world in a brand-new country, I was unable to escape the specter of the Third Reich. What had I done? Had I been some dreadful murdering Nazi in a past life and this constant reenactment was karmic punishment? Whatever, I applauded the story's intrinsic plea for tolerance and Carl Zlinter's delighted discovery of this far country matched my own.

A California Christmas followed with its eve spent amidst Dickensian carol singers with our new friends Barbara and Cary Grant. Cary, true to his British roots, loved saucy humor, presenting me with a "Hand-D-Gas" patent fart replicator. Elegant in a caftan—he could have looked so even wearing a plastic garbage sack—he also showed us his raccoon coat, purchased half a century ago when they were fashion's latest cry, from a Harvard student who lost it—and his shirt— gambling. On the betting front we used to love being invited by Cary to the Hollywood Park racetrack. It was not that I was a great fancier of horseflesh, for, like cricket, the waits in between activity seemed excessive. As with Deauville and the more recent Melbourne Cup, it was the mise-en-scène that mattered—as well as the chance to lunch and chat with this amusing, unusual man. Cary and Barbara's favorite kind of holiday was a bed and breakfast tour of Britain and I was amused to imagine the reaction of the average landlady on opening the door to find Cary Grant standing there!

We spent the remainder of the "holiday period," as it was carefully called, in Arizona, a time memorable for a dawn hot-air balloon trip over the shadowed desert with only the sound of barking dogs to punctuate our progress. For so long Pat and I had been up, up and away in the clouds, blown in every direction. Now we landed squarely on home soil and, for the time being, showed every sign of staying there.

America, America

Tightening my embrace of American culture, I took part in an afternoon special television film. In it, in another welcome trend, I even graduated to having a teenage daughter of my own. It was about the Los Angeles homeless—the bag ladies and the bums reduced by economic and other circumstances to roam the streets—whose plight was becoming shamefully more prevalent, representing the stressful down side to all the bustling, glitzy prosperity.

Homelessness was not the least of L.A.'s problems. The numbers of newly identified AIDS victims were rising alarmingly, the majority centered in the great coastal cities. It was totally unrecognized then that we were facing another kind of annihilation—a disease that would replace nuclear bombs as a threat to the species. Then it was still regarded as a "gay plague." Pat was shocked when approached at a reception by an unrecognizable man who kissed and greeted her enthusiastically. Only his voice revealed it was Rock Hudson, whose eventual death—and "celebrity" factor—did much to force a reluctant public's attention on this dreadful scourge. The entertainment industry was particularly badly hit and, while the bureaucrats procrastinated, it was left to the artists to look after their own with such hard-hitting dramas as *The Normal Heart*. This art was not escapist but combative and had no scruples about daring to speak its name.

The following year, 1986, I was invited by the charming chanteuse Line Renaud to co-host a fund-raising gala for AIDS in Paris. It was a significant time in research into the proliferating disease—the American Dr. Gallo had just joined forces with his French counterpart, Dr. Montagnier. By resolving their differences about who invented what and when, they emphasized that the world's problems now had to be solved on an international scale. We attended the reception at the Pasteur Institute commemorating this medical milestone. Informed, just before the Gala's television broadcast, that I would have to make a speech, I barely had time to improvise it in the limousine to the theater. Fortunately, the Blessed Will came to my rescue with Hamlet's "If it be now . . . the readiness is all" speech, which, even in French, was both appropriate and reassuring at that uncertain stage of AIDS research.

Afterward there was a glamorous supper party at which someone suggested that, instead of perfumes and other standard party favors, a packet of "French letters" should be left gift-wrapped at every table setting. Confirming this sign of the newly responsible times, the most sought-after present for Christmas 1987 was apparently Dior's single condom holder, worn by either sex, like a talisman around the neck.

A retrovirus had spawned a new order of global terrorism, but its more conventional expression was the subject of a new film offer. Michael Anderson called to ask if I would care to make a hat trick of our partnership. *Sword of Gideon* was a film he was directing based on the aftermath of the Munich massacre of 1972 when eleven Israeli athletes had been killed by Palestinian terrorists. In response, the Mossad had formed a hit team to hunt down every single participant in the crime. Playing a British explosives expert, I was one of them. Putting at emotional arm's length my own distaste for armed violence and my ambivalence about the moral justification of an eye for an eye, it was fascinating to get under the skin of an assassin. In a brilliantly directed, suspenseful death scene I was hoisted with my own petard, a bomb hidden in a refrigerator exploding at eye-level. With only a clear plastic panel to protect me from the blast, trust in the special effects man, an Israeli army demolition expert, was absolute!

It was strange though to find myself part of an ensemble instead of in a leading role but, like Rod Steiger and Colleen Dewhurst in this film, and John Gielgud in many others, playing small roles and cameos marked an interesting and rewarding development for me. Each new characterization, whether a full portrait or a miniature, that was added to the gallery contributed in some indefinable way to its worth. I liked being back in Israel, too, finding that the view from the suite of a luxury hotel could be just as enjoyable as that from a kibbutz dormitory. I showed Pat the scenes of my student triumph. Jerusalem cast the same special spell on us both. We stayed at the historic King David Hotel where Pat's father, a British army officer, had been headquartered when it was blown up by guerrillas.

Examining a Muslim text from the Koran in the temple of the Dome of the Rock, it came as a shock to realize it provided a recipe for paradise. How had earthly matters strayed so far from this ideal to countenance the mass murder of the disbeliever? Here indeed was the peace of God that, quite literally, passed all understanding. Although not conventionally religious I found that, after treading the length of the via Dolorosa and meditating in the Garden of Gethsemane, both my hands were imprinted with ruddy stigmata. I hardly dared examine my feet or side. The physical effect lasted for weeks, the spiritual much longer.

The most important action, though, happened offstage. Rick and Serena's first child, a baby girl, was born in London while Pat and I were participating in a Seder in old Jaffa. The words of the Passover text, with their reaffirmation of life, seemed wonderfully appropriate. Alexandra was destined to be a special child. From her earliest days Pat and I had an extraordinary affinity with this beguiling, open child, who, as soon as she could talk, appropriated us as *my* Pat and *my* Michael. But enough! Such dotage can be notoriously tedious. As Victor Hugo observed: "There may be some fathers who do not like their children; there is no grandfather who does not adore his grandson!"

Alexandra came into a world growing daily less wholesome. The explosion of the nuclear power station at Chernobyl marked a significant international parting of the ways. Although not realized at the time, the Iron Curtain was irreparably torn, marking perhaps the last time the Soviet Union would attempt to cover up a significant event. Meanwhile, I had become involved in contributing to, and later publicizing, a collection of essays about the worldwide nuclear threat drawn from an international spectrum of individuals including the Dalai Lama, the Pope and Andrei Sakharov. Called *Voices of Survival,* its dynamic was summarized in an observation of the anthropologist Margaret Mead: "Never doubt that a small group of thoughtful, committed citizens can change the world. Indeed, it's the only thing that ever has."

It seemed to me to be the one issue that transcended all others. Fortunately, as it was also observed, no one requires a professional license to work toward lessening the risk of nuclear war and this time its monstrous threat provoked an unambiguous response. The proliferating arsenals had, it was true, kept the world from war, but peace through fear seemed to me an uncivilized alternative and the size and cost of this stockpile indefensible in a world still full of hunger and disease. Belatedly I joined my schoolboy Aldermaston March, finding myself united with Dudley Moore as a celebrity spokesperson—to use that regrettable American neologism and custom. But reservations over the means—particularly British ones about speaking out—were overridden by the all-importance of the end.

The Chernobyl disaster had its villains but it also created its heroes. Not the least of these was Dr. Robert Gale, the boyish, clog-wearing UCLA physician who, when the accident was admitted, flew there directly to put his expertise in bone marrow transplants to use. I am proud to count this remarkable man—and his equally unpretentious wife, Tamar—among our friends. His courage made me question my own when asked to do a film in Russia just after the accident. A Soviet film director friend had urged me not to come, insisting that the authorities were concealing the scale of the damage.

This advice, however, was further backed up by another remarkable source. Lazaris was an entity channeled by a man called Jach Pursel. This unincarnated spirit had been first manifested several years ago while Jach was meditating, using his voice as a surrogate. At first Lazaris's extraordinary counsel had been confined to a small community near San Francisco. His metaphysical teachings had been disseminated on tape and so by now word had spread of his loving, informative presence.

Pat and I had first been introduced to Lazaris the previous year, just before our Australian trip, when he had given us illuminating insights and prescient, practical advice. He even told us of an infallible travel tip that I am happy to pass on because of its known philanthropic worth. Before this spiritual encounter, our last few long distance flights had been unusually stressful. On the first a salacious drunken couple had argued loudly behind us all the way from L.A. to London.

We landed exhausted. So, on our return flight, we were delighted to see sitting behind us a respectable gray-haired couple, quiet and well behaved. However, not long after the meal service there was a grotesque Neanderthal groaning and, like an outtake from *The Exorcist,* the little old lady proceeded to disgorge her lunch. Months later a steward reported that the plane's cabin had had to be entirely refurbished!

"How can we protect ourselves from such involuntary assaults?" Pat asked Lazaris, who described a routine that we have since followed faithfully. At the airport you imagine the plane you are about to take encircled in a bright pink light and you affirm to yourself that it will fly from here to there in complete comfort and total safety. Once aboard you imagine behind you a guardian—an old man, for example —who is there to protect you and you repeat the affirmation. One of the first occasions we followed this routine, the plane made one of the fastest coast-to-coast flights ever recorded and since then almost all our air trips have been problem-free and enjoyable.

Among the reasons for our mortal incarnation, Lazaris also told us, was not only the need to explore the fullness of love and to consciously create success but, we were delighted to learn, to have fun. I was pleased, too, with his confirmation that I was here to communicate, my present job being integral to my personality in the sense that creativity and spirituality were one. He verified what I suspected, that Pat and I had known each other in a previous incarnation. How else had we so effortlessly picked up where seemingly we had left off?

Lazaris had decided the time was now propitious to extend his teachings to a wider audience and asked Pat and me to introduce him on Merv Griffin's popular television show. At first I had hesitated, suggesting that Shirley MacLaine, another Lazaris devotee who already had a wide public following for her New Age explorations, would be more appropriate, but he had insisted. Pat and I found ourselves along with Jach before the cameras in a Hollywood studio. We were in no way, we insisted, a mouthpiece, as Jach was for Lazaris, but felt that something so beneficent should be shared. The show was remarkable. Jach went into his trance, allowing Lazaris to take over and, with his usual perceptiveness and humor, to instruct and even, given the nature of the circumstances, to entertain.

He was there, he told us, to remind us of what we once instinctively knew. We had to relearn how to take back those powers we used to possess—the powers of choice, of change and of love—in order to return to the harmony we once enjoyed with nature. With the world getting smaller, and everything becoming interconnected, we had to act as a community to make the common choice that it be a more loving place. Inviting us on the "ultimate journey" to discover how completely loved we are and how capable we are of giving love, he reminded us of Magellan's account of sailing his great ships into South American waters where, until their details were delineated, the natives were completely unable to see them. In the same way, those who point to a bleak, empty horizon of doom have to be shown the shapes of the ships of success, of beauty and of happiness that ride at permanent anchor. All that is required is a shift of perspective, reminding me of my favorite remark of Proust's: "The real journey of discovery consists not in seeking new landscapes but in having new eyes."

In life's sequence of hatch, match and dispatch, I was now prepared to face, if not embrace, the last of the triumvirate. Death, moreover, Lazaris also informed us, was a glorious experience, a very celebratory time of life. This was reassuring in a year marked by the passing of many friends. Michael Croft died, worn out by his Sisyphean struggle with the Arts Council and other recalcitrant funding bureaucracies, but not before he had celebrated the thirtieth anniversary of his Youth Theatre. Also in London, Dr. Sharma, who had rescued Pat from her brush with mortality, embraced his own soul's karma. Chris Isherwood died too, leaving Herr Issyvoo to remain immortal. Cary Grant gave his last performance. It happened a week after he had entertained us yet again at the Hollywood Park races. Silver hair gleaming and perennially elegant in tweeds, Cary picked our wits for jokes for his forthcoming—and final—speaking engagement in Iowa. Curiously, on a more serious note, he also spoke to me about dying, saying that when it was his time, he wanted to make a good exit. After delighting yet another packed audience, his wish was surely fulfilled.

We attended the ceremonies commemorating the relighting of that beacon of hope and renewal, the Statue of Liberty. It was an appropriate moment. My green card had just been issued, confirming my American residency. We celebrated amidst the placid lakes and sprawling mountains of the Adirondacks—the real setting of so much of *The Master of Ballantrae* and still the holiday playground of Serena's family. She had memories of going there as a child in a private rail car from New York City and waking up to the splendors of this seemingly unlimited wilderness.

At the end of the year we were back in Monaco to pack up our apartment and to mumble a grateful *Merci* for ten years of enjoyable living in this improbable, high-rising place now slowly beginning to resemble a mediterranean Hong Kong. "The truth is that a man who has won for himself a home in many foreign lands feels in his heart of hearts nowhere truly at home, hardly even in his Fatherland." We put Ibsen's observation to the test with an English Christmas, finding it to be most inaccurate and, notwithstanding, most enjoyable.

We spent a Christmas Day positively bursting with Dickensian bonhomie with Rick and Serena at their new house in Fulham. Rick had enjoyed a profitable year, in particular producing an exquisite film called *Dreamchild* about the elderly Alice of Wonderland immortality. A larger family Boxing Day was shared under the Cwynarskis' roof in Faversham. Also there was May's sister Irene, who had finally returned from Africa. She, too, was now a reluctant alien in her motherland, but was resigned to the wisdom of an old Zulu song:

> *If we go forward we die!*
> *If we go backward we die!*
> *Better go forward and die!*

I felt none of her traumatic dislocation. On the contrary, I was grateful that I could have my Christmas cake *and* eat it, too. I enjoyed being bihemispherical, bestriding a narrowing world with one foot here and one foot there. Fundamentally, "home" was no longer a territorial concept, but a spiritual one.

Nineteen eighty-seven saw Pat and me back in alien, if familiar, territory. In January we returned to the Sahara Desert, retracing our steps, by one of those ironic coincidences, directly back to Erfoud, the very location where I had filmed for de Broca some twenty years before. The wheel turning full circle was a significant new trend.

Morocco had lost none of its potent fascination. In fact, the previous year, attending the celebrations in Marrakech marking the King's twenty-five years on his throne, we had been treated to a stupefyingly photogenic scene. People had come to pay homage from all over the kingdom and, like a Delacroix painting exploding into life, had provided a joyful, noisy and utterly fantastic spectacle. Such extravagant scenes were to be laboriously re-created in *The Secret of the Sahara,* an epic film produced by an Italian television company and the reason for our present return. A story of both ancient and alien worlds, it is generically best described as "The Little Prince Meets the Raiders of the Lost Ark," although making it was more like "Beau Geste Meets the Creature from the Black Lagoon." I was playing an archaeologist. Ben Kingsley was a wise old Arab and Andie McDowell portrayed the beautiful Warrior Queen.

In Erfoud nothing much had changed. The shifting, alluring sand dunes, our film set some fifteen years before, still dominated the horizon. The boy selling postcards and fossils, however, was now comfortably rotund and full of giggled memories of bedridden camels and other youthful exploits. Certainly older and questionably wiser, I still felt charged with the same neophyte enthusiasm. Though the slate was re-wiped with each new project, leaving a thickening residue of past efforts, there was always a clear enough space for further invention and discovery.

We stayed at a new hotel heavily disguised with mud walls and castellations to look like an ancient *ksar*. Inside, its lobby was transformed into an Aladdin's cave of costumes and props, and the pool area resounded to the energetic cries of stuntmen rehearsing fights. It never ceased to amaze me how film crews, like invading armies, could commandeer so effectively or that the worldwide fascination for filming should make everyone countenance such liberties.

Two inauspicious signs greeted us as we checked in. Staggering out was the assistant director, who was being escorted back home, having been temporarily blinded by the sun. Then I was cornered by the American actor playing my villainous nemesis who, blinded by his own self-importance, presented me with pages of detailed notes on the script. They culminated in his master-stroke: we would not now fight a decisive duel in which I, representing the forces of reason, vanquished his evil. Instead, he had contrived a scenario in which he fought entirely with himself! My rapidly sinking heart plummeted still further. Some people—and some actors—are like psychic vampires who thrive by sucking up all the ambient energy. As proved the case here.

Pat and I determined to enjoy ourselves and indeed the experience was not without considerable pleasures. Andie McDowell, my beautiful American co-star, as seductively attractive as her slow Southern accent, was "real nice." She had brought her tiny new baby and the whole company became its adoring adoptive godparents. Taken shopping by the Bedouin maids at the local market, she returned with long, shiny bloomers worn scandalously unskirted. A former model, Andie was adored by the camera. Pat's was no exception, and recorded some beautiful photographic layouts that were published around the world. Assured before a lens, Andie's only lack of confidence stemmed from her accent. I never realized before that Americans could suffer from this British disease. Ignominiously dubbed in a previous film, Andie insisted that if ever she could perform in her own voice, she knew she could make her mark. QED.

The absence of choice in our new life was most agreeable. It simplified existence. Menus remained unchanged and even the lack of newspapers and television, after an initial spasm of panic, induced an alternative appreciation of books and music. Literally awe-inspiring, you understood why the desert was integral to so many of the world's major religions. It was also everywhere. Literally. Sand filled noses and lungs and reddened eyes; it even infiltrated as a microscopic dust inside the heavily clad camera which had to be constantly checked and cleaned. On some days it would blot out the sun, leaving everyone to choke and grope in the swirling yellow air. Looking like the Invisible Woman, Pat photographed with her head entirely wrapped in a cloth.

To scour ourselves clean we took to the local *hammam,* a gloomy, steamy building lit only by a hole in its ancient brick vault. Lying white and self-conscious on the hot brick floor we were doused, pummeled and pounded by unseen hands as our eyes slowly focused on a scene from a medieval torture chamber. Dimly revealed were dark forms scrubbing, massaging and, limb locked in sweaty limb, flexing and stretching.

The most popular activity of all, though, was waiting for a chance to use the lone telephone that sat like a sacred relic in the hotel lobby. There was always a patient group of communicants standing in line for their precious, shouted moments that briefly reunited them with the world beyond the sand dunes. I was thankful that Pat could be with me so constantly. There was no sense of compromise, of putting normal life on hold until hostilities were over. She once returned briefly to London, leaving me with a rare opportunity to unpack my heart on paper: "I feel a little like Chekhov writing to his Olga. 'I miss you.' 'How empty the bed is,' etc., etc. I'm thinking of you winging your way to England. I'm jealous of the person sitting next to you, but hope he carries your bag" (something that invariably happened when Pat traveled alone). "It's strange to be without you. The room seems a shell and *very* empty. It reminds me forcibly how much I love and miss you and how you are an absolutely integral part of my life."

Filming was tough and demanding, not least the constant battle to preserve the script's integrity. The duel *was* fought: between both of us. And I won! There were further equine escapades, especially hairraising as our mounts were barely broken, local Arab horses reined with one hand while the other frequently held a falcon. I also found myself playing another novel role. Our younger, more inexperienced actors required constant encouragement and advice and, as this was not coming from the director or producer, it fell upon me to be self-appointed coach and cheerleader.

I remembered how Dirk Bogarde had oiled and seasoned my own salad days and it gave me great pleasure to do likewise. Ours is such a vulnerable profession, insecure and so eager to please, that the smallest word of encouragement carries huge dividends. It constantly astonishes me that producers can spend millions on special effects and yet ignore the extra special effect that can be so easily obtained in the demeanor of a performer made confident and comfortable. Actors, as Alfred Hitchcock observed, are like cattle. I assume he meant that as a compliment, implying that they are easy to guide, rarely stampede and give of infinite nourishment. Peter O'Toole, too, was correct in saying that, if you replaced Mr. Hitchcock with a chimpanzee, you would always get a performance from the actors as they have a built-in instinct to save their hides, however thickened by experience.

At one point in our Saharan epic I had to simulate being blind and spent a busy day staggering around a dune with eyes held unblinkingly open. The cameraman exulted at being able to film a reflection of the sun in my iris. My eyestrain and headache that evening redoubled in intensity the following morning, and by the weekend was intolerable. I carried on filming, meanwhile ransacking the local market for a cure. Amidst the fruits and fossils, silver teapots and plastic shoes, the only medicament I could find was a dried lizard that was a specific against sore throats.

On the first day off I was sent to a doctor in a nearby garrison town who turned out to be Chinese and very shortsighted. After a fumbled examination with his bedside torch I requested his fee. He mentioned a sum of dirhams that my rusty arithmetic equated to approximately a thousand dollars. Swallowing hard, and fumbling for my wallet, I tried to explain that this was perhaps excessive. It came as much relief—if not for my now unnaturally widened as well as reddened eyes—to learn that the quoted figure represented the gentleman's annual salary!

Eventually another doctor was flown in from Casablanca who discovered that I had burned the retinas of my eyes and prescribed antibiotics. I told him I would prefer to use something more natural and asked what the local people used to treat such an injury. Their remedy, it turned out, was to bathe the eyes in a mixture of garlic, oil and lemon juice! That evening at dinner I was recounting this tale of cruel and unnatural practices when one of the Italian crew nipped my incredulity in the bud. His ninety-year-old grandmother, he informed me, still happily read and sewed without problem—and treated her eyes precisely that way every day!

The rest of the filming was in Italy and indoors, hidden away from a more tentative sun in Cinecittà, where *Romeo and Juliet* had blazed into life. The bar that had once served Renaissance grandees and Titian-haired maidens now swarmed with an orientalist tableau of legionnaires, swarthy desert dogs, Nubian guards and veiled houris. It was another Roman spring of filmmaking and another Easter spent with Franco Zeffirelli, this time with friends and *famiglia* at his beloved villa in Positano.

He had been recently in our thoughts. There was an incident on the exact same stretch of motorway where Franco had almost been killed. Returning from a weekend in Tuscany our driver, who was obviously the worse for drink, went berserk. I stopped the car and asked to take over. Swaying on his feet and wild-eyed, the driver refused to return with us to Rome and so we left him to sober up at a motorway station. Moments later I was arrested. He had called the police, saying his car had been stolen. We spent four unpleasant hours at the police station in Orvieto during which our enraged accuser tried unsuccessfully to smash his bloody way through the window. Traveling in Italy, it seemed, required—for us at least—extra caution. Meeting the veteran director Joseph Mankiewicz later while putting in jury duty at the Venice Film Festival, I was reminded of his remark that "the difference between life and movies is that a script has to make sense—whereas life doesn't."

Our Saharan adventure was to provide one of the most popular programs ever put out on Italian television. Returning to Los Angeles, there was news of real life adventures. In the Great Hurricane that overnight snapped trees like twigs, altering the whole landscape of southern England, both Caroline and Penny had had chimneys fall through the roofs of their houses. There were shocks in America, too. The stock market crashed and Los Angeles tremored from a considerable earthquake, the first in my experience. The noise was even more menacing than the shaking. I was filming again and the studio's lighting gantries overhead went swaying alarmingly just as depicted in the disaster movies of the previous decade, some no doubt made in these very buildings.

The work that had been so rudely interrupted was a guest appearance in a soap opera called *Knot's Landing*. At first I had turned down the invitation to appear in this long-running and very popular series, but curiosity about the nature of series television had eventually prompted my acceptance for a limited time. It was odd to be working alongside actors who had played the same part for almost a decade. As one of them described it, he was retained by "golden handcuffs"— the exorbitant financial rewards making the loss of artistic freedom acceptable. Although fortunately not faced with this dilemma, I didn't really enjoy my employment. It was like performing in some kind of glamorous open prison. There was none of that special sense of uniqueness and unpredictability attendant on every new film venture when you set off with high hopes and brand-new maps to explore virgin territory.

The publicity dividends, however, were extraordinary. Later, when returning through New York from Europe, I was stopped by a customs officer who prefaced his interrogation with a statement that he was going to ask me a most important question to which he wanted an absolutely truthful answer. Rooted to the spot, dry-mouthed and suffused with guilt, I nodded assent. "Why did you stand up Abbey?" he snarled venomously, referring to the lady played by Donna Mills, whom my churlish character, in order to leave the story within the allotted time frame, had been obliged to abandon!

Soon afterward I found myself in more comfortable professional circumstances as the host of a special event that was part of "U.K./ L.A.," a successful celebration of Britain, and especially of her arts, in Los Angeles. The brainchild of the British Consul, he had offered me a novel and interesting role serving on his committee. The resultant festival had showcased a major David Hockney retrospective that included his luminous designs for the recent *Tristan und Isolde* for the new L.A. Opera Company, whose artistic director was now Placido

Domingo. David, incidentally, had recently provided a scenic experience that outdid any staged spectacular. One sunset he took us in a car bristling with stereo speakers along a trail winding into the Santa Monica mountains while playing Wagner at full volume—a journey to rival, in visual and aural majesty, the gods' own progress across the rainbow bridge to Valhalla.

My contribution was a tribute to Noël Coward, memorable for a reunion it provided with his godson Sheridan Morley, in brilliant anecdotal form, and for a clip of the Master's very first screen appearance as a boy pushing a wheelbarrow in D. W. Griffith's 1918 film, *Hearts of the World.* This was his first attempt at "Petty Larceny," Coward's genial and self-effacing response when accused of stealing a picture. Those other Yorks—Prince Andrew and his vivacious Sarah —were chief guests headquartered on the Royal Yacht in L.A.'s far-flung, unlovely harbor. Working hard and enthusiastically, they were a great local success, but I often wondered if, like Prince George, fed up with handshakes and culture, they ever managed to jump ship, don jeans and sneakers and sample some of L.A.'s less U.K. life-style.

The cross-cultural alliance was further cemented by a recording of Arthur Miller's *The Crucible* and Eric Bentley's *Are You Now or Have You Ever Been* by BBC Radio and the L.A. Classic Theater Works. I had been a founding member of the latter company with Marsha Mason, Richard Dreyfuss, Amy Irving and Ed Asner among others, all of whom shared a desire to get back to their stage roots. Our ideal had been an actual theatrical production, but while the company was in formation we did the next best thing, holding staged play readings and recording books and dramas. Drinking at the source with the BBC was a special pleasure. Both radio plays were about witch hunts and the enforcement of orthodoxy and provided a strong double bill.

Technically I was still out of work, but "resting" was far from restful. Our professional lives were ruled by a maddening, seemingly irreconcilable dichotomy. On the one hand, a chance to leisurely smell the jasmine and do those things that active employment prevented, was most welcome. On the other, there was a feeling of being in one's prime and anxious not to waste any opportunity. Was it a puritan work ethic that made actors so ill at ease when not actually engaged on a play or film or were they addicts requiring a regular fix of excitement? Or was it simply the need to attend to that other kind of billing—for laundry and electricity? "Perhaps," Adrian suggested, it was, "that Pirandello idea that an actor's only half a person—the other half being the character he's currently playing? Certainly a director's only half a director when he's at home with a script and pencil."

It was Adrian's fifty-second birthday. Reminding ourselves that Shakespeare had died at this age prompted in us both comparisons about productivity and achievement. "When are you going to do some theatre work again? At your age all the best parts are open . . ." Adrian inquired, triggering in me further ambivalent soul-searching. The fact that our theater company had yet to mount a theatrical production indicated just how hard it was to make that commitment, especially in a company of "stars" who were in constant demand for their individual gifts. Dietrich Bonhoeffer's words, written from prison, began to ring in my mind ever more insistently: "Time is the most precious gift in our possession, for it is the most irrevocable."

I had in fact a trio of film parts—nothing outstanding but nothing unworthy—lined up in Europe, providing a welcome opportunity to renew family ties there and, especially, to see our newest grandchild, Olivia. Crossing over again on the *QE II,* I "lectured" to my trapped shipmates. Compared to our first voyage, the vessel seemed even more like a floating supermarket, although it was reassuring to find steak and kidney pie still aboard along with an aura of heroism that had enveloped the ship after its service in the Falklands War. Back in Europe, I embarked on a curious novelty—filming two projects simultaneously. As one was based in Oxford and London and the other in Berlin, they presented some formidable logistical planning. I made ten trips back and forth and, with luck and Lazaris, never once waited or missed a connection.

One film, a dramatization of the events surrounding the first four-minute mile, provided another Teutonic role—that of the famous coach Franz Stampfl. It was the combination of his genius and Roger Bannister's natural talent that had achieved the world record. As documentary footage of the famous race was available, I was able with wig, cap and duffel coat, to approximate Stampfl's external appearance. His inner characterization, though, was sheer stab-in-the-dark instinct, so I was both relieved and pleased to receive a letter from the playwright and renowned sportsman Ulick O'Connor. "I knew Franz Stampfl well in the fifties and had some coaching from him," he wrote. "Your performance was quite uncanny—in fact, my memory of Franz is now obliterated and replaced by your interpretation." Later, however, I met Sir Roger Bannister himself, who, although also complimentary, charged that the screenplay writer had introduced "conflict" —whereas "we all got on so well!"

Berlin was memorable for two grotesque locations: the slaughter-house at Spandau, complete with bleeding carcasses, and the wall itself, which then seemed as paranoid and immutable as the political order it so jealousy guarded. A highlight of the Oxford shooting was filming on exactly the same spot where I had played a scene in *Accident* twenty-two years before—and finding it just as difficult and, thank-fully, just as enjoyable.

In July, I was given an opportunity to compress all these experi-ences into a sort of credo when asked to give the Commencement Address at the University of South Carolina in Columbia. I tried to put myself back into the shoes of the student I had been all those years ago, facing the future's possibilities and uncertainties. What would I have liked to have heard then? Gowned and robed beside my fellow Doctors of Arts Kitty Carlisle Hart and Lukas Foss, in a bas-ketball stadium the size of a Roman arena, I declaimed an address that included the following wisdom, again inspired by *Hamlet:*

> I am sure that for many of you, education has been a process that revealed your weaknesses. It is now time to find out your *strengths.* And what is strength? It is a combination of awareness and actions. Strength is creativity, which is a kind of awareness, but productivity is the action. Strength is courage but it's also the inspiration that the implementation of courage brings.

Returning to Europe for two more projects, I little realized then that my own strengths were about to be severely tested. The first was a film based on one of Barbara Cartland's popular bodice-ripping ro-mances in which, drowning in a long dark wig, I had the responsibility of playing her favorite merry monarch, Charles II. A mellow Oliver Reed and I met up again on horseback, a warm-up for our next venture —a larger reunion with the cast and creators of the previous *Musketeer* films for yet another outing.

The new film was based on Dumas's own *Twenty Years After* which, itself a response to public demand, recounted the later adventures of D'Artagnan, Athos, Aramis and Porthos. By extraordinary luck, the producer had managed to recruit the same talents that had tickled the public fancy some sixteen years before. Even the Spanish locations were the same. But these were superficial similarities—this film would be an entirely different experience from its predecessors.

Renewal

On the first day, striking a keynote for the rest of the filming, Richard Chamberlain fell—harmlessly—from his horse. On the second, a misdirected stuntman leaped on me, pulling me—harmfully—backward from my horse. The gag, of course, was that he was meant to miss, but the consequences were distinctly unfunny. Hitting the ground, my spine struck the steel pommel of my sword and, hurting intensely, I was taken to hospital. X-rays revealed no vital damage but, I was told, had the blow been another millimeter away I might have been paralyzed for life.

The pain took weeks to abate despite Pat's constant ministrations and the distant healing of Dr. McCready and Dr. Reeves. Scarcely able to sleep at night I nonetheless went through the "comical" physical routines of filming, even jumping on a horse backward the very day after the accident as there was nothing else to shoot. "This film is being made at breakneck speed," Christopher Lee observed darkly.

Then, on Monday, September 19, we were back in Toledo. In the first shot of the morning, the Musketeers were to ride hell for leather over the Alcantara bridge spanning the Tagos river just outside the city walls. As we walked our horses over the ancient structure, their hooves slipped on the cobbles and it was decided that until more earth had been laid down, the ride was too dangerous—"suicidal" was how one stuntman put it. The shot was postponed until the afternoon and we relocated to film some interiors at the Tavera convent where, amidst nuns and washing, I had fought my very first Musketeer duel.

After lunch I drove back down to the bridge with Roy Kinnear, the British actor, generous of girth and good cheer, who played my servant, Planchet. He had been in usual splendid form, setting the table on a delighted roar. I shall never forget, however, the look of apprehension that swept over him when we arrived. He was not a good rider—a fact put to comic, if for him painful, effect in the first films. He had a stunt double but, because the director was shooting with several cameras, one in close-up, the actors had been requested for the scene.

My own apprehension renewed, even though I was informed that the bridge was now considered safe. Besides having a low parapet guarding the huge drop into the deep gorge, it was now lined with extras. Moreover, almost immediately opposite its far end was a restaurant with only a narrow road in between where we would have to turn the horses sharply at full gallop in order to pull them up in the parking lot to the left of the building. C. Thomas Howell, who played the "juve" Raul, afterward admitted that, although the son of one of America's top three stuntmen and having grown up on horseback, he was nervous.

But there is something—literally fatal—in the actor's psyche that responds to such a challenge. Perhaps it is simply the desire to be cooperative, although the sight of an entire film unit waiting for an actor to perform, producers looking meaningfully at watches, photographers anxiously at the light, can be a most powerful inducement to throw natural caution to the winds. There is a general desire to be "good troupers" and not cause a fuss but get on with the show.

"Action!" Heart in mouth, and totally preoccupied with my own selfish concerns, I spurred my horse across, exulting when the speeding animal turned under my command and experiencing genuine relief when it reined to a panting halt alongside Oliver's heaving mount. We both turned around—to see Roy lying motionless on his back in the road. People came running. An ambulance arrived. It had happened. There was a silence heavy with unspoken thoughts. We carried on filming.

The next morning back in Toledo I was again in the first shot. I was told that Roy had passed a comfortable night and that his wife, Carmel, had flown from London to be with him. Though expected to be out of action for at least a week, he had responded to traction treatment. Filming would be unaffected as—ironically—his double could be used.

Back in Madrid at our rented apartment I found Pat about to have lunch with friends in the same building. We made plans to visit Roy that afternoon and, calling the production office for his exact where-abouts, were informed he had been moved to another hospital. By chance a fellow guest at Pat's lunch had connections with this clinic and she offered to telephone to confirm his admittance. A few minutes later Pat returned distraught. Weeping and almost incoherent, she told me she had some dreadful news. I guessed at once, of course. Roy had died.

Soon afterward we were at the clinic. For a moment I had been reluctant to go, afraid we might get in the way and assuming that everything would be taken care of. We walked in just as Carmel was being led out of the intensive care unit, her grief uninhibited and publicly displayed. Together with Frank Finlay, his wife and others who had arrived, we tried to console her in our own shocked, disbe-lieving way. As there was no one present from the production com-pany, Pat's luncheon companion, hitherto a complete stranger, took matters in hand, organizing a room where Carmel could be with Roy's body in privacy—otherwise it would have been sent directly to the morgue. Asked to fill in forms, and unwilling to disturb Carmel, I called Roy's hotel as there was no reply from the production office for details of his passport. Just then his body, lying under a sheet, was wheeled out and down the corridor. I learned that he was only fifty-four.

We suggested to Carmel she return home immediately to tell her three children of their father's death and not risk them learning this from the media. After signing another form for Roy's body, we rushed to the airport to ensure Carmel a seat on the London flight. That night Pat and I wept in each other's arms but these tears would turn cold with news of the subsequent developments.

Oliver, Frank, myself, the director and producer met the following day in the latter's office and decided, if Carmel agreed, to go ahead and finish the film in Roy's honor and memory, and to showcase his already hilarious contribution. A call sheet duly appeared with the trivial, seemingly inevitable, refrain: "What do we do next? Only one answer has come to us—the show must go on."

Reports of the accident filled the press. I was astonished to read that Roy had died of "heart failure," as if this was unconnected with his fall. One newspaper even went so far as to say he was a "heart attack waiting to happen." My anger at this calumny was further inflamed when Carmel returned to Madrid and recounted what had happened during that dreadful last night of Roy's life. "There, but for the grace of God," she told me, "go you." It was no exaggeration. . . .

On the set business was determinedly as usual. There was even some cheery wisecracking. I was withdrawn. Carmel's horrific story had imprinted itself on my mind and was the filter through which I perceived everything. Without wagging or pointing a finger, I tried to suggest there was another story apart from the one being fed to the press.

Pent-up anger reached the exploding point with subsequent revelations and events. A coroner's report, stating that Roy's death was the result of shock and hemorrhage due to fracture and dislocation of the pelvis, confirmed that his heart had been sound. Carmel, incredibly, was being treated with a version of the same callous indifference that she—and Roy—had suffered at the hospital. It was Pat who would meet her at the airport and accompany her on the grim task of returning to the hospital to find Roy's effects. Although he had made many films with her husband, after seven days our director still had not spoken to Carmel.

I assumed that the possibility of a lawsuit had enforced this extraordinary circumspect behavior. Confirming this probability, an English lawyer friend added that, even so, nothing excused the want of human compassion. Not wishing to compromise any potential legal action myself and restricted by contractual obligation, I was unable to discuss the matter to any meaningful extent. It was a dreadfully disillusioning time. It could so easily have been Pat, transformed by a trick of fate into a grief-stricken widow. For what? To split the ears of the groundlings? There had to be a nobler justification for our endeavors. Something positive had to come from Roy's wasteful death. No other actor, I vowed, both personally and later publicly, should ever be put in his position again. There had to be standard, inviolable regulations to protect performers.

. . .

A somberness seemed to hang over the rest of the year, a feeling underscored by another film I made in October. It was based on a novel by Elizabeth Bowen called *The Heat of the Day*. A story of obsession, it had been adapted by Harold Pinter, having apparently obsessed him for much of his creative life. I was happily reunited with my old Vic dressing room chum Michael Gambon, now an actor with a growing, formidable reputation including recent acclaim for his performance as a Dennis Potter alter ego in *The Singing Detective*, produced by Rick. The leading lady, and apogee of our triangular relationship, was Patricia Hodge, an actress of great resourcefulness and cool, elegant beauty.

It was an extraordinary pleasure to again have a Pinter script in one's hands, although, full of half-repetitions and inversions, it was fiendish to learn. Pat and I would perambulate endlessly around Holland Park as she put me through my wordy paces. Once the rhythms were established, however, it played like a marvelous piece of music. Earlier, Adrian had perceptively written about his Belgian production of Pinter's other triangular English play, *Betrayal*, elucidating the complexity of this extraordinary writer.

> Pinter pretends to discourage psychology (Who are we to say why someone does this or that?) chiefly I think because he realises that love and hate, hope and fear, can co-exist—consciously you fear something happening that subconsciously you hope will come about. You can draw somebody to you at the same time as you are fending them off. People like playing with fire. He's deeply English in the way his characters are indirect, trying to stifle their feelings and to disguise them, at the same time hoping that their partners will understand what those feelings are. He's also deeply Jewish, as far as I understand that word, in that a character who feels oppressed, threatened and in a minority, is likely to want to dominate, threaten and win first place as a way of self-defence.

The theme of control, subjugation and the misuse of power to terrorize was crucial to our story of a woman caught between two men and two loyalties. Told by a government agent that her lover, a soldier, is betraying his country, she learns that her informant is reluctant to have him arrested as this will curtail his own relationship with her. The scene where Patricia Hodge confronts me, her soldier lover, wounded both physically and mentally, was played most dramatically

in a studio-bound taxi traversing the blacked-out London streets with
only the spectral traffic lights and the odd nervous cigarette to light
the scene. The setting was the year of my birth, 1942, and the story
perfectly captured the desperate passion and shadowy unease of wartime where a description of Dublin lit up at night had the power to
shock.

Patricia was pregnant at the time of filming, which meant that her
clothes and camera angles had to be skillfully maneuvered. This joyful
eventuality itself and the pleasure of working with her lit up an otherwise difficult shoot. There were clashes of personality that, apart
from intensifying the already somber atmosphere, were otherwise un-
productive and exhausting. I had had my fill of directorial arrogance,
although, as with John Dexter, the end results brilliantly justified their
painful means.

The great nourishing factor in our lives at this drear time was our
families—made even more precious by recent events. Alexandra continued to be a particular joy—we were even lucky enough to be
present at her theatrical debut. Unusually quiet and undemonstrative
at nursery school, she had been cast as a tree in the school play and
stood in a forest of identical tots at the back of the stage. But the
moment the curtains parted and the lights shone, she broke rank to
down stage front center and, waving her leaf at them, told the audience
to "go away!" There was an immediate response of delighted laughter
that doubled when, catching sight of me, she rose to her theme, giggling out a loud, "Go away, my Michael!" A star was born!

This incandescent episode illuminated the end of a year grown sere
and yellow with unhappiness. As if to set a seal on this, Pan Am 103
was blown out of the Christmas skies over Scotland, a forceful reminder that death's pale flag respected nobody and no boundaries.
Yet, although emotionally and physically hurt, we had survived to
face a richer future. Just before we had returned from Spain to London
for Roy's funeral, our old friend Duarte had invited us to stay in his
beautiful house in Trujillo. He had asked us to accompany him to
Mass and on the way to the church, threading through ancient lanes,
Pat felt someone at her elbow just behind her. Turning to see who
had joined us, she had a fleeting but radiant vision of the most exquisite angel in gossamer white and gold, sent, she was instantly convinced, to protect us during this sad time.

We were staying with other great friends in Mexico when the New
Year of 1989 began. Baron and Baroness de Portonova owned an

extraordinary fantasia of a house in Acapulco. At the flick of a switch a waterfall would cascade down the side of the house and its other features—a huge disco, a gargantuan cliff-edge swimming pool and vast terrace where a helicopter could land—were so singular it was no surprise it had been recruited for a recent James Bond movie.

The baron, or Ricky, as he was more familiarly known, sporting his trademark cigars in his special shirts like cartridges in a belt, was matched in kindness by his bright, voluptuous Sandra, whose favorite form of relaxation was to give a seated dinner party for fifty. Fellow guests included Kirk Douglas, Joan Collins and Edna O'Brien. All were successful writers, which drove me to a ferment of authorship, for I had just started to cast a net for these words and memories. I tried never to miss, however, that magical moment when the reddening sun, having illuminated more hours of pleasurable fellowship, dipped below the darkening horizon to miraculously renew itself.

In the same way the wornout year was itself renewed as I continued to review the past ones, pulling the various threads of experience together and trying to see if there was a pattern in the weave. Between paragraphs I kept busy professionally. Ever in search of new disciplines, I agreed to host a live television show. Although a novel departure, the program would take me back down a well-worn trail to Nazi Germany.

The show's rather catchpenny title was *The Hunt for Stolen War Treasure,* but at its heart lay one of the great unredressed crimes of our century. Part of Hitler's megalomania took the form of teaching the world about art and so, when he came to power, he not only decreed aesthetic standards but also systematically stole some 12 million works of art, designing a grandiose gallery for their display in Linz. Sequestered in saltmines during the war, many of these works were not returned to their rightful owners when it was over.

Both galleries and private collections, especially in South America, where the old Nazis went into hiding, hoarded this misappropriated treasure. If one little wrong could be righted as a result of this program with its scripted documentary narratives, unscripted interviews and debates and live satellite linkups to Europe, then, it seemed to me, it would have been worthwhile. It felt agreeable to be the people's tribune, prising open Pandora's box on their behalf. I would like to think that the recent rediscovery of Schliemann's Trojan hoard, stolen by the Nazis, is not unconnected with our efforts.

The actual live broadcast from Washington was literally terrifying, even for someone with my experience before a camera. The impossibility of retakes instilled its own dynamic and eventually my heart and I settled down to enjoy being ringmaster at a public event. By this time, as luck would have it, I had become involved in another project and, by a further extension of Murphy's Law, found that I was required back on the set in California the next morning at seven. There was no other solution but that ultimate fulfillment of every boyhood dream, a private jet. After the end of the broadcast at 10:00 P.M., I raced for Washington's National Airport, which was due to close because of noise restriction laws. A few hours later I was on the set in Pasadena, proving that it was possible to beat the shuttle simulator at its own game and give the illusion of being simultaneously in two places even if, in reality, one's brains stayed on one coast while one's body gamely simulated normality on the other.

This new project, a television version of Judith Krantz's highly popular *Till We Meet Again,* provided one of the most glorious summers of our lives. We filmed first in a vineyard near Santa Barbara, including a sequence where, playing the patriarch of a French champagne house, I suffered a heart attack while out riding, an episode made even more poignant by our recent attendance at a memorial service in London for dear Roy Kinnear. The California weather was its usual balmy perfection and we wondered how its warm light and azure skies could be matched back in gray, dismal England where a major part of the story was to be filmed. In the upshot the latter almost outshone the former. We had "our" weather again—day after day of unbroken sunshine—rendering both sequences seamless.

Although my character aged from his trim thirties to his wrinkled seventies, I only worked intermittently. So rural Sussex and the whole of Yorkshire, wolds, dales and moors, waited to be enjoyed. Basing ourselves in the exquisite medieval city of York, we plundered the treasures of this great-hearted county. Once asked to play James Herriot's famous vet in an early film version of his adventures, I had always regretted missing the opportunity of working amidst such wild beauty and amply made up for that now.

As in York itself, the great churches provided focal points—Bolton Abbey with its lowing herds at sunset and Rievaulx glimpsed in its vale across a carpet of wild garlic. Farther afield we strode along Hadrian's Wall and heard news of other conquests, the massacres in

Tiananmen Square, amidst the Wordsworthian tranquility of Malham Tarn. There were hearty fish and chips in Whitby and genteel cream teas everywhere. In the old manufacturing cities the dark satanic mills had been scrubbed clean and converted into cathedral-like galleries, restaurants and work spaces. England seemed to be sloughing off its tired past like a snake its skin.

Shocked by the unfamiliar, I felt pangs of intense affection for my country. Change was everywhere. I made a nostalgic trip back to Bromley to see my old school before its transformation into a modern coeducational comprehensive. While delighted to meet some of my special prize-winners, including a potter who presented me with an exquisite vase, I was saddened to learn that the school-play tradition no longer existed. *Sic transit gloria* . . .

It also gave slight pause to realize that my own Oxford college, that bastion of male exclusiveness, was now coeducational, too. How different—and how much more fun—college life would have been had women been there in my day. Meanwhile I delivered more scripts to the Bodleian Library. It had all started with a request for the loan of a film script with the explanation that, though crammed with literary treasures, the library was underrepresented in the field of twentieth-century literature—that old Oxford English course failing! "You can have them all," I magnanimously responded, secretly flattered that my tattered, scribbled-over papers should find such an august resting place.

Also on the academic front, I had been asked to teach an acting course at the University of South Carolina. Although tempting, thinking on it further I began to question if what I did for a living could actually be formulated—though acting teachers were as common as agents in my home town. Acting, it seemed to me, was common sense allied to uncommon imagination. Stanislavsky had drawn up a famous and overinfluential set of rules, but his work has to be put in context. He was dealing with the kind of Russian acting then current at the turn of the century—like its English and American counterpart, large, grandiloquent and totally unnatural. He was putting "bridles on runaway horses," as Adrian put it, adding, "His system's no good when there's no bloody horse. A contemporary of Freud's, he urges us to find out how people tick, but 300 years before, Shakespeare was telling us that they don't 'tick'—not in the predictable way of a clock, anyway. Shakespeare was concerned with *in*consistencies of people's behaviour, the *ill*ogicalities, the *in*explicables."

What could be taught was technique—experience being the best teacher—although too much technique detracted from that childlike quality of imaginative inventiveness that was at the heart of the craft. Good acting, it also seemed to me, happened when you were not entirely aware of it happening, when Apollo and Dionysus joined in perfect chorus to drown out your own petty pipings. It was like a good movie, essentially trompe l'oeil and totally engrossing. As someone once remarked, no one takes notes on a love affair. At times I wondered if it could not all be reduced to George Burns's brilliant—and surprisingly truthful—observation: "The secret of acting is sincerity—and if you can fake that, you've got it made!"

Certainly I was impressed with what Jimmy Stewart told me one evening as we drove with our wives to an L.A. function: "Audiences should be partners not customers." It was in this all-important oft-neglected area of audience development that part of our work at the California Youth Theater lay. I was particularly pleased with our recent association with L.A.'s MacLaren Hall for abandoned, abused and neglected children, providing an opportunity for the participants to create as well as perform their own musical. Guttering in a gale of governmental indifference, our bright little torch was illuminating the necessity and the magic of the dream.

In a year when the foundations of Shakespeare's Elizabethan theaters, the Globe and the Rose, lost for years, were unearthed, one of the greatest of the long line of descendants of those early players was lost to us. Laurence Olivier died. I found myself by chance in London on the morning of his memorial service, having slipped away from a film location in Yugoslavia for the weekend. The coincidence seemed fortuitous and I was determined to attend this tribute to the master spirit of our age even though tickets for the service at Westminster Abbey were unobtainable at such short notice. Hoping to be allowed to perhaps stand behind a pillar, Pat and I approached a policeman at the great door, and were passed on to an usher who seated us in the main lobby of the Abbey to pay tribute. The King is dead. Long live the King! The great vaulted building was full of heir-presumptive actors and I wondered to whom the crown would now pass.

In a year that marked my quarter century as a professional actor, my parents celebrated their golden wedding anniversary with a family gathering in mellow Sussex sunshine. Both seemed more vigorous than ever. As with my grandfather before, the local air seemed to have an unusual tonic effect. My father had involved himself in much unsalaried work and was especially pleased that his business acumen had been seized upon by the organizers raising funds for Oxford University. He was living proof of the beneficial physical effects of an active and enthusiastic mind. Returning from an invigorating trip to Sidmouth on the Costa Geriatrica he wrote us: "I was amazed at the number of old, infirm men hobbling around on sticks. They must have been there before, but I had never noticed them!"

Coincidentally, Pat was working on a book called *Going Strong,* a collection of her exquisite photographs and lively interviews with people over the age of seventy-five who still worked and had a great zest for life. The book included two extraordinary people who had provided me employment: the colorful Barbara Cartland, and Lord Grade, who was still happily dancing his way through life. I was reminded of one of the most sublime artistic experiences we had ever had the privilege to experience—Karl Böhm conducting an incomparably bewitching performance of *Così fan tutte* in Salzburg on his eightieth birthday. When so many were being condemned to retirement in their sixties here was proof that talent, joy and vitality had nothing to do with age. I accompanied Pat on several assignments—notably a reunion in Dublin with Dr. McCready—and, like her, relished the wisdom and the dignity we encountered. This work signaled Pat's growing desire to focus away from the familiar purlieus of show business and use her talents to record less ephemeral phenomena. As usual, we were both in sync about this feeling.

My job was everything and nothing, permanent and impermanent, important and meaningless. To David Niven's catechism of questions I now added another: "Why?" The quality of life that my work afforded was taking on an increasing significance. I had only recently discovered the satisfaction of restricting myself to what I enjoyed doing—a pleasure that was doubly enhanced when I found this coincided with what I should be doing. Apart from agreeing to write this book in the time allotted, there is little of the masochist in my makeup, although, as I hope I have demonstrated, I relish a challenge. Above all, the principal energy flow of life is the wave pattern, applying equally to my profession—one moment up, the next down, though at all times charged. Just as you have to draw back to jump higher, so it is the downward momentum of the roller coaster that enables it to speed to new heights.

"Beauty is truth, truth is beauty." The validity of this Keatsian creed was brought home to me when I recorded for a local radio station the entire text of Bruce Chatwin's *Utz*, a remarkable and illuminating meditation on obsession and artistry, on the possessor and his possessions, written just before his untimely death. Like the Czech Kaspar Utz himself, we now owned—or rather, like him, were the temporary guardians of—an extensive collection of porcelain—beauty frozen in time and fused by the heat of the creative moment to defy the mutability of death. While Pat specialized in Chinese blue and white, I slowly added to my Staffordshire theatrical collection, which now included a favorite piece that seemed to reflect my own cross-culturism—the only known surviving figurine of the celebrated American actress Charlotte Cushman, playing Romeo, from 1852. My work is also my collection—a portrait gallery of characters, some more crudely fashioned than others and some modeled with more lifelike detail and truth. Not all, I know, will survive their own fragility, but those that do will, I hope, provide enduring interest, if not pleasure.

Finale

A yearning for democratic government shook Utz's Eastern Europe, fragmenting the Berlin Wall like so much smashed china. The beginning of this annus mirabilis of 1990 saw us back in Pat's tropical birthplace, Jamaica, sharing a holiday house with the McCallums. Here, happily, the world's problems were reduced to the local radio's broadcasts about potholes in the road! Role-playing, too, was reduced to an enjoyable and unfamiliar one—that of grandfather.

Returning to the City of the Angels, we drew up plans for a new terraced garden full of avocado, as well as orange, lemon, and in belated homage to my grandfather, rose trees. This was an exotic treat for someone brought up amidst dank cabbage patches. The real luxury, though, was the water to grow them, which had to be stolen from mountain valleys hundreds of miles away. With L.A. in a fourth year of drought, a letter from May made ironic reading: "Brighton was almost surrounded by flooded streets and we can see flooded fields all around. Yet drought conditions are still in effect! Caroline had quite given up the idea of growing vegetables as last year they just perished from lack of water."

My sister's attention was for the moment on other matters. She was in the process of purchasing a lovely old building in the center of Lewes to convert into an alternative health center. Here treatments would be combined with growth workshops and lectures. We also learned that Kate was well on her way to becoming a fully qualified doctor, and Lucy was about to take her nursing finals.

Pat's and my health concerns, however, were now centered on a tiny fruit-eating fly and the city's controversial program of aerial spraying to eradicate it. Agriculture was big business and a major contributor to California's wealth, but the spraying meant that every glass of healthy orange juice was produced at the cost of bombarding the citizenry with malathion, a dangerous poison first developed by the Nazis. People were told it was harmless yet also advised to stay indoors, cover their pools and cars and safeguard their pets whenever the thunderstorm of helicopters swept over like scenes from a Vietnam War film. The inconsistencies would have been laughable had not many people, Pat and I included, become ill.

Diagnosis on an energetic level having proved the poison's presence, we felt an impotent rage that any government could do this to those they had been entrusted to protect. It brought into focus another mass pollution that normally could be ignored—the television lie that, without constant headaches, wind, incontinence and other mentionable ills, and the resort to their cure by other chemicals, you were somehow abnormal. On a much more sinister level the all-powerful American Medical Association was threatening practitioners of alternative medicine. There was talk of homeopathy being banned in certain states and of practitioners being arrested. It required little cynicism to believe that the drug companies had such a profitable enterprise that actually curing people could be regarded as a threat. All this was while over 30 million Americans were unable to afford even basic health insurance and the general wellness of the nation, apart from some impressive surgical side shows, particularly in the cosmetic department, seemed not significantly improved. Indeed, one of the chief sources of sickness was not so much the proliferation of hard drugs but the addiction to, maladministration and adverse side-effects of, medicaments. There had to be a more natural way.

At least the malathion plague brought some positive benefits. We were recommended a doctor who used the remarkable Interro machine, a totally noninvasive diagnostic system. By linking certain acupressure points to a computer, it was able to determine the body's condition with extraordinary accuracy. Any disease in its energetic pattern he then normalized with the potent, harmless energy of homeopathy. Also at this time, and not without coincidence, I was sent a play about Franz Anton Mesmer that portrayed in historic terms this unresolved battle between conventional and alternative attitudes to health and modes of healing. I had to do it!

Meanwhile, winter in California unfolded dryly, apart from the persistent chemical rains that threatened to make a reality of Hamlet's "foul and pestilent congregation of vapours." Pat and I, ever intolerant of victimization, even contemplated putting our beloved house up for sale and treading anew the path of exile. It was precisely this trail that, turning full circle, led us back to England.

I had gone there on a whim to take part in a student film based on the famous Anglo-Saxon poem *The Wanderer,* an epic lament on the soul-sapping afflictions of loneliness, homesickness and rootlessness. It was one of my favorite poems, and perhaps a certain identification with the "Earth-walker" made the project irresistible. The filming involved just four exhilarating days of work. Weighed down in authentic chainmail and helmet lent by a local group whose bizarre recreation it was to wage "period" wars, I intoned the entire poem within a set that gave *Alfred the Great*'s a run for its groats, and also on top of Wiltshire's lonely, windswept White Horse Hill. I loved every uninhibited minute. The novice filmmakers were open to collaboration and, like the young Orson Welles, broke all the rules. We were using a standard English translation of the ancient text that had taxed and then delighted so much of *my* student time. It suddenly occurred to me we were missing a great opportunity. The original was intended to be spoken aloud in all its sinewy alliterative richness. My suggestion that we return to it was eagerly seized upon and embellished and so we made what I believe is the first and only Anglo-Saxon film!

This gave the lie to all the prevailing breast-beating about the impoverished state of the British cinema. Moreover, a certain creative excitement could be sensed behind the prospect of long-term prosperity and opportunities that Britain's impending physical as well as fiscal union with continental Europe promised. There was hope of this translating into an international European film industry to counterbalance the American behemoth. The problem was essentially not one of financial but of cultural difference and British actors were lucky to speak the lingua franca of the common cinema market.

At Easter we joined up with Rick, Serena and the children for a family holiday in Cornwall at a hotel just around the headland from the Minack Theatre, of which I was now proud to be an official patron. It was a special delight that we could take our little Alexandra and her equally adorable sister, Olivia, to a performance at the theater itself where I had spent that time out of mind summer. Later they both came to see me when I was filming in another theater—the very one in Wimbledon where, at Alexandra's age, I had seen my first panto-mime. Fortune's wheel! Would it never cease revolving? We looked on delightedly as the makeup girl sat them down in front of the lighted mirror and applied lipstick and eye shadow, "Watch me!" "Watch!," I swear I could hear, echoing back from the past. And now the future was sitting there in embryo but already distinctively characterized. Alexandra was a clone of Pat—forthright, disarming, resolute and loving. Like her grandmother she even refused to kiss me wearing a mustache!

My beneficial effect on the weather seemed to have excelled itself when I left London on the hottest day ever recorded—99°F. Sadly, it was more a foretaste of the scorched and shriveled future that global ecological mismanagement had inflicted on our green and pleasant land. I flew out of the frying pan and into the fire of Phoenix for the world premiere of my Mesmer play. Called *Whisper in the Mind,* it was written by Norman Cousins and also by Jerome Laurence and Robert E. Lee, who had created such theatrical masterpieces as *Inherit the Wind.* The drama centered around a meeting between Benjamin Franklin and Mesmer in 1784 in prerevolutionary Paris, where the German doctor was attracting much controversial attention for curing disease with what he termed *biological magnetism.* Such was his fame that he even treated members of the French court, including Marie Antoinette. To investigate the validity of his powers, King Louis XVI appointed a commission of inquiry headed by Franklin, who was then the American Ambassador. So the ultimate man of reason came head to head with the first unwitting psychotherapist. But which was the true representative of enlightenment?

It was a meeting that never occurred historically, but, like the one between Good Queen Bess and Mary Queen of Scots, should, and could, have happened. Mesmer, in fact, sent an assistant to the inquest, but in our play spoke eloquently and passionately for himself. He both explained and demonstrated his use of a power that was later called hypnosis although the term *mesmerize* would, of course, enter the language in permanent tribute to him. As with so many forerunners of great discoveries, the reactionary medical establishment, still engaged in such barbarisms as bleeding, closed ranks to discredit him.

Norman Cousins's interest in the story was obvious. He had written best-sellers about his victory over his body's infirmities using the healing power of positive thought and the intervention of that Swiftian physician, Dr. Merryman. The mind-body relationship in Mesmer's work was in a cruder form and yet its results were just as beneficial. His interest, however, in older disciplines such as planetary influence cast ominous shadows of charlatanism. Even his Viennese friend Mozart lampooned him memorably in *Così fan tutte*. These suspicions were not allayed by the mise-en-scène of his Paris salon where, in a darkened music-filled room, patients were linked by a cord to his magnetized *baquet*, a wooden barrel-like contraption, in an early form of group therapy.

The controversy has been handed down to this day and much of the appeal of the role, apart from its welcome physical and mental challenge, was a chance to reinstate the reputation of a great man. One of the pleasures of rehearsing a brand-new play is that it is work in progress, providing the actor with an opportunity to influence its final shape. Intuitively I sympathized with many of Mesmer's ideas. Radionic healing had convinced me that, if not bathed in his "universal fluid," all life forms were inextricably linked. There seemed to be less and less separation between the physical and the spiritual world—between what was seen and unseen. Overinfluenced by that other Mesmer, the television set, we have abrogated to others the extraordinary healing powers within ourselves.

Franklin was played by E. G. Marshall, a powerful actor and endearing man and the perfect embodiment of open-minded probity. The play's production, however, seemed at first to unfairly condemn Mesmer even before his investigation, having him make his entrance with his *baquet* and patients on a platform elevated from below stage like a raft of damned creatures rising from hell. Rehearsals were fascinating, especially when the old magic trick that I wait for in every performance occurred, and I suddenly found myself thinking like Mesmer, and dictating his—not my—demands. The entrance was reworked with gratifying results.

The play was presented at Arizona State University in Tempe, a tranquil suburb of Phoenix, dominated by a colossal football stadium, the institution's principal dramatic forum. The whole place reminded me of the *Logan's Run* set with its supermodern malls and even an outdoor cafe that blew chilled air over its youthful customers who resembled our extras in their comely blondness and brevity of garments. The theater on campus was brand new and resonated with enthusiasm. Some of our cast were drama students and, as with my Anglo-Saxon filmmakers, it was wonderful to catch the contagion of youthful passion. I was back in the Oxford Playhouse again, doing what I had set out to do: reflecting a spectrum of great ideas and concepts through a dramatic prism. I also found myself in the happy position of being able to return the favors that had been done to me —advising about photos and job-request letters.

It was strange to note that, by coincidence, my return to the theater over the years had happened at almost ten-year intervals. This had so conditioned my reflexes that, after the first night, I felt we had achieved our purpose and was somewhat disconcerted to learn the experience had to be repeated for another three weeks. The play was well received and immediately requested for a Broadway transfer. However, none of us felt that we had got it quite right, and we agreed to temporarily disband while some restructuring took place. This was in civilized contrast to my previous Broadway outing where this was frantically done as we teetered on the edge of a shark pool, before being rudely pushed in.

I had other commitments, too. There was a television film in Canada to be made expressly so that Alexandra, Olivia and Henry could watch me in something appropriate. There was also my Israeli-Hungarian film with Liv Ullmann, due to start toward the end of the year. Called *The Long Shadow,* it had originated from a message left on my answering machine some three years earlier. Someone with my stock-in-trade, a lilting Eastern European accent, explained with elaborate politeness that he had tried to contact me through official agency channels but without success. Apologizing for calling directly, he said there was a script he would like me to consider. Intrigued as usual by this unconventional, improbable happenstance, I called him back. Eventually a thick tome arrived containing the germ of a most powerful story. It concerned a Hungarian actor who learns one day that the father he never knew was Jewish. He goes to Israel and discovers his roots—and, of course, himself. Embracing the Jewish fate that so many previous professional projects had seemed to insist upon, I agreed to do it.

I suggested certain emendations and over the years other improvements and embellishments occurred—notably the addition of the Oscar-winning director of photography, Vilmos Zsigmond, making his debut as director and Liv Ullmann as co-star. After waiting for Liv's availability, the pieces finally fell into place at the end of 1990 when we began the Hungarian part of the movie in Budapest. It all went extremely well and I even had a brief but exhilarating taste of playing Hamlet on stage again. It was with great anticipation that we reassembled in Tel Aviv in the New Year for the remainder of the filming. The threat of war in the Gulf triggered by Iraq's invasion of Kuwait still hung in the air. Despite some fearsome sabre rattling, however, everyone was convinced that, in our rapidly evolving new world order, the crisis would be resolved politically. The United Nations Organization had been motivated to act as a decisive and meaningful authority, another hopeful portent for the planet's future—and for our film.

The Mother of all Wars, however, had been unable to resist devouring her ambitious children. Back in California, I returned to my study where a more innocent-seeming sun streamed over the cuttings, letters, files, notes and papers that had been proliferating for the past two years.

We were in limbo, our lives on hold. But on hearing of the missiles that had robbed the life and ease of the remarkable people who had so recently been our companions, testing their courage and patience, I realized my own impatience was trivial. No make-believe movie, either, could possibly have outdone the crisis in terms of emotional conflict and dramatic content. Was it an epic or a tragedy? Certainly the world had been cruelly disillusioned. The end of the Cold War had seemed to signal the advent of open discussion and the demise of great standing armies to enforce agreement. Then, yet again, plowshares had been beaten back into swords. However, now was the time for optimism, to remember that so many strong and beautiful things are forged in fire. Once the politicians and soldiers had had their way, it would be time for the artists to attempt to make enduring sense of it all. As Martin Gray insists, life must go on.

So fate, ever capricious, gave me an unexpected opportunity to put all these words in order. Many were scribbled far from the solid, unfamiliar desk on which I now have a chance to write—in planes and cars, on busy sets, in strange hotel rooms and, once, during a particularly boring political speech. The enforced hiatus corresponded to the period of this book's composition when I similarly paused to retrace my wandering footsteps over the last half century and plan the most scenic route for what lay ahead. As Adrian had remarked, "I suppose that round about fifty we all start asking ourselves Montaigne's question: 'Que sais-je?' "

After so much indulgent retrospection, I am now firmly convinced that the path will continue upward and that the journey to the undiscovered country, though not without pitfalls and unscheduled detours, will be a grand adventure. The career engine will hopefully still pull the train of life, but the gradient should now afford a smoother ride with more time to appreciate the view.

Revisiting the past has made me even more gratefully aware of how rich my present is, and I wish I could meaningfully acknowledge all those who made the going so good. As with an unfinished performance of a play, however, all the foregoing can in no sense be a summing up; the best, I am convinced, is yet to come, and the last acts and denouement promise to be most interesting and entertaining.

Meanwhile, the wheel continues inexorably to turn. The other week, Braham, my old Oxford companion and now an established theater director, offered me the lead in a musical he is directing. The Mesmer play is now rewritten and ready for performance. Again, that old, delightful problem—choice.

Barbara, my Dutch girlfriend from Youth Theatre days, called after almost thirty years and researching the book has brought me back in touch with many other important people from my past, including Lesley, Julia, Derek and Chris Hill. Dick Vane-Wright, I find, is even a patient of my brother-in-law Marek. Caroline's healing center has now opened. Rick, in continued fulfillment of his mother's Gypsy forecast, is producing a television project that will be filmed all over the world. Perhaps one day he will give me a job! Our grandchildren continue to enchant. "I will always be in your heart and you will always be in mine," Alexandra assured us the other day.

After reading an early draft of this book, my father handed over a scrapbook that, unbeknownst to me, he and May had kept since my theatrical debut. It perfectly illustrates their involvement in my activities—close and caring yet totally unconfining, for which I am continually indebted.

Pat's book, a treasure trove of great thoughts and photographs with an introduction by the sadly now departed Norman Cousins, has gone to press. Consistent with the synchronicity of our lives, it will be published at the same time as mine. She is hard at work on a new book about healers, the direct karmic payoff to those enormously consequential hours in an Indian hospital hovering between life and death.

The Gulf War's wheel of fire rotated, too, the close of hostilities allowing us to resume the film. Meeting up with Liv, Vilmos and the crew again seemed to justify David Ben Gurion's observation that anyone who did not believe in miracles in Israel was not a realist.

As we picked up the pieces of our stalled enterprise, my end was my beginning. In Jerusalem we filmed just around the corner from the theater where, almost thirty years before, I had played my youthful Romeo. On the Dead Sea we returned to stay at the hotel from which, a few momentous weeks before, we had been so hurriedly evacuated. I even found myself driving up the hills again to Arad in the pre-dawn darkness. We were there to film the sunrise. This time the harsh winds were stilled and the first tentative rays of light showed the rocky slopes to be freshly greened with spring's tender leaves of hope. The bright, confidently rising sun gave promise of another splendid day. . . .

Michael York

Los Angeles	Washington	London
Brussels	Bournemouth	Santa Barbara
Uckfield	York	Seville
Columbia	Napa	Salzburg
Edinburgh	Dublin	New York
Zagreb	Frankfurt	Portoroz
Montego Bay	Miami	Acapulco
Lamorna Cove	Hawaii	Canterbury
East Hampton	Jervaulx	Atlanta
Tempe	Toronto	Budapest
Tel Aviv	Jerusalem	Eilat

March 1989–March 1991

Index